THE TIMES HISTORY OF THE WORLD

CONTRIBUTORS

EDITORS:

Geoffrey Barraclough
Late President, Historical
Association
Chichele Professor of Modern
History
University of Oxford

Norman Stone
Professor of History
Bilkent University, Ankara

Geoffrey Parker FBA
Andreas Dorpalen
Distinguished Professor of History
The Ohio State University

Richard Overy
Professor in History
University of Exeter

CONSULTANTS:

David Abulafia	Peter Coates
Daud Ali	Frank Cogliano
F R Allchin	Irene Collins
R W Van Alstyne	Michael Crawford
David Arnold	James Cronin
John Barber	Douglas Dakin
James R Barrett	John Darwin
Iris Barry	Ralph Davis
Peter Bauer	Kent Deng
Christopher Bayly	Robin Dunbar
W G Beasley	I E S Edwards
Ralph Bennett	Robert Evans
Amira K Bennison	John Ferguson
A D H Bivar	Felipe Fernándo-Armesto
Brian Bond	Stefan Fisch
Hugh Borton	David H Fischer
Hugh Bowden	John R Fisher
David Brading	Kate Fleet
Warwick Bray	Michael Flinn
John Breen	Timothy Fox
Carl Bridge	Alan Frost
F R Bridge	Robert I Frost
Michael G Broers	Clive Gamble
Hugh Brogan	W J Gardner
Tom Brooking	Carol Geldart
Ian Brown	John Gillingham
Anthony Bryer	Ian Glover
Muriel E Chamberlain	Martin Goodman
David G Chandler	Graham Gould
John Cannon	D G E Hall
Eric Christiansen	Norman Hammond
Colin Coates	John D Hargreaves

Tim Harper

David R Harris

Jonathan Haslam

Ragnhild Hatton

M Havinden

Harry Hearder

W O Henderson

Colin J Heywood

Sinclair Hood

Albert Hourani

Henry Hurst

Jonathan Israel

Edward James

Nicholas James

Richard H Jones

Ulrich Kemper

Hugh Kennedy

David Killingray

George Lane

Mark H Leff

Karl Leyser

Colin Lewis

James B Lewis

Wolfgang Liebeschuetz

D Anthony Low

David Luscombe

John Lynch

Rosamond McKitterick

James M McPherson

Isabel de Madriaga

J P Mallory

P J Marshall

A R Michell

Christopher D Morris

A E Musson

Thomas Nelson

Linda A Newson

F S Northedge

Joan Oates

David Ormrod

Caroline Orwin

J H Parry

Thomas M Perry

David Phillipson

Sidney Pollard

Andrew Porter

Avril Powell

T G E Powell

John Poynter

Benjamin Ravid

Tapan Raychaudhuri

B H Reid

Michael Roaf

Francis Robinson

A N Ryan

Gören Rystad

H W F Saggs

S B Saul

Peter Sawyer

Chris Scarre

Roger Schofield

D J Schove

H M Scott

H H Scullard

Andrew Sharf

Stephen Shennan

Andrew Sherratt

Peter Sluglett

R B Smith

Frank C Spooner

Jocelyn Statler
L S Stavrianos
Zara Steiner
Sarah Stockwell
Melvyn Stokes
W C Sturtevant
Julian Swann
Alan Sykes
Martin Thomas
E A Thompson
Hugh Tinker
Malcolm Todd
R C Trebilcock
Hugh R Trevor-Roper
Denis C Twitchett

Frans von der Dunk
F R von der Mehden
Ernst Wangermann
Geoffrey Warner
Anne Waswo
D Cameron Watt
Bodo Wiethoff
D S M Williams
Glyn Williams
H P Willmott
David M Wilson
Jon E Wilson
Peter Wilson
George D Winius

CONTENTS

Contributors   v

Introduction: 'The State of the World'   xv

SECTION ONE

HUMAN ORIGINS AND EARLY CULTURES   1

Human origins from *c.* 5 million years ago   2

The spread of modern humans from *c.* 200,000 years ago   4

The Ice Age world, 20,000 to 10,000 BC   7

From hunting to farming: the origins of agriculture, 8000 to 4000 BC   9

Before the first cities: southwest Asia, 10,000 to 4000 BC   11

Early Europe: the colonization of a continent, 7000 to 2000 BC   13

African peoples and cultures to 900 BC   15

Peoples of the Americas to 300 BC   17

Southeast Asia before civilization to 500 BC   19

Australia to 1770   21

Melanesia and Polynesia to the 1700s   23

SECTION TWO

THE FIRST CIVILIZATIONS 27

The beginnings of civilization in the Eurasian world, 3500 to 1500 BC 28
The early empires of Mesopotamia, c. 3500 to 1600 BC 30
Ancient Egypt, c. 3100 to 1000 BC 32
The Near East, 1600 to 1000 BC 34
Peoples of South America and the Caribbean, 300 BC to AD 1300 36
Peoples of Mesoamerica, 300 BC to AD 1300 37
Peoples of early North America, 300 BC to AD 1300 39
The beginnings of Chinese civilization to 475 BC 41
Korea to 1392 43
The beginnings of Indian civilization to 500 BC 45
Minoan and Mycenaean civilizations, c. 3000 to 950 BC 47

SECTION THREE

THE CLASSICAL CIVILIZATIONS OF EURASIA 51

The commercial and cultural bonds of Eurasia, 550 BC to AD 752 52
The Near East, 1000 to 539 BC 54
The empires of Persia, 550 BC to AD 637 56
The spread of Greek civilization, 800 to 336 BC 58
The Hellenistic world, 336 to 30 BC 61
The unification of China, 475 BC to AD 220 63
China and east Asia, 220 to 618 65
India: the first empires, 500 BC to AD 550 67
The peoples of northern Europe, 2300 to 50 BC 69
Africa, 900 BC to AD 700 72
The expansion of Roman power to 31 BC 73
The height of Roman power, 31 BC to AD 235 75
From Rome to Byzantium, AD 235 to 565 77
The rise of Christianity to AD 600 79

SECTION FOUR
THE WORLD OF DIVIDED REGIONS 83

Germanic settlement in western Europe, 341 to 597 84
Pre-Islamic Arabia, to AD 600 86
The spread of Islam from AD 632 88
The expansion of Christianity, 600 to 1500 90
The Jewish diaspora, AD 70 to 1800 92
The rise of the Frankish kingdom, 482 to 814 94
Magyars, Saracens and Vikings in 9th and 10th century Europe,
   793 to 1000 97
Northern and eastern Europe, 900 to 1050 99
Crusading in Europe from the 11th to the 15th century, 1095 to 1492 101
The Byzantine empire, 610 to 1453 104
The first Russian state: Kievan Russia, 882 to 1242 106
The German empire and the Papacy, 962 to 1250 108
Monarchy in Britain and France, 1154 to 1314 110
Economic growth in Europe, c. 950 to 1150 112
Imperial Japan and the early shogunates to 1477 114
Chinese civilization from the T'ang to the Sung, 618 to 1279 117
Iran and central Asia, 600 to 1501 119
The Mongol empire, 1206 to 1405 121
India: the emergence of temple kingdoms, 550 to 1206 124
India: the Delhi sultanate, 1206 to 1526 127
The early civilizations of southeast Asia, 500 BC to AD 1511 129
The Muslim world, 800 to 1100 131
The Muslim world, 1100 to 1350 132
The emergence of states in Africa, 1000 to 1500 134
The rise of the Ottoman empire, 1281 to 1522 136
The crisis of the 14th century in Europe, 1252 to 1381 138
European states in the 14th century, 1300 to 1400 140
South America on the eve of European conquest, c. 1300 to 1535 142
Mesoamerica and the Caribbean on the eve of European conquest,
   c. 1300 to 1520 144
The Renaissance and early modern state in Europe, 1450 to c. 1600 147

SECTION FIVE
THE WORLD OF THE EMERGING WEST 149

The world on the eve of European expansion, *c.* 1500 150
European voyages of discovery, 1487 to 1780 153
Expansion of the trading empires, 1500 to 1700 155
Russian expansion in Europe and Asia, 1462 to 1815 157
North America, 1500 to 1810 159
Latin America and the Caribbean, 1500 to 1825 161
Trade and empire in Africa, 1500 to 1800 163
China at the time of the Ming dynasty, 1368 to 1644 165
Ottoman Turkey, 1522 to 1800 167
Iran from the Safavids to the Qajars, 1501 to 1906 168
Mughal India and the growth of British power, 1526 to 1803 170
China under the Ch'ing dynasty, 1644 to 1839 172
Korea, 1392 to 1953 174
Japan under the shogunate, 1477 to 1868 176
Southeast Asia and the European powers, 1511 to 1826 178
The European economy: agriculture and society, 1500 to 1815 180
The European economy: trade and industry, 1550 to 1775 183
Reformation and Catholic Reformation, 1517 to 1670 185
Europe: the state and its opponents, 1500 to 1688 187
The Mediterranean world, 1494 to 1797 189
The struggle for the Baltic, 1523 to 1721 192
The Holy Roman Empire, 1493 to 1806 194
The ascendency of France, 1648 to 1715 196
The struggle for empire, 1713 to 1815 199
The age of partition: eastern Europe, 1648 to 1795 201
The emerging global economy, *c.* 1775 203
The industrial revolution begins: Great Britain, 1760 to 1820 205
The age of revolt, 1773 to 1814 207
The French Revolution, 1789 to 1797 210
Napoleon and the reshaping of Europe, 1799 to 1815 212

SECTION SIX

THE AGE OF EUROPEAN DOMINANCE 215

Population growth and movements, 1815 to 1914   216
The industrial revolution in Europe, 1815 to 1870   219
The rise of nationalism in Europe, 1800 to 1914   221
Germany and Italy: the struggles for unification, 1815 to 1871   223
The making of the United States: westward expansion, 1783 to 1890   226
The market revolution in the United States, 1800 to 1880   228
Slavery, civil war and Reconstruction, 1820 to 1877   230
The United States: a nation of immigrants, 1776 to 1924   233
Canada since 1810   235
Latin America: independence and national growth, 1810 to 1910   237
The disintegration of the Ottoman empire, 1800 to 1923   240
The Russian empire: expansion and modernization, 1815 to 1917   242
The collapse of the Chinese empire, 1839 to 1911   244
India under British rule, 1805 to 1935   245
Australia since 1770   248
New Zealand since 1800   249
Africa before partition by the European powers, 1800 to 1880   251
The partition of Africa, 1880 to 1913   253
The expansion and modernization of Japan, 1868 to 1922   255
European colonial empires, 1815 to 1914   257
The anti-western reaction, 1881 to 1917   259
European rivalries and alliances, 1878 to 1914   261
The formation of a world economy, 1870 to 1914   263
The First World War, 1914 to 1918   265

SECTION SEVEN

THE AGE OF GLOBAL CIVILIZATION 269

The Russian Revolution, 1917 to 1929   270
Imperialism and nationalism, 1919 to 1941   272
The Chinese revolution, 1912 to 1949   274
European political problems, 1919 to 1934   277

The Great Depression, 1929 to 1939   279
The outbreak of the Second World War, 1931 to 1941   281
The war in Asia and the Pacific, 1941 to 1945   283
The European War, 1941 to 1945   285
Racism and deportations, 1919 to 1953   287
Europe, 1945 to 1973   289
The Cold War, 1945 to 1991   291
Retreat from empire since 1939   293
Japan and east Asia since 1945   296
China under communism since 1949   298
Southeast Asia's long war, 1945 to 1975   300
Southeast Asia since 1975   302
South Asia: independence and conflict since 1947   305
Africa, 1957 to 1989   308
African democratization since 1989   310
Palestine, Zionism and the Arab-Israeli conflict since 1947   312
Nationalism, secularism and Islam in the Middle East since 1945   314
South America: search for stability and development since 1910   316
Mexico, Central America and the Caribbean since 1910   319
The United States: the age of abundance since 1939   321
The United States as a world power since 1945   324
The development of the Soviet Union and Russia since 1929   326
Europe since 1973   329
Europe's civil wars since 1991   331
Warfare since 1945   333
World terrorism since 1945   335
Iraq and Afghanistan: the arc of instability, 1979 to 2007   337
The world in the 21st century   339
The global economy   341
Communications in the modern age   343
The global environment   345

Chronology of significant events in world history   349
Bibliography   373
Index   381

INTRODUCTION

'The State of the World'

The choice of Beijing, capital of China, as the host city for the 2008 Olympic Games has produced an extraordinary, if brief, historic marriage of East and West. The games symbolize the world of classical Greece, whose legacy has played such an exceptional part in the development of the Western world. Greek civilization gave the West professional medicine, geometry, ethical speculation, democracy, an ideal of participatory citizenship, codified law, the first history, a science of politics and an artistic heritage imitated again and again down the ages. Many of our common terms today – from economics to psychiatry – are Greek in origin.

China, on the other hand, is seat of the most ancient and continuous of civilizations. Always the site of the largest fraction of the world's population, China for thousands of years, despite waves of invasions, sustained a way of life and a social structure which proved remarkably enduring. Chinese values and intellectual life were not, unlike Greek civilization, diffused widely outside the frontiers of what was loosely defined as 'China'. Western critics in the 19th century regarded China as a stagnant culture, unmoved for centuries, but the artistic, scientific and intellectual life of China, though very different from that of the West, was rich and diverse. A good case can be made for arguing that China has been a fixed point throughout the period of recorded history, where Greek culture has been anything but continuous, relying for much of its survival on the intercession of the Arab cultures of the Middle East that succeeded the

Roman Empire, in which aspects of Greek thought were kept alive and then re-exported to late medieval Europe.

The China of the 2008 Olympics is still a central part of the world story, but it has come part way to meet the West. From the late 19th century traditional Chinese society crumbled under Western impact. A nationalist revolution overthrew the emperors and the old way of life after 1911. A second communist revolution transformed China into a more modern industrial state after 1949. Over the past 25 years China has undergone a third revolutionary wave by embracing the fruits of modern global capitalism and becoming one of the world's major economic players. China has not become an Asian 'West', but has adapted what the West has had to offer and has turned China into a world 'superpower'. The relationship between East and West has come full circle. For centuries the West pushed outwards into the world exporting, usually violently, a version of Western civilization. China was long resistant to this pressure; now China can exert pressure of its own, challenging the monopoly hitherto enjoyed by the remorseless march of Western economics, political models, consumerism and popular culture.

The meeting of Greece and China weaves together two of the central threads of world history. But the Olympics are also a symbolic fusion of ancient and modern. Although the original games are far removed from the glossy, commercialized, technically sophisticated and ruinously expensive modern version, their revival is a reminder that there are easily understood reference points back to the Europe of more than 2,000 years ago. Boxing, wrestling, javelin-throwing and running are simply what they are, the same for a modern audience as they were for the Greeks. Even the marathon, the icon of the current Western obsession with keeping fit, describes a Greek legend, when a soldier-runner covered 26 miles non-stop under a gruelling sun from the Battle of Marathon to Athens to warn of the approaching Persian fleet, only to drop dead from the effort on his arrival. Distant though the ancient world seems, the span of recorded human history is remarkably short in relation to the long history of prehistoric man and the infinitely longer history of the earth. The span can be covered by just a hundred human lives of 60 years, stretched out one after the other. Only 50 human lives will take you back to those first Olympic Games.

To think about the past as something connected by a continuous thread of human activity runs the danger of imposing a false sense of unity, but for much of the earth's surface, over long periods of time, fundamental change has been absent. Anthropological evidence has for a long time been able to describe practices and beliefs that are clearly connected with a world so distant that it has been transmuted into myth. One hundred human lives laid end-to-end is not very many. To put it another way: it is possible to house an artefact from every major civilization of the past 5,000 years in a single cabinet and to recognize that until the last few hundred years those artefacts – whether a pot, a fertility doll, an arrow-head, a shoe, a coin – bear a remarkable underlying similarity. The recorded history of the world can be read at one level as a unitary experience, a brief 4 per cent of the time modern hominids have been evolving, a hundred human lives.

Of course these lives were not the same wherever they were lived. Whatever homologies can be detected between peoples and civilizations, the experience of world history over the past 6,000 years is a series of fractured narratives, divided geographically and segmented by differing cultures, religious practices and political orders. The whole course of world history has been a process of cultural exchange and discovery, of imperial expansion and decline; sometimes links once made were then ruptured again; at other times communication enriched both cultures. In the past 500 years that process of discovering, mapping and understanding the world as a whole has accelerated, but for most previous civilizations the 'known world' was only what was immediately known. The modern concept of 'world history' which this book encapsulates was meaningless to most human civilizations through most of human history. For large areas of the globe there was no written culture so that 'history' survived as myth or folk memory, dating was arbitrary or non-existent, and the world was circumscribed by the very limited geographical reach of particular peoples. Rome was an exception, but even for Romans the known world was centred on the Mediterranean and the barbarous (meaning alien) outside was scarcely understood or valued. China for centuries regarded itself as the centre of the universe, and the outside world, to the extent that it intruded at all, was supposed to revolve like so many blighted planets around the Chinese sun. The history of the world is a very Western idea and it has become knowable only in the last century or so as Europeans and their descendants overseas produced sophisticated archaeological techniques and scholarly skills to unlock many of the remaining secrets of the past. When the English novelist H. G. Wells wrote his famous *Outline of History*, published in 1920, he was able to do so only on the foundation of an outpouring of new research in the last decades of the 19th century. Wells was preoccupied, he wrote in his introduction, with 'history as one whole', and he was one of the first to attempt it.

The more that came to be known about the many civilizations and cultures that made up human history, the more tempting it was, like Wells, to try to see history as a whole and to explain the process of historical change as a uniform one. This ambition had roots in the 19th century, where it was famously attempted by the German thinkers Georg Hegel and his erstwhile disciple Karl Marx, who both suggested that historical change was dynamic, the result of shifting patterns of thought or the transition from one economic system to another, each stage of human development incorporating the best from the past but each an advance on the one before it, until humankind finally reached an ideal society. The 19th-century view, coloured by the remarkable technical progress of the age, was to try to see a purpose behind historical change – not a mere random set of events, or a set of parables or myths to educate the present, but a triumphant account of the ascent of man. Neither Hegel nor Marx was a historian, and they both regarded China as a backwater that had somehow failed to move like the rest of the world. The 20th century witnessed more historically sophisticated attempts to find a unity in world history. The German philosopher Oswald Spengler published just after the First World War two volumes of an ambitious study of the pattern of all world history. Each civilization, Spengler argued, had a natural life-cycle, like any organism, of birth, growth, maturity and death, a run of approximately 1,000 years each. He called his volumes *The Decline of the West* in order to argue against the optimism of the previous century and to demonstrate that Western civilization, for all its belief that it represented the full flowering of human history, was doomed to go the way of the rest. The British historian Arnold Toynbee thought Spengler's view of history too schematic, but he produced 10 volumes of *A Study of History* between 1934 and 1954 in which he too detected a common pattern in all previous civilizations which explained their birth, rise to cultural fruition and eventual collapse. Both Spengler and Toynbee rejected the idea that the purpose of history was the triumph of the West, but they both thought that history could be understood as a single, repeated pattern, from ancient Egypt to the modern West.

Few historians now accept that world history works like this. The rise and fall of civilizations evidently has causes, many of which are explored in the pages that follow. But it does not follow from this that history ought to progress, or that it follows internal laws or patterns of development. History does not move forward entirely blindly, but its progress is more often than not accidental, not patterned, and the circumstances of its development contingent rather than purposive – a product of a particular set of circumstances at a particular time rather than a necessary progress from one stage to the next. The same objection can be raised to the popular idea that there are turning points in history, key battles or events that have determined the course of history. Some events are clearly more important than others. History might now be written differently if the Roman army had not defeated Hannibal at Zama in 202 BC, but this was just one event in a much wider world of human activity, insignificant in India or China of the 3rd century BC. On balance human history moves forward on a broad front, less affected by 'turning points' than might be expected. If one set of events had never happened, there would just be a different narrative which would now be accepted as part of the past as readily as any other. History has neither pattern nor purpose. It is simply the record of what has been.

There are nonetheless broad common factors that have shaped the development of human communities wherever they have settled. The most important element has been the continuous and complex relationship between mankind and the natural world. Natural phenomena have defined a great deal of the human story. Until quite recently most natural forces were beyond human capacity to control or mediate or even to understand. Some still remain so. In the spring of 2008 a ferocious cyclone, which laid waste large parts of southern Myanmar, and a powerful earthquake in China, killed at least 150,000 people between them. Natural disasters – earthquakes, tidal waves, volcanic eruptions, soil erosion, rising sea levels, crop failure – have been a constant feature of all history. The shaping of the landscape determined patterns of settlement, forms of husbandry, the possibility of exploration and trade. The seas and rivers have been both barrier and pathway. The siting of cities, artificial additions to the landscape, has been determined by access to river communications, or the existence of a natural harbour, or the natural defensive walls provided by high outcrops of rock or hillside. For the past 5,000 years and the introduction of widespread agriculture, the relationship between population size and food supply has added a further natural factor restricting or enhancing the prospects of particular societies, or creating violent tensions between communities that lived by hunting and those with settled pastoral traditions. This competition is not confined to the ancient past, when, for example, waves of hunters from the plains of Eurasia descended on Europe in the 5th and 6th centuries; the near extermination of the North American buffalo in the 19th century by white hunters, an animal on which some Native American tribal societies depended, opened the way for the vast grain-growing prairie belt and the emasculation of the Native American population.

The supply of food, or its absence, famine, is a constant through human history. It exercised the ancient Egyptians, who developed complex irrigation systems to compensate for a buoyant population surrounded by desert; 3,000 years later Adolf Hitler argued that Germans needed 'living space' in Eastern Europe to provide a proper balance between population and food supply; the contemporary world, trying to support a vastly greater population, witnesses famines in Africa side-by-side with an overabundance of food in the richer West. A new food crisis in 2008 has prompted the bleak conclusion that food output must expand 50 per cent by 2030 to meet demand. For most people through most of recorded history the search for food has been unyielding. In hunting communities, as long as there existed a wealth of animal life or fish, food was not a problem. In settled, agricultural communities, on the other hand, the supply of food was restricted either by problems of soil or changeable climate or by the maldistribution of food between rich and poor, or both. Tilling the soil was no guarantee of a decent diet; a Roman feast or a groaning Victorian banquet gives no clue as to how inadequate was the food supply for the slaves who grew and garnered it in Roman Italy, or for the Victorian poor, most of them cut off from the land and dependent on a monotonous starch-rich diet. In post-Renaissance Italy there developed one of the most sophisticated cuisines in the world, informed by a wealth of gastronomic master-works, but the later peasant workers of the Po Valley suffered debilitating pellagra from eating a stodgy maize-based diet that inflated their abdomens and eventually killed them. In settled civilizations, an adequate, varied, artistically presented or innovative diet was the preserve of the rich. It was no accident that the Russian Revolution of February 1917 began with a demonstration for bread by hungry women in St Petersburg (Petrograd).

The relationship between mankind and environment has changed a good deal over the past 200 years. Larger and more regular food supplies together with changes in healthcare have provoked a population explosion. Global population was around 800 million in the 18th century; currently it is an astonishing 6.7 billion. A result has been the massive expansion of the agricultural base, partly from utilising virgin lands, partly from raising yields artificially through plant- and stock-breeding or the addition of chemical fertiliser. These changes have provoked deforestation and the transformation of natural habitat. Heavy hunting has brought thousands of land and sea creatures to the edge of extinction. The world's urban population has grown dramatically since 1900 and now stands at just over 50 per cent of the whole, producing huge sprawling cities and high levels of human pollution. To meet the daily needs of such a population has meant expanding industrial production, depleting the earth's natural resources, and creating a growing chemical imbalance in the atmosphere that has damaged the ozone layer and threatens through so-called 'global warming' to undermine the fragile basis on which 6 billion people can subsist. Demands for a higher living standard from Western populations already rich in resources, and for catch-up living standards in much of the rest of the world, has accelerated the depletion of resources, the transformation of the landscape and the unnatural climate change. The rich United States has 5 per cent of the world's population but generates annually 25 per cent of the 'greenhouse gases' that cause climate change. The most alarming scenarios are now painted of the capacity of man to forge new natural disasters to which there will be no answer – enough methane gas perhaps to cause a global explosion in a century's time, or the release of bacteria from the frozen icecaps millions of years old, from which current populations would have no prospect of immunity. The relationship between man and nature has about it a profound irony. The attempt to master the natural world has simply given nature new and more terrible powers.

Only in one respect has it proved possible to tame nature sufficiently to alter human society for the good. Over the past 150 years, in itself a fraction of the long history of man, it has proved possible to understand and then prevent or cure most medical conditions. For all the rest of human history, disease and disability were an ever-present reality for which there was almost no effective relief. The establishment of cities and animal husbandry combined to create ideal conditions for the establishment of a cluster of endemic epidemic diseases which periodically killed off wide swathes of the human host. The earliest epidemics in the cities of the first civilizations in China, Egypt or Mesopotamia included smallpox, diphtheria, influenza, chickenpox and mumps. With the opening of trade routes and regular invasions, disease could be spread from populations that had developed some immunity to those biologically vulnerable. Athens was struck by a devastating plague in 430 BC which undermined its political power; the Antonine plague in the late-2nd-century AD Roman Empire killed around one-quarter of the populations it infected, probably with smallpox. Bubonic plague, transmitted by fleas carried on rats, killed around two-thirds of its victims. Plague originating in Egypt in 540 AD spread to the Eastern Mediterranean where again one-quarter of the population died. The famous Black Death in the 14th century swept from Asia to Europe, killing an estimated 20 million and reducing Europe's population by one-quarter. Epidemics died out partly because the pathogens had no other victims to kill. Modernity was no safeguard either. Cholera coincided with the industrialization and urbanization of Europe and produced regular pandemics in Asia, the Middle East and Europe between the 1820s and the 1890s. 'Spanish influenza' struck Europe at the end of the First World War with populations unnaturally weakened by lack of food; it was the world's worst pandemic, killing 60 million people in just two years.

The attempt to understand and explain the nature of disease, and if possible cure it, goes back to the very earliest periods of recorded history. Classic Chinese medicine (now usually described as Traditional Chinese Medicine or TCM) is thought to date back almost 5,000 years. The standard text on 'Basic Questions of Internal Medicine' (known as *Neijing Suwen*) was written, according to legend, by the Yellow Emperor around 2,600 BC; the earliest surviving version dates from at least 2,000 years ago. Early Chinese medicine was rooted in a broader philosophical system based in one case on Confucianism, in the second on Taoism. Confucianism rejected the idea of anatomical or surgical invasion in the belief that the body was sacred; instead the use of acupuncture or massage was preferred, influencing internal disease by external means. Taoism saw health related entirely to achieving harmony between the different elements of the world, the Yin and the Yang. Disease was a consequence of lack of harmony. Chinese medicine focused on herbal remedies and acupuncture as means to restore that harmony rather than more violent medical intervention. Close observation of morbid symptoms was regarded as essential to understand what combination of remedies was needed. During the brief Sui dynasty (581–618 AD) a group of doctors composed *The General Treatise on the Causes and Symptoms of Disease* which comprised 50 volumes and described some 1,700 conditions. The classic texts retained an enduring influence down to the 20th century when successive modernising regimes tried to substitute Western medicine with only limited success.

The other classic tradition arose in Greece from the 5th century BC based on the teachings of the secular theorist Hippocrates, born around 460, whose famous 'oath', that doctors should at the least do no harm, is still sworn by Western doctors today. Like Chinese medicine, Greek medicine relied on explaining disease as an absence of harmony in the body between four elements or 'humours' that composed it. The elements were blood, choler (yellow bile), phlegm and black bile. These humours corresponded to the elements identified by Greek science as universal components – air (blood), fire (choler), water (phlegm) and earth (black bile). Cure for any imbalance was based on a range of options – bleeding, diet, exercise and occasional surgery. These views, revived in medieval Europe, exercised a continuing influence down to the time when modern medical science made its first appearance in the European Renaissance, and even beyond it. The problem for Greek as for Chinese medicine was the strong prejudice against direct anatomical research on human cadavers. In all pre-scientific medical systems an absence of proper understanding of the function of the body and the cause of disease meant that cures were largely accidental. Recent tests on 200 Chinese traditional herbal remedies for malaria found that only one, by chance, contained anything that might contribute to a cure.

Only the onset of serious research on how the body worked – perhaps the most famous example was William Harvey's discovery of the circulation of the blood, published in 1628 – made it possible to understand how the body was affected by particular conditions and to suggest prophylaxis. Even then the growing understanding of the body did little to help prevent epidemics until the onset of vaccination (introduced in late-18th-century Britain for smallpox) and the path-breaking research of the French chemist, Louis Pasteur, and the German doctor Robert Koch, which by the 1880s had confirmed that disease was caused by bacteria, each different micro-organism responsible for a particular disease. The discovery of antibiotic properties in penicillin mould in 1928 completed the therapeutic revolution. From the mid-19th century onwards the older medical traditions, which had limited or no medical efficacy, were superseded by a science-based medicine which has pushed the frontiers of biochemistry, neurology, physiology and pharmacology almost to their limits and has, at least temporarily, conquered almost all known diseases and a large number of internal medical disorders.

Only the identification of the HIV virus in the 1980s, which attacks the body's immune system, made it clear that even the most scientifically advanced medicine may not in the future be able to stem new and unexpected forms of epidemic. For the fortunate few generations in the West who have been the full beneficiaries of the medical revolution, the transformation has been extraordinary. For all the rest of recorded human history there was no effective cure for most diseases and humans survived only because of a complex struggle between the micro-organisms and the human immune system. Death was ever-present and social attitudes and religious beliefs had to be rooted in the expectation of high levels of mortality. For those who survived there were disfiguring illnesses, crippling medical conditions, poor eyesight, chronic toothache, and so on. For women throughout history there was the debilitating cycle of births and the ever-present risk of maternal death. Pain, like premature death, was a permanent visitor.

To make matters worse, throughout human history both death and pain have been inflicted unnaturally, the product of deliberate violence on the part of human communities. Man, and almost always the male of the species, is a uniquely aggressive and punitive creature. Although attempts have been made over the past century to demonstrate that other animal species indulge in deliberate violence, animal violence is instinctive, not conscious. Mankind, on the other hand, has throughout recorded history, and evidently long before that, been able to premeditate the use of violence directed at other humans. Some anthropologists, following the 18th-century French philosopher Jean-Jacques Rousseau, have tried to argue that early man was most likely peaceable, and that only the tensions generated by more complex forms of social life introduced higher levels of violence. But the range and sophistication of pre-historic weapons, first stone, then iron and bronze, makes the idea of a pacific pre-historic state implausible. It is of course true that with settled communities, centred on cities, violence came to be organized through the use of armies. The evolution of a specialized human function for organising and legitimating the use of violence is evident in the very earliest recorded history. The soldier, armed with an ever more lethal armoury, runs in an unbroken line from all corners of the ancient world where complex civilizations arose. In tribal communities, without settled urban life, inter-tribal and intra-tribal violence was often ritualized, the young males of the tribe using violence as a rite of passage or a sacred obligation.

There is no single answer to the question of why violence should be such a hallmark of world history, but it can be found on almost every page. The German legal theorist Carl Schmitt, writing in the 1920s, claimed that the human community has always been divided between 'friend' and 'foe', those who are included in the group and those who are excluded. Simplistic though the distinction might seem, the concept of the alien, the other, the barbarian, the enemy, or the excluded also runs as a thread through all history. Treatment of the 'other' has always been harsh, even in the modern age with its vain efforts to impose some kind of restraints or norms on military behaviour and state violence. Yet even this distinction leaves a great deal unexplained. Human beings do not just fight each other in pitched battles using soldiers who know what to expect. They punish human victims in hideously painful and savage ways. Coercive social relationships have been far more common than consensual ones. Victims, even those from among 'the included' who are guilty of crime, have been tortured, executed, beaten, imprisoned in ways so ingeniously atrocious and gratuitously cruel that it is difficult not to assume that violence is the normal human condition and the very recent and limited experience of peace and respect for the individual a merciful historical anomaly. Violence is also universal, not some characteristic of 'savage society' as self-righteous Victorian imperialists like to think. Civilizations, however sophisticated, have indulged in violence of every kind. Religions have often led the way in devising grotesque ways to seek out heresies and exorcize devils. At the Museum of Torture Instruments in Guadalest in Spain (by no means the only such museum) are displayed roomfuls of fearful devices designed to extract confessions from across early-modern Europe, including the unhappy victims of the notorious Spanish Inquisition – iron crowns with spikes which tighten around the victim's head, sharp stakes that could impale the whole length of a human body without killing the victim immediately. Human beings have devoted a deplorable amount of effort to inflicting suffering, and seem to have done so with few moral qualms.

There have been many attempts to explain why wars happen, or why human history is so soaked in blood. There is no single concept of war (though there is 'warfare', the art of fighting) that can embrace all the many forms of war or the thousands of separate historical reasons why particular wars break out, evident from the pages that follow. Early-20th-century anthropologists were inclined to argue that war might have had some important function in primitive societies or in the age of early state formation but they could see no justification for it in the modern age. The idea that war, and other forms of violence, were a throwback to a past age now thinly papered over with 'civilization' was urged by the Austrian psychoanalyst Sigmund Freud when he reflected on the reasons for the prolonged and deadly fighting in the First World War: 'the primitive, savage and evil impulses of mankind have not vanished in any individual, but continue their existence, although in a repressed state'. Freud thought war rapidly exposed the savage persona inside and later argued that the more 'civilized' a people became, the more likely it was that the dam of repression would burst and uncontrollable violence result.

Whether this really is the mechanism that releases violence, Freud proved all too right in his prediction. In the late 19th century it was still just possible to imagine that the barbarities of earlier history, when cities were sacked, their populations put to the sword, fine buildings burned, was a thing of the past (though this did not prevent European troops on a punitive expedition from destroying the stunning Summer Palace in Beijing in 1860, an act of wanton vandalism that witnesses compared with the sack of Rome by the Goths). But the 20th century has been the bloodiest in all of human history, witness to somewhere between 85 and 100 million violent deaths, and millions more wounded, maimed, tortured, raped and dispossessed. It includes the deliberate murder of the European Jews which must rank with anything else in scale and horror from the past 6,000 years. It will be difficult for historians in a few hundred years' time to see what separates the Mongol sack of Samarkand in 1220, which left only a few of the inhabitants alive, from the Allies' destruction of Hamburg in 1943, which burnt the city to the ground and killed 40,000 people in hideous ways in just two days. The second was, of course, quicker and more efficient, but the moral defence usually mounted, that war is war, is a maxim as comprehensible in the ancient world as it would have been to Genghis Khan or Napoleon. So-called civilization displays precisely Freud's divided self – capable of self-restraint and social progress, but capable of sudden lapses into barbarism.

The impact of famine, disease and war on human history was famously illustrated by the English 18th-century clergyman, Thomas Malthus, who argued in his *Essay on the Principle of Population,* published in 1798, that throughout history the dangers of overpopulation were always checked by the operation of these three elements. It is tempting to turn this argument on its head and wonder how it is that the human species survived at all under the multiple assault of violence, hunger and epidemic but it took another English biologist, Charles Darwin, with the publication of *The Origin of Species* in 1859, to explain that species survived through natural selection. The survival of *Homo sapiens* was thus biologically explicable; the stronger survived, the weaker perished. In a crude sense that was true, and for decades thereafter it was assumed that harsh though the realities of history had been, they had been necessary hardships to produce a biologically and intellectually progressive species. Both writers have in the end been confounded by a further paradox of the modern age: population has risen to levels often predicted as insupportable, but growth has scarcely been dented by the incidence of disease or violence or hunger, while natural selection has been overturned by modern medicine and welfare policies. The most violent and deadly century has at the same time been the century with the highest survival rates.

Grim though the past has often been, history has not been an unmediated story of suffering borne by an uncomprehending and victimized humanity. From the very earliest times human societies needed to make sense of the chaos and dangers around them, or to justify the hardships they faced, or the reality of unpredictable or premature death or to find some wider moral universe which sanctioned acceptable forms of behaviour and penalized others. Religion was able to satisfy all these needs and religious beliefs, like warfare, have been a constant for at least six millennia. Consideration of religion raises awkward questions about the nature of 'world history' because for most human societies through most of time, the material world described by modern historians has only been one part of the universe of human experience. Religious communities are connected to other unseen states and unknowable sites which have been, and for many still are, as profound a part of reality as the political structures and economic systems of the visible world. Belief in a world of spirits or an afterlife, or in unseen and divine guardians, or in a sublime universal 'other' has made historical experience multi-dimensional, natural as well as supernatural. For medieval Christians the world was one link in a complex chain between heaven and hell, which included the nether world of purgatory where souls were left to wait entry to paradise. For ancient Egyptians the other world was so real that kings talked and walked with the gods, and when they died took with them their household, animals, and furnishings. So widespread was the belief that the dead, or at least the kings, nobles and priests, needed to take possessions with them beyond the grave that modern knowledge of past cultures has been enormously expanded by the votive offerings and funerary furnishings found in excavated graves.

Belief in the supernatural, the divine, a world of the spirit, the reality of a soul that could live on beyond the decay of the earthly body, magic, superstition and witchcraft created for the inhabitants of all but the most recent communities a sphere of experience that was always larger than the material world around them. Belief was used to explain the apparently inexplicable, to ward off evil, to promote well-being, induce harmony of being and to prepare the mortal body for the world or worlds to come. The link with a world beyond mere physical observation has proved remarkably enduring, even in the secular, liberal West. In southern Italy images of saints and the Madonna are still carried through villages to offer protection against floods or volcanic eruptions or to encourage rainfall. The concept of 'the Limbo of the Infants', introduced as a term by the Catholic Church around 1300 to describe a haven for the souls of babies who died before there was time for baptism, in which they enjoyed a natural happiness, but were denied access to heaven, was all but set aside in 2007 when the Church announced that unbaptized infants should be entrusted to the possible mercy of God. Protests from parents anxious that their dead children should have a sure destination forced the Church to admit that Limbo was still a possibility. All attempts to provide a secular alternative to traditional Islam have foundered on the continuing vitality of the values and practices of the faith which is bound to a world beyond this one. Suicide bombers are recruited on the promise that they will be welcomed at once by the souls of the faithful when they cross the threshold of death.

Religions of every kind have exerted an extraordinary psychological power. This has been served in a number of ways. For thousands of years the finest buildings and monuments have been dedicated to religious purposes; in tribal societies the sacred – totems, ancestral graveyards – have exerted powerful fears and provoked an instinctive reverence. The numerous cathedrals, mosques and temples built in Christian, Islamic and Buddhist communities from medieval times onwards as gateways to the divine are among the richest architecture in the world, constructed in societies where for the poor the monumental buildings were awe-inspiring expressions of the spiritual. Religions were also the source of sanctioned behaviour. The rules laid down for social practice, custom, family life, or sexual conduct, are almost all religious in origin. A great many religions have been vehicles for constructing a male-centred society in which women were compelled to accept an ascribed and restricted gender role or risk severe forms of punishment or social discrimination. Many moral codes or legal systems were constructed by lay authorities – for example, Justinian's *Codex*, or the Code Napoleon – but they relied on a conception of acceptable behaviour that was derived from the core moral teaching of the Church. In traditional Islam there should ideally be no distinction between religious precept and state law. In early Chinese history the emperors were accorded divine status, making the law, but making it as gods. In Japanese society, where the emperors also enjoyed quasi-divine status, to die willingly for the emperor was a moral obligation that overrode all others.

Religious belief was always difficult to challenge because the threat that unbelief or heresy posed was a threat to an entire way of viewing the world. For a great many communities governed by animist or polytheistic systems of belief there were no reasons, and usually no means, for questioning the ground in which such belief was rooted. There was no question of earning salvation, but simply obeying the customary rites and endorsing the beliefs of a given system. Monotheistic religions, in which respect for the deity and reverence for doctrine earned the right to salvation, were altogether more problematic. Arguments about Christian doctrine brought regular schism, provoking the rift between Orthodox Christianity in Eastern Europe and Western Catholic Christianity in 1054, and further schism between Catholic and Protestant Christianity in the

16th century. Fear of heterodoxy, or of the diabolical, provoked Catholicism into regular heresy hunts and the extraction of confessions through torture. Protestant and Catholic were burnt at the stake for their faith in the struggle over the Reformation. Radical Protestantism was also fearful of idolatry or witchcraft and the last witches were famously burnt in Salem, Massachusetts, in 1692. Islam was also schismatic. In 680 AD the faith divided between Sunni and Shiite sects over disagreements on doctrine (including the Shia insistence that Allah could take human form), and the two branches are still engaged in violent confrontation throughout the Middle East. Convinced of the rightness of their cause, monotheistic religions enjoy a strong imperative to convert; those outside the pale, regarded as pagans or infidels, are damned. Conversion was seen as an obligation, part of God's purpose to ensure that among the many competing claims to a divine order only one could be the right one.

To claim no religious allegiance has been a recent and limited option, confined largely to the Western world. Atheism became publicly admissible in the 19th century without fear of punishment but the public denial of God still attracts outrage. Secularists over the past two centuries have been keen to separate Church and state, but have not necessarily been irreligious. The strident rejection of the supernatural was identified with 19th-century socialism whose world view was materialist. Atheism appealed to a progressive intelligentsia hostile to what they saw as stale Christian convention. When the German poet-philosopher Friedrich Nietzsche famously announced in *Thus Spake Zarathustra*, published in 1888, that 'God is dead!', he challenged what he saw as the great lie, dating back 2,000 years, and found a limited intellectual audience more than willing to accept a godless reality. In the early 20th century atheism was formally adopted by the Soviet Union, and communist China after 1949, but in neither case was it possible to eradicate belief. Atheism is now widely regarded as a declining intellectual force in an age of religious revivalism. The wide popular hostility to Richard Dawkins's recently published *The God Delusion* (2006) is testament to how necessary it is even for societies where church attendance is moribund that the material world is not just all there is.

For much of recorded history what was known or believed to be knowable was bound up with religion. Religious institutions and the priesthood were the depositories of knowledge passed down, like the famous Jewish Talmud, from generation to generation. The earliest work of 'wisdom literature' in ancient Egypt, perhaps in the world, was attributed to Imhotep, high priest of Heliopolis under Djoser, king between 2,654 and 2,635 BC. Religious buildings housed valuable manuscripts, not only sacred books but treatises on many subjects. During the early Christian era in Europe, in what use to be known as the 'Dark Ages', monasteries and churches kept alive traditions of teaching, writing and recording. The Venerable Bede, based at the monastery in Wearmouth-Jarrow in the north-east of England in the early 8th century, helped to collect together an estimated 300-500 volumes, one of the largest libraries of books in the then Western world. Western education was dominated by the Church until the 18th century. Knowledge of this kind was limited in several ways. First, it was confined to a very small elite who could read and write. A distinct literary or official language was developed which could be fully understood only by the favoured few. Although the earliest writing can be dated back to the Sumerian civilization in present-day Iraq around 5,000 years ago, and then appearing in Egypt and China, the overwhelming majority of all humans who lived between then and the last few centuries were illiterate. Knowledge for them was limited to what could be conveyed orally, or crudely illustrated. For most people information was passed on through rumour, superstition, ritual, songs, sagas and folk tales. Second, it was limited by the theological or philosophical priorities of those who held the key to knowledge, reinforcing existing views of the known world, or of man's relation to the universe, or of social hierarchy. Knowledge was used instrumentally, rather than for its own sake, confirming the existing order rather than encouraging critical or subversive discourse.

Knowledge in this sense did not inhibit technique. From the earliest settled communities onwards rapid strides were made in the practical skills associated with metallurgy, construction, irrigation, sculpture, and the production of artefacts of often stunning originality and beauty. The contrast between the last 6,000 years and the previous tens of thousands of years is remarkable. Early man made painfully slow progress in the development of sophisticated tools of stone or bone; humans in settled communities, with a division of labour and access to trade, could transfer technologies or fashions in a matter of years. By the time of the late Roman Empire, as any visit to a museum of classical archaeology will confirm, the range and sophistication of everything from daily products to major pieces of engineering was as advanced as anything that could be found for another thousand years. Practical skill was not, nevertheless, knowledge. Understanding of the natural world, like understanding of the supernatural, was conditional. It was possible to build the most technically remarkable and artistically splendid cathedral but still to believe that the earth was flat and hell really existed.

The development of a critical, sceptical, speculative science that did not endorse existing beliefs but deliberately undermined them, was a historical development of exceptional importance. The foundations of a speculative intellectual life were to be found in ancient Greece, whose philosophers, poets and playwrights produced work of real originality whose central concerns, despite the passage of 2,000 years, engaged the enthusiasm of educated Europeans when the classics were rediscovered in the late medieval period. Nineteenth-century intellectuals could write as if little separated their age from that of Plato or Aristotle or Aeschylus. The critical breakthrough in understanding the nature of material reality by thinking critically about accepted world-views was begun, however, during the sixteenth and seventeenth centuries, and associated mainly with the rise of a body of experimental or deductive science based on close observation. The key names are well-known. The Polish astronomer Nicolaus Copernicus dared to argue that the earth revolved around the sun in a book only published the year of his death, in 1543; the Italian astronomer Galileo Galilei extended these observations and in many other ways paved the way for much modern physical science, utilising recent developments in the mechanical sciences; the Englishman Thomas Hobbes laid the foundations of modern political science and human psychology in his *Leviathan*, published in 1651; in 1687 the mathematician Isaac Newton in his *Principia Mathematica* announced the law of gravity and ushered in a new age of mechanical physics. The scientific and philosophical revolution precipitated by the late 17th century in Europe opened the way to developing a modern understanding of nature and natural laws and above all accepting that such things were intrinsically knowable, not part of a Divine Plan whose purpose was not to be questioned. The new principle, according to the late 18th-century Prussian philosopher, Immanuel Kant, was *sapere aude* – 'dare to know'.

Those who pioneered a critical, scientific view of the world ran great risks. In 1616 the Catholic Church banned Copernican teaching, and placed Galileo under house arrest for challenging scripture. Galileo was fortunate: a few years before, in 1600, Giordano Bruno, another Copernican, was burnt at the stake in Rome. Hobbes was forced into exile, suspected of atheism; John Locke, who wrote the founding text of modern liberal representative government in the 1680s was also forced to write in exile, and his works circulated in parts of Europe in secret, too subversive for open sale. Writers of the 18th-century 'Enlightenment', during which critical thinking began to flourish for the first time, had to steer a careful line between what could or could not be said. Rousseau was also banned for life from his native city of Geneva for his radical democratic views. But it was a tide that could not be held back. By the early 19th century most of the modern Western sciences had been established on a firm scientific basis; political and social theory exploded traditional claims to authority (expressed most clearly in the founding of the American Republic in 1776 and the French Revolution of 1789); organized religion in its Western guise was shown to be unable to defend its major contentions about the nature of the universe and of man's place in it and an alternative, naturalistic, rational model of the world was substituted. The triumph of free expression now seems irreversible, but the revolution represented by modern thought was not inevitable and its progress was subject to fits and starts. It is still not entirely clear why the prevailing authorities in Europe came to tolerate the new intellectual wave when a century before it might have been violently suppressed. The publication in 1859 of *On Liberty* by the English philosopher John Stuart Mill summed up what had been achieved in modern Europe. There was no other freedom, Mill asserted, more fundamental than the right to say what you like without fear that you will be silenced.

The formal acquisition of scientific, material knowledge about all aspects of the natural world and its application to human societies has been responsible for transforming world history more fundamentally than any other development in the past 6,000 years. Whatever case can be made for showing that there are strong lines of continuity throughout world history, the possibilities opened up by transcending the narrow world view of a God-centred and God-given universe have been unprecedented. It is a story intimately bound to the wider history of the rise of Europe (which with European expansion to America came to be regarded as the Western world) over the past 500 years. Historians have often been tempted to see this is as a happily progressive narrative while the rest of the world stagnated. From a Western perspective the idea of 'the triumph of the West' has an evident plausibility. Yet it begs the larger question of why Europe did evolve in very different ways, not only from the other civilizations existing alongside, but from all previous civilizations. What has been distinctive about the West, as Karl Marx argued in the mid-19th century, is the fact that it proved capable of expanding world-wide; Marx thought that no other culture or civilization would be capable of withstanding what Europe had to offer or what it forced upon them.

There is no agreed or straightforward answer to the question 'why Europe?' Geography was clearly favourable – a temperate climate, generally adequate food supplies, population growth steady but not excessively large, few of the debilitating, parasite-borne diseases that affected large parts of Africa and Asia with elephantiasis, river-blindness, bilharzia or malaria. The long European shoreline, never very far from any human habitation, encouraged the development of seaborne trade and exploration and the development of early sea power. Seafaring technology was one of the earliest and most important of the technical revolutions and Europeans exploited it fully. Europe also succeeded in stemming the tide of regular invasion which had characterized European history for almost a thousand years from the collapse of the Western Roman Empire. The Tatar invasions of the 13th century and the expansion of the Ottoman Turkish Empire into south-eastern Europe during the early modern period were checked sufficiently to allow central and western Europe to consolidate the state system, to build a settled network of cities, and a regular trading network. The military organization of Europe was transformed by the application of gunpowder and the development of cannon and musket-fire. Although these innovations were usually used against other Europeans, they gave Europeans a clear advantage whenever they found themselves fighting non-European peoples. It is sometimes argued that post-Reformation Protestantism, with its emphasis on individualism, played an important part in making Europe different, but the earliest explorers and imperialists were Catholic Portuguese and Spanish, while the Americas were discovered by an Italian from Genoa, Cristoforo Colombo. The long history of the Crusades against the Arab Middle East showed that there was nothing passive about Catholic Christianity.

The distinctive characteristic of European societies as they solidified into an early version of the modern states' system was their willingness to look outwards towards the wider world. The voyages of discovery were not isolated examples of a lucky piece of exploration, but rapidly embraced the whole globe, making it clear in the process that the earth was round rather than flat. Only Europeans embraced the world in this way: map-making, navigation, inland exploration, elaborate descriptions of native communities and exotic fauna and flora, all contributed to creating a view of the world fundamentally different from the view from Constantinople or Beijing. Not only did Europeans discover large areas of the hitherto unknown (at least to Europeans) but they began a process of aggressive settlement across the Americas, in parts of Africa and India and into the archipelagos of the western Pacific 'spice islands'. If occasionally briefly reversed, European expansion proved irresistible and European appetites insatiable. The Spanish conquistador Hernán Cortés captured the Aztec capital Tenochtitlán in 1520 with 300 Spanish troops and some local allies aided by the fact that around half the city's 300,000 inhabitants had died of imported smallpox. Once the imperial toeholds were established across the oceans, Europeans never abandoned them. They became a source of remarkable wealth, helping eventually to make Europe richer than any rival civilization, and making it possible to defend and extend the imperial frontier.

Wealth itself would not have made Europe distinctive. The rulers of China and India were fabulously rich. What made the difference was how that wealth was used. The application of rational organization and scientific technique made possible a remarkable economic revolution. An important fraction of the wealth generated in Europe was mobile wealth, mobilized to develop yet further wealth by banks and commercial houses, which developed across Europe from the late 17th century. This was the engine that made commercial capitalism possible and it was fuelled by an acquisitive urge that was subject to few customary or religious restrictions. From the late 18th century the mobile wealth was used to fund a second revolution of technique. Although inventiveness was nothing strictly European – Chinese scientists and engineers had anticipated many European discoveries, including gunpowder – the critical difference was the application of invention. The development of steam technology in Britain made possible the mobilization of new and efficient forms of energy quite distinct from the water or horse-powered technologies of other cultures. The development of gas and later generated electricity as an energy source, the mastery of turbine technology, the perfection of rail locomotion, were all

THE TIMES HISTORY OF THE WORLD

uniquely Western, a blend of European and American innovation. In a mere hundred years the gap between Western technique and the rest of the world was unbridgeable, making possible the rapid expansion of European states as imperial powers. The British American colonies won their independence in 1783, and European settlers, enjoying the same technical advantages and territorial ambitions, occupied the whole area of North America between Mexico and Canada by the middle years of the 19th century.

The economic and technical revolutions relied on a high level of social and spatial mobility. Europeans moved abroad in large numbers, bringing with them Christianity, guns, and trade. In western Europe there were few barriers to social mobility, allowing new classes of successful bankers, merchants and manufacturers to play an influential part in public affairs. The establishment of secure property rights and respect for individual wealth-making removed any legal inhibitions on the right to make money. The publication of Adam Smith's classic *The Wealth of Nations* in 1776 provided a sound intellectual basis for the claim that the interests of communities were best served by allowing the free play of market forces and individual pursuit of economic well-being. Economic individualism and belief in the benign concept of the market had no equivalent in other cultures. Internal mobility was also important. The new industries attracted large numbers of rural workers who were no longer tied to the soil, at least in western Europe. Rapid population growth from the late 18th century, which threatened to put a severe strain on food supplies, was absorbed into the new cities; at the same time rising agricultural yields and the application of modern techniques (fertiliser cycles, threshing machines, stock breeding) made it just possible for the mobile urban population to be fed. The new wealth could then be used to fund overseas food production and imported foodstuffs. In 1877 the first refrigerated food was carried on board ship between Argentina and France making it possible to bring meat and fruit half-way across the world.

The economic revolution was accompanied by other important changes. In Europe and the United States the idea of education for all replaced the traditional distinction between illiterate mass and the educated few. Education was basic for most people, but opportunities for higher forms of training or for university expanded throughout the 19th century and became general in the twentieth. Civil rights and the rule of law were applied in most European states and the settler communities overseas, and limited progress was made towards representative forms of government. One of the most striking aspects of the move to greater emancipation was the gradual recognition in the liberal West that women should have equal rights – social, sexual, political – with men, even if the principle has not always worked as it should. Finally, the idea of the modern nation-state, in which identity was derived from being a citizen of a particular nation, defined by territory, shared culture and language, although far from universal even in Europe in the 19th century (and certainly not applied to Europe's empires), set the model that has been subsequently established worldwide. The United Nations now counts 195 sovereign states, all but three as members.

The impact of Western wealth, military advantage, technology and ambition on the rest of the world was catastrophic. India was conquered, the Mughal emperors overthrown, and British rule imposed. China succeeded in keeping the West at bay, but at the cost of regular punitive expeditions, and the final sapping of China's traditional political system by Western-educated Chinese who wanted China to adopt modern politics and economics. The Ottoman Empire crumbled under the remorseless pressure of Europe, which took over the whole of North Africa and encroached on the Ottoman Middle East. The Empire finally collapsed in 1919 at the end of the First World War. Everywhere else traditional societies, long isolated from any contact with a wider world, were visited, annexed, fought over and incorporated into the Western orbit. What resulted was usually an unstable mix of tradition and novelty, the old order sufficiently challenged or undermined that it could no longer function effectively, the new order mediated by surviving social traditions, religious practices and native cultures. The one exception was Japan. Contact with the West in the 1850s was perceived to be an immediate threat. In 1868 the Tokugawa Shogunate was overthrown, the Meiji emperor restored, and a rapid process of modernization undertaken to shield Japan from Western imperialism. Within forty years Japan's modern armed forces could defeat the much larger Russian army and navy in the war of 1904-5; in the 1930s Japan invaded large parts of China and in 1941 Japanese forces launched a swift and successful campaign against American and European territories in the Pacific and South-East Asia which was reversed only by the exploitation of Western technologies yet more advanced.

The changes ushered in by the rise of European and American power have developed exponentially. The history of the past 250 years shows a dizzying transformation: global horizons have narrowed with mass communication and the development of a homogenized consumer culture; a level of knowledge and technical achievement unimaginable a century ago makes it possible to explore planets millions of miles distant, to revisit the earliest moments of the universe, to understand the genetic codes that dictate human biology, to harness lasers and micro-electronic components to produce a technical base not only of exceptional sophistication, but one that is also democratic in its reach. Some sense of the sheer speed of change can be illustrated in numerous ways, but few examples are more remarkable than the difference between the colonial wars of the late 19th century, fought with Gatling machine guns, rifles and small artillery pieces and the Second World War fought only forty years later with tanks, high-speed aircraft, radar, radio, missiles, and, in its late stages, with jet aircraft and nuclear weapons.

The Western experience, for all its technical and social achievements, has nonetheless been profoundly ambiguous. There have been perhaps no other civilizations which have been so publicly anxious about the prospects for their survival, so fearful of pride before a fall. The two world wars, both generated in Europe, compromised that claim to be the heartland of modern civilization and a source of social progress and moral authority, which had been relayed throughout the last decades of the 19th century. Exporting ideas about civil rights and nationhood accelerated the decline and disappearance of the old European empires. The transfer of the British crown colony of Hong Kong to Chinese rule in 1997 marked a symbolic end to a long history of coercive European expansion and acknowledged China's growing international stature. The export of Western technology and commercial skills resulted in the collapse of many European industries and the transfer of large-scale manufacturing to the rapidly growing economies of eastern and south-eastern Asia. The global reach of Western commerce and the remorseless march of English as the global language has produced a backlash against what are perceived to be new forms of imperialism, and against the crass failure of Western states to understand the complex differences that still mark off communities in Asia, Africa, Latin America or the Middle East from the Western model. Islamic terrorism is only one of the many fruits of hostility to the idea that somehow the Western model ought to be appropriate in any cultural or geographical context.

Where, then, is this history going? Accelerated change can be read several ways: it could either mean speeding downhill to the edge of the precipice, or climbing rapidly to a richer, more secure and more peaceable world. Historians would do well do be humble in the face of the future. The unpredictable and unpredicted can be found throughout the chapters that follow. How few commentators and Sovietologists thought in the late 1980s that the Soviet bloc would possibly collapse in a matter of a few years; how many observers thought, wrongly, that HIV/AIDS would provoke an unstoppable pandemic which would decimate the world's population. One thing can be said with certainty: for all the talk of a new unipolar world built around the massive military power of the United States and the appeal of the Western model, the foreseeable future will have China, Russia, India and the Middle East, the great bulk of the world's population, developing in ways that are not consistent with an ideal Western model, capable of exerting a growing influence on global economic structures and the distribution of political influence, able perhaps to restore at least some of that diversity in historical experience characteristic of all recorded history up to the 19th century.

Taking the longer view there is little to be said. A hundred human lives of 60 years will take us to 8,000 AD. Perhaps the acceleration of history will provoke a sudden crash long before that. There remain the awful paradoxes that the more 'progress' there has been, the more violence, discrimination and crime has been generated and the more economic desires are satisfied, the nearer the earth moves to ecological crisis. As Nietzsche remarked more than a century ago, 'the universe does not need man'. Human history may well be finite. On the other hand, the history of the world hitherto has shown man to be a remarkably adaptable, ambitious, unscrupulous, technically adept creature. This history so far is no simple parable of survival and triumph; the future of the world may have to be just that.

Richard Overy, 2008

ONE

HUMAN ORIGINS AND EARLY CULTURES

Recorded history is only the tip of an iceberg reaching back to the first appearance on earth of the human species. Anthropologists, prehistorians and archaeologists have extended our vista of the past by hundreds of thousands of years: we cannot understand human history without taking account of their findings. The transformation of humankind (or, more accurately, of certain groups of humans in certain areas) from hunters and fishers to agriculturists, and from a migratory to a sedentary life, constitutes the most decisive revolution in the whole of human history. The climatic and ecological changes which made it possible have left their mark on the historical record down to the present day.

Agriculture made possible not merely a phenomenal growth of human population, which is thought to have increased some 16-fold between 8000 and 4000 BC, but also gave rise to the familiar landscape of village communities which still characterized Europe as late as the middle of the 19th century and which even today prevails in many parts of the world. Nowhere are the continuities of history more visible. The enduring structures of human society, which transcend and outlive political change, carry us back to the end of the Ice Age, to the changes which began when the shrinking ice-cap left a new world to be explored and tamed.

FROM *c.* 5 MILLION YEARS AGO
HUMAN ORIGINS

Global cooling between five and six million years ago saw savannahs replace the tropical forests of sub-Saharan Africa. The appearance of this new environment was in turn matched by an evolutionary pulse that gave rise to new carnivores and omnivores. Among them were the hominines, the ancestors of modern man.

The earliest hominine fossils, discovered in the Afar region of Ethiopia, are the fragmentary 4.5-million-year-old remains of *Ardipithecus ramidus*. Better evidence is available of the later and more widespread Australopithecenes, or "southern apes". Skeletal and fossilized footprints of *Australopithecus afarensis*, dated to between three and four million years ago, indicate a serviceable if not fully bipedal gait, hands still partly adapted for specialized tree climbing and a brain approximately one-third the size of ours. This species is the probable ancestor both of the robustly built Australopithecines *boisei*, *aethiopicus* and *robustus*, all with large teeth and herbivorous diets, and of our genus, *Homo*, meaning "man". A major discovery thrown up by fieldwork since the 1950s has revealed that these closely related but nonetheless distinctive species not only lived at the same time but side by side in the same habitats. Finds of more species are expected.

From between two and three million years ago, there is evidence of important evolutionary trends in *Homo*: brains became much bigger, a process known as encephalization; and full bipedalism was attained – as the 1974 discovery of the fossil skeleton known as 'Lucy' shows. As larger brains need better diets to sustain them, the increase in brain size could only have occurred as a result of significant evolutionary pressures. The problem was compounded because hominines stayed the same size, with the result that their bigger brains could be achieved only by reducing the size of another organ, the stomach, a trade-off which in turn reduced the efficiency of the digestive tract, which in turn demanded a still better diet.

EARLY TECHNOLOGIES

The most convincing explanation of this development – the expensive tissue hypothesis – holds that a move towards an energy-rich diet, particularly animal proteins, was responsible. And indeed the earliest-known stone tools, found in Gona, Ethiopia, suggest that 2.5 million years ago meat was a central part of hominines' diet, with the sharpened stones used to cut flesh and pound marrow-rich bones from carcasses either scavenged or brought down and then defended against carnivores. Burnt bones found in southern Africa indicate that by 1.5 million years ago hominines had learned to "cook" their food, a development which again would have compensated for smaller stomachs by breaking down animal proteins before digestion took place.

OUT OF AFRICA

This pattern of development was the basis for the first colonization, by *Homo erectus*, 1.8 million years ago of areas outside sub-Saharan Africa. Then, around 500,000 years ago, *Homo heidelbergensis* migrated into north Africa and the Near East, reaching northern Europe about 400,000 years ago (however there is also good evidence in northern Europe for hominines 700,000 years ago). *Homo erectus* and *heidelbergensis* are sometimes considered to have shared a common ancestor, a type designated as *Homo ergaster*, and best known from the skeleton found at Nariokotome in Kenya's Rift valley. By perhaps 1.5 million years ago, all three had brains of about 1000cc (61cu in) and an adaptable stone technology: the weight and careful shaping of the edges of their distinctive handaxes, whether pointed or oval, made them effective butchery tools.

Stone technology was not the only factor in the evolutionary pressures that led to larger brains. It was also to do with allowing hominines to remember, to manipulate, to support and to organize others in more complex ways. Perhaps paradoxically, as hominines developed these more sophisticated social structures, so they simultaneously became less reliant on one another and better adapted to living in smaller groups. This in turn allowed them to colonize harsher barrier habitats such as the Sahara at the margins of their homelands from where they could colonize new, more temperate areas beyond.

MODERN HUMANS

From about 500,000 years ago, this early burst of colonization came to a halt. Instead, though there were undoubtedly many dispersals of populations and much intermingling of genes, regional groups of separate populations living side by side such as the Neanderthals developed. But from 100,000 years ago, another major dispersal began when anatomically modern people – *Homo sapiens sapiens* – emigrated from sub-Saharan Africa. By 50,000 years ago, Australia had been reached, by boat; 33,000 years ago, the western Pacific islands were colonized; 15,000 years ago, the Americas were reached. Major expansion into the Arctic began about 4500 years ago as the continental ice sheets retreated. Finally, 2000 years ago, humans began to settle the deep Pacific islands from where they reached New Zealand around 1200 years ago, 1000 years before the island's discovery by Captain Cook.

FROM *c.* 200,000 YEARS AGO

THE SPREAD OF MODERN HUMANS

DNA studies have revealed that the first anatomically modern humans – *Homo sapiens* – arose in Africa between 200,000 and 140,000 years ago. Though much has still to be discovered about their origins and dispersal, by almost 28,000 years ago *Homo sapiens* had become not only the sole human species but the first truly global one.

The earliest modern-looking human skulls yet found are about 130,000 years old and come from the Omo basin in Ethiopia and Klasies River Mouth in southern Africa, the latter one of the best-researched sites of early human habitation. Perhaps 100,000 years ago, these early populations began to disperse, migrating northwards out of Africa. These migrations were followed by a process known as "bottlenecking" in which population levels among the dispersed peoples remained small for thousands of years. It is possible that a contributory factor to bottlenecking was the eruption of Toba in northwest Sumatra 71,000 years ago, an environmental catastrophe on an extraordinary scale: parts of India were covered with ash up to 3m (10ft) deep, global temperatures were lowered for a millennium. At the same time, the restricted populations generated by bottlenecking had the side effect of encouraging rapid changes in genetic structures thereby increasing the pace of evolutionary change.

Archaeological and genetic evidence then point to a further rapid expansion of modern human populations about 50,000 years ago. The archaeological evidence in particular highlights growing sophistication and the mastery of a wide and increasing range of skills. In some regions, lighter, multi-component weapons have been found, including spears made from skilfully produced stone blades fixed to wooden shafts and handles. There is evidence, too, of textiles and baskets, and of more orderly layouts of camp-sites, including cold-weather dwellings and underground food stores. Trading networks also increased dramatically. Raw materials, particularly stone, which had previously been traded over distances of less than 80km (50 miles), were now traded over several hundreds of kilometres (there is good evidence for this in eastern Europe).

THE NEANDERTHALS

Homo sapiens was by no means the only human species in the world of 50,000 years ago. In East and southeast Asia lived the descendants of those *Homo erectus* populations who had colonized the region over a million years earlier. Among other human populations the best known are the Neanderthals, distinguished from modern humans by their distinctive large and low-crowned heads with prominent brows and big teeth and powerful stocky bodies well adapted to cold. By contrast, the incoming modern people had an African body pattern – slender with long legs and small torsos – that copes better with heat stress. The Neanderthals had brains as large as modern humans and were in many ways highly successful. They adapted well to a wide range of habitats and climates ranging from the relatively arid Middle East to the cold of central Europe; their use of tools was sophisticated; and they were effective hunters of animals in prime condition such as bison, horse and reindeer. The burial of their dead, often with some elaboration, also indicates signs of a recognizably modern humanity. They almost certainly had language, too. But what the Neanderthals seem not to have possessed is the degree of social flexibility and cultural tradition that more than any other characteristic singles out *Homo sapiens* and explains our ultimate success in becoming the only global hominine.

This social and intellectual sophistication reveals itself in a number of ways but the result of it was almost always the same: the evolution of more complex social relations which allowed early humans to thrive in a much wider range of habitats and societies than previous hominine species had managed before. Whether living in large or small groups, *Homo sapiens* was able to overcome its environment to an unprecedented degree. The most striking evidence is provided by the wide variety of artefacts that have been discovered: engraved stones, ornaments, figurines, exotic shells, amber and ivory and, most famously, cave paintings. That the latter were frequently inaccessible and could have been seen only with ladders and artificial light suggests that a variety of factors motivated their creators. Whatever the explanation, these early works of art are an evocative monument to the humanity of these early hunters.

It is significant that the Neanderthals had almost no cultural traditions of this kind. A few incised bones have been found; similarly, the very occasional exotic piece of raw material occurs. By almost 28,000 years ago, both Neanderthals and *Homo erectus* were extinct. Modern humans had already colonized Australia 20,000 years before, and were set to colonize the Americas before 12,000 years ago. Henceforth modern humans were the sole surviving hominine in the world.

20,000 TO 10,000 BC
THE ICE AGE WORLD

By 10,000 years ago, humans had colonized almost the whole of the habitable world. It was an achievement made in the face of the last of a series of Ice Ages, when vast sheets of ice periodically advanced and retreated. The human species today is the product of this long process of adaptation to the varied conditions of the Ice Ages.

There have been eight Ice Ages in the last 800,000 years, each interspersed with warmer periods from 30,000 to 10,000 years known as interglacials, brief and extreme parts of this cycle. The Ice Ages were periods of exceptional cold away from the equator. Ice sheets advanced across the frozen wastes of the northern hemisphere as temperatures fell by up to 15 degrees centigrade. With so much of the earth's water locked into the ice sheets, sea levels fell by up to 150m (500ft). As they did so, land bridges appeared, linking many major land areas and present-day islands into larger continental land masses.

Equatorial regions were also affected: as rainfall diminished, half the land area between the tropics became desert. With each advance of the ice, the plants and animals of the northern hemisphere withdrew to warmer latitudes. As the ice retreated, so they moved northwards again. Humans, too, must have migrated with these changing climates. Yet despite the extremes of cold, the human species continued to develop, spreading from its original African homeland to east and southeast Asia and to Europe. Mastery of fire and the invention of clothing were crucial to this achievement, as were new social and communication skills.

ICE AGE HUMANS

The height of the last Ice Age or LGM (last glacial maximum) was reached about 20,000 years ago. As the ice expanded, human populations contracted into a small number of more favourable habitats. Across almost the whole of the Eurasian landmass between the ice to the north and the deserts to the south, from the glacial cul-de-sac of Alaska to southern France, productive grasslands and steppes were created. Rich in seasonal grasses, they sustained large herds of mammoth, bison, horse and reindeer, all of them important food sources for Palaeolithic (the period of the emergence of modern man, about 2.5–3 million years ago to 12,000 BC) hunters.

Much the same sort of habitat seems to have developed in North America. By the time modern humans migrated there about 15,000 years ago, the rolling grasslands were teeming with animal life: giant bison with a six-foot horn spread; towering beaver-like creatures called casteroides; camels; ground sloths; stag moose; two types of musk-oxen; several varieties of large, often lion-sized cats; mastodons; and three types of mammoth. So effectively did the new human population hunt them that by about 10,000 years ago almost all of them were extinct, including the horse, re-introduced to the New World only by Europeans following in the wake of Columbus.

South of the Eurasian mammoth steppe lay an extensive zone of drier conditions. Indeed parts of the Sahara, the Near East and India became almost entirely arid, forcing their populations along permanent watercourses such as the Nile. Similar patterns of settlement are found in Australia, where cemeteries discovered along the Murray River bear marked resemblances to those along the Nile.

Modern humans were late arrivals in western Europe, replacing Neanderthal populations only from about 35,000 years ago. Yet the new communities developed remarkable levels of cultural expression. In southwest France, the Pyrenees and northern Spain, hundreds of caves decorated with paintings of symbols and animals have been discovered, evidence of a rich cultural tradition.

By 12,000 years ago, the last Ice Age was drawing to a close. As temperatures rose, vegetation spread and animals re-colonized the cold northern wastes. With them went hunters and gatherers. By 10,000 BC in Central America and the Near East, people had begun to move beyond their existing resources and to investigate new ways of producing food and manipulating plants and animals in the first experiments in farming.

FROM HUNTING TO FARMING: THE ORIGINS OF AGRICULTURE

The transition from hunting and gathering to agriculture irreversibly changed human society, but it involved the domestication (selective cropping and planting, or herding and rearing) of relatively few plants and animals and occurred independently in a very few areas. The earliest evidence of agriculture comes from the Levant 10,000 years ago, from where it spread to Europe, northern Africa and central Asia.

Ten thousand years ago, at the end of the last Ice Age, the human population numbered only a few millions and all their food came from wild plants and animals. Then people began to domesticate some species, so that today almost the entire world population depends for food on a relatively small range of crops and domestic animals. During the 150,000 years that preceded the "agricultural revolution", anatomically modern humans had colonized most of the the globe and had learned to survive as foragers, subsisting on a great diversity of plant and animal foods. Foragers moved seasonally in small groups to obtain their food supplies and population densities remained low for many millennia.

FORAGING TO FARMING

By 8000 BC, some groups of foragers had settled down and occupied favourable sites year-round. Their populations increased, as restraints on fertility imposed by the seasonally mobile way of life were relaxed, and they ranged less far for their food. This profound change in human behaviour led to the beginnings of agriculture, enabling more people to be supported on a given area of land – although at the cost of the greater effort needed to cultivate crops and raise domestic animals. The effects of settling down, population increase, and growing dependence on agriculture led to increases in the number and size of settlements, to the development of more complex, less egalitarian societies, and, eventually, to urban life and civilization.

The earliest evidence of agriculture consists of the remains of wild species that have been altered in their morphology or behaviour by human intervention. Foremost among the crops are the cereals and pulses (peas, beans and other herbaceous legumes), the seeds of which provide carbohydrate and some protein and are easily stored. They sustained early civilizations and are still staples today. They were domesticated from wild grasses in subtropical regions, for example wheat, barley, lentil, pea and chickpea in southwestern Asia; rice, soya and mung bean in southern and eastern Asia; sorghum, other millets and cowpea in tropical Africa; and maize and the common bean in Mexico. Root crops have also become staples in many areas, such as the potato, which was domesticated in the Andes and is now a major crop of temperate areas, and manioc (cassava), yams, taro and sweet potato, all of which were native to the tropics.

DOMESTICATION OF ANIMALS

Whereas cereals and root crops were brought into cultivation and domesticated in all the habitable continents except Australia (where agriculture was introduced by European settlers in the 18th century AD), animals were domesticated in relatively few areas, principally in western Asia, where there is evidence for the early domestication of sheep, goats, pigs and cattle, followed later by asses, horses and camels. Some forms of cattle and pigs, as well as chickens, were domesticated in southern and eastern Asia, and cattle and pigs may also have been domesticated independently in Europe. Very few animals were domesticated in the Americas – turkey in North America and llama, alpaca and guinea pig in South America – and none in tropical Africa or Australia.

THE SPREAD OF FARMING

The earliest known transition to agriculture took place in the "Fertile Crescent" of southwestern Asia during the Neolithic period starting about 8000 BC. Sites in the Levant have yielded charred seeds and chaff of barley, wheat and various pulses, as well as the bones of domestic goats and sheep. Grain cultivation began here about 1000 years before goat and sheep pastoralism. Dependence on agriculture increased very gradually, paralleled by the spread of village settlement, the development of techniques of irrigation and terracing, and the cultivation of fruits. By the end of the Neolithic in southwestern Asia, about 6000 years ago, agriculture had spread west and east into Europe, northern Africa and central and southern Asia.

Agriculture began independently in China between 7000 and 6000 BC, in the Americas by about 3000 BC and in tropical Africa by about 2000 BC. By the time of the 16th century AD European expansion in the agricultural and pastoral economies occupied most of Eurasia, Africa and Central and South America.

10,000 TO 4000 BC

BEFORE THE FIRST CITIES: SOUTHWEST ASIA

The period 10,000 to 4000 BC witnessed three critical developments: the origins of settled life; the first farming; and the first cities. The origin of agriculture is often referred to as the "Neolithic revolution", but archaeology reveals only gradual changes in techniques of food acquisition over thousands of years, which by 8000 BC led to villages dependent on food production.

The earliest changes visible in the archaeological record relate not to food production but to social relations, indicated not only in the tendency to reside in one location over longer periods and in the investment of labour in more substantial and more permanent structures, but also in the growth of ritual, an important factor in social cohesion. Indeed it is possible that this "symbolic revolution" was of greater immediate significance than the economic changes we associate with the origins of agriculture.

Lakeshore and riverine sites were important for their rich and varied resources, while the utilitarian date palm flourished in marsh areas in southern Mesopotamia, rich also in fish and waterfowl. The earliest permanent settlements tend to be found at the junctions of discrete environmental zones, with greater access to a variety of resources (for example Abu Hureyra on the boundary of the dry steppe and the Euphrates flood plain, and Ain Mallaha in the Jordan valley). The importance of ritual house fittings and skull cults, perhaps suggestive of the increasing importance of the family and property, is attested at some of the earliest sites (Qermez Dere), while 9th-millennium villages in Anatolia, with early evidence for the cultivation of cereals, contain impressive ritual buildings (Çayönü, Nevali Çori). The carving of stone (Göbekli Tepe, Jerf al Ahmar, Nemrik) and the working of copper (Çayönü) are found well before the appearance of true farming villages. The early use of clay for containers is attested at Mureybet on the Euphrates (9000 BC) and at Ganj

Dareh in the Zagros; white lime plaster vessels are characteristic of the latest pre-pottery Neolithic phases, especially at sites in the Levant and Anatolia.

THE DEVELOPMENT OF VILLAGES

Among the best-known pre-pottery Neolithic sites is Jericho, in the 9th millennium BC already a settlement of some 1.5ha (4 acres) with, uniquely, a rock-cut ditch and stone wall with a huge circular tower ascended by means of an internal circular stair. A millennium later Basta and Ain Ghazal in Jordan are farming settlements of over 9.5ha (24 acres). Human skulls on which faces had been realistically modelled were kept by the inhabitants of these sites, while at Ain Ghazal deposits of cultic statues have been recovered.

In the 7th and 6th millennia BC, developed Neolithic villages appear over much of the landscape. They are characterized by economies dependent on domesticated plants and animals, and on sophisticated technological developments (for example an "industrial" area of two-stage pottery kilns, and the presence of lead and copper at Yarim Tepe around 6000 BC). Well-fired painted pottery characterizes these villages, which are often classified by their ceramic styles. One of the most spectacular early pottery sites is Çatalhöyük, 13ha (32 acres) in area, with extensive evidence for wealth in the form of valuable commodities such as obsidian and semi-precious stones. The house fittings bear elaborate ornaments including wall paintings and the plastered skulls of wild cattle.

TRADE AND TEMPLES

An important development attested in the Neolithic villages of north Mesopotamia and Syria is the earliest record-keeping, effected by the use of combinations of small clay tokens and the stamping of distinctive clay or stone seals onto clay lids and other fastenings (most importantly at Sabi Abyad in the Samarran period and slightly later at Arpachiyah). Such simple methods of validating social contracts and other transactions formed the basis of later literate urban recording systems.

Mesopotamia had no metals or semi-precious stones, and by the 5th millennium BC demand for such luxury goods led to the establishment of small colonies in Anatolia, even as far as the Malatya plain (Değirmentepe) and the sea-borne exploitation of the resources of the Persian Gulf (Dosariyah, Abu

Khamis), even as far as the Musandam peninsula. The first temples were built at this time in southern Mesopotamia, precursors of the institutions around which the earliest urban states were organized. There was a temple on the same site at Eridu for 3500 years, striking evidence of the continuity of tradition which was one remarkable feature of the world's earliest city-states.

Despite their precocious development, sites like Jericho and Çatalhöyük did not form the focus of more complex polities. By 4000 BC the foundations of literate, urban civilization had been laid in Mesopotamia, where it was the organizational and economic potential of the highly productive irrigation economy in the south and the powerful, strategic positions of sites like Nineveh in the north, controlling access to areas rich in raw materials, that saw the growth of the world's first complex states.

7000 TO 2000 BC

EARLY EUROPE: THE COLONIZATION OF A CONTINENT

Farming first spread from the Near East to southeast Europe c. 7000 BC and then along the Mediterranean coast and across central Europe, reaching the Low Countries by 5000 BC. After a brief pause it spread to Britain and northern continental Europe by 4000 BC. It was only c. 2000 BC that farming reached the more northerly parts of European Russia and the Baltic.

The earliest farming villages in Europe, dating to immediately after 7000 BC, were on the western side of the Aegean (eg Argissa) and on Crete (eg Knossos), but by 5500 BC such villages were distributed widely across the Balkans. They consisted of clusters of mudbrick buildings, each with a similar layout of hearth and cooking and sleeping areas. Their economy was based on keeping sheep and cultivating wheat and legumes. Such villages were situated in areas of good soil with a plentiful water supply and were often occupied for hundreds of years.

AGRICULTURAL VILLAGES

Villages of this kind spread inland as far as Hungary but from here northwards a new pattern developed. The mudbrick dwellings were replaced by wooden long-houses whose remains did not build up into settlement mounds. Agricultural settlement spread in a broad band from northeast France to southwest Russia on soils produced by the weathering of loess – a highly fertile windblown dust laid down during the Ice Age. Over this area the characteristic pottery was decorated with incised lines in spiral or meandering bands, a uniformity which reflects the rapid spread of settlement between 5500 and 5000 BC. Cattle were more important than sheep in the forested interior of Europe but wheat continued as the main cereal crop. The settlers did not clear wide areas of land but practised intensive horticulture in the valleys around their settlements.

At the same time as it was spreading into continental Europe, aspects of an agricultural way of life were also spreading westwards along the northern shore of the Mediterranean, reaching Spain by around 5500 BC; in this zone environmental conditions were much closer to those where agriculture started and fewer adjustments had to be made.

Alongside the early agricultural communities, small groups of foragers pursued their way of life in areas untouched by the new economy. Hunting populations were rather sparse in the areas first selected by agriculturists, and the rapidity with which farming spread across the loess lands may in part reflect a lack of local competition, but elsewhere foragers were more numerous. They were especially well-established in the lake-strewn landscapes left by the retreating ice sheets around the Alps and on the northern edge of the North European Plain.

There has been much debate about whether the spread of agriculture was due to the expansion of colonizing populations from the southeast or to the adoption of the new way of life by existing foragers. Current evidence from archaeology and the analysis of the DNA of modern populations suggests that there was a colonizing element, probably associated with the expansion through the Balkans and the loess lands of central Europe, but that in most of Europe the dominant process was the adoption of agriculture and its material attributes by existing populations, perhaps in part because of the prestige of the new way of life.

MEGALITHIC EUROPE

In much of western Europe, farming was first adopted around 4000 BC and the clearance of land in rocky terrain provided the opportunity to build large stone (megalithic) monuments as burial places and mortuary shrines for the scattered hamlets of early farmers. Some of the earliest megalithic tombs were built in Brittany and Portugal around 4500 BC, but particularly elaborate forms were made in Ireland and Spain up to 2000 years later. Alongside the tombs, other kinds of megalithic monuments were constructed in some regions, such as the stone circles of the British Isles.

From 4500 to 2500 BC, important developments occurred which were to change the established pattern of life. Early metallurgy of copper and gold developed in the Balkans from 4500 BC, although whether this was an independent invention or came from the Near East is still in dispute. Fine examples of the products come from the rich Copper Age cemetery of Varna on the Black Sea coast.

From around 3500 BC there is evidence of contact between eastern Europe and the steppe zone north of the Black Sea; some link this to the spread of Indo-European languages to Europe. The time around 3500 BC also saw the rapid spread across Europe of wheeled vehicles and the plough, both associated with the first large-scale use of draught animals. These slowly changed the nature of agricultural production. Widespread clearance of forests took place and flint mines produced stone for large quantities of axes. It was only after 2000 BC that stone axes were superseded by metal ones in western Europe.

TO 900 BC

AFRICAN PEOPLES AND CULTURES

Archaeology is revealing evidence that strongly suggests that the evolution of humans began in Africa. Virtually every stage of our development – stretching back over 5 million years – can be traced in the African record. Almost throughout this vast span of prehistory our ancestors lived in mobile groups engaged in scavenging, gathering and hunting.

From about the 10th millennium BC onwards, conditions in large parts of Africa were wetter than they are today, and human settlements began to spring up by lakes and rivers, from the Rift valley and Sudanese Nile valley in the east, across what are now the central and southern Saharan regions, to the Senegal River in the west. These earliest African settlements were based on fishing and were characterized by certain shared aspects of material culture, most notably barbed, bone harpoon heads. Such similarities between the disparate settlements have led to the view that these communities were part of one cultural complex. However, there is considerable local variation in associated stone-tool industries, and it may therefore be more accurate to consider the appearance of these sedentary hunting-gathering-fishing communities as the result of a broadly contemporary, but independent, adaptation of different groups of people to the changing environment.

It was this ability to adapt to changing circumstances that led to the gradual transition to food production, that is, the cultivation of domesticated plants and herding of domesticated animals. It must be stressed that our current understanding of African food production is far from comprehensive. However, the view that food-producing techniques spread from the Fertile Crescent via the Nile valley to the rest of Africa is no longer tenable as far as plant cultivation (with the exception of wheat and barley) is concerned, and it may not be so for cattle domestication. From the 7th millennium BC onwards there is evidence of cattle-herding in present-day Algeria and the Egyptian Western Desert at Nabta Playa, which may be indicative of local domestication. At about the same time barley, wheat and domestic small stock, such as sheep and goats, were introduced from the Near East into the Nile delta. In central and southern Sahara early food production involved a move from fishing to livestock herding. The domestication of plants in these regions seems to be associated with progressive dessication after about the 5th millennium BC. As water and grazing land disappeared in the emerging desert, cattle-herding communities dispersed. These climatic and demographic factors initiated, or perhaps accelerated, the independent development of tropical agriculture.

However, it was only in the Nile valley that the advantages of food production led to state formation before about the 1st millennium BC. This is seen most spectacularly in the rise of dynastic Egypt at the end of the 4th millennium; but as early as about 2400 BC there is evidence of a substantial town at Kerma, near the third cataract, which includes fortifications, facilities for copper-smelting and eight large mound graves. Because of the many Egyptian artefacts recovered from the site, Kerma was once thought to have been an Egyptian colony. But there is plentiful evidence to support the view that it was a Nubian site and that the indigenous people had a prolonged, primarily commercial, contact with Egypt. Kerma reached a political and cultural peak during Egypt's Second

Intermediate Period (*c.* 1720–1550 BC) but failed to survive the militaristic imperialism of the New Kingdom. The kingdom of Napata, which succeeded Kerma, did not emerge until about 900 BC.

TO 300 BC

PEOPLES OF THE AMERICAS

First colonized by Siberians during the Ice Age, the Americas then developed in complete isolation from the rest of the world. Nonetheless, ways of life and forms of social organization evolved in much the same ways as in the Old World, though languages and customs were distinct as was much of the technology that was developed.

When were the Americas first peopled and by whom? Long controversy is now deepening with the results of new research on genetics. But the general view remains that humans first entered the Americas from Siberia around 15,000 years ago. A second Asiatic immigration in about 8000 BC brought the first speakers of the Na-Dene languages of northern and western North America, and then came the ancestors of the Aleuts and Inuit. From this point on, the Americas remained almost entirely isolated from further human contact until the European discovery of the continent 500 years ago.

Linguistic diversity today shows that these early colonists soon spread. Archaeology confirms that the southernmost tip of South America was inhabited by 9000 BC and northernmost Greenland by 1750 BC (by "Independence" cultures). The way of life – travelling in small bands, gathering, fishing and hunting – encouraged such wide dispersal. Yet in some areas large groups assembled regularly. Buffalo hunts on the Great Plains of North America called for extensive cooperation. Gatherings on this scale would have been annual highlights for the people involved. They continued in remoter areas into the early 1900s, allowing anthropologists to discover something of the organization, knowledge and skills of this largely unchanged way of life.

THE FIRST SETTLEMENTS

With the end of the Ice Age, peoples in the temperate and tropical zones of the region came to rely increasingly on both non-migratory prey and migratory wildfowl, on shellfish beds and on seasonal farming, all of which encouraged settled ways of life and population growth. Along the west coast of North America and the southeast coast of South America, fishing was to remain a mainstay but elsewhere – in Mesoamerica, the Central Andes and Amazonia – gathering and hunting gradually declined in favour of farming. Both cause and effect, villages were flourishing in many areas by 1500 BC.

The most widely grown crop was maize, though manioc (cassava) became important in lowland South America and potatoes and cotton in the Andes. Other early crops included gourds, squashes, beans, tomatoes, avocados, chillies and aloes. Turkeys and dogs were kept for food in Mesoamerica, guinea pigs in the Andes. Herding was restricted to the Andes, where llamas were important as pack animals, and both llamas and alpacas were raised for wool.

Settled village life did not preclude long-distance trade. Sea shells and metal tools and ornaments were circulated widely in eastern North America. Pottery provides evidence that sailors ranged along much of the west coast of South America as well as north to Central America. It is not known whether it is diffusion of this kind or a common and older Siberian heritage that explains the cultural similarities widespread among native Americans even today.

EARLY CIVILIZATIONS

Settled life permitted rising populations. Similarly, the need for farm labour may have encouraged the trend. But how were larger groups to live together? Across the continent, political leaders emerged. They used religious institutions to reflect and mould new forms of organization. Across the eastern half of North America, families gathered around ceremonial earthworks for festivals. Their tombs suggest that funerals were political occasions, too. There is evidence from these burial places of distinctions between rich and poor, governors and governed.

In the Central Andes, temples stood guard over warehouses built to store seasonal surpluses and precious imports. Community assets were the objects not only of local rivalry but of outsiders' jealousy as well. Gruesome sculptures at Cerro Sechín may depict warfare. Later, around 700–400 BC, the Chavín cult transcended local rivalries. Associated with ideas about supernatural spirits, its rites, architecture, sculpture, goldwork and fine textiles were used in many districts, probably partly to justify the privileges of chieftains. These ideas were to last long (*see* p. 36).

In Mesoamerica during the same period religion was almost certainly used to the same ends by the Olmecs, whose cult was also widespread and also part of a tradition that lived on. Chiefs seem to have claimed pivotal roles in the organization of the cosmos. Earthworks, rock art, sculpture and decorated pottery served the cult and illustrated it. Again probably for the same reasons, the Maya adorned their pyramids with similar religious and political symbols.

All the while, chiefs were supposed not to order their people but to depend on them. The break came in Mexico, in about 500 BC, with the foundation of Monte Albán as a new capital for the Zapotecs. Whether or not this move was prompted by a need for local cooperation in managing water resources or by common interests in defence, it was soon evident – from the site's architecture, its symbolism, and the rulers' effects on the surrounding villages and their conquests further afield – that a more powerful and centralized form of rule had arisen: the state. From the same period at Monte Albán is the earliest evidence for hieroglyphic writing: dated records of conquest.

TO 500 BC

SOUTHEAST ASIA BEFORE CIVILIZATION

With its long coastlines, mountain ranges and great river valleys fed by heavy seasonal rains, both the mainland and islands of southeast Asia provided a wealth of resources for early humankind. The diversity of flora and the abundance of metal ores allowed the growth of agricultural communities from at least the 4th millennium BC.

There seems little doubt that *Homo erectus*, the ancestor of all modern humans, was established in southeast Asia west of the biogeographical boundary "Wallace Line" more than one million years ago. But only Java, with its favourable geological conditions, has provided the skeletal evidence; elsewhere only discoveries of stone tools along river terraces and in some limestone fissure deposits reveal his passing.

ARCHAEOLOGICAL EVIDENCE

Abundant archaeological evidence for modern human hunter-gatherers comes only in the Late Pleistocene, and mainly from sites in the limestone mountains: among the best known are Tham Khuong and Nguom in northern Vietnam, Lang Rongrien in Thailand, Leang Burung in Celebes, and Tabon Cave in the island of Palawan in the Philippines. From about 40,000 years ago a varied range of flake stone tools have been found in these caves, left by people who exploited a wide range of plants, small and large animals and molluscs. This way of life persisted until about the 6th millennium BC, with changes in the toolkit from flake tools to pebble choppers – the Hoabinhian tradition, called after the region in north Vietnam where it was first described.

From at least 6000 BC village settlements with evidence for rice-growing and pottery-making have been found in southern China, but perhaps because there has been relatively little research on early village sites in southeast Asia no settlements of rice farmers older than 3000 BC have been found in northern Vietnam and inland areas of Thailand, although Phung Nguyen in the Red River valley of Vietnam and Ban Chiang and Non Nok Tha in northern Thailand have all been well investigated. But the best evidence for late Neolithic occupation of southeast Asia comes from Khok Phanom Di, a 7m (23ft)-deep village mound occupying about 5ha (12 acres) near the coast southeast of modern-day Bangkok. Here over 150 burials and rich occupation layers dated to between 2000 and 1400 BC provide evidence of intensive exploitation of the sea and adjacent mangrove forests, and the beginnings of social differentiation.

METAL TECHNOLOGIES

From early in the 2nd millennium BC bronze tools were added to the existing stone, bone and antler toolkits in central and northeast Thailand and northern Vietnam, where we can refer to a true Bronze Age from about 1500 to 500 BC. The best known Bronze Age locations in Thailand are Ban Chiang and Ban Na Di in the northeast and Nil Kham Haeng near Lopburi in the Chao Phraya valley. In Vietnam more sites of this phase are known including Dong Dau, Viet Khe, Cau Chan, Trang Khen, Lang Vac and Dong Son on the Ma river where a rich burial ground has been excavated since the 1920s and given its name to the late Bronze Age culture of the region, best known for its great bronze drums. These are widely distributed from Yunnan in southwest China to Thailand,

Malaya and many parts of Indonesia where they seem to have been traded in antiquity as objects of great prestige and magical power.

INFLUENCE FROM INDIA

In western and peninsular Thailand, Malaysia, Burma (Myanmar), Indonesia and the Philippines bronze metallurgy seems to have arrived only with iron after about 500 BC and to have been introduced from India as maritime trade routes were extended across the Bay of Bengal. In graves of this period are found glass and semi-precious stone jewellery of great aesthetic and technical sophistication together with iron tools and weapons, while in inland areas large moated-mound settlements and well laid-out cemeteries mark the emergence of powerful chiefdoms whose rulers, attracted by the rituals and prestige of Indian culture, soon adapted these to enhance their own status and power. Sites such as Ban Don Ta Phet, Khao Jamook, Khuan Lukpad, Ban Prasat, Non U-Loke, Ban Lum Khao and Ban Chieng Hian in Thailand, and Giong Ca Vo, Giong Phet, Doc Chua, Long Giao, Hang Gon and Hau Xa in southern and central Vietnam have all produced rich examples from this last stage of prehistoric culture on the mainland of southeast Asia, as have Plawangan and Lamongan in Java and Gilimanuk and Sembiran in Bali, where glass beads imported from south India and a potsherd with a Brahmi inscription serve to mark the end of prehistory.

TO 1770

AUSTRALIA

About 40,000 years ago, when lower sea levels linked Tasmania, Australia and New Guinea, man first ventured onto Sahul, the greater Australian continent. That journey from a southeast Asian homeland was a pioneering one, as it involved at least one major sea crossing. The original Australians were therefore among the world's earliest mariners.

PLEISTOCENE AUSTRALIA

The strange new world that greeted these newcomers was of enormous size, and ranged from tropical north to temperate south. Some of the edible plants found in more northerly latitudes were related to those of Asia and were therefore familiar; but this was not so of the animals. In addition to the mammals that have survived until today, there was a bewildering assortment of giant forms: 3m (10ft) tall kangaroos, various enormous ox-like beasts, a large native lion and rangy, ostrich-like birds. This megafauna was a rich and easily available food source but it was reduced and eventually killed off by the advancing human tide.

Consequently, it was on the plentiful supply of fish and shellfish along the coasts and in the rivers that the newcomers focused their attention, and it was in these areas of Australia that the first human settlements were concentrated. Most of the sites are lost to us, for between 40,000 and 5000 years ago the sea level was lower than it is at present, and the sites now lie offshore, on the continental shelf.

The Pleistocene inhabitants of Australia used red ochre to create elaborate rock paintings, thus laying the foundations of a rich and long-lived Aboriginal custom. Their stone core implements and crude scrapers belong to what is known as the Australian Core Tool Tradition. This tradition, which underwent remarkably little change in more than 40,000 years, is pan-Australian, but there are a number of regional elements that have links with New Guinea and southeast Asia. One of these is the edge-ground axe, which has been dated to 22,000 years in Arnhem Land. Similar ground-stone tools found in Japan are up to 30,000 years old. Ground-stone tools were ultimately developed in most other parts of the world also, but only in a much later period.

ABORIGINAL SOCIETY

About 5000 years ago, following the end of the last ice age, the sea rose to its present level; and while Aboriginal settlements were still concentrated along the coasts there was a rapid increase in the exploitation of inland resources. At about this time a range of small, finely finished flake implements especially developed for hafting sharp tools, and known as the Australian Small Tool Tradition, appeared across the continent. The dingo was also introduced.

Political, economic and religious development continued and by the time the first European settlement arrived in the 18th century, there were about 750,000 Aborigines living in around 500 tribal territories. Although the Aborigines' way of life was still based on hunting and gathering (they never became full-scale agriculturists) they had developed very intricate and finely balanced relationships with their environment. In desert areas, small nomadic groups ranged over thousands of square kilometres, while in richer parts of the continent there were settled, permanent villages. Fish traps were constructed, grasses and tubers were replanted to assist nature, and fire was used systematically to burn old vegetation and encourage the growth of rich new plant cover and the abundant new game it attracted. Rare goods, such as ceremonial axes, shells and ochres, were traded from one side of the vast continent to the other, as were stories down the accompanying "song lines".

TO THE 1700S

MELANESIA AND POLYNESIA

Melanesia and Polynesia were first settled, from around 50,000 years ago, by modern people from southeast Asia. These adventurous people were the world's first great blue-water sailors and seaborne colonists. They moved in waves, initially into New Guinea and its adjacent islands, and over time they gave birth to the Melanesian and then the Polynesian traditions. There were many great migrations, and the furthermost Pacific islands were reached as late as AD 750.

The Pacific islanders' ancient ancestors, the early people or *Homo erectus*, lived in southeast Asia two million years ago. During this period, the Pleistocene, sea levels meant that the land mass of southeast Asia included much of the western part of what is now the archipelago. Remains of these people have been found in Java, part of the ancient continent known as the Sunda shelf, which is, for the most part, submerged today.

FIRST MIGRANTS

Around 50,000 years ago, *Homo sapiens*, or modern people, arrived in the region. These people were hunters and gatherers who drifted the short distance to the ancient continent of Sahul (modern-day Melanesia, which at the time was attached to Australia) around 40,000 years ago. Skulls of *Homo sapiens* found in the area date back to this time. These people had settled the New Guinea highlands by 25,000 years ago. Eight thousand years ago rising seas following the end of the last ice age caused the separation of New Guinea from the continent of Australia.

A second wave of southeast Asian immigrants known as the Austronesians, or Lapita people, arrived in New Guinea 6000 years ago. Lapita is their distinct, red-slipped pottery, often intricately decorated with geometric patterns, which can be traced right across the western Pacific. These new migrants were aided by their revolutionary new technologies, such as the sail and the outrigger canoe, and the development of root crops (taro) and pig and chicken farming. These advances made it possible for the Austronesians to discover and settle the islands across the vast expanse of the Pacific Ocean. Recent archaeology, genetic mapping and linguistic analysis show that this was not a rapid "express-train" migration, as initially thought, but rather a "slow-boat" penetration. Most of the rest of island Melanesia was settled as recently as 4000 years ago, and Fiji (the blurred boundary between Melanesia and Polynesia) was reached as late as 3500 years ago.

In the Tonga (reached 3200 BP (before present)) and Samoan (3000 BP) regions, the Melanesian material culture gradually evolved over a thousand years of relative isolation into what we now call Polynesian. Polynesian mariners using sophisticated navigation techniques and large ocean-going canoes reached and settled the Marquesas as late as AD 300, and from there the remaining Polynesian islands were discovered and settled. Early evidence shows settlement of Easter Island by AD 400, there to give birth to an extraordinary culture. The Society, Cook and Hawaiian Islands were settled by AD 600 and New Zealand by AD 750. Coconuts from southeast Asia reached Panama by AD 1500, and the sweet potato, though native to eastern Polynesia, travelled in the other direction, reaching highland New Guinea in the 16th century.

ISLAND RESOURCES

Between AD 750 and 1300, a multitude of largely independent cultures evolved on these little "island universes". In the New Guinea highlands, where farming flourished, population density was the greatest in the world and easily sustainable. On most Pacific islands a balance was reached between population and natural resources; in less hospitable places, such as Easter Island and New Zealand, initially abundant resources became very depleted and, by the time of European contact in the 17th and 18th centuries, populations were in conflict and decline. When the Maoris arrived in Aotearoa (New Zealand) from about AD 750, they found large numbers of a flightless bird, the Moa. Some of these were gigantic, up to 3m (10ft) high and weighing up to 250kg (550lb). Unafraid of man, the Moa proved a readily available food source, and over the next 400 years they were hunted to extinction. The first Maoris thus established themselves with a Moa-fed burst in population numbers, while succeeding generations had to battle hard to sustain themselves.

TWO

THE FIRST
CIVILIZATIONS

About 6000 years ago, in a few areas of particularly intensive agriculture, the dispersed villages of Neolithic peoples gave way to more complex societies. These were the first civilizations, and their emergence marks the start of a new phase of world history. They arose, apparently independently, in four widely dispersed areas (the early civilizations of America emerged considerably later): the lower Tigris and Euphrates valleys; the valley of the Nile; the Indus valley around Harrappa and Mohenjo-Daro; and the Yellow River around An-yang. The characteristic feature of them all was the city, which now became an increasingly dominant social form, gradually encroaching on the surrounding countryside, until today urban civilization has become the criterion of social progress. But the city possessed other important connotations: a complex division of labour; literacy and a literate class (usually the priesthood); monumental public buildings; political and religious hierarchies; a kingship descended from the gods; and ultimately empire, or the claim to universal rule. A dichotomy already existed between the civilized world and the barbarian world outside. The onslaught of nomadic peoples eager to enjoy the fruits of civilization became a recurrent theme of world history until the advent of effective firearms in the 15th century AD tilted the balance in favour of the civilized peoples.

3500 TO 1500 BC
THE BEGINNINGS OF CIVILIZATION IN THE EURASIAN WORLD

Urban civilizations developed independently in four different areas of Eurasia, as the exploitation of fertile river valleys allowed complex forms of social organization. The sudden growth of cities was a dramatic development in human history, and was accompanied by the beginnings of literacy. From this period it becomes possible to write true history.

The development of urban societies seems to have been triggered by a sudden concentration of population in certain river valleys, which in some cases may have been a result of climate change which made the surrounding areas outside the valleys less attractive for habitation. The need to exploit the fertile land of these valleys and their alluvial plains to feed a growing population then led to the development of irrigation and flood-control mechanisms. In Mesopotamia and China this involved the construction of canals to carry water away to the land around the Tigris-Euphrates and the Yellow River, while in Egypt and India the annual flooding of the Nile and Indus provided fertile silt in which crops were grown.

THE FIRST CITIES

The concentrated populations were able to produce surplus crops which could be exported to areas beyond the rivers in return for raw materials and precious items not locally available, above all bronze. The food surplus also made possible social groups not directly involved in agriculture, whether specialized craftsmen or rulers and military leaders. It was when ambitious individuals and families succeeded in diverting resources into the construction of monumental ceremonial centres that provided a focus for the populations living near them that the first true cities appeared. This took place in Mesopotamia in *c.* 3500 BC and in Egypt in *c.* 3100 BC, while the Indus valley cities appeared in *c.* 2500 BC, and in China urbanism began in *c.* 1800 BC.

The political development of these different regions was not uniform: in Egypt a single unified kingdom emerged almost immediately, extending from the Nile delta south to the first cataract; in China the earliest civilization is associated with the Shang dynasty, although the Shang rulers may have just been leaders of a loose confederacy. In Mesopotamia, by contrast, no one city was able to establish control for any period, and competition for dominance between the leading cities characterized the history of the area for nearly three millennia. The situation in the Indus valley is less clear, but the major cities of Harappa and Mohenjo-Daro appear to have coexisted until the decline of the Indus cities after about 2000 BC. It appears that in all these civilizations, religious, political and military power was concentrated in the hands of a few ruling families.

Trade and exchange were important in the expansion of the first civilizations. The possession of prestige goods and the desire to acquire more resources were instrumental in the emergence of the first empires in Mesopotamia. During the 3rd millennium BC goods were being traded between the Indus and the Mediterranean. In the 2nd millennium BC urbanization spread to Anatolia and the Aegean, and the cultural influence of the Near East can be seen in the bronze-working of the Balkan communities. However, in many parts of Eurasia, including the fertile river deltas of the Ganges and Mekong, the landscape did not favour concentrations of population, and village communities remained the norm until the 1st millennium BC.

The development of writing occurred almost at the start of each of the four civilizations. The earliest known use of writing in China was for divination: the Shang rulers used prepared turtle shells and ox scapulae heated in a fire to establish the will of the gods, and the result of the enquiry was scratched onto the shell or bone. In Mesopotamia, Egypt and the Indus valley writing was used mainly for administrative activities, with inventories and accounts being inscribed on clay. Early examples of writing have often survived because clay tablets were accidentally baked, fixing the messages permanently. Clay inscriptions spread to Crete and Greece by around 1500 BC. In Egypt and Mesopotamia the use of writing developed rapidly, as large public inscriptions, including law-codes, were erected by the rulers as monuments to their wisdom, justice and power. It is from monuments such as these, celebrating their victories or their public works, that the earliest true history can be reconstructed.

c. 3500 TO 1600 BC

THE EARLY EMPIRES OF MESOPOTAMIA

The broad plain through which the Tigris and Euphrates rivers flow gave birth to the world's first cities. Irrigation systems made it possible to support substantial populations and complex administrative structures. With urbanization came more developed economies and trade, while competition between cities led to warfare and the first empires.

The earliest cities appeared in Mesopotamia in the second half of the 4th millennium BC: at Uruk, Ur, Tell 'Uqair and Susa vast and elaborately decorated ceremonial complexes were built as the centres of urban settlements, probably under the leadership of families eager to display their power and their respect for the gods. The fertile plains and valleys watered by the Tigris and the Euphrates produced food surpluses sufficient to support these elaborate new centres and their complex social structures.

The cities were the basic political units of Mesopotamia. Religion was fundamental to their social organization: the rulers of cities presented themselves as favoured servants of the gods, while lower down the social scale agricultural workers had a necessary role in producing the materials for sacrifices and offerings to the gods. The cities established diplomatic and trade relationships with each other, although little is known of the mechanisms for this. Finds of goods from Uruk, the predominant city in Mesopotamia from around 3500 BC, have come from as far afield as Susa and Syria. The effect of trade and gift-exchange between cities encouraged the development of a common culture from the edges of the Persian Gulf to Mari in the northwest and Ashur in the north. Although other languages were spoken, the early use of Sumerian as a written language has led to the use of the term "Sumerian" to describe the culture and society of early and middle 3rd millennium.

THE EMPIRE OF AGADE

Towards the end of the 3rd millennium powerful leaders attempted to expand their influence over a wider area. The first was Sargon (*c.* 2296–2240 BC), who created a new political centre at Agade, also known as Akkad, before conquering the cities of southern Mesopotamia and claiming authority over areas as far west as Byblos. The empire of Agade was enlarged by Sargon's grandson Naram-Sin (2213–2176 BC), but within a generation of his death it had disappeared, as its subject cities reasserted their independence. The rise of Agade had long-lasting effects on the region, with Akkadian (whose variants included Babylonian and Assyrian) replacing Sumerian as the main language of Mesopotamia.

A century later the rulers of the Third Dynasty of Ur (Ur III: 2047–1940 BC), beginning with Ur-Nammu, built an empire in southern Mesopotamia, but in common with the other early Mesopotamian empires it was not long-lasting and its decline left a number of important cities competing for power. The centre of activity moved to northern Mesopotamia, and a new elite emerged – the Amorites – who had previously been excluded from power. The most successful Amorite leader was Shamshi-Adad I, who established a short-lived empire in Assyria in the years after 1750 BC. After his death the region returned to a period of competing rulers, as reflected by the assessment of an advisor to Zimri-Lim of Mari (*c.* 1714–1700 BC): "There is no king who is strong by himself: 10 or 15 kings follow Hammurabi of Babylon, as many follow Rim-Sin of Larsa, Ibalpiel of Eshnunna and Amutpiel of Qatna, while 20 kings follow Yarim-Lim of Yamkhad." Soon after this Hammurabi was able to establish an empire of his own, and Babylon became a leading power in the region for the first time.

THE LAW CODE OF HAMMURABI

Hammurabi is most famous for his law code, inscribed on a large stone with a carving of the king in the presence of Shamash, the Babylonian sun god. Although it is presented as a practical collection of laws including the principle of punishment with "an eye for an eye", the primary function of the document was probably to advertise the achievements of Hammurabi's reign. After his death, his successors in the First Dynasty of Babylon ruled for about 90 years before the city was raided by the Hittites, and a new phase in the history of Mesopotamia began (*see* p. 34).

c. 3100–1000 BC

ANCIENT EGYPT

The history of the ancient Egyptian state is one of successive periods of unification and fragmentation. Counterbalancing this is a pattern of civilization – characterized by such features as the use of writing, an organized system of religion and divine kingship, and dependence on the annual Nile floods for the fertility of the land – which links the different periods together through a span of 3000 years.

Tradition dates the unification of Upper and Lower Egypt to 3100 BC, but it is more accurate to see the emergence of a unified state around this time as the outcome of formative processes stretching back into prehistory. The 4th-Dynasty pyramids at Giza, the largest of which was built by Khufu (Cheops), are the most famous examples of Egypt's monumental funerary architecture, which expressed the divine status and power of the pharaohs of the Old Kingdom. Construction projects on this scale were possible only because of the enormous wealth of the state, derived mainly from agriculture. The pharaohs controlled this resource through a system of assessment, taxation, collection and redistribution. Central rule broke down at the end of the 6th Dynasty. Although the reasons for this are not entirely clear, it is probable that a series of low Nile floods and consequent famines were one factor in the loss of political and social stability that marks the onset of the First Intermediate Period (from *c.* 2181 BC).

MIDDLE KINGDOM REUNIFICATION

Egypt was reunified under Mentuhotep of Thebes, and a new era, known as the Middle Kingdom, began. Thebes became an important centre, and its god, Amun, was identified with the sun god, Re, who had been closely connected with royalty since Old Kingdom times. During the 12th Dynasty, which represented the high point of the Middle Kingdom, trading expeditions were sent to Palestine, Syria, and south to Nubia, where the Egyptian presence was consolidated by the construction of several forts clustered around the second cataract. During the Second Intermediate Period (c. 1720–1550 BC) power devolved to various local rulers until foreigners from the east, known as the Hyksos, extended their authority over a large part of Egypt. The Hyksos were eventually expelled by the independent rulers of Thebes, who reunified Egypt from the south.

EXPANSION AND DISUNITY

During the New Kingdom, military conquests created an Egyptian empire stretching from the Euphrates in the north to Nubia in the south. Within Egypt, imperial expansion was matched by magnificent construction works of tombs and temples. The cult of the most important god Amun-Re was temporarily set back when Akhenaten (c. 1364–1347 BC) built a new capital at Amarna, where the worship of the Aten or solar disc was promoted.

Under Rameses II Egypt reached a pinnacle of wealth and power, but there are clear indications that from the reign of Rameses III onwards there were growing external and internal problems. Egypt's empire in Syria and Palestine was lost. Its eastern and seaward borders were threatened by the sea peoples. On the western border, despite the victories of Rameses III, the Libyans posed a continuing and destabilizing problem. Internally, royal power was eroded by such factors as weak rulers, administrative inefficiency and the growing authority of the high priests of Amun at Thebes. By the end of the 20th Dynasty (c. 1069 BC) Egypt was once again a disunited land.

1600–1000 BC

THE NEAR EAST

The period after 1600 BC saw the fertile lands of Mesopotamia and the Levant become the battleground between rival empires: Hittites, Mitannians, Assyrians, Babylonians, Elamites and Egyptians. After 1200 BC, however, these powers collapsed in a dramatic sequence of events that is still not fully understood by historians. The resulting two centuries of upheaval marked the end of the Bronze Age in the Near East.

Much of the detailed knowledge of the relationships between the warring empires comes from the "Amarna letters". This collection of documents written in Akkadian (the international language of diplomacy in this period), consists of correspondence between the Egyptian pharaohs Amenophis III, Akhenaten and Tutankhamun (1390–1327 BC) and the rulers of the other great powers. The letters reveal the dynastic marriages and gift-giving that typify relations between rulers: the personal and the political were intimately bound together.

The most important new power in the region was the Hittite empire in central Anatolia. The Hittites had been expanding their power from their centre at Hattushash since the reign of Hattusili I (c. 1650–1620 BC). Mursili I (c. 1620–c. 1590 BC) led an expedition that destroyed Aleppo and Babylon, but it was Tudhaliya I (c. 1420–1400 BC) and Suppiluliuma I (1344–1322 BC) who made the Hittites an imperial power. The empire consisted of a large number of small territories governed by client kings who owed their position entirely to the "Great King" who ruled from the capital, Hattusa. Client rulers were required to raise troops for the king's campaigns, and to provide labour and goods for the central administration. They were often bound to the king by marriage ties.

The Hittites faced frequent pressure on their borders from Arzawa to the west and the Gasga to the north, but their biggest rivals were Egypt and the kingdom of Mitanni to the south. Mitanni first appears in the historical record in c. 1480 BC, when its ruler, Parrattarna, is described as controlling Aleppo. For the next 140 years Mitanni was a major power, controlling Assyria by 1400 BC. Mutual concern about Hittite power saw an alliance between Mitanni and Egypt, and the last independent ruler of Mitanni, Tushratta, married his daughter to Amenophis III and, after the pharaoh's death, to his son Amenophis IV (Akhenaten). Tushratta was assassinated in *c.* 1340 BC, and his son Shattiwaza was installed as a vassal of the Hittites. Hostility continued between the Hittites and the Egyptians, leading to the great but inconclusive battle of Kadesh in 1275 BC between the pharaoh Rameses II (1279–1213 BC) and the Hittite king Muwatalli (1295–1271 BC).

Assyrian expansion began under Ashur-uballit I (1353–1318 BC), as Mitanni began to collapse under Hittite pressure. Adad-nirari I (1295–1264 BC) seized what was left of Mitanni from the Hittites, and Assyrian power grew to its greatest extent in the reign of Tikulti-ninurta I (1233–1197 BC), who conquered Babylon and installed a series of puppet rulers. Up until then Mesopotamia had been through a period of stability, ruled from Babylon, which came under the control of the Kassites in *c.* 1595 BC. Little is known about their origins, but they were noted for their horses and chariots, and maintained power for four centuries.

The Assyrian attack on Babylon led to counter-attacks from Elam to the southeast. The Elamite kings Kiden-Hutran (*c.* 1235–1210 BC) and Shutruk-Nahunte (1185–1155 BC) led campaigns into Mesopotamia, the latter capturing Babylon. Despite a Babylonian revival under Nebuchadnezzar I (1126–1205 BC), the general upheaval that brought an end to the Bronze Age saw both Babylon and Elam more or less disappear from the historical record within a few years.

Around 1200 BC there was a wave of destruction throughout the eastern Mediterranean from Greece to Syria and Palestine. Fifty years later several cities in Mesopotamia were also destroyed. There are reports from the city of Ugarit of attacks from the sea, and the Egyptian pharaohs Merneptah (1213–1203 BC) and Rameses III (1184–1150 BC) describe battles with "sea peoples". Although this obscure group was once considered the cause of widespread destruction it is now thought that they were merely taking advantage of a widespread breakdown in political organization. Earthquakes, drought, interruption to the supply of metals, and many other things, have been suggested as the cause of the collapse. It is likely that no one explanation will suffice, and that a number of external factors, combined with the fragility of the centralized power structures of the Bronze Age kingdoms, led to the dramatic end of the civilizations of the Bronze Age.

300 BC TO AD 1300

PEOPLES OF SOUTH AMERICA AND THE CARIBBEAN

By 300 BC most people in South America had become farmers, although some hunter-gathering persisted in the southern part of the continent where farming was difficult. By 750 BC, complex societies were developing in the Andes. As in Mesoamerica, they went through phases of growth and decline, but in the central Andes there was a degree of cultural unity in that artistic differences between the highlands and lowlands were not as marked.

SOUTH AMERICA

The coast of the central Andes is best known, archaeologically, for the graphic pottery of the Moche, dating from AD 100 to 600. It reveals much about daily life and religion. The Moche were the first to assert themselves more widely by conquest. Both pottery and tombs show that, like their contemporaries in Mesoamerica, Moche kings exhibited their authority in elaborate rites.

Yet from about AD 600 the coast succumbed to conquest from the Tiahuanaco and the Huari. Both these civilizations developed elements of the earlier Chavín cult (see p. 19). The city of Tiahuanaco was centred on the Titicaca Basin in Bolivia where the people grew potatoes and herded llamas and alpacas. Renowned for their stone buildings and sculpture, their expansion seems to have been achieved through the establishment of religious and commercial colonies. The reasons for its collapse about AD 1200 are not fully understood, but may have been related to climate change that affected agricultural production. The Huari are often considered to have been the precursors of the Inca. Among the hallmarks of Huari civilization was a network of roads and logistical, perhaps administrative, bases. Following two centuries of political fragmentation, the Moche tradition was revived among the Chimú, consummate engineers who developed vast irrigation systems. They controlled parts of the Andean coast until their destruction by the Incas (see p. 143).

In the northern Andes and southern Central America, along the Amazon and in the plains southwest of the Amazon, there were other large populations. Much of the most telling evidence for them is in the form of extensive field systems. In northwestern South America chiefdoms had emerged, and in the southernmost parts of Central America superb sculpture, goldwork and pottery indicate powerful patrons.

THE CARIBBEAN

There is some evidence that peoples exploiting wild food resources occupied Cuba, Haiti and the Dominican Republic about 4000 BC. However, it was between 500 and 250 BC that farmers began migrating to the Lesser Antilles and Puerto Rico from the Orinoco and other rivers in northeast South America. They introduced the cultivation of manioc (cassava) and brought with them dogs and a distinctive red and white pottery known as Saladoid. Between AD 500 and AD 1000, the population in these islands expanded and spread to parts of the islands of Hispaniola (today Haiti and the Dominican Republic), Cuba and Jamaica. Most of these people were probably Arawak speakers. With population growth the societies became more complex and chiefdoms emerged. These people were later known as Tainos.

300 BC TO AD 1300
PEOPLES OF MESOAMERICA

Many societies in the Americas changed little in the 2000 years before 1300. In Mesoamerica, however, complex societies were developing by the end of the first millennium BC. They then underwent cycles of growth and decline that included periods of outstanding intellectual and artistic achievement.

By 300 BC, almost every way of life that the Europeans would later encounter had developed in Mesoamerica: while some societies in northern Mexico continued to live by hunting, fishing and gathering, most had adopted farming and some were developing into states that extended their influence by trade or force.

THE RISE OF TEOTIHUACÁN

Earlier developments in Mesoamerica were eclipsed in about AD 100 by the sudden rise of Teotihuacán. The city grew to about 200,000, much larger than cities in the Old World at the time. There are doubts about the nature of the city's economy but the centre – with the Temple of Quetzalcoatl and the Pyramids of the Sun and the Moon – was clearly planned for rites that involved human sacrifices. The city also possessed thousands of artisans who produced many items for foreign trade, including many articles made of obsidian, which they obtained from mines they controlled at Pachuca. Whether or not in association with trade, the Teotihuacános' influence spread widely through present-day Mexico and Guatemala and was apparent in their distinctive pottery, crafts and architecture. In the 7th century AD Teotihuacán was attacked either by insiders or outsiders, or both, and its power destroyed, although it continued to function as a town.

THE RISE OF THE MAYA

At the same time the small but brilliant kingdoms of the Maya flourished. Their capitals were pyramid-studded ceremonial centres with densely settled suburbs. Voluminous inscriptions reveal a sophisticated but typically Mesoamerican concern with astrology. For a long time it was not understood how these cities in a tropical forest were supplied with food. It now seems they built terraces, drained fields and made extensive use of game and fish. However, whether it was on account of the chronic wars that are recorded, or of popular discontent, or of environmental degradation by excessive population – or of all of these factors – most of the towns were abandoned between AD 790 and the mid-9th century. Many districts revived later in what is known as the Post-Classic period, but the Maya never regained their grandeur.

THE RISE OF THE TOLTECS

The Maya "collapse" followed the dissolution of Teotihuacán in about 700. But between these poles of power a new generation of thriving towns had emerged, including some of Teotihuacán's protégés, such as Cholula, which established their independence from the traditional order. They appear to have been eclipsed in turn by the Toltecs, soldiers and probably traders, whose influence subsequently extended throughout Mesoamerica and beyond.

In about 1175 their reign, too, ended, possibly on account of refugees from the north driven south by changing climatic conditions. Meanwhile, two Nahua-speaking migrations from central Mexico had extended Meso-american influence to societies on the Pacific coastal plain as far south as Costa Rica.

300 BC TO AD 1300

PEOPLES OF EARLY NORTH AMERICA

The early cultures of North America were predominantly agrarian-based, with small communities developing in and around areas where the natural environment provided rich sources of food. By AD 700 three distinct cultures had developed. These were more urban and culturally diverse, and they were heavily influenced by Mexican civilizations. By the beginning of the 15th century, however, these cultures were in decline.

By 300 BC, the area stretching from Ohio to West Virginia had already been settled. Small communities and villages developed in river valleys, where natural food resources (such as mammals, birds, fish and vegetable foods) were both abundant and close at hand. Horticulture also developed around this time: sunflowers, marsh elder and squashes were cultivated.

Archaeological evidence from this period points to the existence of chiefdoms: the elaborate burial sites, such as that at Hopewell in Ohio, are excellent indicators of the social, religious and trade networks through which imported goods, as well as ideas, filtered. By AD 700, three distinct cultural traditions had emerged in southwestern North America: the Hohokam, Mogollon and Anasazi. Their area of influence covered much of the territory that is now Utah, Colorado, Arizona and New Mexico, and also extended south into Sonora and Chihuahua.

The Hohokam, Mogollon and Anasazi cultures all had contact with Mexico, and this contact became a significant influence on their development. Excavations have revealed ball courts and Mesoamerican-style mosaics, bracelets, effigy vessels and figurines. The architectural layout of the towns (which were used as economic, religious and trading centres) also reveals

Mexican influence, and the Mexicans may even have established Casas Grandes in Chihuahua as the "capital" of the Mogollon culture.

The first true towns in North America appeared in the Middle Mississippi Valley from AD 700. They were characteristically built on large, flat-topped, rectangular mounds, which supported temples and mortuary houses for the elite society and more modest timber houses for the town's merchants and officials. A town generally consisted of up to 20 mounds grouped together around a plaza and enclosed by a defensive wooden stockade. The towns had substantial populations: it is estimated that some reached 10,000 inhabitants.

The large rural population (about 200 people per square km) was based predominantly in the fertile river valleys surrounding the towns. Again, Mexican influence here is evident: after AD 700, a hardier strain of maize, popular in Mexico, was introduced and cultivated. In addition, the introduction of the bow and arrow to replace the spear-thrower and dart meant more efficient hunting of the abundant game on the uplands.

By the time 16th-century French explorers discovered the area, the population had advanced to a ranked, matrilineal society headed by a chief who ruled four well-defined classes. Archaeological evidence from Mississippi to Minnesota and from Oklahoma to the Atlantic coast also bears witness to the widespread existence of a religion known as the Southern Cult. Reaching its peak in 1250, the cult was strongly influenced by Mexican practice, especially in regard to the importance of the four cardinal points and the significance placed upon death.

Disease, caused by unhealthy overcrowding and poor sanitation, heralded the slow decline of the early North American cultures after AD 1300. However, their demise was a but a pale foreshadowing of the destruction that was to befall these cultures when Europeans arrived in the New World.

THE BEGINNINGS OF CHINESE CIVILIZATION

Geographically and climatically China has a range of favourable conditions for human settlement, which took place 500,000 years ago. A turning point was reached at about 1600 BC when China entered the Bronze Age. It was then that Chinese culture took shape, as written languages, philosophies and stable socio-political and economic structures gradually emerged.

China has been inhabited continuously by humans since very early times. Remains of early hominines, which are similar to those from Java, have been found across large areas of southeast China. In about 500,000 BC Peking Man – *Homo erectus* – was living around Pohai and in the southeast and possibly in central and southern China as well. *Homo sapiens* first appeared in Palaeolithic cultures in the Ordos region, in the north and in the southwest in about 30,000 BC. Later Mesolithic cultures flourished in the north, south and southwest and in Taiwan.

EARLY AGRICULTURALISTS

Neolithic agricultural communities, the immediate ancestors of Chinese civilization, arose around 7500 BC in what is now southern China and in the loess-covered lands of the north and northeast, where the well-drained soil of the river terraces was ideal for primitive agriculture. One of the best early sites is Pan-p'o, with round and rectangular houses, pottery kilns and a cemetery area. In the valley of the Yellow River, early agriculture depended heavily on millet, but in the Yangtze delta area evidence of rice-paddies dates from the 5th millennium BC. By 3000 BC, more sophisticated skills developed, including the carving of jade, and small townships rather than villages began to emerge.

Around 1600 BC China entered the Bronze Age with its first archaeologically proven dynasty, the Shang (*c.* 1520–1030 BC). Chasing copper mines, the Shang moved their capital at least six times, and three, at Cheng-chou, Erh-li-t'ou and An-yang, have been excavated. Many smaller Shang sites have been found and some are now known from the Yangtze valley in central China indicating the

Shang expansion southward. In addition, the Shang had trade relations with most of the northern and central east Asian mainland.

THE CHOU DYNASTY

In the 11th century BC the Shang territory was conquered by the Chou, of different ethnic origin, who inhabited the northwest border of the Shang domain. The Chou gradually extended their sovereignty, including the entire middle and lower reaches of the Yellow River and parts of the middle basin of the Yangtze. At first their capital lay near Hsi-an. The Chou territory was divided into numerous domains among the king and the elites – a system of delegated authority similar to the later European feudal system.

Until the 8th century BC the Chou constantly extended their territory. About 770 BC, however, internal disorders broke the kingdom into numerous units and forced the Chou king to abandon his homeland in the Wei valley and move to the eastern capital at Lo-yang, where his power diminished. Over the next two and a half centuries wars caused more than 100 petty units to be swallowed up by some 20 of the more powerful ones, among whom there emerged a clear pecking order.

The Shang and early Chou periods were differentiated from their predecessors by their political organization and their bronze technology, and also by the use of writing; their culture was already recognizably "Chinese". Their cities maintained a hierarchy of nobles, royal officers and court servants. They drew support from communities of craftsmen working in bronze, jade, wood, stone, ceramics and textiles. Peasants working the various domains that belonged to the landed classes produced revenues and foodstuffs. Market activities were common and mint currencies were in use.

Bronze was used for ritual objects and a wide range of weapons and tools, with the exception of farming equipment. Farmers working in the fields continued to use stone implements, growing rice, millet, barley and hemp and raising pigs, poultry and silkworms.

Towards the end of the period, the old social order began to collapse. The more powerful units employed bureaucrats rather than the hereditary nobility of older times. A new group of administrators (*shih*) emerged. A leading figure among this group, Confucius, formulated a new ethos, which was to have currency far into the future and far beyond China's territory.

TO 1392
KOREA

The area now known as Korea was the mountainous eastern edge of the Eurasian continent until the Yellow Sea formed and the west coast emerged to define a peninsula. Peoples migrated into and through the peninsula to the islands. Chinese political culture and Buddhism followed on, and states emerged. With Chinese aid, one of three competing kingdoms conquered the peninsula, but instability led to anarchy by the late 9th century. The successful kingdom created a bureaucratic state with strong aristocratic characteristics and established a Korean identity.

During the last glacial maximum, "Korea" was high ground across a low plain (Yellow Sea) at the eastern end of Eurasia. Sea levels rose and a peninsula appeared between 14,000 BC and 6000 BC. Humans from 22,000 BC; villages from 10,000 BC; rice between 6000 and 4500 BC. Bronze was worked from 1000 BC and dolmens appeared.

By 108 BC, the Han Empire had established colonies to trade for iron. Only the Lelang colony near Pyŏngyang survived until AD 313, when it was destroyed by a tribe from the middle reaches of the Yalu River, the Koguryŏ, who first revolted against the Chinese in AD 12. Over several centuries, the south politically evolved into Paekche in the southwest, Silla in the southeast, and the iron-rich principalities of Kaya in between.

By the 6th century, the peninsular states were importing Chinese law, bureaucratic government, and land was monopolized by the state to centralize power. Koreans and Japanese fashioned compromises between the Chinese ideal of centralization and the native system of aristocracy, which resulted in semi-centralized political orders based on inheritance. Buddhism permeated every corner of the peninsula by 540 and was exported to Japan.

An alliance between T'ang China and Silla destroyed Paekche in 660 and Koguryŏ in 668. The T'ang had promised to withdraw but betrayed Silla, attempting to seize the whole peninsula. By 676, Silla drove T'ang out, demonstrating that outside powers were unable to succeed on the peninsula without a local ally. T'ang completely retreated, and a new state called Pohai (Korean *Parhae*, 712–926) formed in Manchuria from tribal elements and Koguryŏ refugees.

From the 8th century, northeast Asia saw peace: great cities, long-distance trade, and a cosmopolitan, state-oriented Buddhism. Kyŏngju, Silla's capital, was a world city known to Arab traders. Ch'ang-an may have had nearly two million inhabitants, and Kyŏngju approached 900,000, swollen by slaves from the wars. Monks, merchants and diplomats wandered among Ch'ang-an, Kyŏngju, and Nara in Japan. Thereafter, "Korea" and "Japan" began to form separate identities.

Sillan central control lapsed, and in 918, Wang Kŏn, a general outside the old aristocratic order, emerged to found a new dynasty named Koryŏ. Wang Kŏn peacefully absorbed the Sillan court in 935. His successors inherited the aristocratic pretensions of Silla and the desire to centralize. During the 10th century, a bureaucratic state was created, with examinations, ideology, salary ranks and centralized provincial appointments. Where Silla had conquered, Koryŏ unified. In 1126, the Liao (Jurchen) destroyed the Chinese Song Empire and Koryŏ faced a dilemma of identity: take the opportunity to expand out of the peninsula or accept its limitations. A rebellious faction argued for continental destiny in Manchuria. Kim Pu-sik, the general who suppressed them, produced an official history (*Samguk sagi, c.* 1145) that defined Koryŏ's heritage as peninsular. After the Mongols invaded in 1232, an unofficial history (*Samguk yusa, c.* 1283) reaffirmed a peninsular identity and recorded foundation myths.

Koryŏ nearly slipped into feudalism when abuse of civil privilege sparked a military coup d'etat in 1170. Military dictators did not create a new government, but ruled through the central government. Perhaps Koryŏ never disintegrated into feudalism because of the threat from northern barbarians, a threat Japan never faced. The Mongols invaded in 1232, but the Korean court resisted until 1270. The Koryŏ kings became sons-in-law to the Mongol Khans, and Koryŏ was press-ganged into supporting Mongol efforts to conquer Japan in 1274 and 1281. Both invasions failed.

From the mid-14th century, Japanese piracy appeared to ravage Korea. In the north, the Mongols weakened and, in 1368, the new Ming dynasty dislodged the Mongols. Indecision at the Koryŏ court over whether to support the Mongols or the Ming resulted in a coup d'etat in 1388 and a new dynasty, the Chosŏn, was founded in 1392.

TO 500 BC

THE BEGINNINGS OF INDIAN CIVILIZATION

India was the home of one of the oldest civilizations of history, which grew up along the banks of the Indus river. The Indus valley culture and the Vedic culture, which succeeded and was influenced by it, were the basis for the development of later Indian society, in particular for the major religious systems of Hinduism, Buddhism and Jainism.

The early history of India is very difficult to recover. Archaeology can reveal something about the way of life of its earliest inhabitants, but little can be learned from written evidence. The earliest works of Indian literature, the *Vedas*, were composed in the centuries after 1200 BC, but they were not written down until probably the 5th century.

HARAPPA AND MOHENJO-DARO

Although the subcontinent had substantial human occupation from the Stone Age onwards, the first great Indian civilization was the Harappan culture which emerged in the Indus valley in the 3rd millennium BC. Like the slightly older civilizations of Mesopotamia and Egypt it was based on flood-plain agriculture, as the cultivation of the fertile land on either side of the Indus was able to provide enough of a surplus to support a complex urban society. Several substantial cities were built, of which the best explored are Harappa and Mohenjo-Daro.

The Indus civilization also developed writing, and about 2000 seals with short pictographic inscriptions on them have been discovered. The script has not been deciphered, and until it is, little will be known about the political structure or religious beliefs of the Indus civilization.

The presence of cylinder seals from Mesopotamia at Mohenjo-Daro and of Indus seals in Mesopotamia is evidence of trade between the two areas via the Persian Gulf, and tin and lapis lazuli from Afghanistan and Central Asia also made their way to the Indus. However around 2000 BC the 'Harappan period' came to an end, as the cities ceased to function and were replaced by a settlement pattern of agricultural villages and pastoral camps.

POST-INDUS INDIA

From around 1500 BC a new culture becomes apparent in India, characterized by a new language and rituals, and the use of horses and two-wheeled chariots. The traditional way to explain the changes was to talk of an "Aryan invasion", with mounted bands of warriors riding in from the northwest and conquering the indigenous Indus population before moving eastwards to the Ganges. Support for this picture was claimed from one of the Vedas, the Rig Veda, where the Aryans are presented as conquering the cities of the darker skinned indigenous Dasas. Archaeological evidence offers little support for this theory however. The styles of pottery associated with the Indo-Aryans, known as Painted Grey Ware, which appears from c. 1100 BC, is similar to earlier Painted Black and Red Ware, and this may indicate that Indo-Aryan speakers were indigenous to the Indus plain. Whatever their origins, Indo-Aryan languages, from which Sanskrit developed, became widespread through Northern India.

THE SOUTH

Southern India was left largely untouched by the civilizations of the north. There were probably trading links between the Indus valley and the southern tip of the peninsula, but there was no urbanism in the south, where villages were the normal form of social organization. However, some limited form of common culture in the south is suggested by the distinctive megalithic tombs found over most of the area.

In the north, where, unlike the hilly, fragmented geography of the south, great plains lent themselves to large-scale agriculture and the growth of substantial kingdoms, cultural coherence became more widespread as, in the period after 1000 BC, the new civilization spread gradually east from the Indus to the Ganges. Evidence from finds of pottery characteristic of particular periods suggests that there was also movement southwards. The late Vedic texts depict the early first millennium BC as a period of frequent warfare between rival tribal territories. During this period the society of Northern India became increasingly stratified, and this culminated around 600 BC in the emergence of states ruled by hereditary monarchs. Trading networks developed, agricultural activity increased, and this led to a new phase of urbanism in India. Once again cities began to be built, although they were not on the scale of Harappa and Mohenjo-Daro, being constructed largely from mud-bricks. No known public buildings survive from this period. Yet by the 5th century BC there were political entities that might be called states or polities, most significantly Magadha, with its substantial fortified capital at Pataliputra (*see* p. 69).

VEDIC RELIGION

Religious practices in India in the first millennium BC were influenced in part by the earlier culture of the Vedas, and animal sacrifice had a central role in it. The religion was polytheistic, and the Rig Veda includes hymns to a number of deities, including the warrior god Indra, the fire god Agni, and Soma, identified with a mind-altering drug of some kind, possibly derived from mushrooms. These cults were the forerunner of Hinduism, and the urban societies that developed along the Ganges were the communities among whom appeared in the 5th century Mahavira, the founder of Jainism, and the Buddha himself.

c. 3000 TO 950 BC

MINOAN AND MYCENAEAN CIVILIZATIONS

In the late 19th century, Heinrich Schliemann and Sir Arthur Evans unearthed the remains of previously unknown civilizations. Although the names of Troy, Mycenae and Knossos were familiar from the poems of Homer, the Bronze Age societies of the Aegean revealed by these excavations had much more in common with contemporary Near Eastern societies than they had with later Greece.

Substantial settlements appeared in mainland Greece and Crete by the end of the 3rd millennium BC. These were subsistence farmers, with households producing goods for their own consumption. The subsequent appearance in Crete of large stone-built complexes marked the emergence of a new form of social organization. There are some parallels between these "First Palaces" and Near Eastern buildings, and they are accompanied by other signs of such influence, including the appearance of a form of hieroglyphic writing in Crete. However, it is likely that local needs as much as outside influence determined the island's overall development.

There is no agreed explanation for the later destruction of the "First Palaces", but in their place the large complexes of the "Second Palace Period" emerged. These were not fortified, but they were the focus of the economic and religious life of the Minoan communities.

By 1700 BC Knossos had achieved a dominant position within Crete, and the palace there reveals much information about Minoan society. Surviving frescoes depict scenes of communal activity including processions, bull-leaping, dining and dancing. It is clear from Knossos and other palaces that Cretan society depended upon intensive agriculture – the palaces incorporate large storage areas where crops could be gathered for later redistribution to the population. Outside the towns, especially in eastern Crete, large "villas" had a similar role, and acted as processing centres for grape and olive crops.

The two hundred years of the Second Palace Period witnessed considerable destruction and rebuilding at a number of sites. The eruption of Thera in 1628 BC left its mark on sites in eastern Crete but otherwise appears to have had little long-term impact. More significantly, a little over a century later many Cretan settlements were widely devastated, possibly as a result of invasion from the Greek mainland.

MYCENAEAN GREECE

Mainland Greece did not share in the prosperity of Crete and the Aegean islands until after *c.* 1700 BC, when rich burials, especially in the "shaft-graves" at Mycenae and in *tholos* tombs, point to the emergence of a powerful warlike elite. After 1500 BC mainlanders, called Mycenaeans, appear to have been in control of Knossos, where the palace functioned for another century. It was only after then that palaces started to appear on the mainland. While they owed something to Minoan models, and, like them, acted as centres for agricultural storage and redistribution, they were fortified and less luxurious. The Mycenaeans spoke a form of Greek, and wrote in a syllabic script, Linear B, adapted from the still-undeciphered script in use in Crete, Linear A. Documents inscribed on clay tablets reveal a strongly hierarchical society, with the ruler (*wanax*) at the top, lesser lords below and the mass of the people at the bottom.

Soon after 1200 BC, more or less simultaneously, the palaces on the mainland were destroyed. In the centuries following there is no trace of Linear B writing, nor of the figurative decoration that characterizes Mycenaean art. When written Greek appears again in the 8th century, it uses a version of the Phoenician alphabet.

The absence of firm evidence – mirrored by the lack of firm dates for this period – has led historians to examine myths in the search for historical facts. On this basis it has been suggested that the Mycenaeans fell victim to Dorian invaders from the north, or that a long war against Troy caused revolution in the Greek homeland. Neither finds support from archaeology, and an agreed explanation for the complete social breakdown of Mycenaean society is yet to emerge. One contributing factor may have been major political upheavals further east, cutting off access to the tin needed to make the bronze on which the Mycenaean rulers based their power. Certainly the society which emerged from the "dark age" that followed the collapse was reliant on the more widely available iron.

The massive ruins of the Mycenaean palaces remained visible to the Greeks of later times, and these, together with a tradition of oral poetry that developed over the following centuries, led to the invention of a heroic world, most famously celebrated in the epic poems of Homer, that was very different from Bronze Age reality.

THREE

THE CLASSICAL CIVILIZATIONS OF EURASIA

The earliest civilizations arose at a few scattered points in the vast and sparsely inhabited Eurasian landmass. Between 1000 BC and AD 500 the pattern began to change. Although America, Australasia and Africa south of the Sahara still stood outside the mainstream of world history, and were to stay so for a further thousand years, the civilizations of Europe and Asia now formed a continuous belt. By AD 100, when the classical era was at its height, a chain of empires extended from Rome via Parthia and the Kushana empire to China, constituting an unbroken zone of civilized life from the Atlantic to the Pacific.

This was a new and important fact in the history of the

Eurasian world. The area of civilization remained narrow and exposed to unrelenting barbarian pressures, and developments in the different regions remained largely autonomous. But with the expansion of the major civilizations and the elimination of the geographical gaps between them, the way lay open for inter-regional contacts and cultural exchanges which left a lasting imprint. In the west, the expansion of Hellenism created a single cultural area which extended from the frontiers of India to Britain; in the east, the expansion of the Chinese and Indian civilizations resulted in a kind of cultural symbiosis in Indo-China. These wider cultural areas provided a vehicle not only for trade but for the transmission of ideas, technology and institutions, and above all for the diffusion of the great world religions. Beginning with Buddhism, and continuing with Judaism, Zoroastrianism, Christianity and Islam, religion became a powerful unifying bond in the Eurasian world.

550 BC TO AD 752
THE COMMERCIAL AND CULTURAL BONDS OF EURASIA

The rulers of the empires of the ancient world had no commercial policies, and were seldom interested in trade. Yet the activities of traders, operating at the margins of society, and rarely mentioned in ancient literature, had a profound effect on the development of the world, transmitting not only goods, but also cultural ideas – and occasionally deadly organisms.

The quantity of goods passing across the Eurasian landmass varied enormously depending on the political conditions of the time. Between 200 BC and AD 200 stable regimes in the Roman Mediterranean, the Persian Parthian empire, the Kushan empire and China under the Han dynasty, helped to stabilize the routes between Europe, Persia and China. Such favourable conditions for the movement of goods and people did not recur until the 8th century AD. These earlier empires, however, were not directly interested in facilitating trade. Chinese campaigns in the area of the Silk Road in Sinkiang, north of Tibet, such as that of Pan Ch'ao against the Kushans in *c.* AD 90, confronted a military rather than a commercial threat. The Han emperors certainly wanted valuable commodities like horses from Ferghana, but they expected to receive them as diplomatic gifts, tribute or booty from war.

Since the time of Assyrian merchants in Anatolia in the second millennium BC there are examples of communities of traders who settled in foreign territories to import goods from their homelands. In the 8th century BC Greek and Phoenician trading posts were established across the Mediterranean for the same purpose. These "trade diasporas" made possible effective communication between different cultural groups. The people who made up the diaspora communities were not wealthy merchants, but of much lower status. The "Roman" traders who sailed across the Indian Ocean or visited the Chinese court would not have been Italians, but inhabitants of the eastern provinces, who were probably not even Roman citizens.

Trade was not the only way in which goods travelled across this route. The Han rulers of China maintained peace on their northwest frontier by regular gifts of large quantities of silk and lacquerware to the Hsiungnu tribes outside the Great Wall. Some items would have been passed on in dowries or as gifts, and gradually made their way to the Mediterranean where silken clothing was sought by Roman senators, much to the distaste of more austere emperors.

While silk was the major import from China to the Mediterranean, a variety of goods found their way westwards. The Roman writer Pliny (AD 23–79) complains that the desire for eastern goods was draining the empire of its gold and silver, but this is not supported by the archaeological evidence. Glass was certainly sought after, but slaves were probably also a significant item of trade, and there are references in Chinese sources to "Syrian jugglers" reaching the Chinese court.

MARITIME TRADE

Maritime trade developed at the same time as the overland routes, making increased use of the monsoons for trade between southern Arabia and south

India. Vital information about the goods traded between the Roman empire and the east comes from *A Voyage around the Red Sea*, an anonymous handbook for traders written in the 1st century AD, which describes the coastal routes from the Egyptian Red Sea ports of Myos Hormus and Berenice to east Africa and the Ganges delta. The author knows of China as a vast city, but east of India his geographical knowledge is hazy.

The exchange of goods might have profound cultural effects. Begram in Gandhara was the location of the summer palace of the Kushan emperors. A rich hoard from there dating from around AD 100 included lacquer from China and ivory from India, as well as bronzes, glassware and pottery from the Mediterranean. The Kushan interest in Mediterranean artefacts illustrated by the Begram hoard had a profound effect on local practices, acting as a catalyst for the development of Gandharan art which emerged in the 2nd century AD, in part modelled on Greco-Roman styles.

1000–539 BC

THE NEAR EAST

As the Near East recovered from the upheavals of the late Bronze Age, Assyria re-emerged as the great regional power. At its greatest extent Assyrian territory stretched from the Mediterranean to the Persian Gulf, and from southern Egypt to Lake Van. At the height of Assyrian power, internal conflict saw the Babylonians replace the Assyrians as the rulers of the empire, but less than a century later they, in their turn, were overthrown by the Persians.

Our knowledge of this period is drawn largely from Assyrian, and later Babylonian, documents, but some idea of how neighbouring states saw Assyria can be gained from the Hebrew Bible, which contains historical material from the 8th century BC onwards. Although its narrative was revised several times in later centuries, the Bible provides information about the kingdoms of Israel and Judah, which emerged in the area of Palestine in around 1000 BC, initially as a single kingdom with its centre at Jerusalem. Over the next 300 years Israel and Judah came increasingly into the Assyrian sphere of influence, with their kings adopting varying attitudes to the neighbouring superpower.

Assyrian expansion started in the reign of Ashurnasirpal II (883–859 BC), who rebuilt and expanded the city and palace of Nimrud to be his capital. His successor Shalmaneser III (858–824 BC) extended the power of the kingdom westwards, partly by conquest and partly by accepting tribute from the local rulers in Syria and the Levant. In the following century Assyrian expansion turned south and east under three powerful rulers, Tiglath-pileser III (744–727 BC), Sargon II (721–705 BC) and Sennacherib (704–681 BC). Repeating the achievements of the 13th-century kings they conquered the city of Babylon and brought Mesopotamia under Assyrian control.

At this time a new power was growing on Assyria's northern border in the shape of Urartu. Little is known about this state, which had its capital at Tushpa on Lake Van. Many Urartian sites were heavily fortified, and the state flourished from the 9th to the 7th centuries BC. If the Assyrians did try to conquer it, they had little success. Along with its western neighbours, Phrygia and Lydia, Urartu had grown up after the collapse of the Hittite empire, but a number of "neo-Hittite" city-states also emerged in the region of northern Syria.

A little before 700 BC Egypt was beginning to recover from the disorganization of the Third Intermediate Period after the end of the New Kingdom, and attempted to influence affairs in the Levant. In response Esarhaddon (680–669 BC) and Ashurbanipal (668–627 BC) led campaigns into Egypt, going as far south as Thebes and more or less installing pro-Assyrian rulers in the country. Ashurbanipal also invaded Elam, extending his empire further than ever before. His death in 627 BC however marked the end of Assyrian power: within 15 years his capital, Nineveh, had been sacked, and his empire had come under the control of Babylon.

It has been suggested that the transformation of the neo-Assyrian empire into the neo-Babylonian empire should be seen as the result more of an internal dynastic conflict than of conquest. With the help of the Medes, who were settled on the northeastern borders of Assyria, the first neo-Babylonian ruler, Nabopolassar (626–605 BC), took advantage of quarrels within the Assyrian ruling house to seize control of the whole empire. In the process, Median and Babylonian armies destroyed Ashur, Nimrud and Nineveh, but, with the exception of Egypt, the empire that these cities controlled held together under its new rulers.

When the Egyptians tried to take advantage of the upheaval, Nabopolassar and his successor Nebuchadnezzar (604–562 BC) marched to the Levant, drove the Egyptians away, and at the same time captured Jerusalem and deported its leaders. The wealth of the empire was used to rebuild the cities of Mesopotamia, and above all Babylon. Excavation in the early 20th century revealed the splendour and the sheer size of the city as it was rebuilt by Nebuchadnezzar.

After Nebuchadnezzar's death there was a period of instability, which ended with a palace coup that placed Nabonidus (555–539 BC) on the throne. Although he had a long reign, his religious reforms appear to have made him unpopular with many leading members of the kingdom. This may have critically weakened Babylonian military strength when, in 539 BC, the city was taken by the Persians under Cyrus I (752).

550 BC TO AD 637
THE EMPIRES OF PERSIA

The Iranian plateau was the heartland of three great empires whose territory stretched from the ancient centres of civilization in Mesopotamia to India. For more than a millennium, the Persian empire was governed successively by the Achaemenid, Arsacid and Sasanid ruling families, and offered a constant challenge to the Mediterranean lands to the west.

The downfall of the Assyrian empire around 612 BC was brought about by the Babylonians and the Medes, a loose confederacy of tribes in western Iran. It was the Persians, however, who proved to be the main beneficiaries. The Persian state emerged in the 7th century BC on the edge of the area dominated by Assyria, and in 550 BC its ruler, Cyrus (559–530 BC), defeated an invading Median army at Pasargadae. The next 11 years saw attempts to stop the growth of Persian power by both Croesus of Lydia and Nabonidus of Babylon. Both were defeated, leaving Cyrus in possession of Anatolia, the Levant and Mesopotamia.

The absorption of Lydian territory into Cyrus's empire brought Persia into contact with the Greeks. He then turned his attention eastwards, gaining control of much of Afghanistan and south central Asia. Though Cyrus's successor, Cambyses (530–522 BC), added Egypt to the empire in 525 BC, his death was followed by the first of several upheavals within the empire as uncertainty over the succession encouraged widespread revolts.

These were quickly suppressed by Darius (522–486 BC), who also incorporated northwest India into the empire. The northwestern boundary of the empire remained a problem, but after the failure of expeditions into Europe by Darius and Xerxes (486–465 BC), the Persians protected their interests by a series of peace treaties with the Greek states.

Achaemenid rule was brought to an end by the invasion of Alexander the Great in 334 BC. Dynastic struggles in the 330s may have had an effect, but no entirely satisfactory explanation has been given for the rapidity with which the Achaemenid empire fell.

THE PARTHIAN EMPIRE

After Alexander's death, Iran and its neighbouring territories became part of the Seleucid kingdom. In the 3rd century BC internal disputes and conflict with other Hellenistic kingdoms weakened Seleucid control of their eastern territories. Bactria broke away to become an independent kingdom, and the provinces of Parthia and Hyrcania were taken over by Arsaces, leader of the Parni in 238.

The early history of the new kingdom of Parthia is uncertain, but under Mithradates I (171–138 BC) its territory was extended into Mesopotamia and as far east as the mouth of the Indus, its success, like that of Sasanid Persia later, largely the result of the use of mounted archers and armoured cavalry. In the years after Mithradates's death the empire was threatened by the Tocharians and the Shakas in the east, but order was restored by Mithradates II (123–87 BC). From the 1st century BC onwards, in spite of further severe Shaka incursions from the east, the main threat to Parthian security was Rome. But although there were a number of wars between the two empires, they were well matched militarily and Arsacid, or Parthian, rule remained secure until it was challenged from within.

SASANID PERSIA

Considerable autonomy was left in the hands of local ruling families, and it was from one of these in Persis that the new rulers of Persia arose. The first Sasanid ruler, Ardashir, defeated his Arsacid overlord Ardavan in AD 224 and rapidly took control of the whole of Parthia's empire and the areas beyond. Roman and Byzantine rule in Mesopotamia, Syria and eastern Anatolia was constantly challenged over the next centuries. The last century of Parthian rule had seen the rise of the Kushana empire in the east (*see* p. 68). This ended in 225 and Gandhara, Bactria and Sogdiana were brought under Sasanid control. From the 4th century this territory was threatened by Hephthalite and Chionite Huns and in the 6th century by the Turks.

The Arabs were a constant presence to the southwest of Persia's empires. The Achaemenids had established some control over northern Arabia, but in the Parthian period an independent state of Characene emerged at the head of the Persian Gulf, whose rulers styled themselves "kings of the Arabs". The Sasanids ended the independence of Characene, but maintained friendly relations with the Lakhmid Arab kingdom of Hira in western Mesopotamia which supported them against the Romans. Southern Arabia was never brought under Persian control, and in *c.* 604, after the Sasanid Chosroes II had ended Lakhmid independence, the Persians were defeated in battle by a confederacy of Arabs from the south. Success created confidence and increased Arab unity to such an extent that with further victories at Al Qadisiyya (637) and Nihavand (642) they brought Sasanid power to an end.

800 TO 336 BC
THE SPREAD OF GREEK CIVILIZATION

The Greek heartland is an area of islands and plains divided by mountains. After the collapse of the Mycenaean palace system, a new form of political and religious community emerged here, the *polis*, or city-state, which became the Mediterranean world's dominant form of political organization.

The 8th century BC was a period of great transformation in Greece. It saw the appearance of the first monumental public buildings, and with them other indications of the emergence of new communities, including changes in burial practices and artistic styles. At the same time literacy was reintroduced into Greece, with a new alphabet. Though contact with the wider world had not been totally broken in previous centuries, it now increased dramatically, above all on the island of Euboea. Although it is impossible to be certain what produced this transformation, one important factor was the activities of the

Phoenicians, who at this time began to explore and settle throughout the Mediterranean.

THE AGE OF EXPANSION

From the middle of the century, following in the wake of the Phoenicians, groups of Greeks began to create settlements around the Mediterranean. The earliest were in Italy and Sicily, but by the middle of the 6th century there were numerous Greek communities in north Africa and, to the east, along the Black Sea coast. These colonies were set up for a variety of reasons. Some of the earliest were trading posts, which over time developed into permanent settlements. Others were formally dispatched as a response to land shortage in the mother city. Others may have been founded by bands of discontented young men looking for a new and better life away from old Greece. It is probable that the experience of the colonists had an effect on the political development of their mother cities.

From its earliest existence, decision-making in the Greek *polis* lay with an assembly of adult male citizens. Leadership, however, would have been in the hands of the wealthy elite. Increasing wealth and overseas contact in the 7th and 6th centuries led to the emergence in many city-states of powerful individuals, known as tyrants, who were able to impose their will on the community, usually with popular support. The "age of the tyrants" was a period of urban development, with new buildings, in particular enormous temples such as those of Hera on Samos, Artemis at Ephesus and Olympian Zeus at Athens. City-states published law-codes on large stone tablets, advertising to the world that they were communities governed by the rule of law. Poetry flourished, with the *Iliad* and *Odyssey* of Homer and the poems of Hesiod appearing in the early 7th century, followed by the great lyric poets, among them Archilochus, Anacreon and Sappho. Certain religious sanctuaries, above all Olympia and Delphi, gained "pan-Hellenic" status, and became meeting places for the leading members of the different Greek communities.

THE ATHENIAN EMPIRE

The experience of the Persian invasion of Greece under Xerxes encouraged the Greeks in the Aegean and Asia Minor to join together to defend themselves from future threats. Athens, which had by far the largest fleet, took command, turning this alliance of city-states into an Athenian empire. Member states were required to pay tribute to finance the Athenian fleet, which guaranteed security. The existence of the Athenian empire considerably affected life in Athens. The fleet gave employment and status to the poorer citizens, who served as oarsmen and were able to participate in political activity to an extent unequalled elsewhere in the Greek world. A proportion of the tribute, along with some of the booty from successful naval campaigns, was given to the gods, funding great building programmes in Athens. The last three decades of the 5th century were also the period of Athens' most enduring literary achievements. Following the work of Aeschylus earlier in the century, Sophocles and Euripides wrote tragedies, and Aristophanes his comedies, for performance at the great dramatic festivals, the City Dionysia and the Lenaea. Herodotus, the first historian, lived in Athens for some time, while sophists, philosophers and rhetoricians flocked there to make their names and their fortunes. Athens also produced its own great historian, Thucydides.

At the same time, Athens' growing power was seen as a threat by the states of the Peloponnese, above all Sparta. After some inconclusive conflicts in the mid-century, in 431 BC Sparta declared war on Athens. This, the Peloponnesian War, developed into a conflict which ended 27 years later in the defeat of Athens and the disbanding of its empire.

THE RISE OF MACEDON

The economies of all Greek city-states were dominated by agriculture, and, except perhaps in Sparta, which relied on the labour of its conquered Messenian subjects (the "helots"), most of the population was made up of small-scale farmers, who were available for military service in the periods of less intense agricultural activity. One effect of this was that even prolonged periods of warfare had little long-term impact on the economies of the city-states involved. Thus within a decade of surrendering to the Peloponnesians, Athens was again at war with Sparta, this time supported by several of her former opponents.

The Spartans had originally defeated the Athenians with Persia's help. In 387 BC the Persian king attempted to impose a peace settlement on Greece, and the next 30 years saw Athens, Sparta and Thebes vying for dominance in Greece, looking always for backing from Persia. In 359 BC Philip II became king of Macedon. He united the country and took advantage of conflicts elsewhere in

Greece to gain control of Thrace to the east and Thessaly to the south. This gave him a firm base for involvement in Greek affairs, and, after Philip had brought to an end the "Sacred War" of 356–46, Macedon was left as the major power in Greece. In 338 BC Philip defeated the Athenians and Thebans at Chaeronea, and imposed a settlement on the whole of Greece, the "League of Corinth". His death two years later left his son Alexander a more or less united Greece, from which he was able to launch his invasion of the Persian empire.

336 TO 30 BC
THE HELLENISTIC WORLD

Alexander the Great's conquest of the Persian empire transformed the eastern Mediterranean and Middle Eastern world. The spread of Greek culture and political organisation which followed in his wake shaped the region for a millennium. Greek became the common language, and the city-state the common form of social organisation.

Along with the kingdom of Macedon, in 336 BC Alexander inherited from his father the leadership of a league of Greek states that he had intended to use to campaign against the Persian empire. Through his ambition and brilliant generalship, by the time of his death less than 13 years later at the age of 32, he was recognized as legitimate ruler of an empire stretching from Egypt to India. From the moment he died there was competition between his closest companions and generals. Until the assassination of Alexander's young son in 307 BC, the contenders, for all that each had ambitions to take over the whole empire, could at least claim to be acting as regents. Thereafter, they were fighting for themselves, rapidly styling themselves as kings, and attempting to carve out areas of personal influence. By 276 BC, a division of the empire into three main kingdoms – Antigonid Macedon, Seleucid Asia and Ptolemaic Egypt – had been established.

CULTURAL LIFE IN THE SUCCESSOR STATES
The basic political units of these new kingdoms was the city-state, some nominally independent, but most owing allegiance to one of the successor kings. The cities of old Greece, such as Athens, retained their prestige, but they were

eclipsed by the newly created or reorganized cities of the east, named inevitably after their founders or rulers: Alexandria, Seleucia, Antioch. The new cities had all the elements of their older counterparts, with gymnasia, theatres and temples to the gods, and regular festivals, some including athletics, which might be attended by Greeks from far afield. Citizenship was restricted almost entirely to the Greek and Macedonian minority, and the land was in the hands of citizens or of the kings and their friends. The local populations might farm the land as tenants or as labourers, but they were excluded from administrative positions. The network of cities helped the spread of a common Greek culture and language throughout the region: Clearchus, a pupil of Aristotle, brought a collection of maxims from Delphi in central Greece to the city of Ai Khanoum in eastern Afghanistan. In a number of cities, but above all in Alexandria, with its access to papyrus, and Pergamum, from where parchment got its name, the kings established great libraries, and these became centres for literary work.

Even before Alexander's conquest, some communities within the Persian empire had adopted aspects of Greek culture. This "Hellenization" continued, at least among the elites: conflict between "Hellenizers" and "traditionalists" in the 2nd century led to violence in Jerusalem. However, especially in Seleucid territories, elements of older cultures, including cuneiform writing, remained important, and in those areas which were to become the Parthian empire (*see* p. 57), Greek culture was never firmly established.

There were advances in geometry and mathematics, especially with Euclid of Alexandria and Archimedes. The great Alexandrian librarian, Eratosthenes of Cyrene, attempted with some success to calculate the circumference of the earth. However, this was not a period of great technological change. The basis of the Hellenistic economy was agriculture, and this changed little. Merchants continued to trade, and writers of the time praise the range of goods available in the great cities, but there is evidence too of an increasing gulf between rich and poor. Only in warfare were there major developments, with the creation of ever more advanced artillery and siege engines, and the introduction by the Seleucids and the Ptolemies of elephants onto the battlefield.

From the late 3rd century, a new player entered the game. Threats to Roman operations in the Adriatic, and Macedonian support for the Carthaginian Hannibal, led to a Roman invasion of Greece and Asia Minor. The Macedonian phalanx proved inferior to the Roman legions.

THE GROWTH OF ROMAN POWER

Wars gave Roman commanders an opportunity for booty and glory, and initially they withdrew their forces after each campaign; but as Rome acquired more allies in the east, the reasons for maintaining their presence grew. After the battle of Pydna (168) the kingdom of Macedon was divided into four independent republics. 18 years later it was made a Roman province. The involvement of Cleopatra VII in the civil war between Mark Antony and the future emperor Augustus led after the battle of Actium (*see* p. 75) to the Roman annexation of Egypt, the last major successor kingdom. A few small client kingdoms, tolerated by the Romans for a while, were all that remained of Alexander's territorial inheritance.

475 BC TO AD 220

THE UNIFICATION OF CHINA

The process of China's nation- and empire-building began with the political anarchy of the Warring States period but ended with a highly centralized state headed by a single monarch and an efficient bureaucracy that reached village level. The new system attained its full glory under the Han, whose wealth and territory matched the Roman empire.

Throughout the Warring States period (475–221 BC) seven major rivals contended for supremacy. At first, following the decline of the power of the Chou king, the principal contenders were the old-established dukedoms of Ch'i, Ch'u, Han and Wei. But from the beginning of the 3rd century BC the border state of Ch'in established firm control over the northwest and west, adopting the title "king" in 325 BC, and during the latter half of the 3rd century BC it began gradually destroying its rivals.

Throughout China, it was a period of constant warfare, waged on a massive scale by powerful and well-organized political units. But at the same time, this Warring States period coincided with major economic and social changes. The introduction of iron tools from about 500 BC and the use of animal power for cultivation greatly increased agricultural productivity. Population multiplied, commerce and industry flourished and large cities emerged. It was also a period of innovation in technology and science, and of philosophical ferment, in which the main schools of thought – Confucianism, Daoism and Legalism – took shape.

That the Ch'in emerged from this period to unify China under their leadership was at least in part due to the success of the "Legalist" system adopted by them in the 4th century, whereby a universal code of rewards and punishments was established that induced a high level of popular obedience and military discipline. Under this system, a centralized bureaucracy took measures to improve the production and distribution of grain, and organized the population to provide manpower for construction works and for the army, enforcing the system through a ruthless penal code.

THE FIRST EMPEROR

When the Ch'in king, Shih Huang-ti, was crowned the first emperor of China in 221 BC, the "Legalist" institutions were extended throughout the country. But although the emperor tried to eliminate all hostile factions, under the burdens imposed on the people by his military campaigns and vast construction works, his dynasty collapsed in a nationwide rebellion in 206 BC, shortly after his death.

After a period of civil war a new dynasty, the Han, was established by Liu Pang (256–195 BC). Copying the general outlines of the Ch'in system, but softening its harshness and in part restoring a system of feudal principalities, the Han gradually evolved an effective central government and system of local administration. The "Legalist" approach was replaced by Confucianism which emphasized benevolent rule and good statesmanship.

HAN EXPANSION

The Ch'in had taken strong defensive measures against the nomad Hsiungnu (Huns) in the north. Under the emperor Wu-ti (140–87 BC), though probably driven by his generals in the north, Han China again took the offensive against the Hsiungnu, and opened up the route to central Asia known as the Silk Road. A large export trade, mainly in silk, reached as far as the Roman empire. The Han also reaffirmed the Ch'in conquests in the southern region, eliminated the Yüeh kingdoms of the southeast coast, and occupied northern Vietnam. Chinese armies also drove deep into the southwest, seeking to establish Han control. In addition, Wu-ti's armies placed parts of northern Korea under Chinese administration.

The Han empire grew extremely prosperous and China's population reached some 57 million. Many large cities grew up and the largest, the capital Ch'ang-an, housed a population of a quarter of a million and was the centre of a brilliant culture. At the beginning of the Christian era the Han empire rivalled that of Rome in size and wealth.

But under a series of weak emperors during the latter half of the 1st century BC, the authority of the throne was challenged by powerful court families. In AD 9 Wang Mang usurped the throne. His reign (the Hsin dynasty, AD 9–23) ended in a widespread rebellion that restored the Han (Later Han, AD 25–220), and the capital was moved to Lo-yang.

THE COLLAPSE OF THE HAN EMPIRE

After some decades of consolidation, in the late 1st century the Chinese resumed active hostilities to drive the Hsiungnu westward to central Asia. But trouble with the Chiang tribes of the northwest and virulent factionalism at court had seriously weakened the Han state by AD 160. A wave of agrarian distress culminated in 184 in a massive uprising led by the "Yellow Turbans", a religious movement based on popular cults. Although the Han survived in name until 220, power now lay with regional commanders. In 220 the empire was divided into three independent kingdoms, ushering in a long period of territorial fragmentation.

220 TO 618
CHINA AND EAST ASIA

The period after 220 was one of the most chaotic and bloody in Chinese history. Not only was the north lost for long periods to non-Chinese regimes, but the governments in the south often lost effective control as well. Political instability was the norm across the country, and economic growth was minimal until the advent of the Sui dynasty.

The Han empire broke up into three kingdoms in 220: the Wei in the north;

the Wu in the south; and the Shu in the west. The militarily strong Wei had conquered the Shu in the southwest by 263, but in 265 a military family, the Ssu-uma, took over the Wei kingdom through a coup d'état. They then proceeded with a series of military campaigns to unify China under the name of the Western Chin dynasty. The target of unification was finally achieved in 280.

THE WESTERN CHIN

The new authorities granted farmers land-holding rights to re-establish household farming in accordance with the Han model. "Salary land" for officials was granted and cultivated by tenants. Overall, this helped the recovery of the agricultural economy. The adoption of a laissez-faire Daoism by the new rulers as the state philosophy was also precedented in the Han. At the same time Buddhism became increasingly widespread.

Politically, however, the ruling class was deeply divided. In the period from 291 to 306, there were numerous assassinations and violent struggles within the royal family, known as the "Wars between Eight Princes". The unitary empire existed only in name. The weakness of the Western Chin regime created opportunities for the non-Chinese peoples within and on the borders of the empire – the Hsienpei, Hsiungnu, Chieh, Ti and Ch'iang – to move in and establish their own kingdoms, as many as 16 at one time. This was known as the "Five Barbarians' Disruption of China" and practically ended the Western Chin. The Chinese regime survived under the Eastern Chin only in south China. Its territory was much smaller than the area controlled by the non-Chinese regimes in the north and its authority over the population severely weakened. Tax avoidance became endemic.

During the years of the Eastern Chin, north China saw near permanent conflict among the non-Chinese regimes. The unification of the north finally arrived in 382 under the Ch'ien Ch'in and after their failed invasion of the south in the following year an era of co-existence was ushered in between the non-Chinese regime in the north and the Chinese one in the south. Based on this ethnic division, the period is called the "Northern and Southern Dynasties".

In the south the Eastern Chin dynasty ended with its overthrow in 420 by one of its generals, who established the Sung dynasty. There followed another three short-lived dynasties, each in turn brought down by either a general or another member of the ruling family, although outside the court there was a measure of peace and prosperity.

THE NORTHERN WEI

In the north a dynasty of Hsienpei descent, the Northern Wei, managed to conquer all of north China in the early 5th century, but split into two lines in 534, to become, in 550 and 557 respectively, the Northern Ch'i and Northern Chou. Although the latter was smaller and poorer, it had a more efficient military organization, and overcame the Northern Ch'i in 577. Within a few years, however, its ruling family was overthrown by one of its partly-Chinese generals, Yang Chien, who went on to conquer the south and establish the Sui dynasty. Although it was itself short-lived, the Sui had at last reunified China.

500 BC TO AD 550

INDIA: THE FIRST EMPIRES

From 500 BC to AD 550 south Asia witnessed a succession of metropolitan empires centred in north India – the Mauryas, the Kushanas and the Guptas. Although centralized political control was often weak, for the first time the entire subcontinent was integrated within a single but diverse cultural field.

By about 500 BC north India sustained 16 well-articulated polities, or "mahajanapadas", some of which were still essentially tribal republics and others were already monarchies. This region witnessed tremendous change, as the consolidation of settled agriculture led to the emergence of cities and more complex political systems. Such changes made the older sacrificial cult of the Vedas, which had its origins in the pastoral communities of the Aryan tribes, increasingly obsolete. In its place, at the end of the 5th century BC in the heart of the Gangetic plains, the founders of Buddhism and Jainism formulated their radical new teachings.

THE FIRST EMPIRE

During the 5th century BC the number of mahajanapadas diminished to four – Vajji, Kosala, Kasi and Magadha. After a century of wars, the single kingdom of

Magadha dominated, with its splendid new capital of Pataliputra. This was to be the nucleus of the first Indian empire. Shortly after Alexander's incursion into India in 327 BC, the Mauryan prince Chandragupta seized the Magadhan throne. Chandragupta then conquered the land east of the Indus, swung south to occupy much of central India, and in 305 BC decisively defeated Alexander's successor in the northwest, Seleucus Nicator. The Mauryan empire that Chandragupta founded reached its zenith under his grandson, Ashoka, who established his rule over most of the subcontinent. Ashoka's empire was composed of a centralized administrative system spread over a number of thriving cities and their hinterlands. After his conquest of Kalinga in 260 BC, Ashoka publicly converted to Buddhism and adopted a policy of "conquest through righteousness", or *dhammavijaya*. In a number of public orders inscribed on pillars and rockfaces throughout the subcontinent, Ashoka called for peace, propagated moral teachings (*dhamma*), and prohibited Vedic animal sacrifices. These edicts, written in Prakrit, are the first specimens of royal decrees in south Asia.

THE KUSHANA EMPIRE

Mauryan rule did not long survive Ashoka's death in 232 BC. In the 2nd century BC, the northwest was repeatedly invaded, both by Greeks from Bactria and Parthia, and then by new nomad groups themselves displaced from central Asia. First among these were Scythian tribes called the Shakas who overran Bactria and the Indus valley in the 1st century BC. Then the Kushana branch of the Yüeh-chih horde, who had settled in the Oxus valley after 165 BC, gradually extended their rule inland, subduing the Shakas in western India and reaching Varanasi in the 1st century AD. As well as the Oxus and Indus valleys, large parts of Khotan were included in their cosmopolitan empire, centred in Purusapura. Kushana India was a melting pot of cultures. The empire reached its height of power and influence under Kanishka, who patronized Buddhism and became extensively involved in political conflicts in central Asia.

Both the Shakas and the Kushanas took Indian names and were the first kings to adopt Sanskrit at their courts – the first courtly poems in Sanskrit date from this period – though the native kingdom of the Satavahanas of the Deccan continued to use Prakrit. In the northwest Mahayana Buddhism emerged at this time from more conservative teachings known as Theravada, and developed a more eclectic outlook, emphasizing compassion and worship in an enlarged Buddhist pantheon.

In the same period, India's ancient trading links with the west were revitalized and greatly extended as the Roman empire rose to power. Ports such as Barbaricum, on the Indus delta, and the entrepot of Barygaza exported turquoise, diamonds, indigo and tortoise-shell, receiving in return a flow of pearls, copper, gold and slaves from the Arab and Mediterranean worlds. Much of the Chinese silk traffic found its way to the city of Taxila, before caravans took it further west. Trade led to other exchanges, as Buddhism spread to central Asia and China.

By the middle of the 2nd century AD the south had also witnessed economic development. The Satavahanas of the Deccan developed a powerful empire and established overland and coastal trading networks and the weaker Tamil-speaking kingdoms of the south established ports on both coasts of the peninsula.

THE GUPTAS

In the 4th century, the native dynasty of the Guptas imposed a new rule, based again in Pataliputra. Following the campaigns of Samudragupta and his son Chandragupta II, their suzerainty was acknowledged over an area almost as great as that of the Mauryan empire. Until repeated Hun incursions ended Gupta power in the 6th century, the Gupta period saw the blossoming of earlier cultural trends, and has become known as the "classical" or "epic" age of Indian history.

2300 TO 50 BC
THE PEOPLES OF NORTHERN EUROPE

The late Bronze Age saw a number of developments in northern Europe. The use of metals increased, new crops were cultivated, and burial practices were transformed. The "urnfield culture", with which these changes are associated, spread over a large part of Europe and laid the foundations for the rise of the Celts, whose warrior bands briefly threatened the Mediterranean world.

Central Europe had rich supplies of copper ores, which for several centuries had been exploited to produce bronze for tools and weapons. After 1300 BC the extent of bronze-working increased dramatically, and new techniques, including the lost-wax method of casting, led to major developments in art. Delicately worked gold ornaments found in some rich graves indicate that there were also improvements in gold-working at the same time. In agriculture, the staples of wheat and barley were supplemented by legumes and oil-rich crops such as linseed. There was also an increase in the domestication of animals, with horses having a greater presence, especially to the east.

THE URNFIELD PERIOD

The most dramatic change, however, was in burial practices, and it is this that has given the urnfield period its name. Inhumation had been the usual practice in earlier centuries, but from 1300 BC there was a move towards cremation and the burial of ashes in large communal cemeteries known as urnfields. Although there were differences from region to region, and even within cemeteries, there was a considerable decrease in the quantity of grave goods buried with the dead. Some burials, such as the so-called King's Grave at Seddin, were particularly rich, and presumably belonged to local chieftains, but most were simple. A change of practice like this may in part have reflected a change in attitudes to death, but it probably also reflected changes in social organization. Large cemeteries containing graves with little social differentiation suggest the emergence of large communities and more developed social structures.

Another feature that points to social change during this period is the large number of fortified sites. These were centuries in which there was fighting between rival communities, and the archaeological evidence points to a growing warrior culture.

THE CELTIC WORLD

The 8th century BC saw the re-establishment of contact with the centres of civilization in the eastern Mediterranean and beyond as well as with the new Greek and Phoenician colonies in the western Mediterranean and the emerging Etruscans in Italy. At the same time the techniques of iron-working were widely adopted. This development had little impact on the Atlantic coasts of Europe, which were still characterized by small-scale trade between communities with little interest in Mediterranean luxury goods. But to the east the Rhône valley provided a trade-route from the Mediterranean, especially after the foundation of the Greek colony of Massilia (Marseilles). It was this that led to the development of a "prestige goods economy" in Burgundy, seen in the rich finds from Mont Lassois and Vix, which acted as staging posts between the Mediterranean and central Europe, as well as farther east at the hill fort at the Heuneburg on the upper Danube. Contact with the steppe communities on the eastern flank of the Celtic world also continued, and by this route goods from the Far East could reach central Europe. This is well illustrated by the discovery in a burial mound beside the Heuneburg site of textiles embroidered with Chinese silk.

Among the chief exports to the Mediterranean from this period onwards was slaves, which raised the status of warriors who were able to trade prisoners of war for prestige goods from Etruria and Greece. This "West Hallstatt system" collapsed when the Etruscans started to make direct contact with the area around the Marne and Moselle. The same period also saw the emergence of a distinctive decorative aristocratic style known as "Celtic" art. Spectacular finds have been made at sites such as Somme-Bionne and Basse-Yutz.

The Celts are the first peoples of northern Europe to appear in the historical record. They are mentioned by several Greek and Roman historians, and these writings give us some insight into their social organization and their religious practices – although they have to be used with caution. Later Celtic traditions are recorded in the epic literature of Ireland and Wales, but it is not clear how much they can tell us about early Celtic Europe. What is not in question is the Celtic interest – and skill – in warfare.

After 600 BC, Celtic war-bands spread out from central Europe into Italy and Greece – Rome was attacked in 390 BC, Delphi in 279 BC – and settled as far south as Galatia in Anatolia and Galicia in Spain. Other areas, such as western France and Britain, were absorbed into the Celtic world by peaceful means, with the native aristocracies adopting the new continental fashions of art and warfare. From the 3rd century BC fortified urban settlements known as "oppida" became more common, and unified Celtic states began to appear.

Celtic social organization was increasingly influenced by the growing power of Rome, and the Celts were the first peoples of northern Europe to be incorporated within the Roman empire. Already by the end of the 2nd century BC the Mediterranean part of Gaul was a Roman province. Julius Caesar's conquests in

Gaul then brought the western Celtic world under Roman control as far as the English Channel by 50 BC. Thus the most economically advanced areas of the barbarian world were rapidly integrated within the Roman world.

900 BC–AD 700
AFRICA

Written sources from this period increasingly help to reconstruct the history of north Africa, the Nilotic Sudan, Eritrea and Ethiopia. For the rest of Africa, archaeology remains the primary source and, since research and evidence are currently meagre, for large parts of the continent the past still awaits discovery.

In the last millennium BC, north Africa was inhabited by the ancestors of the modern Berbers. At the coast these people came into contact with a variety of foreigners. The first were the Phoenicians, seafaring merchants who established trading settlements westwards from Tripoli and founded Carthage towards the end of the 9th century. Egypt at this time was politically weak and succumbed to a variety of foreign powers, among them the kingdom of Kush, based at Napata, whose kings ruled as the 25th Dynasty (c. 770–664). From the 3rd century BC, Rome began to assert its power in the region, successfully challenging Carthaginian supremacy in the western Mediterranean. Thereafter Roman control was extended along the north African coast and, in 30 BC, Egypt was conquered. By the time the Roman empire began to weaken in the 4th and early 5th centuries AD, Christianity was widespread in its African provinces and remained unchallenged until the Arab invasions of the 7th century brought Islam to Africa.

By the 4th century BC the Kushite kingdom had moved south to Meroë, where it flourished until the 2nd century AD. Its subsequent decline was probably owed, in part, to the rise of the Aksumite kingdom in northern Ethiopia. In the mid-4th century, Aksum adopted Christianity as its official religion. Although Christian influences must have spread southwards from Egypt into Nubia towards the end of the Meroitic period, it was not until the 6th century that Christianity was introduced into the region. In the following century, the Arab invasion of Egypt began a process of Islamization that spread slowly southwards into Nubia. The rise of Islam was also a factor in the decline of Aksum, which had ceased to exist as a political entity by about AD 700.

IRON-WORKING AND FARMING

Almost certainly it was the Phoenicians who introduced bronze- and iron-working to north Africa. In west Africa, iron was being used by the mid-first millennium BC. The development of an urban settlement at Jenne-Jeno from about 250 BC onwards, was probably facilitated by the use of iron tools, which helped agriculturalists to till the heavy clay soils of the inland Niger delta. The earliest evidence of iron use in southern west Africa is associated with the Nok culture, famous for its terracotta sculptures. The early iron-using communities of eastern and southern Africa show such a remarkable degree of homogeneity that they are viewed as a single cultural complex, which first appeared on the western side of Lake Victoria around the mid-1st millennium BC and had spread as far south as Natal by the 3rd century AD. In addition to iron technology, this complex is associated with the beginnings of crop cultivation, livestock herding and settlement. South of Tanzania it is also linked to the manufacture of pottery. In Namibia and Cape Province, which were not settled by these iron-using farmers, some groups had acquired domestic sheep as early as the first two centuries AD. At about the same time a distinctive Cape coastal pottery appears, but others continued with their ancient way of life, living in mobile groups, hunting, gathering and making stone tools.

TO 31 BC

THE EXPANSION OF ROMAN POWER

Rome, a city-state governed by aristocratic families leading an army of peasant soldiers, came to control an empire that stretched from the Atlantic to the Euphrates and from the English Channel to the Sahara. But military success brought social disorder; rivalries between warlords led to civil war; and republican institutions became an autocracy.

The city of Rome grew up on the Tiber at the lowest point the river could be bridged. Although several of Rome's hills were settled from around 1000 BC, the earliest signs of urbanization date from the 7th century. According to tradition,

Rome was ruled by a line of seven kings, and the expulsion of the last of these in 511 BC resulted in the creation of a republic ruled by two annually elected consuls or magistrates. It is probable, however, that the government of the emerging city-state was less formalized than tradition suggests and that republican systems reached their developed form only in the 4th century BC.

Consuls held office for no more than a single year and ruled with the support of the Senate, a council of former magistrates and priests. Legislation proposed by them had also to be ratified by a popular assembly. However, their main task was to protect the city, which in effect meant to lead military campaigns. Success in war brought material gains to the people of Rome and prestige to the commanders making imperialism an inevitable feature of Roman policy.

THE PUNIC WARS

By 264 BC Rome controlled the whole of the Italian peninsula and had emerged as a powerful confederacy and the principal rival to the other major power in the western Mediterranean, Carthage. The Romans were forced to develop naval skills to defeat Carthage in the First Punic War (264–241 BC), in which Rome drove the Carthaginians out of Sicily; soon after Corsica and Sardinia were seized as well. In the Second Punic War (218–201 BC), Rome was invaded from the north, when Hannibal brought his army and elephants from Spain over the Alps into Italy. Though Rome suffered devastating defeats at Lake Trasimene (217 BC) and Cannae (216 BC) it was able to draw on great reserves of Italian manpower to drive Hannibal out of Italy and defeat him at Zama in north Africa (202 BC). With Spain added to Rome's provinces, the city now commanded the whole of the western and central Mediterranean.

EXPANSION TO THE EAST

In the following 50 years, Roman commanders turned their attention eastwards, leading expeditions into Greece, but withdrawing their troops once victory was assured, in part from fear that Italy, always most vulnerable to attack from the north, would be invaded. Nonetheless, in 146 BC Macedonia was added to the empire, with the province of Asia following in 133 BC.

Among the consequences of Roman victories abroad was an influx of goods and people into Italy. Works of art were taken from Greek temples to adorn private Roman villas, while Greek literature, rhetoric and philosophy had a profound effect on the nature of Roman politics. Wars also provided cheap slaves, who were brought to Italy as agricultural labourers, threatening the livelihoods of Italian peasant farmers and leading to the rapid growth of the urban population of Rome itself.

FROM REPUBLIC TO EMPIRE

The period from 133 BC saw increasing turbulence within Rome and Italy. Rome's continuing expansion provided opportunities for ambitious men to use their military commands to dominate Roman politics, and the institutions of the republic were powerless to regulate the competition between them. Slave revolts and the Social War with Rome's Italian allies (91–89 BC) increased disorder within Italy. The last generation of the republic saw the system collapse in a series of civil wars which ended only in 31 BC when Octavian emerged triumphant at the battle of Actium and found himself in a position of such dominance that he was able to rebuild the government of Rome and make it capable of administering an empire.

31 BC TO AD 235
THE HEIGHT OF ROMAN POWER

Augustus, the first emperor, transformed the government of the Roman empire. He brought an end to internal conflicts and created a standing army to guard the empire's frontiers and extend its power. As Roman culture and organization spread throughout the empire, it laid the foundations for the development of the Mediterranean world.

In 31 BC Octavian, the future emperor Augustus, was undisputed master of Rome. His popularity as adopted son of Julius Caesar and victor over Cleopatra and Mark Antony at the battle of Actium allowed him to rebuild the shattered Roman republic into a system of government capable of controlling a vast empire, reforms which were to bring Rome a new and intense surge of life and two and a half centuries of almost uninterrupted peace and prosperity.

Augustus's reforms were far-reaching. He restored the prestige of the Senate, though not, in practice, its influence. He reorganized the army and, in 27 BC, took command of those parts of the empire where legions were stationed. From then on responsibility for the defence of the empire lay with the emperor alone. At the same time he took the religiously significant name Augustus, and stressed his relationship to the now deified Julius Caesar. Among his many priesthoods was that of Pontifex Maximus, chief priest, and from the time of Augustus onward the emperor became the focus of all Roman religious ritual.

In 19 BC Augustus was given the power to rule by decree, and although he continued to pay due respect to the Senate, whose members he needed to command the legions and to administer the provinces, his authority was now absolute. The vast wealth he had inherited and won (his defeat of Antony and Cleopatra left Egypt as his personal domain) was further increased by bequests from the rich throughout the empire. At his death his property was worth thousands of times as much as that of even the richest senator. That his heir should also inherit his position as head of the empire was inevitable.

In the event, Augustus had great difficulty in finding an heir, eventually settling on his stepson Tiberius (AD 14–37), who had been a successful military commander but took on the role of emperor with reluctance. Neither he nor his successors were able to maintain good relations with the Senate, and the failure of Nero (54–68) to prevent revolt in the provinces led to his enforced suicide and the end of the Julio-Claudian dynasty. After a year of civil war, Vespasian (69–79) restored order. He was succeeded by his sons, Titus (79–81) and Domitian (81–96). Though the latter was generally regarded as a cruel and probably insane tyrant, many of his imperial policies were adopted by his successors, especially Trajan (98–117), who began the practice of appearing before the Senate not in a toga but in the purple cloak and armour of a triumphant general. This was to become the uniform of the emperor for the next thousand years.

STABILITY AND STRIFE

Domitian's assassination was followed by nearly a century of stability as emperors without sons of their own chose their successors from the Senate. Civil war returned in 193, from which Septimius Severus (193–211) emerged victorious. He ruled with his sons Caracalla (198–217) and Geta (209–12), setting a pattern that was to be followed in the following centuries. Caracalla was murdered, and after him came a series of short-lived emperors, of whom

Severus Alexander (222–35) was the last who could claim a dynastic link to his predecessors.

THE NATURE OF ROME

The emperor's figure was central to the empire: everywhere statues and coins were constant reminders of his presence. In the former Hellenistic kingdoms the kings had been the objects of religious worship, a practice which continued with the cult of the emperors. In the western provinces, temples and altars dedicated to the emperor became focuses of Romanization.

The early 2nd century saw important cultural developments: Greek and Latin literature flourished; and the distinction between Italy and the provinces dissolved as rich men from all over the empire were admitted to the Senate, with some, such as Trajan and Hadrian (117–38), even becoming emperor. For the poor there were fewer benefits, and differences in the rights and privileges of rich and poor grew. By the time Caracalla extended Roman citizenship throughout the empire in AD 212, it gave little advantage to the newly enfranchised citizens. Later in the 2nd century, pressures grew on the frontiers. Marcus Aurelius (161–80) spent much of his reign at war with barbarian invaders, and his successors faced threats both from the north, and, after 224, from the rejuvenated Persian empire under the Sasanids.

AD 235 TO 565
FROM ROME TO BYZANTIUM

The 4th century AD saw Roman emperors still ruling an empire that stretched from Spain to Syria. In the 5th century the two halves of the empire experienced different fortunes. Roman administration in the west dissolved in the face of increasing barbarian settlement, but in the east Byzantine civilization, combining Greek and Roman practices and culture, grew and flourished.

The empire emerged from the storms of the 3rd century intact but not unchanged. Diocletian and his successors owed their position to the army, not the Senate, and the military now provided most of the provincial governors. Rome itself ceased to be the centre of empire, as the emperors based themselves in cities nearer the frontiers: Mediolanum (Milan) in Italy; and, after AD 330,

Constantinople in the east. The emperors were surrounded by large courts, increasingly turning to eunuchs as their closest advisors. To maintain the army, the taxation system was reformed and military service became a hereditary obligation. But as the senators in Italy and other rich landowners were increasingly excluded from power, so they became less inclined to support the emperor, a development which was to have a profound effect on the western half of the empire.

THE RISE OF CHRISTIANITY

But the greatest change to the empire was religious. In 312 Constantine defeated his rival Maxentius outside Rome, and he came to attribute his victory to the support of the Christian god. In his reign and that of his son Constantius II the churches received many favours from the emperor, and Christianity began to establish itself as the dominant religion of the empire. The last pagan emperor, Julian, died in AD 363 on campaign against the Persians before he had the opportunity to reverse the trend. Bishops such as St Ambrose in Milan (374–97) became increasingly powerful figures in the empire.

Barbarian incursions continued to erode central control of the empire. The arrival of the Huns in eastern Europe in 376 drove many Goths across the Danube, forcing them into Roman territory. Having in 378 defeated the Romans at Adrianople, in 405 they invaded Italy. In the winter of 406 German tribes then crossed the frozen river Rhine in unstoppable masses. The situation deteriorated throughout the century. The Vandals marched through Gaul and Spain before crossing to Africa where they captured Carthage, the chief city, in 439 and set up their own kingdom.

Where in the 4th century the Roman army had made use of barbarian officers, now the western emperors had little choice but to make grants of land for the invaders to settle on and to employ them in the army. With landowners unwilling to allow their tenants to fight, what had been a Roman citizen army became a barbarian mercenary one. Since the frontiers were no longer preventing barbarians from entering the western empire, and since the army was itself largely barbarian, the role of the emperor in the west was effectively redundant.

In 476 the *magister militum* (the chief military officer of the western empire) Odoacer, a German, deposed the emperor Romulus Augustulus, and did not replace him. With the eastern emperor making no attempt to resist this, the western empire ceased to exist. In 490 the Ostrogoths took control of Italy, and by 507 the Franks had established an extensive kingdom in Gaul (*see* p. 94). Yet Roman institutions survived: the Roman Senate continued to sit, and Latin remained the language of government.

THE RECONQUESTS OF JUSTINIAN

The eastern part of the empire possessed greater resources than the west, and eastern emperors could use their wealth to persuade would-be invaders to move away westwards. Although Roman culture continued to flourish in the eastern part of the empire, there were growing cultural differences between east and west: when Justinian launched his attempt to reconquer the former western empire, he was trying to impose a Greek-speaking administration on Latin-speaking territories.

Justinian's reign was a mixture of triumph and disaster. In Constantinople it saw the building of the great church of St Sophia (532–63) as well as a devastating plague in 542. His general Belisarius took Africa from the Vandals in 533–4 while in 554, after a campaign lasting 20 years, Ostrogothic rule in Italy was ended. But Justinian's successes in Italy were short-lived: the Lombard invasion of 568 left only Ravenna in Byzantine hands. Meanwhile in the east there was war with Persia (540–62): Antioch was sacked in 540 and peace was eventually bought only at great financial cost. Justinian's wars left Byzantium seriously weakened. The dream of a reunited empire died with him.

TO AD 600

THE RISE OF CHRISTIANITY

Christianity began as a small sect within Judaism, but gradually established itself as a significant religious and intellectual force throughout the Roman empire. It offered both a promise of eternal salvation to individuals and, from the 4th century onwards, a powerful new vision of an empire united under a Christian ruler which was to be of enormous significance for the future of Europe.

The earliest Christians did not see themselves as founders of a new religion but as witnesses to the fulfilment of God's promise to provide his people, the

Jews, with a Messiah or redeemer. By raising him from the dead, they believed that God had shown that Jesus of Nazareth was this Messiah and that the risen Jesus had commissioned his disciples to preach the good news of God's kingdom.

Though the earliest Christians were Jews, they did not interpret the message of Jesus in political or national terms. Christianity was attractive to people besides Jews for its promise of eternal life and for the spiritual benefits of membership of a close-knit, supportive community. So the conversion of gentiles soon began in the cities of the eastern Roman empire and was enthusiastically advocated by Paul, a converted Pharisee and former opponent of Christianity. With the rejection of Christianity's claims by the majority of Jews, Christianity had become a distinct religion by the end of the 1st century. Christian expansion was much slower in the west: while there was a Christian community in Rome by AD 50, the earliest evidence for Christianity in France and north Africa is to be found from the late 2nd century.

At first Christianity was a religion mainly of the urban poor, but it gradually spread to higher social groups. Its growth went largely unnoticed by the Roman authorities. There were sporadic episodes of persecution, such as those under emperors Nero (AD 64) and Decius (250), but these were aimed more at finding scapegoats for major disasters than at systematically eliminating Christianity. Even the "Great Persecution" of 303–12, under the emperors Diocletian and Galerius, had a more profound effect on the leaders of the churches than it did on their followers, as disputes arose over how they had responded to the arrests and confiscations that occurred then.

By this time the church had grown from a network of small communities, meeting in the homes of richer members, into a well-organized body owning buildings and burial grounds, and led by a ministry of bishops, presbyters and deacons. It was well placed to benefit from the changes that began in 312.

CONSTANTINE

In that year, the emperor Constantine gained a victory in the civil war against his rival Maxentius, which he came to attribute to the power of the Christian God. In the following year, with his fellow emperor Licinius, Constantine declared toleration for all religions in the Roman empire. These events marked a turning point in the history of Christianity, as Constantine came to see himself as a Christian ruler endowed with divine authority, and gave privileges to Christian churches. With these privileges came some loss of autonomy for the bishops, as Constantine attempted through a series of Councils to establish orthodoxy of doctrine on the churches. But Constantine did not make Christianity into the state religion of the empire overnight. This was a gradual process, interrupted by the reign of the pagan emperor Julian (361–3), which was to reach its conclusion – the banning of the pagan rites, which Christians found so offensive – only in the reign of Theodosius (379–95).

In the 5th century there were still many pagans, even at court, but the empire was gradually Christianized through a programme of church building and the demolition of pagan shrines. Monks took a leading role in evangelization from the 4th century onwards. Meanwhile, Christianity had also spread east to Persia and west among the barbarian tribes which were eventually to invade and destroy the western Roman empire.

DOCTRINAL DEVELOPMENT

From its roots in Jewish monotheism, early Christianity underwent a good deal of doctrinal development. Many theologians from the 2nd century onwards attempted to combine the teachings of Christianity with the intellectual assumptions of Greek philosophy. In the 4th and 5th centuries the church embodied its beliefs about God and Jesus in a succession of doctrinal statements intended to prohibit heretical views. The statements of faith in the Trinity and the Incarnation produced by the church councils of Nicaea (325) and Chalcedon (451) were especially important. In them, the early church bequeathed to later Christianity a set of doctrinal assumptions that were not to be seriously challenged until the Reformation in the 16th century and which remain the basis of their faith for many Christians even today.

FOUR

THE WORLD OF DIVIDED REGIONS

The period around AD 500 saw upheaval throughout the Eurasian world, when nomads from the steppes of Asia descended upon all the existing centres of civilization. Although the gains of the classical period never entirely disappeared, contacts dwindled between China and the West, between north Africa and Italy and between Byzantium and western Europe. For the next few centuries each region was thrown back on its own resources and forced to fend for itself.

In western Europe this period is traditionally known as 'the Middle Ages'. The description may be appropriate for European history but it makes little sense in the wider perspective of world history. Here, two outstanding events dominated: the rise and expansion of Islam after 632; and the emergence of the Mongol empire in the 13th century. At the same time, important developments transformed hitherto isolated regions. The appearance of the Maya, Aztec and Inca civilizations in America, the creation of the empires of Sri Vijaya and Majapahit in southeast Asia, and the rise of the empires of Ghana, Mali and Songhay in Africa all attested to a new vitality and to the expansion of the area of civilized life.

Europe, by comparison, remained backward. Even here, however, it was a formative age, when primitive societies were welded into feudal monarchies. But the process of consolidation was slow, interrupted by barbarian incursions and by economic setbacks. Not until the second half of the 15th century did Europe begin to draw level with the other world civilizations, laying the foundations for overseas expansion with a series of path-breaking voyages of exploration. Even then, however, it remained overshadowed by the expanding power of the Ottoman Turks for another century.

341 TO 597
GERMANIC SETTLEMENT IN WESTERN EUROPE

With the foundation of barbarian kingdoms within the western Roman empire, Europe began to take on the configurations of the medieval period. The Germanic kingdoms were in a real sense the heirs of Rome, and local populations accommodated the barbarian groups, many of whom originally settled among them as Roman allies or "federates".

The settlement of Germanic and, later, Slav peoples within the former Roman empire was part of a general political and cultural shift within the Mediterranean world in relation to the rest of Europe. Trading and diplomatic relations – both secular and ecclesiastical – between eastern and western Mediterranean and between the Mediterranean and northern Europe were not interrupted.

The origins of the various Germanic tribes are obscured by their own and Roman ethnographers' legends about them, but long before the Christian era West and East Germanic groups (distinguishable on linguistic grounds) probably migrated from the far north of Europe and east central Europe respectively. Between 370 and 470, the build-up of the Asiatic Huns on the eastern fringes of the Roman empire, despite their pastoral economy and lack of political integration, presented a powerful concentration of force and their attack on the Ostrogoths forced the latter to settle, with Roman permission, south of the Danube in Thrace.

The Huns' advances appear to have forced other groups into Roman territory, some of whom were recruited to defend the Romans and given the notional status of "federates" or allied peoples. The relationship with the Romans on occasion could turn sour: the Goths, for example, inflicted a major defeat on the Emperor Valens at the battle of Adrianople (378), but it was Romans and Germanic tribes who together defeated Attila and his Huns on the Catalaunian Fields near Troyes in Gaul in 451.

FRANKS AND VISIGOTHS

With the cooperation of the Romans among whom they lived in Spain, Gaul and Italy, the military role of the federate groups became a governing role as well. In northern Gaul Clovis, the Frankish leader, ruled over Gallo-Romans and Franks (settled in Toxandria probably since the 4th century) from 486. The Visigoths, military allies of the empire who had briefly set up their own emperor in Rome itself, founded the kingdom of Toulouse in Gaul in 418. They subsequently expanded their territory in Gaul, but were pushed south into Spain by the Franks at the beginning of the 6th century. The Burgundians founded a kingdom around the city of Worms, but were settled in Savoy in 443. The Sueves founded a kingdom in Galicia, though this was in due course absorbed into the Visigothic kingdom. The Vandals and Alans crossed from Spain into

Africa in 429, and in 442 the imperial government recognized their king, Gaiseric, as an independent ruler of the former Roman province.

OSTROGOTHIC ITALY

In 476 the last Roman emperor in the west, Romulus Augustulus, was deposed by Odoacer, the commander-in-chief of the Roman army. Odoacer then ruled Italy peacefully until the Ostrogothic leader Theodoric, sent from Constantinople under an arrangement with the Eastern emperor, defeated him and established an Ostrogothic kingdom in Italy in 493. This was effectively destroyed in the middle of the 6th century by the Byzantine emperor Justinian's wars of reconquest, led by the great general Belisarius. He briefly secured the Vandal kingdom of north Africa and the Ostrogothic kingdom until the Byzantines were ousted by the Arabs and Lombards respectively.

THE EUROPEAN PERIPHERY

Meanwhile in Britain, during the 5th and 6th centuries, Angles and Saxons occupied the eastern and southern coastal areas, from which the Roman garrisons had been withdrawn. The early history of the peoples of southeast Europe is more obscure; but by the end of the 8th century independent Croatian, Serbian and Bulgarian kingdoms were taking shape. In all of these centres of settlement and assimilation, a fusion of Greco-Roman institutions, Germanic traditions and the Judaeo-Christian legacy together transformed the Roman world and heralded the emergence of early medieval Europe.

TO AD 600
PRE-ISLAMIC ARABIA

In ancient times the vast Arabian peninsula was largely inhabited by nomadic tribes, which wandered in search of grazing and water for their camels and sheep. Almost all these nomadic tribes spoke Arabic, and they shared certain customs and systems of kinship. Despite these common ties, they had no political unity and no political organization. Ties of kinship were the essential social cement and, in the absence of any system of law enforcement, each tribe was usually hostile to its neighbours.

While most of the peninsula was arid desert, there were towns, villages and quite large settled areas. The most important of these was Yemen, in the southwest corner of the peninsula, where the monsoon winds bring water to a mountainous landscape heavily populated with towns and villages. In antiquity Yemen had supported a thriving urban and mercantile community that prospered from the trade in incense between the area of Suhar, where the frankincense trees grew, and the Mediterranean. Cities such as Marib and Shabwa boasted fine stone-built temples and palaces and a developed language and culture.

By the 6th century, this ancient civilization was in decline. The trade routes were bypassed when the Romans and Byzantines discovered how to use the monsoon winds to bring goods by water up the Red Sea. This decline was symbolized by the collapse of the great dam at Marib, which had irrigated a large inland oasis in about 570. It was never repaired. With the break-up of the old states, Yemen became the target for outside invaders: it was conquered first by the Ethiopians, Christian allies of the Byzantines, and then by the Sasanian Persians.

There were other cities and settlements in Arabia. There were Jewish communities, notably at Yathrib (later called Medina) and Khaybar, and Christian ones at Najran and in the areas bordering the Gulf. There were others, which were pagan shrines. Arabia had a number of ancient holy places where tribesmen who would normally be at war could meet together in the sacred enclave (*haram*) to arrange treaties and trading arrangements. By the late 6th century, the most important of these was the Ka'aba, the shrine at Mecca, whose guardians were the Quraysh tribe. The Prophet Muhammad was born into this tribe in around 570, and the reputation and skills of the Quraysh were an important ingredient in his success.

The old incense trade had been replaced by other forms of commerce, and the merchants of Mecca sent caravans to Syria, especially to Bostra and the Mediterranean port of Gaza, to Iraq, Yemen and Ethiopia. Incense itself had been replaced by gold and silver, and there is both written and archaeological evidence for the mining of precious metals in the hinterland of Mecca.

Arabia lay on the borders of the two great empires of late antiquity, the Byzantine and the Sasanian Persian. Until the early 7th century, both had supported client Arab rulers, known in Greek as phylarchs: the Ghassanids in

Syria and the Lakhmids at Hira in Iraq. Their function was to manage the Arab tribes and keep the borders safe. The collapse of these kingdoms left the way open to nomad advance.

FROM AD 632

THE SPREAD OF ISLAM

In the century after the death of Mohammad, Islam was spread by Arab armies through much of the Middle East, North Africa and Spain. This Muslim world retained a considerable degree of cultural unity. In the Middle Ages it conserved much ancient Greek learning, enabling its later transmission to medieval European civilization.

Islam means "submission to the will of God". Muslims believe that God's message to mankind has been expressed through a series of prophets, culminating in Mohammed, the Apostle and Prophet of God; that God has spoken through Mohammed; and that the Koran (meaning "recitation") is the Word of God. Mohammed is the final Prophet, and no others will come after him.

Mohammed was born in Mecca in about AD 570. The city was the principal commercial centre in western Arabia, and was also an important pilgrimage centre because of its shrine, the Ka'ba. Mohammed received his first revelations in about 610 and his followers soon grew in number. However, the hostility of the merchant aristocracy in Mecca developed into persecution, and Mohammed and his followers withdrew to Medina, some 450km (280 miles) northeast of Mecca. This "migration", *hijra* in Arabic, on 16 July 622 marks the beginning of the Islamic era and thus of the Muslim calendar.

THE MUSLIM CONQUESTS

In Medina, Mohammed organized the Muslims into a community, and consolidated his base with the assistance of his Medinan hosts. He returned to Mecca in triumph in 630 and cast out the idols from the Ka'ba, transforming it into the focal point of the new religion of Islam. At Mohammed's death in 632, his authority extended over the Hejaz and most of central and southern Arabia.

The first of Mohammed's successors, the caliph Abu Bakr (632–4), completed the conquest of Arabia and entered southern Palestine. Caliph Omar (634–44) advanced to Damascus, and followed victory over the Byzantines at the Yarmuk river in 636 with thrusts east into Mesopotamia and northwest into Asia Minor. By 643 Persia had been overrun, and the last Persian emperor, Yazdigird, was killed in 651 at Merv. The conquest of Herat and Balkh and the fall of Kabul opened the way to India; Sind, in northeast India, fell to the Muslims in 712.

Simultaneously, Arab forces pushed west into Egypt, occupying Alexandria in 643, and advancing across north Africa into Cyrenaica and the Maghreb. Independent Arab forces under the leadership of Tariq ibn Ziyad and Musa crossed the Straits of Gibraltar in 711 and conquered the southern part of Spain (al-Andalus). Raids into southern France, however, were successfully deflected by the Franks. In the east, the Byzantines succeeded in preventing the Arabs from capturing Constantinople and retained control of much of Asia Minor until the 11th century.

Initially, Islam did not particularly encourage, far less insist upon, conversion. The Koran enjoins Muslims to respect the "people of the book", that is, members of the other monotheistic religions with written scriptures. The peaceful co-existence of substantial Christian (and, until comparatively recently, Jewish) communities throughout the Muslim world is ample evidence that this injunction was heeded. Under the Abbasid dynasty (750–1258), however, large-scale conversion to Islam became common.

POLITICS AND CULTURE

From 661 the vast Muslim Empire was ruled from Damascus by the Umayyad Caliphs. The reign of Abd al-Malik (685–705) saw the development of Arabic coinage, the use of Arabic in the administration and the construction of the first great monument of Islamic architecture, the Dome of the Rock in Jerusalem. Many Muslims were dissatisfied with the regime and looked to the family of the Prophet to provide leadership, forming the Shi'ite sect. In 750 the Umayyads were overthrown by the Abbasids, descended from Muhammad's uncle Abbas. Islam continued to expand as a religious force. This expansion was due to both conquest and, notably in southeast Asia and west Africa, missionary activity by traders and preachers.

600 TO 1500

THE EXPANSION OF CHRISTIANITY

Having begun as a Middle Eastern religion, Christianity became a predominantly European one during the Middle Ages. Christianity gave ideological unity to medieval Europe, especially in the west. But by 1500, divisions within the Church and criticism of its teaching and institutions had paved the way for the religious turmoil of the Reformation.

In the first five centuries of its history, Christianity was largely confined to the Roman empire. The emergent barbarian successor states in the 5th and 6th centuries were also Christian, although some followed the teaching of Arius rather than Catholic doctrine. The Franks, who were pagan, accepted Catholic Christianity between 496 and 508. Nonetheless by AD 600 Christianity had become the dominant religion of the Mediterranean world. However, from the 7th century the Islamic conquests deprived the Christian Byzantine empire of its lands in the Middle East and north Africa: after several centuries of Islamic rule only small Christian minorities remained in these areas. Despite the tolerance extended by Islam to Christians, the rise of Islam isolated the churches of Europe from the Monophysite and Nestorian Christians of the east, who carried out their own missions in Asia in later centuries.

In Europe various independent missionary efforts were made by Irish and Frankish missionaires in the lands of their eastern and northern neighbours. After being converted by Roman missionaries sent by Pope Gregory (590–604) the English were also active in propagating the Christian faith. Differences between Irish missionaries already active in England and Roman missionaries over issues such as the date of Easter were the result of over a century of independent development in the Irish church (since *c.* 450). Nonetheless these disputes were resolved in the 7th century.

ROME AND CONSTANTINOPLE

The same was not true of the differences between the Roman and Byzantine churches, which grew steadily greater during the early Middle Ages. Though theology played a part, many of the disputes were over liturgical practices (for example, the use in the west of unleavened bread in the Eucharist) or questions of church government and spheres of influence, especially after the conversion of the Slavs of central Europe had been inaugurated by Cyril and Methodius at the end of the 9th century.

The Byzantines were used to a regime in which the Constantinople patriarchs governed the Church under the protection of a Christian emperor, and distrusted the growing power of the western Popes. Although the schism between Rome and Constantinople that occurred in 1054 was not technically a permanent breach, it was an important symbol of the gradual separation of the two Churches. The Orthodox Church in Byzantium eventually came under the authority of an Islamic ruler when Constantinople fell to the Turks in 1453. From then on, Russia, converted to Christianity from 988, was the most important Orthodox Christian power in Europe.

THE POWER OF THE PAPACY

From the 11th century the Papacy assumed a position of leadership in western Europe, which included presiding over the organization of the Crusades (*see* p. 102). Gregory VII (1073–85) campaigned to end simony (the purchase of ecclesiastical office) and to enforce clerical celibacy. Innocent III (1198–1216) continued his work and was probably the most powerful Pope of the Middle Ages. Papal pretensions to superiority over secular rulers often led to political conflicts. In 1302 Boniface VIII propounded the theory of the "two swords", which held that both temporal and spiritual leadership in Christendom should be under the control of the papacy.

The wealth and political pretensions of the Church in the west also led to opposition at a popular level. From the 11th century, heretical movements existed in western Europe. The Cathars of southern France revived the ancient gnostic and Manichaean belief that the flesh was evil, but attracted popular support because of their holiness of life and rejection of the power of the Church. Though the Cathars, like other heretics, were brutally suppressed, some churchmen realized that reform of the Church, rather than the violence of the Inquisition, was the answer to heresy. The foundation of orders of friars by Dominic (1172–1221) and Francis of Assisi (1181–1226) was a response to the need of the Church for anti-heretical preachers. The friars played an important role in preaching the gospel in later medieval Europe, as well as leading a few attempts at converting Muslims to Christianity.

In the 14th century there were further challenges to the Church in western Europe. The English scholar John Wyclif (1330–84) led a movement of protest against both its wealth and some of its teachings, and there were similar protests elsewhere. The papal schism of 1378 to 1415, when two rival claimants to the papacy were supported by different secular rulers, did much to encourage calls for reform. Though such proposals came to nothing during the Middle Ages, hostility to the papacy played a large part in the Reformation of the 16th century (*see* p. 185). Nonetheless, by 1500 Europe was a wholly Christian civilization. Despite protests against the papacy, there is little to suggest that the Catholic Church did not continue to provide adequately for the spiritual needs of most west Europeans.

AD 70 TO 1800

THE JEWISH DIASPORA

After their persecution in Palestine by the Romans in the 1st century AD, Jews settled across much of north Africa and then Europe, contributing decisively to the cultural, intellectual and economic development of their new countries. Further expulsions in the Middle Ages led to a new round of enforced Jewish migrations, above all to Poland and Lithuania.

For over 2000 years the history of the Jews has combined external dispersal with internal cohesion. The decisive dispersal of the Jewish people took place under Rome. Although the Jewish revolts of AD 66–73 and 132–5 and their vigorous suppression by the Romans, as well as Hadrian's measures to de-Judaize Jerusalem, caused rapid deterioration in the position of the Jews in Judaea, elsewhere in the Roman world their legal and economic status and the viability of their communities remained unaffected. This stimulated a constant flow of migration from Palestine, Mesopotamia and Alexandria to the western and northern shores of the Mediterranean. Consequently, widely scattered but internally cohesive Jewish communities developed all over the west and north of the Roman empire: in Italy, in Spain and as far north as Cologne. The Cairo community was a major element in Mediterranean commerce and has left its detailed records (the Cairo "Genizah") of life there during the Middle Ages.

MEDIEVAL JEWRY AND THE EXPULSIONS

The resilience of Judaism can be chiefly ascribed to the evolution of the Jewish religion following the destruction of the First Temple in Jerusalem in 586 BC, and the gradual emergence of a faith based on synagogue and communal prayer. New local leaders of Jewish life, the men of learning, or rabbis, emerged. Jewish religious and civil law was gradually codified in the *Mishnah* (AD 200) and the commentary and discussions systematized as the *Talmud* (AD 500).

During the High Middle Ages Jews from the Near East and north Africa settled in southern Italy, Spain, France and southern Germany. They flourished in Spain under the first Umayyad caliph of Córdoba, 'Abd ar-Rahman III (912–61), and continued to play a major role in society, learning and commerce until 1391. Despite the massacres which attended the First Crusade in the 1090s, the 11th and 12th centuries constituted the golden age of medieval German Jewry.

A series of expulsions from western Europe, beginning in England in 1290, led to a steady eastwards migration of German Jews (*Ashkenazim*) to Prague (from the 11th century) and Vienna. Jewish communities arose in Cracow, Kalisz, and other towns in western and southern Poland in the 13th century and, further east, at Lvov, Brest-Litovsk and Grodno in the 14th. The period of heaviest immigration from the west into Poland-Lithuania came in the late 15th and 16th. Most of the expelled Spanish and Portuguese Jews (*Sephardim*) settled in the Ottoman empire and north Africa, though in the late 16th century a trickle migrated to Rome and northern Italy.

THE REVIVAL OF JEWISH LIFE

After the disruption of the Thirty Years' War (1618–48), Jews from central and eastern Europe, as well as the Near East, were once again able to settle, usually in ghettos, with the permission of both trading cities and princely governments, in northern Italy, Germany, Holland and, from the 1650s, in England and the English colonies in the New World (first those in the Caribbean and later in North America). Small groups also migrated from Germany to Denmark and Sweden. In the central European cities of Vienna, Berlin, Hamburg and Budapest, Jewish communities grew considerably during the 18th and 19th centuries and made major contributions to the development of their countries, in particular engaging in financial enterprises forbidden to Christians. During the 17th and 18th centuries, some of the largest and wealthiest, as well as culturally most sophisticated, communities in the Jewish world lived in Amsterdam, Hamburg, Frankfurt, Livorno, Venice, Rome, Berlin and London. Amsterdam's Jews were especially important in the areas of commerce, finance, printing and book production.

EASTERN EUROPE

Nevertheless until the 1940s by far the greater proportion of world Jewry continued to live in eastern Europe. The small Jewish populations in Hungary and Romania in 1700 increased in the 18th and 19th centuries through immigration from Poland and Czech lands. Under the tsars, the bulk of the Jewish population in the Russian empire was confined by law to western areas (the "Pale of Settlement"). The demographic preponderance of eastern Europe in world Jewry ended with the Nazis: Jewish life in Poland, Czechoslovakia and the old Pale of Settlement was largely destroyed though large Jewish populations survived in the USSR, Romania, Bulgaria and Hungary.

482 TO 814

THE RISE OF THE FRANKISH KINGDOM

The kingdom of the Franks in Gaul was the most enduring of the barbarian successor states to the Roman empire. Under the Carolingians the Franks dominated western Europe. They combined remarkable political and cultural coherence with crucial developments in kingship and government, culture, education, religion and social organization.

The Merovingian Kingdom of the Franks in Gaul (so called because the kings claimed Meroveus, a sea monster, as their legendary ancestor) proved to be the most enduring of the barbarian successor states to the Roman empire. The conquests of Clovis and his sons and grandsons created a powerful basis for Frankish hegemony and one which was built on by their Carolingian successors who later dominated western Europe. Frankish rule in western Europe was a time of remarkable political and cultural coherence, combined with crucial, diverse and formative developments in almost every sphere of life.

THE MEROVINGIANS

The splendid grave of Clovis's father, Childeric (*d.* 481), discovered at Tournai in 1653, shows that, although a pagan, he had ruled as Roman military governor in the north of Gaul. Clovis's conversion to Catholicism was a major factor in winning over the Gallo-Roman population to acceptance of his rule. Gallo-Romans and Franks merged; by the 7th century it is not possible to determine who among the counts and bishops who were so prominent in Merovingian administration and politics was descended from Gallo-Romans and who from Franks. It is symptomatic of the assimilation of peoples in Gaul that the French language has developed from Latin, though it was not until the 9th century that the first small adjustments to the orthography of the written language began to be made. For the whole of the period of Frankish dominance in Europe, Latin was the language of law, religion and education. West of the Rhine it was the vernacular as well.

Under Clovis's descendants, Frankish power was largely concentrated north of the Loire and especially in the areas known as Neustria and Austrasia. From 613 the kings increasingly relied on officials known as the "mayors of the palace" and other aristocrats who governed the far flung regions of the realm. It was from Austrasia's most powerful family, the Arnulfings, later known as the Carolingians, that the most concerted challenge to Merovingian rule emerged. It was led by Pippin II, mayor of the palace, for whom the Battle of Tertry in 687 was a crucial if short-term victory. It was Pippin II's son Charles Martel, however, who rebuilt the family's and Frankish fortunes in the face of opposition from the Neustrian mayors of the palace, the Frisians, Aquitainians and Saracens. By the time of his death in 741 Charles, although still nominally only the mayor of the palace, handed on to his sons Pippin and Carloman a greatly enlarged and strengthened realm.

It was Pippin III who in 751, on the advice and with the consent of the Frankish magnates, made himself king and so established the new Carolingian dynasty. Pippin's position was further strengthened in 754 when the Pope crossed the Alps and anointed him and his sons as the rightful rulers of the Franks. The realm was again expanded under Pippin III to include Alemannia and Aquitania.

CHARLEMAGNE

Pippin's son Charlemagne conquered the Lombard kingdom and annexed Bavaria. In a series of bloody campaigns he then beat the Saxons into submission and obliged them to accept Christianity. Despite the setback at Roncesvalles (778) immortalized in the *Chanson de Roland,* Charlemagne established control of the Spanish march. He also achieved a celebrated victory against the Avars (796). Charlemagne's rule over many peoples was recognized in his coronation as emperor on Christmas Day 800, though this event was largely symbolic and did not materially affect Charlemagne's status or power: it had more to do with the role of the Frankish king in relation to Italy and his protection of Rome. Later generations, however, were to capitalize on its implications. The arrangements for the succession, devised in 806 but never put into effect, did not in fact preserve the imperial title. However, with the death by 813 of all his sons save one, Louis, Charlemagne crowned him as his successor. The triumphalist narratives of the 9th century created a strong image of Carolingian continuity and success which inspired later rulers in Europe.

CAROLINGIAN GOVERNMENT

The Carolingian conquests were accompanied by the consolidation of the Christian Church. The support as well as the protection of the Papacy, the close relationship with the Church, the clerics' key role in all aspects of government alongside lay magnates and the status of the Carolingian ruler as Christian king, responsible for the faith and welfare of the Christians under his dominion, are hallmarks of the Carolingian regime. Scholars, poets and artists from all over Europe were gathered at the court, centred on Aachen from the end of the 8th century, and at other cultural centres throughout the realm. Many innovations were made in government, not least the reform of the coinage and of weights and measures, and a restructuring of the administration, relying heavily on written communications, to rule the vast territories effectively. Laws were compiled and officials charged to ensure justice in society. Christian learning and education, church and monastic life were all regulated and supported systematically. Copies of specified liturgical books for use in the churches, as well as of a corrected Bible text and canon law (ecclesiastical law) were prepared by Carolingian scholars under court auspices for dissemination throughout the kingdom. Although many may have come reluctantly under the Frankish yoke, the Carolingian realm knit together a great diversity of peoples in a remarkable way and laid the foundations of modern western Europe.

793 TO 1000
MAGYARS, SARACENS AND VIKINGS IN 9TH AND 10TH CENTURY EUROPE

Three main groups – Magyars, Saracens and Vikings – launched raids on Europe in the 9th and 10th centuries, as well as being involved in trade. It was the Vikings who proved the most adaptable colonists. Settlements established by them in the north Atlantic and North Sea, Russia and the Mediterranean developed into strong independent states.

The relatively effective rule of the Carolingians in western Europe (*see* p. 95) and of the various kings in Britain gave some assurance of security from attacks both to religious communities and merchants. By the 8th century abbeys and markets were not fortified and the masonry from Roman defences was often used for other building work. The wealth accumulated in such places offered tempting bait to external raiders. They came from countries whose rulers and people were often also partners in trade, the objects of missionary activity and political overtures or attempts at control, and who interacted with the politics of the countries their countrymen raided by entering into political agreements with them or acting as mercenaries. In the 9th and 10th centuries western Europe suffered attacks in particular from bands of Saracens, Magyars and Vikings.

After the Muslim occupation of Sicily, begun in 827 (though conquest was not complete until 902), Saracen pirates, possibly mainly from Crete and the eastern Mediterranean, established temporary bases such as Bari and Taranto on the coast of southern Italy, and later in southern Gaul, from which they were able to attack centres in the western Mediterranean until ousted by Byzantine armies in the late 9th century. Corsica and Sardinia were frequently attacked and many monasteries and towns in central and southern Italy (including Rome itself) were pillaged.

THE MAGYARS

The nomadic Magyars, who may have moved into the Hungarian Plain from the east in the last years of the 9th century, plundered the neighbouring areas: northern Italy, Germany and even France. Their skill as horsemen and their advantages of speed and surprise made opposition difficult. They also acted as mercenaries against the Moravians and the Bulgars. Major defeats were inflicted on east Frankish armies between 899 and 910, but thereafter the German rulers achieved important successes, culminating in the defeat of the Magyars at the Lechfeld in 955. In the east, the threat of Magyar raids was halted by a joint enterprise by the ruler of Kiev and the Byzantine emperor. A Magyar embassy to the German emperor Otto I in 973 marked the beginning of a more settled way of life for the Magyars. Missionary activities thereafter from Regensburg and Passau resulted in Stephen (977–1038), the first Christian king of Hungary, being given the right to set up the Hungarian Church with its own bishoprics.

THE VIKING RAIDS

Frankish expansion into Frisia and Saxony in the 8th century may have prompted defensive aggression on the part of the Danes. Franks and Danes were able to conclude various agreements in the first half of the 9th century, including the conversion to Christianity of a number of leading Danes and the settlement of Viking groups at strategic points to defend outlying regions of the Carolingian empire. However, raids on Lindisfarne in 793 and on the important trading emporium of Dorestad in 834 were the beginning of a grim record of attacks on both France and England until the end of the 9th century. Although the raids were no doubt described in exaggerated terms by survivors, they undoubtedly caused much misery and distress; for example the bishop of Nantes and all his clergy were murdered in 842. Increasingly effective defence (including buying time with tribute payments and the building of new fortifications) against the raids was mounted by the Frankish and English rulers. The practice of ceding the Vikings territory in order to act as a buffer culminated in the granting of the county of Rouen in 911 to Rollo, which with hindsight can be recognized as the foundation of Normandy.

The Vikings were highly adaptable colonists as well as traders and raiders and their shipbuilding and seafaring prowess enabled them to journey far afield. The Danes settled in England as well as France. The Norse ventured to Ireland,

Man, Scotland, the Orkneys, the Faroes, Iceland, Greenland and even as far as Newfoundland. The Swedes travelled down the great rivers of Russia and founded the kingdom of the Rus based at Kiev and Novgorod where they formed links with Byzantium.

900 TO 1050

NORTHERN AND EASTERN EUROPE

Stable political regimes in some northern and eastern European regions outside the former Roman empire emerged only in the period from 850 to 1050. Their conversion to Christianity created essential bonds with the rest of Latin Christendom, despite political tensions and enmities between them.

Political conditions were not as favourable to political consolidation in northern and eastern Europe as they were further south and west. In England the kings of Wessex were only gradually able to absorb the Scandinavian-controlled Danelaw and most settlers were apparently able to retain their land, giving a partly Scandinavian character to the customs and place-names of the region. The conquest of the Danelaw and an expanding economy paved the way for the unification of "England" and for the religious reforms introduced by Eadgar (959–75). Nonetheless England remained subject to Danish attacks, and these culminated in the reign of the Danish king, Cnut, who ruled Norway and Denmark as well as England and introduced many Danish and "Norman" connections into English politics. Emma of Normandy, descended from Vikings, married first Aethelred "the Unready" and then Cnut. It was her son by Aethelred, Edward the Confessor, who succeeded to the English throne in 1042. Emma symbolizes the international sphere of politics at this time. In the wake of the Norman Conquest of England in 1066, links with France, Flanders and the Mediterranean were strengthened still further at the expense of those with the Scandinavian world.

IRELAND, SCOTLAND AND WALES

Ireland at this time was characterized by political fragmentation. The Irish were rarely united and much of the period was punctuated by war between the various Irish and Viking dynasties, notably the northern and southern Uí Néill.

Brian Boru became king of Munster in 976 and then made himself king of Ireland. But the Vikings of Ireland, Orkney, the Hebrides and Man together with the Leinstermen defeated Brian in 1014. His successors, concentrating on the possession of Dublin, still attempted to establish their rule over the whole country until defeated by the Norman invasion of the 12th century.

In Scotland, too, Scandinavian control hampered the consolidation of political power. Vikings settled in the western and southern parts of Scotland from the beginning of the 10th century, and different groups of Picts, Scots (originally from Ireland) and Norsemen formed many shifting alliances until a measure of stability and unity was achieved under the Scottish king Malcom II (1005–34). Relations with England fluctuated; there was frequent border warfare, and a firm boundary was fixed only in the 13th century. In Wales a similar process of consolidation took place: the dynasty of Rhodri Mawr established their rule over much of Gwynedd and Dyfed. Ultimately the instability of the conglomeration of Welsh kingdoms made them vulnerable to Norman attack.

SCANDINAVIA

In Scandinavia itself, powerful kingdoms began to emerge out of the disarray of the Viking age. Most notable was the emergence of Denmark under three kings, Gorm, Harald and Sven. By the 10th century Denmark had become a powerful kingdom, and, under Cnut (1014–35), the centre of an Anglo-Scandinavian empire. Much of southern Norway was united under the rule of Harald Finehair after the battle of Hafrsfjord in the 890s, but after his death in the 930s Norway occasionally came under Danish lordship. Sweden, meanwhile, was united only at the end of the 11th century under the kings of Uppland. On the fringes of the Scandinavian world Iceland was, by 930, an independent commonwealth (without a king) while Greenland was colonized by Norwegians from about 985.

EASTERN EUROPE

In eastern Europe, Moravia was attacked in 906 by Magyar invaders, but a new phase of political consolidation began shortly thereafter, probably in response to pressure from the Saxon kings Henry I and Otto I. Although the Slav peoples along the Elbe successfully resisted the Germans in the great Slav revolt of 983, they remained disunited and loosely organized. It was in Poland that a major Slav state arose: Mieszko I (960–92) united the tribes of northern Poland,

and his son, Bolesław Chrobry (992–1025), extended control to the south. Meanwhile the Magyars, led by Duke Geisa (972–97) and his more famous son, King Stephen (997–1038), the first Christian king of Hungary, established their kingdom. Bohemia, caught between Germany and Poland, had also emerged as a political unit by the time of the Přemyslid prince Bolesław I (929–67). The creation of Bohemia, Poland and Hungary – by the Přemyslid, Piast and Arpád dynasties respectively – was based on agricultural development, suppression of tribal differences and independent tribal aristocracies, and on the organizing and civilizing influence of the Church. All three dynasties made use of western institutions and connections to strengthen their position, though a notable feature in eastern Europe in the succeeding centuries was the power of the nobility as distinct from that of the monarchs. Nonetheless Bohemia, Poland and Hungary did not lose their identities, although it was only in the 14th century that a restoration of royal power took place there.

1095 TO 1492

CRUSADING IN EUROPE FROM THE 11TH TO THE 15TH CENTURY

A Crusade was a Christian war concerned with the recovery and defence of lost lands. For those taking part it was a means of salvation. Starting with the First Crusade in 1096–9, the crusaders altered the political balance in the eastern Mediterranean for many centuries. Christian holy war also remained a recurrent feature of northern European politics.

Christians had made pilgrimages to the Holy Land since the 2nd century AD. The combination of religious tourism and spiritual inspiration offered by pilgrimage had greatly increased the number of visitors after the conversion of Constantine and the discovery by his mother, Helena, of the supposed True Cross in Jerusalem. Many new churches and monasteries were built in the Holy Land, often on newly identified holy sites of both Old and New Testament events. Jerusalem in particular held pride of place in the imagination and hearts of Christians everywhere, which not even its conquest by Arab forces in the 7th century could overturn. Indeed, access thereafter was far from denied and throughout the 8th, 9th and 10th centuries there are reports from travellers from

Britain, France and Italy who prayed at the holy sites. A constant stream of souvenirs and holy relics, furthermore, reached the west and were treated with great reverence in churches across Europe. Allied to the importance of pilgrimage to the Holy Land were the missionary endeavours to convert pagans conducted in western Europe. Between the 6th and 11th centuries this saw the conversion of the English, the Frisians, Saxons, Slavs, Scandinavians, Bulgars and Rus by Irish, Roman, English, Frankish, Saxon and Byzantine missionaries. Within the Christian Church, moreover, there were intense bouts of eradication of heresy. Pilgrimage, the striving to achieve orthodoxy and the conversion of pagans, coupled with the religious piety and devotion of the laity, came together in the crusading movement of the central and later Middle Ages.

The movement was concerned not only with the recovery of the Holy Land from those who were regarded by the Christian Church as "infidels". There were also crusades against the Albigensian heretics in southern France from 1208, the pagan Slavs in Livonia in the Baltic from the end of the 12th century and the Reconquista of Spain from the Arabs by the Catholic monarchs of northern Spain which became a national liberation movement. Even such European rulers as the Emperor Frederick II of Germany and King Beta of Aragon were the objects of Crusades to defend the Catholic faith and liberty of the Church against their rulers' alleged depredations.

THE FIRST CRUSADE

The crusading movement was precipitated by a plea from a Byzantine embassy to Pope Urban II in 1095 for help to defend the eastern Church against the Turks who had overrun Asia Minor. In November of that year the Pope preached the First Crusade at the Council of Clermont. The enthusiasm for the call to wage Christian holy war was remarkable. Nobles and knights made considerable sacrifices which affected both themselves and their families in order to go on crusade, for it was a genuinely popular devotional activity. Many sold their patrimonies to raise money for the expeditions, though only a minority actually "took the Cross" and went to fight. Only a few noble families from France joined the First Crusade, though kings, notably Richard I (the Lionheart) of England and Louis IX of France, were involved in later expeditions to the east.

THE CRUSADERS

Crusaders made a public, formal vow to join a military expedition in response to an appeal by the Pope on Christ's behalf. It was a legal obligation and Crusaders became subject to the jurisdiction of the ecclesiastical courts. In return special privileges were granted to a crusader including the protection of their families' interests and assets while they were absent, and major spiritual privileges in the form of Indulgences to reduce the time spent in purgatory atoning for sins on earth. Closely associated with the crusading movement were the military orders, such as the Templars and Hospitallers, whose members had made a permanent commitment to wage holy war. Both the Templars and Hospitallers had their headquarters in Jerusalem, but soon acquired extensive properties in the west. The rulers of the Crusader states, frequently starved of manpower, entrusted great strongholds and large stretches of land to the military orders and by the 13th century they formed the backbone of the military strength of the crusading states.

THE LATER CRUSADES

The First Crusade led to the foundation of the Latin kingdom of Jerusalem following the Crusaders' capture of Antioch and Jerusalem in 1098 and 1099 respectively. The focus of subsequent expeditions was the defence, ultimately unsuccessful, of these gains against Muslim attack. The Second Crusade (1146–8) was inspired by the loss of the city of Edessa to al-Din Zengi, the Muslim ruler of Aleppo, while the Third Crusade (1189–91) was launched as a response to the conquest by Saladin of most of the crusader territories in the Levant, including the catastrophic loss of Jerusalem. Although the city was not recovered, the Crusaders reoccupied most of the coastal ports, so ensuring the survival of the Crusader states.

In Spain the Reconquista – or recovery of land – from the Muslims was given impetus by crusading ideals. In contrast to the Crusades to the east this was a local affair, with little help received from outside. Yet in Spain, too, military orders such as Calatrava (from 1158) and Santiago (from 1170) contributed vitally to the war against Islam. In 1212 the armies of Castile, Navarre and Aragon crushed the Muslim army at Las Navas de Tolosa, winning the most important victory of the whole Reconquista. In 1492 Christian armies took Granada, the last remaining Muslim stronghold in Spain.

The crusading movement was seriously compromised in 1204 by the blood-shed of the capture of Constantinople by an army of Latin Christians, who diverged from a planned campaign in Palestine. They dismembered the Byzantine empire and, together with the Genoese and Venetians, set up Latin states around the Aegean. The crusading ideal, however, lived on. Further Crusades targeted Egypt and the Levant. The Crusader states in the east survived until the late 13th century, with the loss of the last stronghold at Acre in 1291. Even then further Crusades were still mounted against the Muslims as late as 1444 (the Crusade of Varna), and the language of crusading was employed to describe the struggle against the Ottoman Turks and Spanish incursions into north Africa in the 16th century. Crusades were launched against heretics, such as the Hussites in Bohemia (1420–31) and by the Teutonic Knights in the Baltic against pagan Prussians from 1309.

610 TO 1453
THE BYZANTINE EMPIRE

The Roman empire in the east continued – as Byzantium – long after the political transformation of the west by the barbarian successor states. Its distinctive, Greek-speaking, Christian and culturally diverse civilization dominated the east Mediterranean, exerting a crucial cultural influence on western Europe despite the steady loss of territory to the Turks.

Although Heraclius (610–41) had ended the struggle with the Sasanid rulers of Persia, for so long Rome's most formidable rival, before his death the southern and eastern frontiers of the empire came under attack from the forces of Islam. Constantinople withstood two Arab sieges, in 674–8 and again in 717–8. At the same time the Bulgars settled in the Balkans with armed outposts less than 100km (60 miles) from Constantinople itself.

RENEWAL AND RETREAT

Within Byzantium major disruption to society between 726 and 843 was caused by the controversy over the banning of Christian images, known as iconoclasm. Not long after images in churches were restored, a fresh and vigorous Macedonian dynasty of emperors embarked on a new era of expansion. Between

863, when a strong force of Arabs was annihilated at Poson, on the Halys river in Anatolia, and the death of the great warrior-emperor Basil II (976–1025), a series of dramatic victories pushed back the frontiers, often close to where they had been in the heyday of Rome. In the southeast the Arabs at one stage (976) retreated to the very gates of Jerusalem; the Rus were held and routed at Silistra on the Danube (971); and Bulgaria, after long bitter campaigning, became a group of Byzantine provinces. But the new frontiers, exhaustingly won, proved indefensible, especially as the previously invincible Byzantine armed forces now found themselves starved of funds by a civilian administration fearful of a military coup. In 1071, the Byzantine army was heavily defeated by Seljuk Turks at the battle of Manzikert. The Turks then established a permanent occupation of the Anatolian plateau. In the same year, the empire's last Italian possession fell to the Normans.

THE COMENENI AND THE CRUSADES

Paradoxically, the 11th and 12th centuries proved to be among the most fertile in Byzantine history in artistic and theological terms. Yet for all their genius, the emperors Alexius I (1081–1118), John II (1118–43) and Manuel I (1143–80) ultimately proved unable to recover much of the vast territory that had been lost, though they succeeded by diplomatic means in maintaining a strong balance of the various interests between themselves and their neighbours. The First Crusade (1096–9) had certainly created serious difficulties for the Byzantine rulers while the ferocious assault of the Christian Latin Crusaders in 1204 inflicted great damage on both Constantinople and the empire.

Byzantium's strength, apart from its religious cohesion, was two-fold: the *themes* (administrative divisions) with their independent freeholding peasantry, ready both to farm and to defend its land; and an army and a navy often manned by native officers and troops. By the 11th and 12th centuries, mercenaries – themselves often Seljuk, Muslim or Norman – came to form the bulk of the armed forces, and the important civilian posts in the civilian bureaucracy fell more and more under the control of a few rich dynasties. These owed much of their new wealth and power to the *pronoia* system, under which key state functions, including tax collection, were handed over to large local landowners – originally for their lifetime, but increasingly on a hereditary basis. In religious matters, Rome and Constantinople moved even further apart. There had been tension, if not actual schism, between the Roman and Orthodox Churches since 1054 (*see* p. 90).

THE LAST CENTURIES

Both Seljuks and Normans resumed full-scale frontier aggression in the 1170s and many Byzantine provinces were lost. The immediate beneficiary of the Fourth Crusade (1204) was the rising power of Venice, whose fleets had carried the Crusaders and who established colonies on the Aegean islands and Crete. A Latin empire was created with many principalities in Thessaly, Athens and Achaia and Greek enclaves at Nicaea and Epirus. The Greeks still constituted a majority within the truncated empire and in 1261, aided by Genoa, a rival of Venice, they drove out the westerners. But the Greek empire was only a shadow of the Byzantium of the past and was unable to prevent the steady advance of the Ottoman empire into Anatolia, Thrace, Macedonia and Bulgaria in the 14th century and the conquest of Constantinople itself by Mehmet the Conqueror in 1453.

882 TO 1242
THE FIRST RUSSIAN STATE: KIEVAN RUSSIA

Russia first emerged under the Vikings (or Rus) in the 9th century. Steppes, forests and rivers determined the course of the history of Kievan Rus. It received Christianity from Byzantium, was attacked by Mongols and split into various principalities. When the Kievan Rus lost their southern steppe territory to nomads they resumed eastward colonization.

The rivers between the Baltic and the Black Sea assumed great importance from the 9th century with the coming of the Vikings or Rus, who established, dominated and exploited trade routes along these rivers and adjoining lands. The polity the Rus established ran north and south across forests and steppes; these barriers ultimately proved too strong for a river-based north–south alignment to survive. The main waterway route established ran from the Gulf of Finland up the river Neva, the river Volkhov and thence by portages to the Dnieper and on across the Black Sea to Byzantium. As Viking control spread south, Novgorod, Smolensk and Kiev (in 882) became headquarters. Kiev grew rapidly from the early 10th century, and strong links developed with Byzantium, its chief trading partner. It was from Byzantium that Christianity was introduced to Kiev during the reign of Vladimir Svyatoslavich (980–1015).

EXPANSION OF KIEVAN RUS

At the time of the Viking incursions the Khazars and the Magyars held the steppes. The Rus succeeded in dominating the lands of the lower Prut, Dniester and Bug, and in controlling the upper Dnieper route to the Black Sea and thence to Byzantium. Grand Prince Svyatoslav (c. 962–72) determined to strengthen and expand Rus power by crushing the relatively peaceful Khazars. But by destroying them, he opened the way to the fierce Pechenegs (Turkic nomads) who dominated the south Russian steppes until displaced by the equally warlike Polovtsy in the 12th century. Vladimir I had some defensive success against the Pechenegs, constructing a steppe-frontier south of Kiev, and the Rus princes held the initiative over the nomads during most of the 11th and first half of the 12th centuries.

The southern Rus lands, relatively secure and prosperous, became the bone of contention between rival branches of Vladimir's offspring and from the mid-12th century disputes proliferated. But the resulting multiplication of princely seats opened up outlying areas to Christianity and commerce. Uniquely, Novgorod's oligarchy was powerful enough to "hire and fire" princes and to organize the collection of tribute in the form of furs from as far north as the Arctic Ocean. However, in the early 13th century, Novgorod increasingly came under the sway of the princes of Vladimir-Suzdal, who were emerging as the dominant Rus princes. On the eve of the Mongol attack of 1237, Vladimir-Suzdal was about to challenge the Volgar Bulgars whose stranglehold on the middle Volga obstructed further Russian expansion eastward. Nizhniy Novgorod was built as a first move in this campaign.

THE MONGOL INVASIONS

The Mongols, led by Khan Batu, attacked the middle and upper Volga regions in 1237–8. They displaced the Polovtsy who fled to Hungary where they settled between the Tisza and the Danube rivers and came to be known as Kuns. That winter, when the protective rivers were frozen, the Mongols overcame the Volga

Bulgars and set upon Vladimir-Suzdal, destroying its wealthy towns. Only the approach of spring saved Novgorod, as the invaders dared not be caught by the thaw among its surrounding marshes. In 1239 it was the turn of the southern principalities of the Rus. Kiev itself was sacked in 1240. Novgorod escaped the Mongol fury but was threatened by incessant attacks from Swedes and Germans in the Baltic region. Its prince, Alexander Nevsky, beat the Swedes decisively on the River Neva (1240) and the Teutonic Knights on the ice of Lake Peipus (1242).

The Mongols established the Kipchak Khanate or Golden Horde which came to control the lucrative trade routes between central Asia and the Black Sea. Much of western Rus, however, came under Lithuanian or Polish rule in the 14th century. At first based in Kiev, the metropolitan of the Orthodox Church moved to Moscow in the early 14th century. This lent prestige to the princes of Moscow and contributed to Moscow's emergence as the predominant Rus polity in the northeast.

962 TO 1250

THE GERMAN EMPIRE AND THE PAPACY

The right to allocate the Imperial title, to consecrate kings and nominate new bishops or the Pope was vital in medieval Europe. Individual German emperors or popes attempted to assert either Imperial or Papal prerogatives. Popes ultimately sought to promote the authority of the bishops, while the Emperors' priority was to rule their vast territories.

For all their differences, the separate Frankish kingdoms created between 840 and 843 were nonetheless bound together by many cultural, religious and kinship ties, as well as by the retention of the Imperial title in the Carolingian family. In 911, however, the Carolingians were replaced in the East Frankish (German) kingdom first by the Franconian noble Conrad and then by a member of the Saxon Liudolfing family, Henry I (911–36). Henry I's son, Otto I (936–73), consolidated his position, extended his influence over the German duchies and into Italy and defeated the Magyars. His Imperial coronation in 962 was the symbol of his aspirations and the southern and Italian orientation of his policies.

IMPERIAL GOVERNMENT

Government in the German empire was intensely personal with the king constantly on the move with his court. Only 13th-century Sicily possessed a centralized administrative system. The Ottonians stayed in their royal residences, supplied by the produce of their estates, as well as at royal convents, presided over by female members of the royal house. Bishops, notably those from the reformed monastic houses of Gorze in Lorraine, played a major role in government. The rulers themselves were devoted supporters of the Church and were behind many of the missionary efforts and founding of new bishoprics, where Christianization and political expansion went hand in hand. It was the royal women, many of whom became abbesses, on the other hand, who appear, together with the bishops, to have done most to patronize culture and learning. The Salian and Staufen emperors continued these traditions.

THE PAPACY AND THE EMPIRE

The connection forged between Church reformers and the Papacy inaugurated a long dispute between the Emperors and the popes over who had the authority to appoint bishops or depose kings (the Investiture controversy). The conflict came to a head under Pope Gregory VII (1073–85). Gregory excommunicated and deposed the emperor Henry IV in 1076, forced him to perform public penance at Canossa, and allied with the Emperor's enemies – the Normans of southern Italy, the recalcitrant German nobility, and a chain of states around the periphery which feared German power. Although Gregory failed in his immediate objectives, the launching of the First Crusade (see p. 102) by Pope Urban II (1088–99) testified to the success of the claims for papal authority. The Investiture dispute was settled in 1122 by the Concordat of Worms when the emperor granted canonical election and the free consecration of bishops.

The political involvement of the Papacy in the struggle for the control of Italy became clear when Pope Alexander III (1154–81) allied with the Lombard League to resist the attempts of Frederick I (1152–90) to restore German Imperial authority in Italy. The issue was settled by a compromise but the Papacy failed to prevent the Hohenstaufen from acquiring the Norman Kingdom of Sicily in 1194.

THE APOGEE OF PAPAL POWER

Only the early death of Frederick's son, Henry VI (1190–7), and civil war in Germany enabled Pope Innocent III (1198–1216) to achieve the temporary supremacy of the Papacy. He successfully protected Rome and he claimed the right and authority of examining the person elected Emperor. At the same time Innocent compelled the French king to be reconciled with his wife and become his ally. The Pope also forced King John of England to submit to him. He also had some success in dealing with anti-clericalism. The heretics of southern France were viciously suppressed in the Albigensian Crusade (1208), but Innocent also encouraged the evangelism of the new orders of friars, the Franciscans and Dominicans, and sought to remove sources of discontent with the Church by reforming clerical behaviour. However, like Alexander III before him, Pope Innocent IV (1243–54) allied with the Italian cities to resist the Emperor Frederick II, but the Papacy only succeeded in undermining German influence in Italy when Pope Clement IV (1265–8) called in Charles of Anjou, the brother of Louis IX of France, to evict the Germans from Italy. Disputes thereafter with the increasingly centralized French monarchy over taxation of the clergy and royal sovereignty led to open conflict. Pope Boniface VIII (1294–1303) was kidnapped by his French and Italian enemies. In 1305 his successor took up residence in Avignon, under direct French supervision.

1154 TO 1314

MONARCHY IN BRITAIN AND FRANCE

Within a distinctive blend of public office and landholding in medieval Britain and France, great stress was laid on authority, especially that of kings. Contemporaries did not think in terms of borders or national entities so much as of territorial and legal jurisdictions, where varied social bonds and political obligations and rights were interdependent.

Despite the growth of principalities in France and the strength of the earls in England in the 10th and 11th centuries, kingship survived. The king's position at the apex of the social hierarchy was hallowed by religious and legal sanctions which might bear little relationship to the realities of political power. In the 12th century kings used their position and fortuitous agglomerations of territory to assert their prerogatives. In the hands of the Emperor Frederick Barbarossa and later of the French Capetians, Roman law became a powerful instrument of royal authority. But the main weapons used by 12th- and 13th-century kings were the king's rights as "liege lord"; the duty of tenants-in-chief to render service; the theory that all land was held of the king; and all rights of justice were delegations of royal authority, which therefore reverted, or "escheated", to the crown in case of abuse or treason. Grave misdemeanours (felonies) were reserved to the king's courts or "pleas of the crown". Much of this process was piecemeal; but by the middle of the 13th century the great lawyers (Bracton in England, Beaumanoir in France) had created a systematic theory of royal government, which kings such as Edward I of England (1272–1307) and Philip IV of France (1285–1314) proceeded to implement.

THE NORMANS AND ENGLAND

The process was most rapid in the Norman kingdoms of England and Sicily, both of which were acquired by conquest. In England this enabled William the Conqueror (1066–87) to retain and build up the fiscal and jurisdictional prerogatives inherited from his Anglo-Saxon predecessors. Henry II's coronation as king of England meant that Anjou, Normandy, the Touraine, Aquitaine and Gascony also came under his rule, creating an Angevin "empire" which, at least initially, held together quite successfully.

THE CONSOLIDATION OF FRANCE

In France, on the other hand, Louis VI (1108–37) spent his reign asserting authority over the petty barons of the Ile de France, and it was scarcely before the reign of Philip Augustus (1180–1223) that expansion of the royal demesne began in earnest. The turning point was the conquest of Normandy in 1204 which effectively meant the destruction of the Angevin empire. After 1214 English continental possessions were limited to Gascony while a third of France was now under royal control. Much of Languedoc was subdued in a campaign against the Albigensian heretics (1209–29) and royal authority was extended south of the Loire.

Kings exercised powers of taxation and legislation (often in consultation with parliaments or "estates of the realm") and controlled the administration of justice. Nowhere was the network of overlapping rights and jurisdictions more complex than in France. Indeed, the determination of the French kings to assert their lordship over these lands and over Flanders gave rise to a series of major wars.

THE LIMITS OF ROYAL POWER

Meanwhile the English kings were asserting similar claims in Scotland, Wales and Ireland. Henry II's attempt to conquer Ireland (1171) achieved only a precarious foothold, but in 1284 Edward I subdued Wales. He tried to repeat the process in Scotland in 1296, but met with resistance under Wallace and Bruce, and his son Edward II suffered a crushing defeat at Bannockburn in 1314.

Edward's failure in Scotland was matched by Philip IV's failure in Flanders. Defeated by the Flemings at Courtrai (1302), the French king, who had seized Gascony in 1294, was compelled to restore it to the English in 1303. In England Edward I was compelled in 1297 to confirm and extend the concessions wrested by the barons from his grandfather, King John, in 1215. In France the Estates-General met for the first time in 1302. Everywhere, nobles, many of them well versed in the law, were challenging royal jurisdictions and prerogatives.

c. 950 TO 1150

ECONOMIC GROWTH IN EUROPE

As new archaeological evidence reveals, the early Middle Ages was a vital period of economic activity, in which important new developments in the northwest, the opening up of new trade routes, wealth created by new agricultural land and the foundation of trading towns all built on the earlier economic patterns of the Roman empire.

From the 7th century onwards the northwest of Europe grew in importance as a trading area. In the North Sea and the Baltic region, the Scandinavians built on trading networks already established by the Frisians, Franks and English. The extension of Scandinavian activity overseas coincided with the growing demand for goods that could only be obtained from the north; walrus tusks were at that time the main source of ivory in Europe, and furs from the arctic regions of Scandinavia and Russia were greatly prized. There was a growing commerce in coastal markets called *wics*. The greatest was Dorestad at the mouth of the Rhine, but there were many others, including Quentovic (near Boulogne), Ipswich, London and Hamwic, later to develop into Southampton. Other small trading towns flourished, such as Starya Ladoga in Russia, Birka in Sweden, Wastergarn in Gotland, Kaupang in Norway and Ribe and Haithabu in Denmark.

THE SCANDINAVIAN WORLD

Scandinavians now sought even further afield for fresh supplies of skin, furs and tusks. A 9th-century contemporary account by a Norwegian, Ottar, narrates the voyage he made from his home in northern Norway into the White Sea in search of walrus. Dublin's fortunes fluctuated politically but her function as the chief of the Scandinavian towns in Ireland (founded in the 9th century) is emphasized by the striking of the first Irish coins there in the 990s. From the late 10th century her economic power and international connections grew apace, and the existence of continuous building and growth up to the 12th century bears witness to her prosperity. The town served as the chief market for the Isle of Man, the Western Isles of Scotland and the Atlantic islands, all of which remained under Scandinavian control throughout the period.

THE OPENING OF NEW REGIONS

By 1000 it is estimated that the population of western Europe may have reached a total of 30 million and 150 years later it may have increased by a further 40 per cent. Most of this was concentrated in France, Germany and England and was probably related to the opening up of new land by clearing forests. It took three main forms: steady encroachment by the peasants of the old villages on the woods which surrounded their fields; the migration of settlers, presumably driven by land-hunger to the uninhabited uplands and mountains, where they carved out scattered fields and enclosures from the forest and scrub; and planned development by lay lords and monasteries, wealthy promoters and speculators who founded villages and towns, at the foot of a castle or outside a monastery gate, with the aim of increasing their income. All three types of clearing are found juxtaposed in all countries, and their history is revealed by field patterns and by place-names – Newport, Neuville, Neustadt, Bourgneuf, Nieuwpoort. In a few regions – the Po valley of northern Italy, Flanders, the country around the Wash in England – marshes were drained and land reclaimed from the sea.

MARKETS AND TRADE

The agricultural surplus further stimulated the foundation and growth of towns, markets and fairs (notably the fairs of Champagne) which initially served a local market but became internationally renowned after 1150. In the Mediterranean, the survival of silks, pottery and other goods indicated a continuation of connections across the Mediterranean and with northern Europe.

In Italy, Pisa, Genoa and Venice extended their overseas trade, assisted by the opportunities offered by the crusading movement in the eastern Mediterranean. North of the Alps, rivers such as the Rhine, Seine, Danube and Rhône, conveyed bulk transport and connected the cloth towns of Flanders and the Rhineland with the south. The western Alpine passes (Mont Cenis, Great St Bernard) were in regular use. The central passes (St Gotthard, Splügen) and the Brenner in the east were developed in the later 12th century. The Rhineland was a major focus of artistic, intellectual and economic life. Cologne, in particular, was at the height of its prosperity, but the cathedral-building throughout the region, as at Mainz and Worms, is a testimony to the wealth which "the great age of clearing" had made available.

TO 1477

IMPERIAL JAPAN AND THE EARLY SHOGUNATES

The early Japanese state achieved stability in the 8th century when the great families clustered around the emperor swapped military power for rank in a Chinese-inspired bureauracy. This ruled for four centuries until, in 1185, its own warrior clients founded the first in a series of shogunates, which were to rule Japan until 1868.

Japan is first mentioned in Chinese records of the 3rd century AD. These state that the archipelago was divided into a series of small kingdoms, a number of them tributary to the Chinese emperor and most acknowledging the spiritual leadership of the Empress Himiko. Over the next three centuries, a line of emperors, possibly Himiko's descendants, unified most of what is today Japan either by absorbing or destroying other leading families.

THE INFLUENCE OF CHINA

Early Japan was consistently overshadowed by its much larger and more powerful neighbour, China – so much so that Japan consciously tried to model itself on China. Embassies were dispatched, imperial records drafted on the Chinese model and Buddhism introduced. The changes culminated in the Taika revolution of 645, when a new emperor, backed by the powerful Fujiwara family, first tried to mirror the role played by the Chinese emperors. Further impetus to reform came in 668 when T'ang Chinese and Sillan armies unified the Korean peninsula, in the process decisively defeating at Paekmagang River (J. Hakusukinoe) a Japanese fleet sent to help the allied kingdom of Paekche in Korea. Fear of invasion proved a powerful spur to reform.

Early in the following century, Japan accordingly sought to model itself more closely still on the highly centralized Chinese state, continuing the "Taika" process begun in 645. A new Chinese-style capital was established at Nara in 710 and provincial governors and magistrates, all answerable to the emperor, were appointed. At the same time, all rice-growing land was declared the property of the emperor – was in effect nationalized – and then allotted to households on a per capita basis. Farmers paid the government a tax in the form of rice and were obliged to perform military service.

Soon, however, this structure proved unworkable. After smallpox epidemics had slashed the workforce and conscript armies had been mauled by the northern Emishi tribesmen, conscription was abandoned and the tax system simplified. Whereas earlier land had been allocated to farmers by the state only for life, now private individuals owned income-bearing land-rights (*shiki*), which they could pass on to their descendants. The type of *shiki* varied with the owner's status. At the bottom of the hierarchy, a farmer's *shiki* gave him some of the crop for tilling the soil. A *samurai's shiki* conferred on him a portion of the harvest from the lands he managed. At the top of the scale, an aristocrat's *shiki* gave him income in return for defending the legality of the *shiki* belonging to those below him. Thus the castes were linked by chains of fealty, which were known as *kenmon*.

These changes radically altered the power structure of the country. Previously the imperial family had been dominated by the Fujiwara family, who provided the emperors' consorts. Most emperors were children, very much under the influence of their maternal Fujiwara relatives and, moreover, after coming of age the emperor was required to "retire". However, by the 11th century the imperial family had begun to reassert itself, and the retired emperors had organized themselves as a *kenmon*. With the other new *kenmon* emerging, the Fujiwara now faced real competition, and the scope for factionalism grew.

Now government became merely the arena where *kenmon* heads hammered out their differences. The *kenmon* were largely autonomous, but, when there was a need for military operations beyond the scope of any one *kenmon*, *kenmon* heads would meet and commission as general a Taira or Minamoto, clans who over the generations had acquired a reputation for producing able military commanders. But recurrent factional feuds, culminating in the Genpei Wars (1180–5), allowed one of these generals, Minamoto Yoritomo, to emerge as Japan's first military leader (*shogun*).

THE FIRST SHOGUN

Yoritomo based his regime not in the existing capital of Kyoto, but far to the east in Kamakura. There, he gave justice and protection to any *samurai* who swore him allegiance. After Yoritomo's death, his two sons were eliminated by his Hōjō in-laws, who then dominated the Kamakura shogunate. Initially, the shogunate deliberately limited its role to defending the interests of its warrior clients within the existing framework of *shiki* and *kenmon*, but in the wake of two major crises, its authority grew: in 1221 a bid by the Emperor Go-Toba to re-establish imperial primacy was crushed in the Jōkyū War; and in 1274 and 1281 two Mongol invasions were thwarted.

But the Hōjō family, with no genealogical rights, overreached themselves in their efforts to control ever-larger swathes of the country. The Hōjō's fall came about in 1333 through an alliance between the Emperor Go-Daigo and Ashikaga Takauji, one of the surviving scions of the Minamoto. Within three years, however, the emperor and Takauji had fallen foul of one another. The emperor was forced to flee with his supporters to the mountain fastness of Yoshino, where he established what came to be known as the "southern" court. In his absence, Takauji replaced him in Kyoto with a puppet "northern" emperor. Civil war sputtered on between the two groups until 1392.

The reunion of the courts began a period of cultural effervescence. An official "tally" trade was opened with Ming China. At the same time, Japan's pirates grew more audacious, raiding widely on the coasts of Korea and, later, China itself. Nonetheless, the country remained politically highly unstable. Government was possible only when the *shogun* could impose order on what by now had become a series of powerful regional magnates, or *daimyō*. After the assassination of the despotic *shogun* Yoshinori in 1441, feuding between alliances of *daimyō* led by the Yamana and Hosokawa led to open warfare in 1467, the Ōnin Wars. As Japan fragmented, the *daimyō* houses, now cut adrift from the state, themselves found it impossible to maintain internal cohesion and one after another they were brought down by their own retainers. It would be more than a century before Japan was unified again.

618 TO 1279

CHINESE CIVILIZATION FROM THE T'ANG TO THE SUNG

Under the T'ang dynasty, China's military and cultural hegemony in the Far East was firmly entrenched. Its successor dynasty, the Sung, was a less dynamic external power but nonetheless reinforced China's position as the world's most sophisticated country until the disruptions of the Mongol invasions in the 13th century.

After centuries of disunion (*see* p. 65), China had been reunified in 589 by the Sui dynasty (581–618). This collapsed, partly from the burden imposed by public works like the Grand Canal, partly from expensive attempts to conquer Koguryo (northern Korea).

The T'ang rose from the widespread rebellions that followed to become a strong centralized empire with an effective administrative system. Underpinning T'ang rule was the Imperial Examination System, which was designed to recruit well-educated citizens to serve the empire. It was to endure until the early 20th century.

After some years of internal consolidation the T'ang began to expand abroad. By the 660s T'ang armies had intervened in India, had occupied the Tarim Basin and Dzungaria and had briefly set up protectorates in Tukharistan, Sogdiana and Ferghana. In the same period Koguryo was finally conquered. By the 660s the Chinese empire reached its greatest extent until the 18th century. Chinese culture and administrative methods were spread alongside its military exploits, establishing a Chinese cultural hegemony in the Far East that would endure long after T'ang power had decayed.

In 755 An Lu-shan, a frontier general, mutinied, severely weakening the T'ang. In the years of turmoil which followed, China withdrew from central Asia and became more inward-looking, in part also as the result of the spread of Islam, which by the 8th century had reached Ferghana and later became dominant in Turkestan. Internally, imperial authority was much reduced. Power passed to the provinces, and many provincial capitals grew into large and wealthy metropolises. At the same time there was a massive movement of population to the Yangtze valley, where new methods of farming developed. Trade boomed, and a network of small market towns grew up.

THE RISE OF THE SUNG

At the end of the 9th century, massive peasant uprisings reduced central authority to a cipher. China split into ten states with an imperial rump controlled by five successive short-lived dynasties. Control was lost of the northeastern area to the Khitan (Liao) who set up an empire in Manchuria and Inner Mongolia. In the northwest another powerful kingdom, the Hsi-hsia, was founded by the Tanguts. These areas remained under foreign domination until 1368.

Following a coup d'état at the palace of the last of the "Five Dynasties", the Later Chou, a new dynasty, the Sung, seized power, led by a skilled military and political operator, determined to reunify China and nullify the threat from the north. The new state that emerged was organized on less uniform lines than the T'ang, and was weaker militarily as well. However, the imperial examinations for the recruiting of officials were further streamlined and a meritocracy of career bureaucrats became established. This, too, was a period of rapid economic growth. Between 750 and 1100 the population nearly doubled, trade reached new levels with the help of paper currency and a great concentration of industries arose around the early Sung capital, K'ai-feng. But the Sung paid a heavy price for its weak military defence along the northern border. In 1126–7 the Tatar Chin conquered north China. The Sung territory was soon reduced to central and southern China, and was only maintained by paying vast ransoms to the Tatars.

Nevertheless, economic growth continued in the south. The population continued to increase rapidly, trade and industry boomed and the new capital, Hang-chou, became indisputably the world's greatest city. This was also a period of great cultural achievement ranging from the visual arts to literature and philosophy. New heights were reached in science and technology also, most significantly in metallurgy, porcelain manufacture, ship-building and compass-guided navigation. Education became more widespread, aided by the dissemination of block printing. Merchants established complex commercial organizations with credit systems. In the countryside a free market in land emerged. Since the old overland routes to central Asia and the Middle East were no longer in Chinese hands, the Chinese became a major sea power, regularly trading with southeast Asia, south Asia and the Persian Gulf. A powerful navy was also built.

In the 13th century, the pace of change slowed markedly. This was mainly the result of the immense destruction and social disruption caused by the Mongol invasion and conquest of both Tatar and Sung territory. Nonetheless, 13th-century China remained far more populous and wealthy than contemporary Europe.

600 TO 1501
IRAN AND CENTRAL ASIA

The history of Iran was dominated by the interaction between the settled Persian-speaking people of the cities and villages and the repeated invasions of Turkic nomads from the east. The Seljuks in the 11th century, Mongols in the 13th and Timur's followers in the late 14th, all conquered Iran but were in turn converted to Islam and adopted Iranian styles of government. Despite the political chaos, architecture, literature and painting flourished.

The conquest of Iran by Arab armies between 636 and 650 brought Islamic rule to the lands of the old Persian empire. In medieval times, the area of Iranian culture and civilization extended beyond the borders of modern Iran to include Afghanistan and the central Asian republics of Turkmenistan, Uzbekistan and Tajikistan. Until *c.* 860 the Iranian lands were provinces of the Abbasid Caliphate with its capital in Baghdad. From the end of the 9th century power passed into the hands of local Iranian dynasties, beginning with the Saffarids in Sistan from 867 and the Samanids in Khurasan from 892. These rulers were all Muslim but encouraged the revival of Persian language and culture.

From 1040 Iran was taken over by Ghuzz Turks, originally from the steppes east of the Caspian Sea, led by the Seljuk family. They took Baghdad in 1055 and established an empire which stretched from the Mediterranean to central Asia. The Seljuk period (1055–*c.* 1200) also saw the building of the first great monuments of Muslim architecture in Iran, including the great Mosque of Isfahan.

MONGOL INVASION

This period of comparative peace and prosperity was brought to an end by the invasion of the Mongols under Chingiz (Genghis) Khan (*d.*1227) from 1218 onwards. Many of the cities of the ancient Khurasan, such as Merv, Nishapur and Balkh, were devastated and never recovered while cities in the south and west, such as Isfahan and Shiraz, were spared the worst ravages. With the arrival of the Mongol khan Hülegü in 1256 Iran became independent under the rule of his descendants, known as the Il-Khans. They established their centre of power in the uplands of Azerbaijan, around Tabriz and their new capital at Sultaniya. Ghazan Khan (1295–1304) converted to Islam and adopted much of traditional Iranian culture. This was also a period when commercial links with other Mongol successor states along the "Silk Road" flourished and merchants regularly travelled between the Middle East and China.

The collapse of the Il-Khanid empire after 1335 led to another period of political division in Iran. The 1370s saw the growing power of Timur (Tamerlane). Timur was a Turkish tribal leader from the area south of Samarkand. Although a Muslim, he showed himself as brutal and effective a conqueror of Islamic lands as his predecessor, Chingiz Khan. At the same time, he made his capital Samarkand one of the great cities of Iran and patronized vast building projects in the city. By 1400 all of Iran was under his control but in 1405, just as he was making preparations for an invasion of China, he died.

Left: The Neanderthals present the earliest evidence of hominine species taking care of one another. This 60,000-year-old skeleton of a powerfully built male, found at Kebara Cave in Israel, had been carefully placed in a shallow grave. Neanderthals are distinguished from modern humans by their large and low-crowned heads with prominent brows and big teeth, and powerful stocky bodies well adapted to cold. They had brains as large as modern humans.

Below: A bison from the caves at Altamira, near Santander, in northern Spain. This 14,000-year-old masterpiece comes from the painted ceiling of a chamber covered with depictions of near life-sized animals. It remains among the most potent and vivid images created by the artists of the late Ice Age in Europe.

Top: Stonehenge, in the west of England, was a sacred site of such significance that it was maintained for over 1000 years. The work involved in quarrying, transporting and erecting the stones in *c.*2500 BC make it one of the most astonishing monuments of prehistoric Europe.

Bottom: Examples of ancient rock art survive in various parts of Africa and represent an important source of evidence for African prehistory. This example, from the Messak Plateau in south-western Libya, is thought to date from 5000 BC.

Left: The sphinx and pyramid at Giza, Egypt. They are over 6000 years old. Works such as this required both large-scale labour and considerable organisation to construct. The great pyramid is the only remaining monument of the Seven Wonders of the Ancient World. The sphinx is the largest single-stone statue in the world.

Below: The Parthenon on the acropolis, Athens, 6th century BC. It is the most important surviving building from Classical Greece.

Above: Zapotec ball court at Monte Alban in Mexico. A distinctive feature of Mesoamerican culture, it was not only a ball game but a complex ritual based on religious beliefs. After the first millennium BC Mesoamerica underwent cycles of growth and decline that included periods of outstanding intellectual and artistic achievement.

Right: Warrior from the tomb of the first Chinese emperor Shih Huang-ti. The Ch'in unified China, laying the foundations for the longest-lasting state in world history.

Below: A silver denarius of 44 BC, bearing the image of Julius Caesar. Rome came to control an empire that stretched from the Atlantic to the Euphrates and from the English Channel to the Sahara. Roman culture and organization laid the foundations for the development of the Mediterranean world.

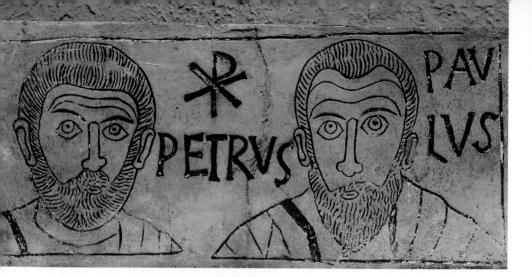

Top: Christianity began as a small sect, but gradually established itself as a prominent religious and intellectual force. It was to have a significant effect on the future of Europe. This shows a stone slab of the Apostles Peter and Paul from the sepulchre of the child Amellus dating from after 313.

Bottom: Borobudur Buddhist temple, Java, Indonesia. Built in the ninth century, it is both a Buddhist pilgrimage site, and a shrine to the Lord Buddha. Buddhism has over 350 million adherents worldwide.

GENGISKAN,
Grand Mogol.

Opposite page: The minaret from which the muezzin chants the call to prayer is attached to all mosques and is a distinctive feature of Islamic religious architecture. Islam spread through much of the Middle East, North Africa and Spain after the death of Mohammad in 632. Shown here is the mosque of Ahmad ibn Tulun in Cairo.

This page, top left: The Mongol empire was the greatest land empire in world history. It was secured by the ruthless and brilliant cavalry armies of Genghis Khan.

Top right: The great gate of the citadel at Aleppo. Mostly constructed by al-Malik al-Zahir (1186-1216), it is one of the greatest fortresses of the medieval Muslim world.

Left: Chu Yüan-chang (1328-98), founder of the Ming dynasty. China enjoyed an economic boom under the Ming.

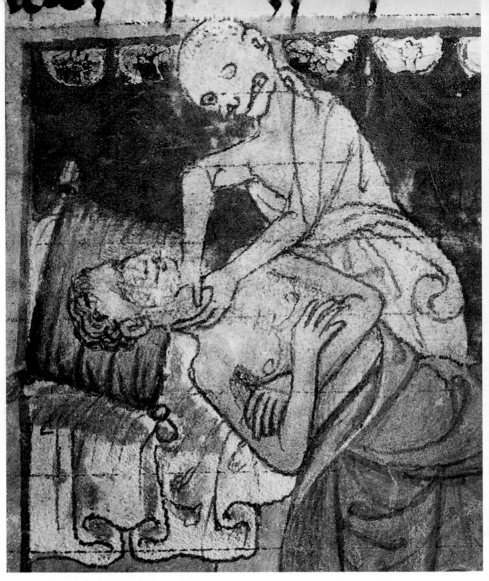

CÕTADOR MAÏORITE3ORERO
TAVANTINSVIOOVIPOC
CVRACA·CON DOR·CHAVA

con tador ytesovero   con ta dor

Above: This illustration from the Stiny Codex shows death strangling a plague victim. In Europe and the Islamic world between a quarter and a half of the population died of the plague, known as the Black Death, in the 14th century.

Left: The Inca empire expanded rapidly in the 15th century. Although they did not have a form of writing, the Incas kept account of numerical data on knotted strings known as quipus. This is a record keeper drawn by an Inca, Felipe Guanam Poma de Ayala.

After his death, his empire began to disintegrate, but the 15th century was a period of great cultural achievements in architecture and book-painting. Under Timur's son Shah Rukh (1405–47), Herat became the capital while his grandson Ulugh Beg (d.1449) built an observatory in Samarkand whose reputation reached western Europe.

The final years of the 15th century saw renewed chaos in western Iran, which opened the way for the rise of the Safavids.

1206 TO 1405
THE MONGOL EMPIRE

The Mongols, pastoral nomads from the depths of Asia, achieved conquests of unrivalled range, from the eastern frontiers of Germany to Korea and from the Arctic Ocean to Turkey and the Persian Gulf, though their invasions of Japan and Java failed. Whole peoples were uprooted and dispersed, permanently changing the ethnic character of many regions.

Through their devastating conquests of the 13th century, the Mongols established the largest ever contiguous land empire. Mongol-speaking tribes had lived for centuries in the general area of present-day Mongolia, but it was to take an extraordinary leader to unite not only the Mongols but all the Turco-Mongol tribes of Eurasia and transform them into a world power. Genghis Khan was born Temüjin in around 1167, the son of a minor Mongol tribal chief. In 1206, after years of personal struggle following the murder of his father, he was proclaimed leader of the united Turco-Mongol tribes. Originating in barren lands, the Mongols themselves were relatively few, but from the outset Genghis recruited members of other Turkic tribes. Using traditional battle tactics that relied on light cavalry, he conducted what were initially raids of pillage and plunder from the steppe into the towns. In 1211 he invaded northern China, subduing the independent Chin empire, and crossing the Great Wall aided by the semi-nomadic Khitans. Genghis Khan then turned his attention westward in campaigns against the Kara Khitai, whose Muslim merchants and administrators would form the backbone of his emerging state. Then, reluctantly, he turned against Khwarizm, the first Muslim state to experience the full fury of the Mongol onslaught after their murder of the Great Khan's envoys.

Proclaiming himself the "Punishment of God", Genghis Khan unleashed the bloody raids and merciless devastation that have made his name synonymous with barbaric mass slaughter. The trail of blood and massacre led from central Asia through Iran to the Caucasus and north into the plains of Russia. The establishment of the Mongol-led armies throughout Asia and eastern Europe in the first half of the 13th century traumatized the world.

One effect of the Mongol conquests was that trade routes flourished, linking east to west across Asia. Tabriz in northwest Iran became a cosmopolitan centre of trade, culture, and learning. The Venetian merchant Marco Polo came this way in 1271, and after 1300 Italian merchants settled as far away as Zaitun in China. The Great Khan Qubilai opened China to the world and, though his empire was riven by cracks, the Yuan dynasty of China and the Ilkhanate of Persia remained close and became beacons of sophistication, commerce and art.

MONGOL CONQUESTS IN EUROPE

Genghis Khan died in 1227. Unlike those of other steppe emperors, his sons and successors were able to maintain and extend his power and territories. Before his death, he had appointed Ögödei his successor and divided his empire among his four sons. Batu, son of the eldest son, Jochi, was bequeathed the peoples of the west, and it was he who directed the invasion of Europe. The northern Russian principalities fell in a lightning winter campaign in 1237–8; Kiev was razed in 1240; Poland and Hungary were attacked, Cracow was burned and abandoned; and in 1241 a Silisian army was annihilated at Legnica. Mongol troops even reached the coastline of Croatia near Trogir (Trail). The death of the Great Khan Ögödei in December 1241 saved Europe; Batu withdrew eastwards to immerse himself in affairs of state as a Grand *Quriltai* (council) was convened to decide on the succession.

MONGOLS, ISLAM AND CHRISTIANITY

The Mongol conquerors came into contact with three main religions: Buddhism, Islam and Christianity. The Mongol elite was shamanist, although many Turco-Mongols adhered nominally to other faiths. However, they were attracted by the high culture associated with the great religions. Many of their administrators were Muslims, Buddhists and Christians, and the Mongol courts had become truly multi-cultural, multi-ethnic and multi-religious. The

Mongols universally exercised religious tolerance, although many have assumed that they were merely hedging their bets with the Almighty. In 1258 the Islamic capital, Baghdad, was captured and plundered, the caliph slain and massacres perpetrated, but the operation was overseen by Muslim advisors, carried out with the assistance of local Muslim rulers and their soldiers and supported by the caliph's Muslim subjects, Kurds and Shi'ites. Even though the Mongols had sometimes promoted Nestorian Christianity and Buddhism in Persia, in 1295 the Mongol ruler, Ghazan Khan, tactically declared his state nominally Muslim. In China meanwhile, the Yuan Mongols had endorsed Buddhism, thereby strengthening the position of that faith in the Far East. Despite their religious differences Iran and China remained politically, commercially and culturally intimate during the first half of the 14th century. With the Christian rulers of western Europe, the Mongol rulers of Iran – the Ilkhans – played up their Christian credentials, which included the presence of Christian queens and princesses at the royal court and the support of their staunchly loyal Christian allies, the Armenians. The Ilkhans made overtures to the Pope, hopeful that a Christian alliance against the Mamluk sultans of Egypt in the Holy Land might emerge.

Just as Europe was saved by the death of Ögödei, it has been said that the death of the Great Khan Möngke in 1259 saved the heartlands of Muslim Asia. Möngke had targeted both Sung China and western Asia for conquest. His brother, Hülegü Khan, returned eastward on hearing news of Möngke's death, leaving only a skeleton military force in Syria – of which the Mamluk sultan took advantage when his army defeated the Mongols at Ain Jalut (1260). The Mongol advance in the west was never seriously renewed, and the myth of their invincibility was dispelled forever. Following the death of Möngke, the empire was plunged into factional wars and the dream of a heavenly mandate for universal rule was forgotten.

THE LAST MONGOL CONQUESTS

The death of Möngke saw the khanates of Chagatai and the Golden Horde break away from the empire and the Ilkhans of Persia achieve independence. In Persia and China the Mongol dynasties lasted under a century, while in Russia the Golden Horde lasted for more than 200 years, and the Crimean khans reigned until the late 18th century. In the second half of the 14th century, until

1405, the world once again trembled under the hooves of a Eurasian conquering army. Tamerlane, who claimed descent from Genghis Khan, had a dramatic and bloody rise to power, but his murderous reign marks the final phase of the Mongol age of conquests; his achievements included a victorious march through Anatolia where he defeated, captured and humiliated the Ottoman sultan, Bayezid.

The Mongol conquests were achieved through a mixture of bold strategy, iron discipline, brilliant propaganda, charismatic leadership and the disorganization and ineptitude of their adversaries. The Mongol empire and its armies were directed by able generals and proficient administrators who eventually began to believe their own propaganda: that they had a mandate from heaven to rule the world. Within a couple of generations the Mongol elite had transformed themselves from rude and coarse nomadic steppe warriors to cultured and sophisticated statesmen commanding the respect and obedience of their cultured subjects. Where once the appearance of their tents and armies stabbed fear and horror into whole cities and provinces, their courts later became magnets for seekers of adventure, glory, culture and wealth from around the world. Genghis Khan terrified the world with his cruel and plundering horsemen, but he gave birth to a legacy of splendour.

550 TO 1206
INDIA: THE EMERGENCE OF TEMPLE KINGDOMS

The integration of early India led to agrarian expansion, the proliferation of rival states and the triumph of Hinduism over its rivals. The political centre of India gradually shifted southward to powerful agrarian empires such as the Rashtrakutas and Cholas. As north India fragmented, it became vulnerable to Turkic incursions from the northwest.

The thousands of inscriptions that have come down to us from medieval India reveal an intricate mosaic of kings, lords and priests superimposed on an agrarian populace. Overall, civilization and its revenue-extracting agents now penetrated into regions previously beyond the reach of the more urbanized polities of ancient India. The great metropolises of earlier times contracted as the countryside became filled with smaller settlements integrated into local trade networks. Temple Hinduism triumphed over Buddhism and provided the political theology of royal courts as well as the religious sentiments of the peasantry.

DYNASTIC STRUGGLES

Politically, this epoch was composed of successive "imperial formations", hierarchies of dynastic empires in struggle and alliance, vying for paramountcy. After the decline of the power of the Guptas (*see* p. 69), north India suffered political instability until the Huns were gradually pushed northward from India by local rulers. Not long afterwards, three major dynasties emerged as powerful contenders for imperial paramountcy – the Pushyabhutis of Kanauj, the Chalukyas of Badami and the Pallavas of Kanci. Harsha Pushyabhuti, who hosted the famous Chinese traveller Hsüan-tsang, was defeated in 630 by the Chalukya king Pulakesin II, although the location of this battle is not known. The Chalukyas, who claimed descent from the Satavahana dynasty that had held sway in the south 500 years earlier, gained initial victories against the southern Pallavas, but were later defeated by them and finally faced rebellion by one of their ablest underlords, the Rashtrakutas, who rose to become the chief power in south India for nearly 200 years (*c.* 750–950). The Rashtrakutas, builders of the famous Kalaisanatha temple at Ellora, were perceived by the Arab traveller Masudi as the most powerful dynasty of India. Their rivals were the Pratiharas to the north and the Palas of eastern India, followers of Mahayana Buddhism and patrons of the Buddhist university at Nalanda.

THE RISE OF THE CHOLAS

By the close of the 10th century these empires had weakened and contracted as the ancient Chola lineage of the south revitalized itself to become the dominant force in a new imperial formation that would last nearly 250 years (*c.* 950–1200). The Cholas made daring military expeditions to north India, Sri Lanka and southeast Asia, gaining tremendous wealth with which they constructed elaborate imperial temples and patronized Brahmin religious elites. In the Deccan, two families revived the Chalukya dynasty and further north the Pratihara empire fragmented into a number of smaller kingdoms warring amongst themselves, that eventually came to be known as the Rajputs. Perhaps the most powerful of these smaller dynasties were the Paramaras based in Dhar. The political instability of north India made it particularly vulnerable to the militarily superior Turkic armies, which under the leadership of Mahmud of Ghazni conducted looting raids in the 11th century.

From the time of the Pallavas the dynasties of eastern India – particularly the Palas and the Cholas – established trade links and cultural exchanges with the kingdoms of southeast Asia. Several Buddhist kings of southeast Asia patronized Buddhist institutions in eastern India and maintained trading enclaves at coastal cities. After the decline of Rome, trade links with southeast Asia were further strengthened, as peninsular India eventually became an important depot in a trans-regional trade circuit connecting China to the Arab Middle East. Despite these trading links, medieval Indian empires remained primarily agrarian in nature. Their royal families, courtly officials and ritual specialists enjoyed the revenue extracted from vast tracts of land cultivated by the lower orders, who in turn were divided into hierarchies of cultivators, tenants and labourers. The Cholas, for example, relied on the flourishing wet-cultivation of rice in the Kaveri river delta. Political authority was not directly administered but was sustained through relations of tribute and dependence among a hierarchy of lords, giving India an almost feudal complexion.

TEMPLE HINDUISM

Saivism and Vaisnavism, the two main orders of theistic Hinduism, which centred their philosophy and ritual around the exaltation of the gods Shiva and Vishnu respectively, facilitated this chain of medieval lordships. These religions, which had been growing since the time of the Guptas, gained the commitments of most royal courts by the 7th century. Two of the most important early texts of these theistic orders were the *Ramayana*, a tale of the mythical king Rama of Ayodhya, and the voluminous *Mahabharata*, recounting the war between two royal families for paramount sovereignty of the earth. The latter contained the *Bhagavad-gita*, which developed the theology of devotion called "bhakti". Through theocentric histories called "Puranas", ancient pedigrees and divine identities were provided for medieval rulers, and images of Hindu gods were housed in royal fashion in hundreds of temples which dotted the countryside, reinforcing the ideology of sovereignty and devotion integral to the authority of kings. Occasionally devotion to god ("bhakti") could be turned against the chain of secular lordships, but such subversions were limited. Temples became the beneficiaries of royal and lordly largesse, accumulating considerable wealth and emerging as significant landholders by the end of the medieval period. This no doubt explains their attraction for the raiding Turks who laid the foundation of Muslim rule in India.

1206 TO 1526
INDIA: THE DELHI SULTANATE

The Delhi sultanate spread Muslim rule throughout most of south Asia. It created the circumstances in which large numbers of Indians began to convert to Islam. In the mid-14th century the sultanate reached the peak of its power after which India began to divide into many smaller sultanates, making it an easy target for invaders from the northwest.

From the beginning of the 11th century the Turkish Muslim rulers of central Asia and Afghanistan had been expanding their power into north India. First Mahmud of Ghazni (927–1030) invaded India 17 times, bringing the Punjab under his sway. Then, from 1175, having overthrown Mahmud's successors, Muhammad Ghuri built his power in northwest India. In 1206, Qutbuddin Aibak, a Ghurid general who had risen from slave status, established in his own name the sultanate of Delhi.

Over the following 320 years northern India was ruled from Delhi by five dynasties of Turkish and Afghan extraction: the Slave Kings (1206–90); the Khaljis (1290–1320); the Tughluqs (1320–1414); the Sayyids (1414–51); and the Lodis (1451–1526). For the first century and a half they strove to spread their rule throughout India. In 1311 the army of Alauddin Khalji (1296–1316) reached the sub-continent's southern tip. Under Muhammad bin Tughluq (1325–51) the sultanate reached its maximum extent, drawing taxes from more than 20 provinces. Greater security was promised, moreover, by the decline of the Mongol threat from the northwest. But controversial decisions by Muhammad to levy higher taxes and to transfer the population of Delhi to a new capital in the Deccan led to the disintegration of the sultanate as it reached its peak. In 1341 Bengal broke away to form a separate sultanate; in 1347 so did the Bahmani rulers of the Deccan. Between 1382 and 1396 Khandesh, Malwa, Jaunpur and

Gujerat followed suit. The invasion of Tamerlane in 1398, when Delhi was razed, rendered the sultanate's power nominal, and allowed the emergence of regional powers. From the mid-15th century the Afghan Lodis managed to stretch Delhi's sway once more over northern India. Dissensions among them between 1517 and 1526, however, facilitated the final overthrow of the sultanate by Tamerlane's descendant, Babur.

THE HINDU SOUTH

From the mid-14th to the mid-16th century the south was not disturbed by powers from the north. Here the Bahmani sultanate of the Deccan and its successors faced a strong Hindu polity in the Vijayanagar empire, founded in 1336, which under three dynasties dominated south India until its fall in 1565. It is a mistake, however, to regard this competition as simply one of Muslim versus Hindu. Men of each faith fought on both sides.

INDIA AND ISLAM

One consequence of the Muslim conquest of much of India was that it came to be linked more closely with central and western Asia. Large numbers of scholars, poets and craftsmen, often uprooted by the havoc wrought by the Mongols and their successors, came to seek their fortunes at Indian courts, providing a great stimulus to Indian arts. Persian became the leading language of literature and government. The dome and the arch became major features of Indian architecture.

Another consequence was the conversion of Indians from all levels of society, but particularly from the lower levels, to Islam. This was a largely peaceful development in which Sufi saints played an important role. One third of the world's Muslims now live in the region.

There was much interaction between Hinduism and Islam, particularly at the mystical level. Teachers emerged who drew from both traditions, for instance Kabir (1440–1518) and Nanak (1469–1539), who founded Sikhism. There was fruitful interaction, too, in literature and architecture, where distinctive traditions developed in the regional kingdoms. Nevertheless, orthodox Muslims continued to find much in Hinduism that offended their belief in the unity of God and His revelation through the Prophet Mohammed.

Hindu culture also saw important achievements. Bhakti devotionalism (love of God) spread from south India to Bengal, leading to a revival of the worship of Vishnu as the Universal God in eastern and northern India. Magnificent temples were built in the rich Hindu civilization of Vijayanagar in the south. Nevertheless, in this period Delhi was established as the political centre of India. It was to remain so until the 19th century.

500 BC TO AD 1511
THE EARLY CIVILIZATIONS OF SOUTHEAST ASIA

Maritime trade routes linked India with southeast Asia from the last few centuries of the pre-Christian era. By the middle of the first millennium AD the influence of Indian Hindu-Buddhist civilization extended throughout the region, but by 1300 Islam was expanding into the island world of Indonesia and the Philippines.

Following earlier trends (*see* p. 19), from about the 3rd and 4th centuries AD there was an increasing adoption of Hindu and Buddhist cults among the local rulers of southeast Asia. They adopted Sanskrit titles and personal names, constructed numerous religious monuments and commissioned statuary modelled on Indian prototypes. In addition and largely through local initiative, Indian scripts and languages came to be used for political and religious texts. By the 6th century Buddhist images and votive inscriptions in Sanskrit had spread over continental southeast Asia, Sumatra and Java.

EARLY KINGDOMS
By the 6th century AD numerous kingdoms, whose locations are not always easy to identify, seem to have emerged. They were in frequent conflict with one another yet most maintained commercial and political relations with China, which welcomed tribute missions from the south. An ancient port has been found at Oc Eo (3rd–6th centuries AD), and from at least the 7th century Hindu temples were being built in lower Cambodia, notably at Angkor Borei, on the Dieng Plateau in central Java and in the valleys of central Vietnam. Buddhist shrines have been excavated at Beikthano and Sri Ksetra in central Burma (Myanmar) and in Thailand (Siam) at U-Thong, Ku Bua and Nakhon Pathom.

The best-studied temple complexes are those of Borobudur and Prambanan in central Java (8th–10th centuries); around Angkor in Cambodia (9th–13th centuries); at Pagan in Burma (11th–13th centuries); and the Cham Shivite temple towers of central Vietnam (7th–13th centuries). All combined Hindu and Buddhist elements to varying degrees.

A centre of Buddhist culture developed from the 7th century at Srivijaya in southeast Sumatra, the capital of the maritime empire of Srivijaya, which for centuries controlled trade passing through the straits of Malacca and Sunda. However, by the 14th century Malacca, on the west coast of Malaya, had replaced Srivijaya as the dominant regional power.

DECLINE OF THE TEMPLE STATES

The Salendra kingdom, centred on the temple complexes at Prambanan, was devastated by volcanic ash falls in the early 10th century, and was replaced by a succession of smaller states and, eventually, the Majapahit empire. On the mainland, Pagan was sacked by Mongol invaders in the late 13th century. The Khmer rulers, under pressure from the Thai kingdom of Sukhothai from the 14th century, abandoned Angkor for the greater security of Phnom Penh.

Sukhothai was itself in decline by the late 14th century and the Thai political centre moved south to Ayutthaya and regional capitals were established at Chieng Mai in the northwest and Luang Prabang on the Mekong river. About this time in Burma new political centres emerged at Ava on the upper Irrawaddy and at Toungoo on the Sittang; Pegu became the capital of a new Mon kingdom in the south.

THE RISE OF VIETNAM

Northern Vietnam had been incorporated into the Chinese empire following the Han invasions of the 2nd century BC (*see* p. 64) but broke free at the end of the 10th century. Despite Chinese attempts at reconquest, a new Vietnamese kingdom emerged which gradually absorbed the Cham principalities to the south, annexing their last capital of Vijaya in 1471. However, with the advent of the Ming dynasty in China from the late 14th century Vietnam again fell within China's tributary system.

The political changes of the 14th and 15th centuries were accompanied by significant religious developments and the expansion of the region's international trade. While Theravada Buddhism spread through the mainland, Islam, which had a foothold at Aceh in northern Sumatra before 1300, expanded through the archipelago as far as Mindanao in the Philippines. Rulers of the north Javanese trading ports and those of Ternate and Tidore converted to Islam, whose advance was only halted by the Portuguese capture of the prosperous Sultanate of Melaka in 1511 (*see* p. 178) and the Spanish settlement in the Philippines from the 1560s.

800 TO 1100

THE MUSLIM WORLD

The three centuries 800–1100 were a period of great political turmoil in the Islamic world: the united Caliphate of the early Islamic period broke up, and a major divide between the Sunni Seljuk Turks and the Shi'ite Fatimids divided the Muslims into two camps. At the same time, this was a period a great cultural and commercial development, especially in Egypt and Iran. Meanwhile, in Spain and Sicily, Christian invaders were gradually conquering Muslim lands.

By 800 the great Muslim conquests were effectively complete. It was only in Pakistan and parts of central Asia that Muslim rule expanded during these three centuries. From 1050 onwards, much of Turkey was conquered by the Turks and came under Muslim domination for the first time. At the same time, in Sicily and Spain, Muslim territory was being occupied by Christian powers from the north and Islam was in retreat.

In the *Dar al-Islam* the main change during the three centuries between 800 and 1100 was the break up of the Caliphate and the emergence of successor states. In 800 the whole Muslim world, except for Andalus (Spain and Portugal), was ruled from Baghdad by the Abbasid Caliph Harun al-Rashid. His death in 809 was followed by a civil war, which saw the beginning of the disintegration of this unity. In 868 Egypt became independent under the rule of the Tulunids, and in 900 the Samanids established their independent rule in most of eastern Iran. By 945 the once powerful Abbasid Caliphs were no more than figureheads in their palace in Baghdad: real power in Iraq was seized by Daylamite military adventurers from northern Iran.

The political unity of Islam was further fractured in 909 when a rival Caliph from the Fatimid dynasty, who claimed direct descent from the prophet Muhammad through Muhammad's daughter Fatima, took power in Tunisia. In 969 the Fatimids conquered Egypt and became the leading power in the Muslim world. In 929 the Umayyad ruler of Andalus proclaimed himself Caliph, so there were now three Caliphs in different areas of the *Dar al-Islam*.

These centuries also saw major economic changes in the region. The rich agricultural system of central and southern Iraq was impoverished by the constant disturbances and civil wars, and much of the agricultural land was abandoned as irrigation canals were neglected or destroyed. At the same time, Egypt enjoyed a period of great prosperity under Fatimid rule: the textile industry boomed and Cairo and Alexandria became the entrepots of trade between the Indian Ocean and Mediterranean basins. Cairo, founded by the Fatimids in 969, came to rival Baghdad as a cultural centre, attracting immigrant scholars from Iraq.

The dominance of the Fatimids was challenged in the 11th century by the arrival of the Sunni Seljuk Turks in Iran after 1040. In 1055 they took Baghdad, proclaiming themselves champions of the Sunni Abbasid Caliphs against the Shi'ite Fatimids. The two great powers came into conflict in Syria and Palestine as each tried to control the eastern seaboard of the Mediterranean. In 1071 the Seljuk sultan Alp Arslan defeated the Byzantine army at Manzikert, laying the way open for Turkish penetration of Anatolia.

In the 11th century, Italian merchants began to frequent the ports of Egypt and Syria, buying fine textiles, pepper and spices. Cities such as Alexandria and Tripoli became thriving ports once more. But the Italians were also forerunners of the Crusaders, who took Jerusalem in 1099.

1100 TO 1350

THE MUSLIM WORLD

After 1100 the Muslim countries of the Middle East were subject to attack from the Christian Europeans from the west and the pagan Mongols from the east. In the west, most of Spain was lost to the Christians by 1250, but in the Middle East the Mamluks of Egypt successfully drove the Crusaders from the Levant and resisted the advance of the Mongols.

During the 12th and 13th centuries, the Islamic world was attacked by outsiders from all directions. In some areas, the Muslims were permanently subjugated or expelled but, in others, Muslim forces counter-attacked and repelled or converted the invaders.

THE CRUSADES

On the Iberian peninsula (al-Andalus) the Muslims came under intense pressure. In the east, Zaragoza was taken by the Christians in 1118; in the west they took Lisbon in 1147, and the city immediately became the capital of the emerging kingdom of Portugal. The Christian advance was halted for almost a century by the Almohads, a Berber religio-political movement. From their capital at Marrakesh, the Almohad Caliphs ruled north Africa as far east as Tunis and all of Spain and Portugal, then in Muslim hands. In 1212, however, they were decisively defeated by Alfonso VIII of Castile and his Christian allies. The main cities of Muslim Spain fell rapidly – Corboba and Valencia in 1236, Seville in 1248 – and Muslim rule was restricted to the mountainous kingdom of Granada, which survived until 1492.

In the Middle East, the Crusaders occupied the lands at the eastern end of the Mediterranean in a long strip from Antioch in the north to Baza and the Red Sea in the south. They were aided by the Muslim world's divisions between the Shi'ite Fatimids of Egypt and the Sunni Turks of Syria and Iraq. In 1174, however, Saladin (d.1193) united Egypt and Syria, and in 1187 he defeated the Crusaders at the Battle of Hattin. Despite the launch of the Third Crusade (1189–91) and subsequent expeditions, the Christians never recovered the territory they had lost. Only a few coastal ports remained in Crusader hands until the fall of Acre in 1291.

A more serious threat to the Muslim world was posed by the invasion from the east by the pagan Mongols under the leadership of Genghis Khan (d.1227). From 1218 they launched a devastating series of attacks on the cities of Iran, and in 1258 they sacked Baghdad, putting an end to the Abbasid Caliphate. In 1260, a Mongol army was defeated at 'Ain Jalut by a force of Mamluk soldiers from Egypt. This setback proved to be a turning point. Mongol rule was confined to Iran and Iraq while the Mamluk sultans ruled Egypt and Syria. The Mongol ruler of Iran, Ghazan Khan (1295–1304), converted to Islam, and his dynasty, known as the Il-Khans, ruled until 1335.

The main rivals of the Mongols were the Mamluks of Egypt. These Turkish soldiers, many of them originally slaves, took power in 1260. They built up a formidable military machine, and it was the Mamluks who destroyed the last vestiges of Crusader power in the Levant. They also prevented further attempts by the Mongols to take Syria and Egypt. Under their rule, Cairo replaced Baghdad as the largest city in the Arab Middle East and became the leading intellectual and cultural centre.

1000 TO 1500
THE EMERGENCE OF STATES IN AFRICA

The period from 1000 to 1500 saw the emergence of states over much of Africa, crucially assisted by the need to control and secure trading routes and by the wealth which flowed from them. The spread of trade often went hand in hand with the dissemination of Islam. By 1500, sub-Saharan African states had made their first contacts with European explorers.

The period from 1000 to 1500 saw two principal developments in Africa: the spread of Islam and the emergence of organized states throughout the continent. In many places these were linked. By 1000 the Maghreb (northwest Africa) had been in Islamic hands for over three centuries. Between 1000 and 1500 Islam spread south: up the Nile into the Christian kingdoms of Nubia; along the northern and eastern coasts of the Horn; and across the Sahara into the states of the "Sudanic belt", stretching from the Senegal to the Nile. Muslim merchants crossed the Sahara with caravans of camels which regularly made the hazardous journey from trading depots on either edge of the desert, such as Sijilmassa, south of the Atlas Mountains, and Walata in Mali. This dangerous trade carried luxury goods (and, in time, firearms) and salt to the black African lands of the south. In exchange, leather-work, slaves and gold went northwards: by 1250 the economies of both the Muslim Middle East and Christian Europe depended to a great extent upon African gold.

THE STATES OF WESTERN AFRICA

Although the beginnings of urbanism in the Sudanic belt can be traced as far back as the last centuries BC, expanding trans-Saharan trade gave an impetus to the growth of states. Two of the earliest of these were Ghana and Mali. Ghana, an essentially African polity, which flourished from the 8th to the 11th centuries, was established north of the Senegal and Niger rivers, far from the modern state which has taken its name. Its successor, Mali, extended from the Atlantic across the great bend of the Niger. In 1324 the Mali king Mansa Musa went on pilgrimage to Mecca, and is said to have taken so much gold with his retinue that he caused inflation in Cairo. The empire of Mali gave way to that of Songhay, centred on the Niger cities of Gao and Timbuktu. East of Mali lay the city states of Hausaland, some of which – Zaria, Kano, Katsina – became extremely prosperous, although they never united to form a single state. Further east was Kanem, founded by desert people to the east of Lake Chad. Their ruling dynasty, the Kanuri kings, retained authority until their final overthrow in the 19th century.

By the late Middle Ages, at a time of crisis in western Europe (*see* p. 138), the black kingdoms of the western and central Sudan flourished. A number of African kings, among them Mansa Musa and Sunni Ali (of Songhay), enjoyed renown throughout Islam and Christendom for their wealth, brilliance and the artistic achievements of their subjects. Their capitals were large walled cities with many mosques and at least two, Timbuktu and Jenne, had universities that attracted scholars and poets from far and wide. Their power derived from a mixture of military force and diplomatic alliances with local leaders; their prosperity was based on control of rich local resources; their bureaucracies administered taxation and controlled trade, the life-blood of these empires.

To the south of the Sudanic states, Hausa and Malinke merchants traded among the peoples on the edge of the tropical forests, especially in the gold-producing regions. The prosperity this trade brought led, by 1500, to the foundation of many forest states, such as Benin. Around this time, also, the first contacts occurred with Portuguese sailors exploring the seas of the west African coast.

THE STATES OF EAST AND CENTRAL AFRICA

In the east, after the decline of the kingdom of Aksum, the centre of political power in Christian Ethiopia shifted southwards, first under the Kushitic-speaking Zagwe dynasty in the 11th century and then, in the 13th century, under the Amharic-speaking Solomonids who later clashed with the Muslim coastal states of the Horn of Africa, notably Adal.

Along the east coast there arose a string of Muslim city states. Kilwa Kisiwani, with its handsome mosques and palaces, prospered as the entrepôt for the gold of Zimbabwe, brought via Sofala. The arrival of the Portuguese in 1498 marked the beginning of European encroachment in this lucrative system of oceanic trade.

Meanwhile, in the interior of the southern half of the continent, many other African peoples coalesced to form states. These processes are best known in two regions: the upper Lualaba where wealth was accumulated in the form of metal, and south of the Zambezi where, from the 10th century, prosperous cattle-herders gave rise to the polity centred at Great Zimbabwe. Other states, many of them Bantu-speaking, emerged south of the lower Congo river, and in the area between the great lakes of east Africa.

1281 TO 1522

THE RISE OF THE OTTOMAN EMPIRE

Originally a petty principality in western Anatolia, from the late 13th century the Ottoman state was transformed into an astonishingly dynamic imperial and military power. By 1522, it had expanded to embrace the Balkans, the Black Sea and the Middle East and had become a major player in the international power politics of the day.

The retreat of the Mongols from Anatolia into Iran in the 13th century created a vacuum in Anatolia which a series of rival Turcoman states fought to fill. Among them was a small polity based on Sögüt. With the accession in 1281 of Osman, after whom the Ottoman dynasty came to be called, it began a period of rapid expansion. By 1354 it had gained its first foothold in Europe with the acquisition of Gallipoli. By 1361 the Ottomans had taken Edirne (Adrianople), which they made their capital. The decisive defeat of the Serbians and Bosnians at Kosovo in 1389 then established Ottoman supremacy in the Balkans. By 1393, Bulgaria had been absorbed as had most of the remaining independent emirates of Anatolia. Ottoman rule stretched from the Danube to the Euphrates.

DEFEAT AND RECONSTRUCTION

The invasion of Tamerlane from the East saw the Ottomans' first serious setback. Though his empire broke up with Tamerlane's death in 1405, his victory at Ankara in 1402 had provided the opportunity for the Balkan states and the Anatolian emirates to escape Ottoman hegemony. But reconstruction of the Ottoman state by Mehmed I (1413–21) and renewed campaigns by his son Murad II (1421–51) again brought most of eastern and central Anatolia and the southern and eastern Balkans under Ottoman control.

The emergence of the Ottoman state as a world power was the work of Mehmed II, Fatih, "The Conqueror" (1451–81), whose conquest of Constantinople in 1453 made possible Ottoman expansion into northern Anatolia and their dominance of the Straits and southern Black Sea. The conquest of Serbia, Herzegovina and much of Bosnia now left Hungary as the major European power facing the Ottomans. Mehmed's failure to take Belgrade in 1456 established the Danube and lower Sava as the Ottoman boundary with Hungary for over 60 years.

With the final re-absorption of Karaman in 1468 the last of the independent Anatolian emirates disappeared. Farther north, Mehmed established a bridge-head in the Crimea by the capture of Kefe (Caffa) from the Genoese in 1475, bringing the Khanate of the Crimea under Ottoman control.

In Europe, the middle years of Mehmed's reign saw the ending of Byzantine and Frankish control over the Morea, and the erosion of Venetian and Genoese power in the Aegean and the Black Sea. Mehmed's death in 1481, which occurred soon after the Turks overwhelmed Otranto in southern Italy, put paid to his ambition to conquer Rome. The struggle for the succession between Bayezid II (1481–1512) and his brother, Jem, was then skilfully manipulated by the West, protecting it from further Ottoman incursions for many years. However, with the conquests of Akkerman and Kilia the land route from Constantinople to the Crimea was secured in 1484, while the Ottoman-Venetian war of 1499–1502 underlined the growing Ottoman naval power.

EXPANSION IN THE MIDDLE EAST

The last years of Bayezid II's reign, and most of that of his successor Selim I (1512–20), were taken up with conquests in the Middle East. The rise of the Safavids in Iran after 1501 brought to power a state militarily strong and ideologically hostile to the Ottomans. Risings among the Turcoman tribes of eastern Anatolia in the last years of Bayezid II's reign were a prelude to the war which broke out in the reigns of Selim and Shah Isma'il (1501–24), culminating in the defeat of the Safavids at Çaldiran in 1514. Eastern Anatolia was secured and the threat of religious separatism removed.

Selim's annexation of the emirate of Dhu'l-Qadr in 1515 brought the Ottomans into direct contact with the Mamluk empire for the first time. Over the next two years Selim swept the Mamluks aside, conquering Aleppo and Damascus in 1516 and taking Cairo in 1517. As well as bringing Syria and Egypt under Ottoman control, his campaign added the holy places of Christendom and Islam to the empire. His successor, Suleiman the Magnificent was to continue Ottoman expansion (*see* p. 167).

1252 TO 1381

THE CRISIS OF THE 14TH CENTURY IN EUROPE

The 14th century saw dramatic change in Europe and Asia as the Black Death spread westward, reaching the Black Sea in 1346, Sicily in 1347 and most of Europe by 1350. In Europe and the Islamic world between a quarter and a half of the population died of plague. The economy and society of East and West underwent radical transformations as a result.

The intense pressure on the land of a densely packed population combined with a succession of poor harvests to cause the Great Famine in northern Europe of 1315–17. Yet though Europe was to be afflicted with a series of further harvest failures, this was also a period of expanding markets, meeting the needs of increasingly active regional trade in wine, grain, dyestuffs and raw materials. Further new opportunities grew after the Black Death, when labour, previously in surplus, leading to low wages, suddenly became scarce.

BLACK DEATH AND ECONOMIC CRISIS

Signs of crisis were visible before the Black Death. Textile manufacture in Flemish and Italian cities was in decline on the eve of the plague. Banking failures, beginning with the Buonsignori of Siena (1298), culminated in the collapse of the great Florentine banking houses of Bardi and Peruzzi in the 1340s. The plague struck in 1346, and by 1350 had swept through most of Europe. Population levels did not recover until the late 15th century because of the recurrence of plague, which became endemic in Europe, though outbreaks were increasingly localized.

Yet though the effects on the European economy were profound, there were many who benefited from the new economic climate, and this was not necessarily a period of severe depression. Thus English cloth exports expanded greatly, as did Castilian wool exports. Farmland was converted to pasture for sheep in England, Italy and Spain and for cattle in the Netherlands, Spain and northern Germany. New products such as saffron were cultivated in southern Germany, where Nuremberg and Augsburg were front-runners in a new wave of economic expansion, partly based on the mineral resources of the lands to the east.

On the other hand, monopolistic guild restrictions meant that some of the once prosperous cloth towns in northern Europe lost out to more agile competitors in the restructured economy of the late 14th century. Florence, too, lost its pre-eminence in woollen cloth, and attempted to become a major centre of silk production instead; but by now there were several lively competitors. Barcelona found a market for its upper-middle quality cloths, but financial crises and internal power struggles sapped the city's energy and Valencia took over as the powerhouse of western Mediterranean trade. In the north, the German Hansa became a powerful confederation of trading cities which dominated Baltic and North Sea trade in fish, grain, dairy goods and furs, operating through bases at London, Lynn, Bergen, Bruges and Novgorod; for long it was able to keep competitors such as the Dutch and the English at bay.

PEASANT UNREST AND REVOLT

Economic change brought new wealth to some and undermined the wealth of others, such as landlords who lost their source of cheap labour. Villages were abandoned in areas as far apart as the English Midlands and Russia, as peasants moved – often without permission – to the lands of lords who made less demands on them or which had more fertile soil. Many moved to towns, especially when villages were abandoned to make way for sheep. Yet some peasants were able to accumulate large amounts of land, as relatives died of the plague and left them their possessions. To many it seemed that the world was turned topsy-turvy. Social unrest became strident in town and country, exemplified by the Ciompi rebellion in Florence (1378) or the Peasants' Revolt in England (1381), particularly among those whose depressed social status did not match their rising economic status. Generally, however, serfdom was a thing of the past in much of western Europe by 1400; in eastern Europe it was, in contrast, reinforced, as landlords such as the Teutonic Knights sought to produce grain for their Hanseatic customers.

The 14th century saw severe readjustment, with the restructuring of economies in the wake of massive depopulation. However, by the end of the century the Hansa was enjoying its Golden Age, the maritime trade routes that linked Italy and Catalonia to England and Flanders (opened around 1277) were flourishing, and Venice and Genoa had secured a strong hold on eastern markets: the Genoese mainly in the Black Sea, from where they brought grain and dried fruits; the Venetians in Egypt and Syria, from where they brought spices and cotton. The Black Death was a dramatic demographic earthquake, with severe aftershocks, yet the European economy was successfully rebuilt on its own shattered remains.

1300 TO 1400
EUROPEAN STATES IN THE 14TH CENTURY

The 14th century was a tumultuous period of state building in which rulers sought to define frontiers and develop centralized bureaucracies. They were challenged by parliaments of nobles, knights and townsmen, seeking concessions in return for taxation. Furthermore, the cost of frontier wars forced rulers back into the arms of their subjects.

War added to the turmoil caused to 14th-century Europe by famine and plague. Italy was particularly affected. The struggle for Sicily after 1282 between the French house of Anjou and Aragonese invaders (the War of the Sicilian Vespers) continued long after its formal ending in 1302 by the Treaty of Caltabellotta. Around 1300 northern Italy remained divided between competing cities, themselves often torn apart by Guelph and Ghibelline factions, the former able to count on the support of Naples or the Papacy. As regional despots gained power over the cities, conflict within their walls died, culminating in the conquest of large areas of Lombardy and Tuscany by Giangaleazzo Visconti, duke of Milan. Few Italian republics stood firm against the trend, though Florence made much capital out of its self-proclaimed dedication to the cause of republican liberty.

The pope himself decamped in 1305 to Avignon in southern France, a more peaceful city than Rome. Papal centralization was visible in the tighter control over Church appointments and taxation, successes that generated bitter criticism from reformers such as Wyclif in Oxford and Hus in Prague. The return of the Papacy to Rome in 1376 led to deep divisions among the cardinals and the outbreak of a schism that lasted nearly 40 years.

The conflict between France and England (*see* p. 110) for control of France, above all Gascony, erupted again in 1294 and then in 1337 (the Hundred Years' War). Initial English successes coupled with internal strife gravely weakened France and great princes such as the Valois dukes of Burgundy exploited this royal debility to create powerful statelets of their own.

RULERS AND SUBJECTS

Against this disturbed background, rulers sought to create a sound financial base for themselves. Often this meant, as in Germany and Aragon, negotiating with parliaments that controlled their budget. Conflicts between rulers and their leading subjects led to the deposition of Edward II and Richard II in England (1327, 1399), and of Wenzel in Bohemia (1400). In Germany, the great princely houses vied for the crown, but were more concerned to strengthen their own patrimonies than to stabilize the German monarchy. A web of leagues emerged, of which the Swiss Confederation (from 1291) was the most successful.

In the Mediterranean, the Crown of Aragon consolidated its hold. Sardinia, promised by Pope Boniface VIII to the Aragonese in 1297, was invaded in 1323–4, though it took many decades before Aragonese rule became a reality; Majorca, an autonomous kingdom since 1276, was reconquered in 1343, giving access to prime trade routes; by the end of the century Sicily, too, was under Aragonese rule. Castile, on the other hand, was wracked in mid-century by civil war, and social tensions took a brutal toll on the Jewish communities of Spain during the pogroms of 1391. A new dynasty gained power in Portugal, and began to look across to Africa for expansion. In 1415 the Portuguese captured Ceuta.

SCANDINAVIA AND EASTERN EUROPE

In eastern Europe, the century saw the emergence of large, well-endowed states that escaped many of the economic difficulties afflicting western Europe. Hungary at its peak dominated an area between the Adriatic (acquiring Dalmatia from Venice in 1352) and Poland, though an attempt to gain permanent control of the Polish crown failed. Lithuania had possessions from the Black Sea almost to the Baltic, and the marriage of its newly baptized duke, Jagiello, to the Polish heiress in 1386 extended its territories still further. In Bohemia, religious dissent flourished by 1400 among the Hussites of Prague, a city that hugely benefited from the rule of Emperor Charles IV (*d.*1378), who endowed it with a great university. In Denmark, Norway and Sweden, Margaret of Norway acquired loose control of all three kingdoms by the Union of Kalmar in 1397. Yet they were not permanently united and the supremacy of the aristocracy persisted.

Amid these rivalries, a sense of national identity, generally built more around language than race, was emerging in areas such as Catalonia, Bohemia and England. Frontiers between states were being drawn, some of which lasted into the 20th century.

c. 1300 TO 1535

SOUTH AMERICA ON THE EVE OF EUROPEAN CONQUEST

In 1492 the great diversity of physical environments in South America – which ranged from snow-capped mountains in the Andes, to tropical forest in the east, and desert on the Pacific coast – were home to an equally diverse range of human societies, which encompassed all forms of social organization that had arisen in the course of human history.

Europeans began exploring south from Panama in the late 1520s, but their first contacts with the Incas, who were still extending their empire, did not occur until the early 1530s. The size and sophistication of the Inca empire attracted most Spanish attention, but there were also important chiefdoms in Colombia, Venezuela and Bolivia. Tribal groups dominated most of Amazonia, but even here some societies were becoming larger and more complex. Hunter-gatherers continued to inhabit cold and arid lands to the south.

THE INCAS

The Inca empire was very different from that of the Aztecs, partly because of its Andean location. However, it was similarly an empire of conquest, and its expansion often met fierce resistance. It has been estimated that in Ecuador perhaps 100,000 people were killed in wars resisting the Incas. Once the Incas had established political control they began to set up an administrative structure that aimed to integrate the empire. To this end they built a road system, more than 20,000km (12,500 miles) in length. They also imposed a common language, Quechua, which is still spoken by large numbers of Indians in the Andes today, and a common religion, which involved the worship of the sun god, Inti, of whom the emperor was regarded an earthly manifestation.

The Incas developed many techniques for enhancing agricultural production, including terracing, irrigation to channel snow-melt from the high Andes, and raised or sunken fields. To straddle such diverse environments the Incas developed a means of internal exchange between peoples living in different zones, so that unlike the Aztecs they needed few markets. The Incas also attempted to maximize production, or increase security, by relocating large populations. In the early 16th century, the Inca ruler Huayna Capac was said to have resettled some 14,000 people in Cochabamba, moving them from areas as far apart as Cuzco and what is now northern Chile. The Incas also developed a system of storehousing; the storehouses were useful in times of food shortage, but they were used primarily to support bureaucratic and religious elites.

Although different in character, the Inca empire revealed some of the structural weaknesses of the Aztec. While the tally of human sacrifice was less extravagant, religion still strained resources as a result of the vast households maintained for the cults of dead rulers. The costs this involved may have contributed to divisions among the elite, which developed into the devastating civil war raging at the time of the Spanish conquest. Also, some subject peoples, particularly in outlying regions, found the burden of Inca rule so oppressive that they were willing to collaborate with the invader. However, in general, the Incas succeeded in creating an empire that was integrated to the extent that resistance to Spanish conquest was greater in the Andes than in Mexico, and the last Inca ruler, Tupac Amaru, was not defeated until 1572.

AMAZONIA

In 1492 most Amazonians practised shifting cultivation combined with hunting, fishing and gathering along the banks of the large rivers, notably the Amazon itself. However, there is evidence for the emergence of chiefdoms, notably the Tapajós chiefdom at Santarem, whose domain may have covered 25,000 square km (9,500 square miles). Although they had a warlike reputation, the Tapajós were also engaged in more domestic pursuits, producing many items for trade, and in their religion, which involved the worship of idols stored in sacred structures.

c. 1300 TO 1520

MESOAMERICA AND THE CARIBBEAN ON THE EVE OF EUROPEAN CONQUEST

When Europeans arrived in Mesoamerica they often failed to recognize the profound diversity of societies that existed there and the people's resourcefulness in dealing with their natural environment. Instead they regarded them as technologically backward and as candidates for civilization and conversion to the Catholic faith.

In 1492, when Columbus set sail on his historic voyage, the continent he would open to European conquest was already peopled by highly developed societies. In Mesoamerica the Aztec empire had spread its influence throughout much of Mexico and south into Central America. In northern Mexico many other groups still obtained their food by hunting and gathering, while in Panama and on the island of Haiti chiefdoms had emerged.

THE AZTEC

The origins of the Aztec empire, which dominated the Valley of Mexico at the time of European discovery, are shrouded in myth. It probably began near the beginning of the 14th century with nomads settling among the agrarian states of the Lake Texcoco area. Through military conquest or alliance, their lake-bound city of Tenochtitlán slowly achieved dominance over neighbouring communities. In around 1500, Aztec armies extended the sway of their system of tribute-exaction as far as the Pánuco river in the north and Soconusco province in the south. Borne by trade, their influence reached across the northern deserts into southwest North America, over the Caribbean to the Taino of Haiti (who adopted their ritual ball games with stone courts), and to the east past Xicalango (where the remotest Aztec garrison was stationed) into Yucatán.

The population of Tenochtitlán probably exceeded 150,000 – much greater than any European city at the time. To help meet the needs of such large numbers, the Aztecs developed an elaborate system of drained fields called *chinampas* on which they grew maize and beans, and exploited fish and waterfowl. However, although agriculture was highly productive, the city could not be supported entirely locally, so huge quantities of food, clothing and ritual goods had to be levied and transported from far afield. A surviving tribute-roll (which may itself be incomplete) lists over 225,000 bushels of maize and 123,400 cotton mantles, with corresponding quantities of beans, herbs, such as sage and purslane, as well as chillies, cacao, lime, salt, incense and other precious exotica due every year. Other Aztec cities had comparable rates of consumption. The daily market of Tlatelolco, Tenochtitlán's neighbour, was said to be regularly patronized by 50,000 people.

The Aztec empire was prodigious in other fields. Its material culture featured monumental stone building, vital sculpture, sumptuous goldwork and extravagant featherwork, all requiring intensive labour and expensive raw materials. Its religion exacted a fearful toll in human sacrifices. According to the varying estimates of European colonial sources, between 10,000 and 80,000 sacrifices were offered at the dedication of the main temple of Tenochtitlán in 1487, most of them acquired through capture in war or ritual exchange of victims with other communities. Human sacrifices were required to give strength to the warrior god, Huitzilopochtli, the empire's patron. The voracious appetites of the Aztec system, while forcing its beneficiaries to be skilled in war, also made it vulnerable to a concerted withdrawal of tribute by suppliers. Isolated by the diplomacy of the Spanish invaders after 1519, the Aztec capital was starved into surrender.

THE MAYA

Following the decline of the Toltec-Maya, a new Maya-dominated state emerged at Mayapán in northern Yucatán. There its Cocom rulers kept the lords of tributary provinces as virtual prisoners to ensure the payment of tribute, but in 1441 they rebelled and destroyed the city. Subsequently the lowland Maya dissolved into 16 rival states, whose merchants managed a coastal trade in salt, cotton, cloth, cacao, honey, jade, feathers, obsidian and copper.

OUTSIDE THE MESOAMERICAN HEARTLAND

Hunters and gatherers continued to dominate the vast dry lands of northern Mexico, but further south changes were occurring. Mesoamerican influences spread into Central America through trade and through the migration of the Central Mexican peoples called the Pipil and Nicarao. In 1492 much of Central America was inhabited by militaristic chiefdoms. In Nicaragua the population was supported by the rich volcanic soils found on the Pacific coast. To the east and south the main cultural influences were from South America rather than Mesoamerica. Here many tribal societies continued to practise shifting cultivation, but militaristic chiefdoms, such as the Guaymí and Cuna, had emerged in southern Costa Rica and Panama. They were renowned for their manufacture of pottery, jade, copper and gold, the abundance of which led the Spanish to give these regions names such as "rich land" (Costa Rica).

THE CARIBBEAN

At the time of Spanish conquest the Taino were also organized into a complex series of chiefdoms that might encompass as many as 100 villages and tens of thousands of people. Stone-lined ball courts and ceremonial plazas were constructed, and there was a flourishing of art styles in pottery, woodcarving and stonework. Meanwhile the Lesser Antilles had been occupied by Island Caribs who had migrated there, probably from the Guianas.

1450 TO *c.* 1600
THE RENAISSANCE AND EARLY MODERN STATE IN EUROPE

Increasing knowledge of the classical past and a desire to return to the Greek and Roman roots of European civilization stimulated the movement known as the Renaissance, which, beginning in Italy, spread rapidly around Europe after the invention of printing. This awakening of interest in its classical past was to affect Europe's politics profoundly.

The Renaissance saw a flowering of literature and the arts across Europe. Writers and artists, seeking to emulate the cultures of Greece and Rome, developed new techniques and formulated new ideas in their attempts to apply the knowledge of the Ancients to the very different world of the 16th century. Important scientific and technological advances were made. At the same time, increased exploitation of the invention of printing promoted the emergence of literate secular elites and created a new political environment as secular rulers used artists to display their power visually and written propaganda to appeal directly to their most important subjects.

STATE CONSOLIDATION

Such incipient secularization of political life enabled monarchs to challenge the power of the Church: in concordats with the Holy Roman Emperor (1448), France (1516) and Spain (1523), the Papacy was forced to concede far-reaching rights over the national churches, while in a number of Protestant countries the ruler openly assumed control of spiritual affairs.

These changes aided the internal consolidation of states across Europe after 1450, now recovering from the economic and demographic ravages of the 14th century (*see* p. 138), when so many apparently powerful states had proved ephemeral. The strengthening of the principle of male primogeniture, under which only the eldest son inherited his father's property, thus keeping estates intact, ensured that states could be consolidated more effectively as well as stimulating desires to recover lost territories. Such "reunifications" brought conflict across Europe, since there were inevitably rival claims to be considered and rulers now enjoyed an enhanced capacity to wage war. This was in part the result of increasing economic prosperity and demographic recovery after 1450. By increasing the tax base of all European states, rulers gained greater access to credit, which enabled them to afford the new military technologies made possible by the development of gunpowder. Large artillery trains destroyed the castles of over-mighty subjects, most of whom were usually in no position to compete financially, while only states could afford the new large, infantry-based armies and elaborate fortifications.

The result was a series of large-scale dynastic and territorial wars. In the east, Muscovy, the Ottoman empire and Poland-Lithuania struggled for control; in the west, Burgundy, the rising star of the 15th century, was partitioned after Charles the Bold was killed in 1477, while in 1453 the English were expelled from France (except Calais). In Spain, Castile and Aragon were united in 1479 and in 1492 consolidated their rule of Spain when their combined forces completed the conquest of the Muslim kingdom of Granada. In England, though defeat by France in the Hundred Years' War had provoked civil war ("the Wars of the Roses"), after 1485 the new Tudor dynasty restored order and extended royal control in the turbulent north and west. In Germany, a series of dynastic alliances united the Habsburg lands with those of Luxembourg and Burgundy (in 1477). All these possessions, and later those of the Spanish crown, came to Emperor Charles V (1519–56), making him the greatest Christian ruler since Charlemagne.

THE MODERN STATE

Yet royal dynasticism did not triumph unchecked. Growing interest in the classical past sparked debate about the nature of legitimate authority. Where monarchs sought to justify their claims to absolute power by reference to Roman law and the Roman empire, their opponents sought counter-arguments from the classical past, citing Rome's republican traditions and arguing for a balanced constitution. While most Italian city-republics succumbed to princely power, the republican tradition triumphed to a greater or lesser degree in the northern Netherlands, Poland-Lithuania and in parts of the Holy Roman Empire. This clash of values stimulated the gradual emergence of recognizably modern secular states, in which politics were divorced from religion and organized around an impersonal, centralized and unifying system of government, whether monarchical or republican.

FIVE

THE WORLD
OF THE
EMERGING WEST

The Indian historian K. M. Panikkar described the period from 1498 to 1947, from Vasco da Gama's discovery of the sea route to India to Indian independence, as the European age in history. Others have pointed out the element of exaggeration in this definition: if, in 1750, the Europeans had abandoned their isolated settlements on the coasts of Asia and Africa, they would have left few traces. Nevertheless, around 1500 the balance, which hitherto had weighed on the side of Asia, began to change, and after 1750 that change was momentous.

Before 1500 civilization had been essentially land-centred, and contacts by sea relatively unimportant. If the year 1500 marks a new period in world history it is because thereafter direct sea contact linked the continents. This resulted not only in the integration in a global system of regions which hitherto had developed in isolation, but in a challenge to the age-old, land-centred balance between the Eurasian civilizations.

Nonetheless, the impact of European expansion should not be exaggerated. The 16th century saw a remarkable resurgence of Muslim power in the Ottoman empire, Safavid Persia and Mughal India. China, meanwhile, remained the world's most advanced state. Indeed to many in 18th-century Europe, Turkey and China were the exemplars of civilized living. The industrial revolution put Europe ahead; but the fruits of that process – some of them poisonous – were only garnered in the 19th century. Europe between 1500 and 1815, for all its thrusting novelty, was still an agricultural society of lords and peasants, closer to its agrarian past than to its industrial future.

c. 1500

THE WORLD ON THE EVE OF EUROPEAN EXPANSION

The central feature of world history between 1500 and 1815 was the expansion of Europe and the gradual spread of European civilization throughout the globe. Until 1500 the world had, on the whole, pressed in on Europe. After 1500, Europe increasingly pressed out on the world. By 1775 a new global balance was in existence.

In the early 16th century, Europe – introspective, uncertain and technologically immature – still stood on the periphery of the civilized world, overshadowed by the Ming empire in China, the most powerful and advanced state of the period, and by the rising Ottoman and Safavid empires of the Middle

East. Both in wealth and population, China, with more than 100 million people (more than the whole of Europe), loomed far ahead. Islam, meanwhile, was still actively making converts in central and southeast Asia and among the peoples of sub-Saharan Africa.

The area occupied by the major civilizations, roughly equivalent to the area under plough cultivation, was still relatively small in 1500. Over three-quarters of the world's surface was inhabited either by food gatherers or herdsmen – as in Australia and most of Siberia, North America and Africa – or by hand cultivators, especially in southeast Asia, parts of Africa and central and South America. But the plough cultivators were more productive and it is probable that between two-thirds and three-quarters of the world's population was concentrated in the relatively small area which was being farmed by the plough.

This concentration of people and wealth closely matches the location of the major Eurasian civilizations. The comparative fragility of the Aztec and Inca civilizations in the Americas and of the African kingdoms immediately south of the Sahara, all of them highly developed in many respects, may be partly explained first by their geographic isolation and lack of external stimulus and second by their dependence on hand cultivation. After 1500, when the expansion of Europe brought all continents into direct contact with each other for the first time, these non-Eurasian civilizations sometimes found themselves unable to put up more than feeble resistance to outside aggression.

THE TEMPO OF CHANGE

It is nevertheless important not to exaggerate the tempo of change. Although in America the Aztec and Inca empires were destroyed by 1521 and 1535 respectively, elsewhere the political impact of Europe was extremely limited before the second half of the 18th century. China and Japan remained intact, and in India the Europeans were kept at arm's length for 250 years following the arrival of Vasco da Gama in 1498. There, as in west Africa and southeast Asia, the European presence was largely confined to isolated coastal trading stations. The cultural influence of Europe was even more negligible: Christianity, for example, made little headway except where it was imposed by force in the Philippines and the Americas until it was backed by the resources of western industrial technology in the mid- to late 19th century.

THE GLOBAL IMPACT

On the other hand, the European discoveries opened the way to a global redistribution of resources: migrations of peoples, diffusions of animals and plants, release of mineral wealth, expansion of cultivation and re-alignment of trade. The spread of food plants – almost all domesticated by prehistoric man in various parts of the world – had proceeded slowly until 1500. Thereafter, they became common to every continent. In addition, the American Indians pioneered two major cash crops: tobacco and cotton (derived largely in its commercial form from varieties they had domesticated, though other species were known and used in the Orient before 1500). Cane sugar, introduced by Europeans into Brazil and the West Indies from the late 16th century, also quickly became a staple of foreign trade.

This interchange of plants produced an enormous surge in food supplies, which made possible the unprecedented population growth after 1500. It also initiated a corresponding increase in intercontinental trade. Before 1500, this trade was limited to Eurasia and Africa and involved mostly luxury goods. After 1500, the combination of regional economic specialization and improved sea transport made possible the gradual transformation of the limited medieval luxury trade into the modern mass trade of new bulky necessities – hence the flourishing "triangular trade" of rum, cloths, guns and other metal products from Europe to Africa, slaves from Africa to the New World and sugar, tobacco and bullion from the New World to Europe.

It was not until the 19th century, with the opening of the Suez and Panama canals and the construction of transcontinental railways in Canada, the United States, Siberia and Africa, that areas and lines of commerce which had previously been separate finally blended into a single economy on a world scale (*see* p. 263). But the first stages of global integration were completed in just over two centuries beginning in 1500.

1487 TO 1780
EUROPEAN VOYAGES OF DISCOVERY

Between 1480 and 1780, European explorers discovered and mapped almost all of the world's seas and the outlines of almost all the continents. Impelled by a variety of motives – trade, personal enrichment, glory and, by the 18th century, scientific knowledge – their legacy is today's world map, a common resource of all mankind.

In 1480 the principal seafaring peoples of the world were separated not only by great expanses of uncharted sea but by continental landmasses whose extent and shape were unknown. Regular European shipping was still mainly confined to the north Atlantic, the Mediterranean and the Baltic. The west African coast had been explored cursorily and only very recently by Europeans, while the coast from Gaboon to Mozambique was unknown to any regular long-range shipping. In the Americas, limited raft and canoe-borne sailing took place on the Pacific coasts of Ecuador and Peru and in the Caribbean, but there was no communication with Europe nor, so far as is known, with other parts of the Pacific.

In the east, several seafaring peoples overlapped. Indian, Persian and Arab ships plied the northern Indian Ocean. Chinese shipping, which in the past had sailed intermittently to east Africa, by 1480 usually went no farther than Malacca, sharing the shallow seas of the Malay archipelago with local shipping, chiefly Javanese. To the east, it went no farther than the Philippines. No shipping used the southern Indian Ocean: Javanese contacts with Madagascar had long ceased. The great expanses of the central Pacific were crossed only occasionally and perilously by Polynesian canoes. In the north Pacific, except in Japanese and Korean coastal waters, there were no ships at all.

THE SPANISH AND PORTUGUESE
The European voyages of discovery began early in the 15th century when Portuguese navigators advanced southward, round the west coast of Africa, in search of gold, slaves and spices, until in 1487 Dias and de Covilha brought them into the Indian Ocean. Thenceforth voyages of exploration multiplied,

particularly after the resurgence of Islam made the old route to the east via Alexandria and the Red Sea precarious.

While the Spanish sailed west, the Portuguese explored the eastern route to Asia. Once in the Indian Ocean they quickly reached their goal: Malabar (1498), Malacca (1509) and the Moluccas (1512). The Spanish search for a western route to the Spice Islands was less successful but its unintended and momentous result was Columbus's discovery of the New World in 1492 followed by the Spanish conquest of the Americas (*see* p. 159). But it was not until after 1524, when Verazzano traced the coastline of North America as far north as Nova Scotia, that the existence of the new continent was generally accepted.

Meanwhile the search for a western route to Asia continued, leading to extensive exploration of the Caribbean. Finally, in 1521 Magellan rounded South America, entered the Pacific and reached the Philippines, but his route would prove too long and too hazardous for commercial purposes. In 1557 the Portuguese occupied Macao and after 1571 Spanish galleons traded between Manila and Acapulco in Mexico. The combined effect of these Spanish and Portuguese voyages had been to show that all the oceans of the southern hemisphere were connected. At the same time, for about a century Spain and Portugal were able to prevent other Europeans from using these connecting sea passages, other than for occasional raids.

THE FRENCH, BRITISH AND DUTCH

As a result, the exploration of the Pacific was delayed until the 18th century. In part at least it was inspired as much by scientific curiosity as by hope of commercial gain. It was the work of British, Dutch and Russians seeking a navigable passage via the Arctic between the Atlantic and the Pacific and hoping also to locate a hypothetical southern continent. Both proved illusory but the result was the charting of New Zealand and the eastern coast of Australia, both opened in a few years to European colonization.

Meanwhile, England and France, unwilling to recognize the monopoly claimed by Spain and Portugal in the Treaty of Tordesillas of 1494, had embarked on a series of voyages intended to reach Asia by a northern route. All these proved abortive and were abandoned after 1632, but they resulted in the opening of North America to European settlement. The English, French and Dutch were also unwilling to abandon the profitable trade with south and southeast Asia to the Portuguese and Spaniards and the later years of the 16th and first half of the 17th centuries saw a determined and ultimately successful effort to breach their privileged position (*see* p. 178).

After 1500 direct sea contact was established between continents and regions which hitherto had developed in isolation. It was necessarily a slow process and for a long time the European footholds in Asia and Africa remained tenuous. But by the time of the death of the last great explorer, James Cook in 1779, few of the world's coastlines remained to be explored.

1500 TO 1700

EXPANSION OF THE TRADING EMPIRES

Portuguese 16th-century traders established Europe's trading links with Africa, India, the Malay archipelago, China and Japan and dominated the African trade in gold and slaves. But by the 17th century growing Dutch, British and French competition was challenging both Portugal's position and Spain's dominance in the West Indies.

The discoveries by European explorers in the late 15th century were rapidly exploited. By 1500, Portuguese possessions outside Europe included several island groups in the Atlantic and the Gulf of Guinea, and a number of trading stations on the west coast of Africa – above all the fortress-factory of Elmina. A dozen or so ships made the voyage between Portugal and Guinea every year, bartering hardware and cloth for slaves and gold dust.

After the sea route to India was discovered, the Portuguese attempted to become the main suppliers of spices to Europe by capturing or leasing trading posts and fortified bases on the east coast of Africa, around the north shores of the Indian Ocean and in the Malay archipelago. By the mid-16th century, they had a tenuous string of more than 50 forts and factories. Strategically, the most important were Mozambique (1507), Goa (1510), Ormuz (1515) and Malacca (1511). East of Malacca, the Portuguese position was precarious and their activity completely commercial. In 1557, with the agreement of the Chinese, they established a base at Macao. From there, they traded to Nagasaki, where they were welcomed as carriers of Chinese goods, since the Chinese themselves were forbidden to trade with Japan. At Ternate, they maintained a warehouse until 1575, when they were expelled by a league of Muslim princes.

PORTUGAL'S TRADING EMPIRE

All these Far Eastern enterprises, together with the gold of the Zambezi basin, exported through Sofala, paid for the pepper and other spices shipped annually from Goa to Lisbon for distribution to western Europe. Though the Portuguese never achieved anything like a monopoly, their power was sufficient to channel much of the Indian Ocean trade through harbours under their control, and for 100 years they had no real European rivals. Only the Spanish, whose main interest lay in the Americas, showed a parallel interest in the Far East (see p. 159).

Once the Portuguese had started to settle Brazil in the 1530s, the Brazilian demand for slave labour breathed new life into the Portuguese trading stations in west Africa, where the gold trade had dwindled as the gold became exhausted and caused traders to extend their operations from Guinea south to Angola. The Portuguese slave depot of Luanda was founded in 1575 and slave ships shuttled directly between Angola and Brazil, with the slaves paid for by Brazilian tobacco.

DUTCH EXPANSION

From the opening years of the 17th century, the Portuguese in the East began to experience significant competition from other European countries. This usually organized itself in the form of joint stock companies, empowered to trade, settle, conquer, administer and defend. The most formidable, at least to begin with, was the Dutch East India Company, formally incorporated in 1602. In 1619, this vast concern, the biggest trading corporation in Europe, established its eastern headquarters at Batavia, well to the south (and east) of Goa and Malacca, thus acquiring a permanent strategic advantage. Its ships pioneered a direct route to Batavia, provisioning (after 1652) at the new Dutch settlement at the Cape of Good Hope, then running east before the "roaring forties" and entering the archipelago by the Sunda Strait. By acquiring bases in strategic locations, by bringing pressure on local rulers and by squeezing other Europeans out, it established a monopoly of the more valuable trades of the archipelago.

Elsewhere in the East it traded in competition with native and European merchants on terms dictated by local rulers, though throughout the 17th century it held its own against all European rivals.

EUROPEAN RIVALRIES

The English East India Company, incorporated in 1600, was a rather smaller concern and usually proved unable to resist Dutch pressure in the archipelago. It engaged principally in trade in cotton goods and pepper from India, first at the Mughal port of Surat, later at stations of its own at Madras, Bombay and Calcutta. In 1685 it began a modest trade with China, purchasing tea and porcelain at Amoy and later at Canton, where from 1698 its agents found themselves in direct competition with the French Compagnie de Chine.

As a result of the commercial competition and naval aggression of these corporations (which continued irrespective of whether there was formal war or peace in Europe), the Portuguese Estado de India shrank both in territorial extent and in commercial profit. The Red Sea and the Persian Gulf both became commercial backwaters as the joint-stock companies carried more and more of the trade between Europe and Asia in their own capacious and well-armed ships. Meanwhile, the Dutch West India Company – less well entrenched than its eastern counterpart, but formidable nonetheless – conquered the Brazilian coastal region of Pernambuco in 1630 and over the next few years seized the Portuguese slaving stations in west Africa, without which the Brazilian plantation system appeared unworkable. But in the 1640s, with the end of the long period of union (1580–1640) of the Spanish and Portuguese crowns, the Portuguese recovered the Angola slave-pens and in 1654 drove the Dutch from Brazil. The West India Company now turned its attention to the Caribbean.

1462 TO 1815
RUSSIAN EXPANSION IN EUROPE AND ASIA

The Grand Duchy of Muscovy emerged in the late 15th century as a powerful state with claims to the legacy of Kievan Rus. Though it spread rapidly east and south, expansion in the west was blocked by Lithuania, which included many of the lands of Kievan Rus. Only after 1648 did Muscovy prevail, laying the foundations of the Russian empire.

The ebbing of Mongol power and the collapse of the Byzantine empire opened the way for the emergence of Muscovy as a European power. Proclaiming Muscovy's independence from the Mongols in 1480, Ivan III (1462–1505) laid claim to the heritage of Kievan Rus and, by marrying the daughter of the last Byzantine emperor and adopting the double-headed eagle as his emblem, to that of Byzantium. The last independent Orthodox state after 1453, Muscovy proclaimed itself the leader of the Orthodox world, with Moscow raised to a metropolitanate in 1448 and a patriarchate in 1589.

Muscovy's growing power was manifested in the ruthless annexations of Novgorod (1478) and Pskov (1510) and the seizure of Smolensk from Lithuania (1514). The conquest of the khanates of Kazan (1552) and Astrakhan (1556) conferred control of the Volga and opened the way to the east and the south. Expansion was not so easy to the west, where the tsars' claim to rule "all the Russias" was challenged by the grand dukes of Lithuania, most of whose subjects were eastern Slavs with elites increasingly attracted by the participative political system of Poland. The 1569 Union of Lublin between Poland and Lithuania, which saw the direct incorporation of Lithuania's Ukrainian territories into the kingdom of Poland, led to the creation of a sophisticated noble democracy with a common *diet* (parliament) and an elective monarchy that was in stark contrast to the centralized Muscovite autocracy.

Between 1558 and 1634, Poland-Lithuania repulsed all Muscovite attempts to expand westwards. Ivan IV's attempts to take Livonia were beaten off, Sigismund III regained Smolensk and Chernigov at the Treaty of Deulino (1618/19), while during the "Time of Troubles" (1605–13), Sigismund's son Wæadysæaw was elected tsar by a group of boyars, and a Polish garrison occupied the Kremlin (1610–12). A Muscovite attempt to retake Smolensk in 1632–4 was repulsed decisively.

GROWTH OF EMPIRE

The turning-point came during the Thirteen Years' War (1654–67). At the 1654 Treaty of Pereyaslav, Tsar Alexis Mikhailovich (1645–76) extended Muscovy's protection to the Zaporozhian Cossacks, who had rebelled against Poland in 1648. Although Alexis failed to hold on to the large areas of Lithuania annexed in

1654–5, the 1667 Treaty of Andrusovo granted Muscovy those areas of the Ukraine on the left bank of the Dnieper and, albeit only for three years, Kiev, though in 1686 the Poles were forced to recognize its permanent loss. The capture of Kiev and left-bank Ukraine made good part of the tsars' claim to rule all the Russias; the Ukraine was dubbed "Little Russia" in contrast to "Great Russia", the empire's Muscovite heartland. Muscovy had become Russia.

As Poland-Lithuania weakened, Russian expansion continued. The military improvements under Alexis were completed by his son, Peter I (the Great), who captured Azov from the Ottomans before turning his attention northwards. In a long war, marked by his great victory at Poltava in 1709, Peter finally wrested Estonia and Livonia from Sweden at the Treaty of Nystad (1721), acquired the ancient port of Riga and founded the new one of St Petersburg.

His successors reverted to the policy of expansion in the south, which was carried to a successful conclusion by Catherine II (the Great) in her first (1768–74) and second (1787–92) Turkish wars. The Crimea was annexed, and Russia now controlled the northern shore of the Black Sea from the Dniester to the Caucasus. The period from 1772 to 1815 then saw the Russian land frontier advanced by 965km (600 miles) at the expense of Poland. By the partitions of 1772, 1793 and 1795 (*see* p. 202), Russia obtained much of the former Polish-Lithuanian Commonwealth, in the process acquiring a further 5.5 million inhabitants. Indeed throughout the period as a whole the population of Russia expanded dramatically from an estimated 10 million in 1600 to nearly 43 million in 1812.

1500 TO 1810

NORTH AMERICA

While the Spanish and the Portuguese had established large and lucrative empires in the south of the Americas, their northerly European neighbours focused on the lands to the north. John Cabot, commissioned by the English king Henry VII, made the first documented voyage to North America (since the Vikings) in 1497.

After John Cabot's voyage, fishing vessels from England, France, Portugal and the Basque country soon travelled in large numbers to the rich cod grounds off Newfoundland and Nova Scotia. However, these fishing voyages led to relatively little interest in the continent and did not result in settlement. French imperial interest in North America began with Jacques Cartier's voyages in the 1530s. However, unlike Spanish and Portuguese colonization to the south, French and English attempts to colonize the north in the early 16th century failed. Jamestown, Virginia (1607), Quebec (1608), the Mayflower communities of Massachusetts Bay (1620), and New Amsterdam (1626) represented the first successes in establishing European colonies in North America. Beset by many difficulties, these colonies grew slowly and often at the sufferance of surrounding aboriginal groups. Swedish and Scottish attempts at colonization remained small-scale. The more significant Dutch settlement in New Amsterdam (New York) was taken over by the English in 1664. Tobacco, grains and furs proved valuable commodities for export to the mother countries.

The European arrivals brought new military dangers as well as opportunities for the aboriginal peoples. While some groups were exterminated by the Europeans (in the Massachusetts area, for instance), other groups (such as the Iroquois of the Great Lakes region) were able to play one group of foreigners off against another and to expand their areas of influence. North American aboriginal peoples maintained a strong military role – as valued allies or feared opponents – at least until the War of 1812; and some groups, such as the Comanches, continued to resist the incursions of foreigners into their territories until late in the century.

Spain, too, made its presence felt in what is now considered North America – in Florida, Texas, New Mexico, and later Louisiana. Settlers in the British colonies tended to be from minority religions or religious sects, while in the French and Spanish colonies non-orthodox Catholics were strongly discouraged from settling. Relatively few French settlers made their way across the Atlantic, and the majority of these returned home. Nonetheless, given the high birth rate – made possible by living conditions that were better than in the mother country – the population of New France grew dramatically. It did likewise in the British colonies to the south, where a stronger stream of immigrants boosted the population from generation to generation. At the time of the American Revolution, some 2.5 million people lived in the colonies which rebelled against British rule.

In the interior of the continent, more varied communities developed. These combined aboriginal and European bloodlines and cultures. Métis (mixed blood) communities became vitally important to the success of the fur trade, which led the French down the Great Lakes and Ohio and Mississippi systems. However, while diversity reigned in the 18th century, these communities could do little to resist the expansion of American settlement in the 19th century.

POLITICAL HOSTILITY AND MILITARY THREAT

Despite its small size, the French contingent, with its aboriginal allies, represented an ongoing military threat to the English colonies. In 1713, the Treaty of Utrecht ceded peninsular Nova Scotia to the British, and withdrew French claims to Newfoundland and the Hudson Bay fur-trading posts. With the War of the Austrian Succession (1743–48) and the French and Indian War (1754–60), also known as the Seven Years' War, the battle between British and French interests came to a head. At the battle of the Plains of Abraham, the French were defeated and Britain temporarily unified the eastern half of the continent under its rule.

The costs of this war – and the English government's desire to exact some payment from the American colonists who had ostensibly benefited from the removal of the French threat – contributed to the outbreak of hostilities between Britain and the colonies in the American War of Independence (1775–83). The war's end saw the forced removal of thousands of erstwhile loyalists, many of whom moved to remaining British colonies to the north.

1500 TO 1825

LATIN AMERICA AND THE CARIBBEAN

Within 40 years of Columbus's discovery of America, the Spanish had overturned the rich empires of the Aztec and the Inca. For over a century longer, the Spanish and the Portuguese dominated the "New World", but in the 17th century the French, English and Dutch began to establish footholds in the Caribbean islands and the Guianas. New colonial societies were emerging, however, which sought to cast off European control.

By 1500, in the wake of Columbus's voyages, around 6,000 Spaniards had already immigrated to the New World. For over a century the Spanish were to dominate the settlement of the Americas. The pace of colonization accelerated enormously after the discovery and conquest of two fabulously rich empires: the Aztec in Mesoamerica and the Inca in the Andean region. Relatively small Spanish forces were able to conquer these societies fairly easily by exploiting existing divisions within them; they were further assisted by the native people's heavy population losses brought about by the introduction of Old World diseases. The Spanish set up a vast bureaucratic system to administer the new colony, and they established many towns, very often on the sites of pre-existing Indian settlements. Mexico and Peru had rich deposits of gold and silver, so they became the main focuses of Spanish settlement in the New World. Few exports could compete with silver, but some sugar, cacao, indigo and cochineal were also shipped to Spain. As a result of conquest, disease and ill treatment, the Indian population fell by about 90 per cent within the first 150 years of European arrival.

THE PORTUGUESE

By the Treaty of Tordesillas in 1494 the Spanish and Portuguese had established a line of demarcation between them in the New World, with the Portuguese allocated the territories east of the line. However, in the early years the Portuguese traded only on the coast of Brazil for dyewoods, and it was not until 1549 that their administrative capital was established at Bahia (today Salvador). In the absence of a large native workforce, African slaves had to be imported to work the sugar plantations. In the 1690s gold was discovered in the Minas Gerais – meaning General Mines in Portuguese – and this provoked massive immigration from Portugal and led to the growing importance of Rio de Janeiro.

BEYOND THE FRONTIERS

Few Europeans ventured outside the main centres of settlement and commercial activity, where the Indian populations were smaller and the opportunities for wealth creation fewer. However, both nations were obliged by papal bulls to convert the indigenous people to Catholicism. They therefore supported the activities of the missionary orders, notably the Jesuits and Franciscans, who through their establishment of missions gradually pushed back the frontier of settlement.

At the same time the French, Dutch and English tried to challenge Spanish and Portuguese power. At first they did this by sponsoring pirates, but later they began promoting settlement in areas where Spanish and Portuguese control was weak, notably in the Caribbean islands and the Guianas, from where they attempted to undermine them economically through contraband trade.

MOVES FOR INDEPENDENCE

Conditioned by the new environment, the mix of traditions brought by the various settlers and the indigenous peoples they encountered, the societies that emerged in the New World were very different from those that the first settlers had left behind in Europe. During the second half of the 18th century, there were increasing moves to gain independence from Spain, with Mexico achieving independence in 1821 and most other countries, apart from Cuba and Puerto Rico, by 1825. Brazil had to wait until 1889 for political independence, although in 1822, when the Portuguese court returned to Europe following the defeat of Napoleon, it acquired considerable economic independence.

1500 TO 1800

TRADE AND EMPIRE IN AFRICA

From 1500 to 1800 African history was dominated by three main processes: the expansion of large political units; the spread of Islam; and the increasing involvement of Europeans. By 1800 Africans had made great progress in evolving distinctive social and political forms, but their independence was already seriously compromised.

From the late 15th century, large political units multiplied in Africa. In 1464, Sunni Ali became ruler of the Songhay people around Gao in the eastern Niger bend. Under Askia the Great (1493–1528), Songhay became a great empire, incorporating a number of important commercial cities including Timbuktu and Jenne, which developed into centres of learning and Muslim piety. In the savannah and forest country to the south, trading communities gave rise to comparable polities. Well before 1500 Oyo and Benin had emerged in the woodlands to the west of the Niger delta, producing superb terracottas and bronzes.

Elsewhere, similar processes gave rise to centralized states of iron-working agriculturists and cattle-keepers. Increased populations, diversified economies and trade promoted stronger political control. When the Portuguese arrived south of the Congo mouth in 1484, they established close relations with the Kongo kingdom. Inland and to the south were other Bantu-speaking African states including those of the Luba and Lunda, while in the fertile lands between the east African lakes a series of states evolved, notably Rwanda and Buganda.

Equally prosperous was the Zimbabwe plateau with its kingdom based initially at Great Zimbabwe, later replaced by a number of successors including the Mwenemutapa empire centred northeast of modern Harare. At its peak Great Zimbabwe was the political and religious centre of a major state with trade links extending as far as China.

THE SPREAD OF ISLAM

Between 1500 and 1800 Islam consolidated its position in the Sudanic lands, and spread southward along the east African coast. Bitter rivalry between Christian Ethiopia and Muslim coastal states in the Horn then developed: Sultan Ahmad Gran of Adal invaded the Christian highlands in the 1520s, and was only defeated by Portuguese intervention.

Meanwhile, in 1517, the Ottomans conquered the Mamluks in Egypt, and subsequently extended their control over Tripoli and Tunis; Algiers was ruled by corsair princes subject to the Ottomans. Only Morocco remained independent, governed for much of this period by Sharifian dynasties. In 1590, Morocco invaded the Songhay empire and set up a client state, disrupting economic life throughout the region. Later, in the 18th century, the politics and commerce of Muslim west Africa recovered again in a burst of Islamic proselytizing.

EUROPEANS AND THE SLAVE TRADE

Throughout the period, Europeans became more involved in Africa, seeking gold, ivory, wood and, above all, slaves to work the mines and plantations of the Americas. Although by 1800 the number of European territorial possessions was small, their domination of oceanic trade had considerable effects in many parts of Africa. In southernmost Africa, Dutch and French Huguenot settlers arrived after 1652 and subjected the Khoisan peoples, but by 1800 they encountered serious resistance from the southeastern Bantu-speakers.

Europeans established "factories" along the coast from Senegal to Angola and bought slaves from Africans. Between 1450 and 1870 some 11,500,000 slaves were exported, first to Europe and then to the Americas. The death rate probably totalled 25 per cent. Most came from west Africa, though by 1800 east Africa, which had long provided slaves to the Muslim world, was contributing to the Atlantic system. The precise effects of the slave trade are unclear. Overall, Europeans gained and Africa's development was inhibited.

1368 TO 1644
CHINA AT THE TIME OF THE MING DYNASTY

By the late 14th century a new Chinese dynasty, the Ming, had overthrown the Mongols. For 200 years it brought order and prosperity to much of China. The population more than doubled, new crops were introduced, industry flourished and trade greatly increased. By the early 17th century, corruption, external attack and crop failures conspired to weaken Ming rule and bring about its collapse.

By the late 13th century Mongol rule in China had brought a measure of stability even to the north of the country, which had endured the worst of the Mongol depredations 50 years earlier. But the death of the Mongol emperor Kublai Khan in 1294 sparked further instability as rival claimants fought for the imperial throne. By the 1340s and '50s, dynastic decline was accelerated by floods, droughts and disease. Together with increasing discontent with Mongol rule, these touched off a series of uprisings against the government. The most serious was in central and southeastern China where, in 1368, Chu Yüan-chang, the most powerful of the rebels, proclaimed a new dynasty, the Ming. By 1388, the Mongols were driven back to the steppe and the Ming controlled all China.

CONSOLIDATION
Under the Ming, stability was restored and numerous improvements to the country's agricultural base made. Throughout the period, new agricultural techniques enabled the country to feed its rapidly growing population more efficiently. New crops were introduced — some, such as yams, maize, peanuts

and potatoes, by the Portuguese and Spanish – and new areas opened up to cultivation. To facilitate the movements of products and people, the Grand Canal, which would eventually stretch 1600km (1000 miles), from Hang-chou to Peking, was built. Upwards of 20,000 barges carrying 200,000 tons of grain a year used the canal. The administration of the burgeoning Chinese state was simple and practical. Though it discouraged innovation and, being highly centralized, was dangerously dependent on the emperor, it proved effective. Control over the vast population was effected largely through the "gentry", or *shen-shih*, degree-holders who had been through the education system and shared the values of the bureaucracy without actually holding office.

Within the new stability provided by the Ming, industry boomed. The great cities of the Yangtze delta – Nanking, Su-chou, Wu-hsi, Sung-chiang and Hang-chou – developed as major industrial centres, particularly for textiles. The enormous volume of trade that flowed through them gave rise to a number of powerful groups of merchants, whose influence came to extend across the country. By the late 16th century, the economy was further stimulated by inflows of silver from the New World, which were used to pay for Chinese exports of tea, silk and ceramics.

OVERSEAS EXPANSION

Ming China, especially under the Yung-lo emperor, successor to Chu Yüan-chang, was exceptionally expansionist and aggressive. Campaigns against the Mongols in the far north, the occupation of Annam from 1407 to 1427 and a series of immense seaborne expeditions extended China's reach to new and unprecedented limits. But the return on these extravagant ventures was never enough to justify them. Following a further and abortive attack against the Mongols in 1449, which ended with the capture of the Ming emperor himself, China reverted to its traditional defensive posture. Renewed Mongol attacks coupled with a succession of political and economic demands placed the empire under increasing strain. It was made considerably worse by persistent attacks on the south coast by Japanese-based pirates and smugglers. By the 1550s, the seas around China were infested by heavily armed bands who terrorized coastal regions. Exacerbating China's difficulties, at the end of the century Japan launched a costly and destructive invasion of Korea, obliging China to send huge armies to aid their vassal.

These threats both coincided with and were partly responsible for a decline in Ming power, a process made worse by growing government corruption and a series of crop failures in the north. By 1636, much of the country was in rebellion, with the Manchus in the forefront. Though it was to be another rebel leader, Li Tzu-ch'eng, who in 1644 toppled the Ming, his regime was itself overthrown almost immediately by the new Ch'ing dynasty from Manchuria. It was to exercise its iron grip over China until 1911.

1522 TO 1800

OTTOMAN TURKEY

In the early modern period, the Ottoman sultanate dominated the Balkans, Anatolia, the Middle East and much of north Africa. Despite increasing political paralysis after the death of Suleiman the Magnificent in 1566, the Ottoman army and navy remained formidable. In the 18th century, the sultanate came under increasing threat from Russia and the Habsburg empire, but it was also a period of great cultural achievement.

In the first three decades of the 16th century the frontiers of the Ottoman empire expanded rapidly. In 1514 the defeat of the Safavids (*see* p. 168) at Çaldiran ensured that eastern Anatolia remained under Ottoman rule. In 1517 the troops of the sultan Selim the Grim took Syria and Egypt from the last of the Mamluks. Under his son, Suleiman the Magnificent (1520–66), the empire reached its height. The Ottoman janissaries were the most disciplined and formidable fighting force of the time. The administration, headed by the grand vizier, was both effective and honest. Suleiman embarked on campaigns of conquest in the Balkans, and in 1526 his victory at Mohács led to the incorporation of most of Hungary into the Ottoman empire; in 1529 he came close to taking Vienna. The supremacy of the Ottoman fleet in the Mediterranean made possible the conquest of Rhodes in 1522 and of Algiers in 1529, but they failed to take Malta from the Knights of St John after an epic siege in 1565. Naval bases were established at Suez in 1517 and Basra in 1538 to enable Ottoman ships to sail the Red Sea and the Gulf. Suleiman was also the patron of the great architect Sinan, whose buildings – notably the Suleimaniye mosque and tomb complex – still dominate the skyline of Istanbul.

THE EMPIRE UNDER PRESSURE

Although the expansion faltered after the death of Suleiman, Ottoman power remained strong. The naval defeat at Lepanto in 1571 was only a temporary setback. The sultans were able to take Cyprus in 1571, Tunis from the Habsburgs in 1574, and Crete from the Venetians in 1662. Campaigns in the east led to the conquest of Yerevan in Armenia in 1635 and the taking of Baghdad from the Persians in 1638. As late as 1683 the Ottoman army, led by the grand vizier Kara Mustafa, was able to lay siege to Vienna.

The years after the death of Suleiman saw the internal administration of the empire becoming increasingly paralysed as palace officials and the harem took over political power. The queen mother or *sultan valide* was often the most important person in the sultanate, and the army was dominated by the janissaries, which were by now an ill-disciplined rabble who resented any attempts at reform and deposed any sultan or grand vizier who threatened their privileged status. The rule of the mad sultan Ibrahim (1640–8) saw the nadir of the sultan's power, but under the Köprülü viziers (1656–76) the administration was once again established on a firm footing.

In the 18th century the empire came under increasing pressure on its European frontiers, and the Ottomans were forced to cede Hungary and Transylvania to the Habsburgs and the lands north of the Black Sea to the Russians. In the east, the collapse of the Safavids in 1722 meant that the frontier with Iran remained largely peaceful. The 18th century was also a period of cultural achievement typified by the "Tulip Age" patronized by the cultivated bibliophile Sultan Ahmet III (1703–30). Nevertheless, in 1800 the Ottoman empire was still the major power in the Middle East and southeast Europe.

1501 TO 1906

IRAN FROM THE SAFAVIDS TO THE QAJARS

The rule of the Safavid and Qajar dynasties saw the consolidation of Iran within its modern frontiers and the adoption of Shi'ite Islam as the national religion. The 18th century was a period of great disruption and violence. In the 19th century, the Qajar Shahs struggled to retain their independence from Russian and British influence. Afghanistan became an independent kingdom in the 19th century but the Uzbek Khanates were unable to resist Russian power.

In 1501 a new era in the history of Iran began with the coming to power of the Safavid Isma'il I. The Safavids came from Ardabil in Azerbaijan and their first capital was at Qazvin in northern Iran. Under Isma'il I (*d.*1524) the frontiers of Iran were consolidated. In the northeast, the lands beyond the Kopet Dag mountains, including Merv, Bukhara and Samarkand, were lost to the Uzbek Shaybani Khans and the modern frontier of Iran was established. In the west, the forces of the Safavids were defeated by the Ottomans at the battle of Çaldiran in 1514 which ensured that eastern Anatolia remained firmly in Turkish hands. It was at this time too that Shi'ite Islam became the state religion, clearly differentiating the Safavid empire from the Ottomans and the Uzbeks, both of whom were Sunnis.

The high point of Safavid power was reached under Shah Abbas I (the Great) (1588–1629) who established a new capital at Isfahan, which was expanded and endowed with a series of mosques, palaces and bridges, forming one of the glories of Persian architecture. In 1623 the Safavids took Baghdad and much of Iraq but this had to be surrendered to the Ottomans in 1639. By the early 18th century the Safavid empire was in decline and in 1722 Isfahan was sacked by the Ghilzai Afghans.

The 18th century was a period of violence and confusion in Iran. The throne was seized by a military adventurer called Nadir Shah, who invaded India and sacked Delhi in 1738–9 but was murdered in 1747. From 1750 to 1779 the main power in the land was the peaceful Karim Khan Zand, ruling from Shiraz.

In 1779 the leader of the Qajar Türkmen of northeastern Iran, Agha Muhammad Khan, established his control over most of the country and the Qajars were to rule as Shahs of Iran until 1924. In 1786 he moved the capital to Tehran which until then had been only a small village. In the period of Qajar rule, Iran came under increasing pressure from Russian influence in the north and the British in India and the Gulf, but the country retained its independence. However, they were forced to cede their claims to sovereignty in the Caucasus to the Russians at the treaty of Turkmenchay in 1828, and Herat to the Afghans in 1857. In 1906 political resistance to the absolutism of the shahs led to the granting of a constitution.

In the east, Dost Muhammad (1819–63) proclaimed himself Amir of Kabul and laid the foundations of modern Afghanistan, playing off the British and the Russians to secure the frontiers of his state. In the lands to the northeast, the Uzbek rulers established the Khanates of Bukhara, Khiva and Kokand, but they were unable to resist Russian encroachment and lost Tashkent in 1865 and Khiva in 1873. By 1900, the Qajars and the Tsarist Russians shared common frontiers in Azerbaijan and northeast Iran.

1526 TO 1803
MUGHAL INDIA AND THE GROWTH OF BRITISH POWER

Founded in the early 16th century, the Mughal empire was at its height from the 1550s to the 1650s, presiding over a golden age of religious cooperation and cultural synthesis. But in the 18th century it rapidly disintegrated, with the British emerging as the victors over the French and the Maratha Hindus in the struggle for the succession.

In the 1520s Babur, who counted both Genghis Khan and Tamerlane among his ancestors, invaded India from Afghanistan. After defeating the Lodi sultan at Panipat in 1526, he began the establishment of the Mughal empire, but died before the foundations were secure. His son, Humayun, was expelled by the Afghans of Bihar under Sher Shah and it took a full-scale invasion, brilliantly consolidated by Babur's grandson, Akbar (1556–1605), to restore Mughal rule. This now stretched from Bengal in the east and the Godavari river in the south, to Kashmir in the north and the Indus Valley in the west. Most of the Hindu Rajput princes became tributary allies, and the empire was administered by a new class of bureaucrats, the *mansabdars*, ranked in a military hierarchical system.

Akbar's reign is one of the golden ages of Indian history. A standardized tax system was introduced; there was agricultural prosperity and buoyant trade. Policies of tolerance were adopted towards the non-Muslim majority and Akbar himself took wives from Rajput families. His patronage laid the foundations for a remarkable synthesis of Persian and Indian cultural forms. He presided over the development of Mughal miniature painting, which combined the traditions of the Safavid and Rajput schools. Under his son Jahangir (1605–27), Mughal painting reached its peak. Akbar's red sandstone capital at Fatehpur Sikri expressed a striking synthesis of Islamic and Hindu traditions of architecture. The new style reached its climax under his grandson Shahjahan (1628–57), the builder of the Taj Mahal.

Akbar's political inheritance included a ceaseless thrust towards territorial expansion, especially southwards. Under Aurangzeb (1658–1707) this brought confrontation with a new Hindu power, the Marathas, a kingdom founded by Sivaji in 1674. By 1700 the Marathas were ravaging the land from the Deccan to Bengal. There was also open internal disaffection from Rajputs, Sikhs and Jats. It used to be thought that these developments were the outcome of Aurangzeb's revision of Akbar's policies of toleration. It now seems clear that they arose from weaknesses in the economic and administrative structures of the empire.

MUGHAL DECLINE

After Aurangzeb's death the empire quickly declined. The finishing stroke came from Persia when Nadir Shah's army sacked Delhi in 1739. The former Mughal provinces of Oudh, Bengal and Hyderabad now offered only nominal allegiance to Delhi. In the south the Muslim state of Mysore grew into a formidable power under Haidar Ali and his son, Tipu Sultan. Over the course of the century the Maratha chiefs spread their territories deep into north, west, central and eastern India. The Mughal emperor became no more than a Maratha protégé.

THE EAST INDIA COMPANY

Simultaneously, India was undergoing its first major invasion from the sea. By the 1760s the English East India Company, having both defeated the French and been granted control over the revenues of Bengal by the Mughal emperor, was firmly established on the Indian shore. With these resources the Company was now able to sustain an army of over 100,000 men. Through military victories over the Marathas and Mysore, it came to occupy a continuous band of territory from the Gangetic plain to India's southern coasts. In addition, by a system of subsidiary alliances, its suzerainty was recognized by many Indian rulers beyond its actual borders. In 1803 the Mughal emperor himself accepted British protection. British supremacy was now widely acknowledged.

1644 TO 1839

CHINA UNDER THE CH'ING DYNASTY

Under the Ch'ing dynasty China doubled in size and experienced a century of peaceful prosperity. But by the late 18th century economic decline brought about by rapid population growth sparked repeated revolts. The developing crisis was exacerbated by growing government inefficiency and Western economic intervention. By the 1830s China's problems demanded urgent and radical change.

The Ch'ing dynasty was founded by a non-Chinese people, the Manchus, who in the early 17th century established a Chinese-style state in Manchuria with its capital at Mukden. When the Ming were toppled by the rebel Li Tzu-ch'eng in 1644, the Manchus invaded China and proclaimed a new dynasty. Though Ming resistance continued in the south and west for several decades, notably in the rebellion of the Three Feudatories of 1674–81, from 1652 Manchu rule was effectively established. The Ch'ing brought to China more than a century of internal peace and prosperity under three rulers of great ability, the emperors K'ang-hsi (1661–1722), Yung-cheng (1722–35) and Ch'ien-lung (1736–96), who also led the expansion of the Chinese empire into central Asia until it was almost doubled in size.

The Manchus maintained their predominant place in government, and above all in the military, but also established good working relationships with their Chinese officials. Only towards the end of the 18th century, as they became more and more influenced by Chinese education and culture, did the distinctive Manchu identity begin to fade. Exploitation by Chinese and Manchu alike led to many rebellions of peoples on the periphery: in Yunnan in 1726–9, among the Chinese Muslim minority in Kansu in 1781–4, among the Yao people of Kwangsi in 1790, among the Miao people of Kweichow in 1795–7, and most notably the massive Chin-ch'uan tribal risings in western Szechwan in 1746–9 and again in 1771–6, when order was finally restored only after ruinously expensive military operations.

POPULATION GROWTH

From the end of the 18th century rebel movements began to take new forms. The background was a developing economic crisis. The area available for agriculture, which had been expanded by the introduction of maize, sweet potato, ground nuts and tobacco in the 16th and 17th centuries, was now fully used. The population, meanwhile, grew inexorably, from 100 million to 300 million between 1650 and 1800 and to 450 million by 1850. This constantly growing population had to be fed by ever-more intensive cultivation of a limited area. By the end of the 18th century, there was widespread hardship and impoverishment which in turn sparked rebellions, usually inspired by secret societies: the rebellions of the Heaven and Earth Society, 1787–8; the White Lotus, 1796–1805; and the Eight Trigrams of 1813, which was accompanied by an attempted coup in Peking. Further risings took place among border peoples.

THE CRISIS OF GOVERNMENT

The developing economic crisis was exacerbated by the strains that external expansion placed on imperial financial administration and by a sharp decline in the quality of government. Corruption became endemic at every level of administration while the government itself failed to keep up with population growth, delegating more and more power to local gentry. A further factor was the import of opium by foreign powers into China to help pay for their extensive purchases of tea, silk, porcelain and handicrafts. By the 1830s opium imports were leading to a substantial drain of silver from China with concomitant damage to the economy and state finances.

By this time Manchu China was the world's largest and most populous empire, directly controlling vast territories in inner Asia and treating as tributary states still larger areas: Korea, Indo-China, Siam, Burma, Nepal. But within this huge empire, effective Ch'ing administrative and military control was gradually declining, while inexorable economic pressures increased which could be cured only by large-scale technological innovation and radical reorganization. Neither was imminent and in the meantime China faced new pressures from the expansionist Western powers.

1392 TO 1953
KOREA

The transition from Koryŏ to Chosŏn rule in Korea was essentially smooth, as the same ruling clans retained power, although Chosŏn exchanged Buddhism for Neo-Confucianism. The Chosŏn dynasty survived a Japanese invasion of Korea in 1592, but it was ultimately Japanese imperialism which destroyed it in 1910. The harshness of Japanese rule gave rise to a liberation movement, but ideological divisions within it led to a bitter and damaging war in the 1950s and the division of the peninsula. It was only in the 1960s that economic recovery occurred and then only in the non-communist south.

The clans of the Koryŏ era (918–1392) maintained power in the transition to the Chosŏn dynasty (1392–1910), but the new dynasty broke with the past by rejecting other-worldly Buddhism and embracing Sung Neo-Confucianism as the new orthodoxy. The new dynasty brought in a "golden age" of governance. King Sejong (1418–50) commissioned agricultural and medical manuals for general welfare, expanded the world's oldest use of moveable metal type and, in 1446, promulgated a new script that he had a personal hand in producing.

Chosŏn Korea was a model Confucian state. Dress was Ming; law was Ming; government organization and recruitment were Ming; and Korea established its own international order by accepting tribute from Manchurian tribes and Japanese, while the Ming took tribute from Korea. Social ideals derived from *The Family Rites of Zhu-xi* (Chu Hsi): reject Buddhism; practise ancestor rites; establish primogeniture; and enhance clan cohesion. Everyday life was metaphysical, and philosophy became politicized. Chosŏn was not plagued by powerful eunuchs, but court factionalism emerged to produce political gridlock.

In 1590, the Japanese threatened to invade China through Korea. Court opinion split along factional lines and nothing was done. The Japanese came in 1592, and did not withdraw until 1598. East Asia fell into war, with Japanese fighting Chinese in Korea using European arquebuses. Even a Portuguese priest accompanied Christian samurai to Korea. Korea was devastated. Japanese atrocities and pillage left lasting scars, and the war confirmed Korea as the geopolitical pivot of East Asia.

Korea again prospered by the late 1600s, developing balanced agricultural production, cash crops and trade. Because ideology preferred subsistence agriculture, urban centres never developed the commercial focus that they did in China or Japan. Aside from occasional disturbances, peace reigned, and Chinese and Japanese relations were cordial.

From 1800, a succession of boy kings resulted in weak leadership and strong in-laws. Corruption expanded and government became impotent from the 1860s. Systemic decline and climatic disturbance produced vulnerability to Japanese imperialism, which used gunboat diplomacy to obtain an unequal treaty in 1876. In 1882, Korea signed its first treaty with a Western power (USA), opening the country to Christianity and further trade. Economic dislocation and a new religion produced a peasant revolt in 1894. Japanese and Chinese troops intervened and stayed to fight each other in Korea for the first time since 1592. With victory over China, Japan then turned to eliminate a Russian threat and was victorious in the Russo-Japanese War (1904–5). Japan annexed Korea in 1910.

Harsh policies established a compliant agricultural colony and a peaceful independence movement in 1919 was brutally suppressed. Japan industrialized during World War I and relied on Korean rice for Japanese labourers. After 1920, Japanese capital launched Korean industrialization but used it to meet military needs as Japan expanded into Manchuria (1931) and then into China (1937). As the China War expanded, extreme assimilation policies were imposed on Korea. Names were Japanized, men were abducted as labourers and women abducted as sex slaves.

Korea became the forward base for the China theatre but was never attacked. In 1945, US and Soviet troops divided the country at the 38th parallel and, by October 1948, a communist north, under Kim Il Sung, and a non-communist south (Republic of Korea) had appeared. With Russian and Chinese support, Kim Il Sung attacked southwards in 1950 hoping to reunify Korea. The UN fielded an international (mostly American) force to repel the invasion. As UN forces approached the Yalu River Chinese armies intervened, just as the Ming empire had driven Japanese invaders south in 1593. Seoul exchanged hands four times. Battle lines stabilized near the 38th parallel, where the truce line runs today. Infrastructure was reduced to rubble. Millions died, and barbed wire still divides the peninsula. Post-war recovery was not apparent until the 1960s, when socialist planning in the north produced surplus, and military dictatorship in the south began an industrialization programme that took the Republic of Korea from US$85 per capita in 1962 to US$20,000 per capita in 2002.

1477 TO 1868
JAPAN UNDER THE SHOGUNATE

By 1600, the Tokugawa *shoguns* had pacified Japan. They tamed the feudal barons, controlled Buddhist institutions, disarmed the peasantry, harnessed imperial authority and monopolized diplomacy. Not until 1868 did the Tokugawa fall, powerless in the face of economic crisis, the return of Western powers and new enthusiasm for imperial rule.

With brutality and military brilliance, as well as much political imagination, Oda Nobunaga (1534–82) and Toyotomi Hideyoshi (1536–98) laid the foundations on which the centralized feudalism of the Tokugawa shogunate was constructed. It was to prove remarkably enduring. After the fall of the last stronghold opposed to the rule of the Tokugawa shogun Ieyasu in 1615, Japan enjoyed over two centuries without war and with rapidly increasing prosperity.

THE DAIMYŌ

The Tokugawa effectively emasculated the power of the 260 or so *daimyō* or feudal barons. Though left largely autonomous in their domains and required to pay no taxes to the shogun, the *daimyō* were obliged to spend alternate years in Edo, where participation in elaborate courtly ceremonials was demanded as evidence of submissiveness.

If this "alternate attendance" system turned Edo into the most populous and thriving capital in the world, it also imposed massive burdens on the *daimyō*. With huge retinues to transport to and from the capital and residences and servants to maintain once there, the financial fragility of the *daimyō* was guaranteed and their potential for rebellion accordingly curtailed. However, the submission of the most powerful of these barons, the tozama or "outside lords", such as Satsuma and Choshu, was always grudgingly given and more widespread resentment against the shoguns began to surface around 1700 as the debts to the rising merchant class, run up by the *daimyō* to finance their courtly rituals, deepened.

If the *daimyō* and their samurai retainers, together only 7 per cent of the population of Tokugawa Japan, constituted the most privileged of the social classes, a comparatively low status was accorded to merchants. This was because Confucianism, used by the Tokugawa as an ideological buttress, despised money-making. Paradoxically, Japanese merchants, based in cities such as Osaka, Kyoto and Edo, were left alone to develop their commercial contacts and a number, such as the Sumitomo family, acquired fabulous wealth. Though excluded from all forms of government, they left an increasingly important mark on the development of Japan. From around 1700, a brilliant and sophisticated alternative culture developed characterized by kabuki drama in Osaka in the 18th century and wood-block prints in Edo in the 18th and 19th centuries.

The bulk of the population, perhaps 80 per cent, consisted of the peasantry. The tax burden they owed their *daimyō* could be crippling, however, especially at times of poor harvests. Rural and urban uprisings in the 1730s, 1780s, 1830s and 1860s were directed at the *daimyō* and the merchant class alike and exposed the contradictions inherent in the Tokugawa system.

TOKUGAWA CONTROL

Aware of the emperor's potential as a rival focus of authority, the Tokugawa isolated and carefully controlled the imperial court. The emperor himself, silent and symbolic, served to bestow legitimacy on Tokugawa rule. It was not until the 1850s, when the arrival of Westerners demanding trade with Japan effectively paralysed the Tokugawa, that the imperial court, backed by unrest at the inability of the Tokugawa to stand up to the West, reasserted itself.

But long before this undermining of their authority, the Tokugawa had established complete control over the country, monopolizing foreign trade and diplomacy and expelling most European merchants and missionaries. Yet however self-sufficient and hierarchical, Japan did not withdraw entirely from contact with the wider world. Formal diplomatic and trade relations were maintained only with Korea, but Japan traded with the Chinese and Dutch.

Nonetheless, by the end of the 18th century financial crisis and rural unrest prompted attempts at reform by the Tokugawa. All ended in failure. In 1854 and 1855, the Americans, British, Dutch and Russians extracted "friendship" treaties from the Tokugawa. These aggressive foreign intrusions coupled with the weak

Japanese response provoked crisis. For once unsure of itself, the Tokugawa solicited advice from the *daimyō* and authorization from the imperial court, thus drawing both groups on to the political stage. In 1858, the Tokugawa signed trade treaties, with the Americans, then with the British, but without first seeking imperial approval. A wave of radicalism swept Japan which led to the fall of the Tokugawa.

1511 TO 1826

SOUTHEAST ASIA AND THE EUROPEAN POWERS

At the beginning of the 16th century the first Europeans, lured by the lucrative spice trade, arrived in southeast Asia. Though the Spanish and Portuguese established the first European settlements, in the longer run the Dutch and the British, exploiting divisions among the southeast Asians themselves, were the major beneficiaries.

When European traders and adventurers broke through into the Indian Ocean at the close of the 15th century, the great prize drawing them forward was the spices of southeast Asia. Here was untold wealth to be tapped. But here also, at one of the world's main crossroads, where cultural influences from China and India intermingled, they found themselves in a region of great complexity – politically fragmented and divided between three religions (Buddhism, Hinduism and Islam) and many different types of state.

On the mainland, rival peoples and dynasties competed for hegemony. In the Malayan archipelago, the empires of Srivijaya and Majapahit were little more than memories, having split into many small states with little cohesion between them. This was the situation when Europeans first arrived in the region in the person of Alfonso de Albuquerque who in 1511 conquered the great international emporium of Malacca for the king of Portugal.

The Portuguese presence changed little at first. Albuquerque and his successors were there to dominate the spice trade and to this end built a chain of fortified trading stations linked by naval power. Provided this was accepted, they had no wish to interfere with the native potentates. Far more important, after the arrival on the scene of the Dutch and the English, was the challenge to the

Portuguese trading monopoly presented by their European rivals. For most of the 17th century, this rivalry was the dominant factor.

THE DUTCH AND ENGLISH CONQUESTS

The Dutch in particular began a systematic conquest of the Portuguese settlements, capturing Malacca in 1641, before turning against the British. But in doing so, they were drawn into local politics. After establishing a base at Batavia in 1619, they interfered in succession disputes among the neighbouring sultans, to ensure their own position, and in this way gradually extended control over Java, expelling the British from Bantam in 1682. They had already driven them out of the Spice Islands at the "Massacre of Amboina" (1623) and by the seizure of Macassar (1667), as a result forcing the English East India Company to turn instead to the China trade. With this in view, the British acquired Penang on the west coast of Malaya in 1786, the first step in a process which was ultimately to make them masters of the Malay peninsula.

But this was still exceptional. Though European activities encroached on the outlying islands they had little impact on the mainland monarchies, which had no direct interest in European trade and were mainly concerned with extending their power at the expense of that of their neighbours. At the same time all the main centres were under pressure from the hill peoples of the interior, always waiting to assert their independence. But the main lines of development include the advance of Annam (Vietnam) at the expense of Cambodia, the rise of a new Burmese empire under Alaungpaya (1735–60) and successful Siamese resistance to Burmese enchroachment, in spite of Burmese conquest in 1767.

These events occured for the most part without European involvement even if, during the struggle for empire between France and England in the 18th century (*see* p. 199), some states were implicated. Already under Louis XIV, France had intervened in Siam against the Dutch. But such was the popular hostility engendered by French meddling in Siam that the dynasty they supported was overthrown and the French themselves were expelled. During the Anglo-French war in India after 1746, France supported the Mon rebellion in Burma, provoking the English East India Company to seize in reply the island of Negrais at the mouth of the Bassein river. Later, when the Burmese, foiled in their attempt to capture Siam, switched their efforts to the north, the British, fearing for the security of Bengal, again intervened. The result was the first

Anglo-Burmese War (1824–6) and the British annexation of Assam, Arakan and Tenasserim.

ANGLO-DUTCH AGREEMENT

In Malaya there was similar encroachment on the native states when the British, rulers of Penang since 1786, established Singapore in 1819 as a free trade port after its acquisition by Sir Stamford Raffles, the British Lieutenant-Governor of Benkulen in Sumatra. This led to a conflict of interest with Holland which was only settled by the Anglo-Dutch Treaty of London of 1824, under which the British withdrew from Sumatra in return for Dutch withdrawal from Malacca.

But if by the early years of the 19th century the future Dutch and British colonial empires in southeast Asia were taking shape, the control directly exercised by the European powers was still loose, more concerned with trade than with imperial rule. The Portuguese and Dutch had dominated the spice and pepper trades, but they were largely content to receive surpluses produced by local peasants; it was not until 1830 that the Dutch introduced the "Culture System" in which the Javanese were forced to devote one-fifth of their lands to export crops. Only with the impact of the industrial revolution in Europe, and the rapidly expanding market for raw materials and the increased exports of finished goods it created, were the lives and fortunes of the peoples of the region seriously affected by the European presence.

1500 TO 1815
THE EUROPEAN ECONOMY: AGRICULTURE AND SOCIETY

European agriculture as a whole improved only slowly between 1500 and 1800 and with marked regional contrasts. Southern and eastern Europe, the latter severely handicapped by feudalism, saw slow growth. But in northern Europe there were dramatic increases in agricultural productivity, above all in Britain and the Low Countries

From the early 16th century Britain and the Low Countries enjoyed an agricultural revolution which by 1800 had produced a highly efficient, commercialized farming system. But elsewhere in Europe agricultural techniques and levels of productivity had hardly changed since Roman times and most peasants produced only about 20 per cent more a year than they needed to feed their families and their livestock and to provide the next year's seed. Consequently, in many countries about 80 per cent of the people worked on the land. In Britain and the Low Countries, however, the proportion fell rapidly during the late 18th century as improved agriculture met the food needs of the growing urban population.

THE NEW CROPS

Except in Britain and the Netherlands, most improvements came from the introduction of new, more productive crops, mainly from America. Thus the potato became a basic staple in western Europe, starting in Spain and Italy. In Ireland it allowed such a massive increase in population (from 2.5 to 8 million) that disaster struck when the crop failed in 1846. American maize, like the potato, gave a far higher yield than the established cereals – barley, millet and sorghum – and was widely adopted in southern Europe. Buckwheat, useful on poor soils, entered northern Europe from Russia while in the Mediterranean sugarcane, rice and citrus fruits had arrived from Asia before 1500. Sugar production declined after 1550, however, in the face of competition from Madeira, the Canaries and, after 1600, the West Indies and Brazil.

These slow crop changes contrasted strongly with the rapidly developing northwest. The Dutch began the process by pouring capital into reclaiming land from the sea. Naturally wishing to avoid having to leave land fallow every third year (necessary under the traditional system), they discovered that fertility could be maintained by simple crop rotation involving the alternation of arable with artificial grasses and industrial crops such as rapeseed, flax and dyestuffs. Turnips, on which sheep could be grazed in winter to produce manure as well as mutton and wool, were especially important, as were peas, beans and clovers. English farmers copied and developed these innovations. Irrigation, drainage schemes and woodland clearance increased the productive area, while land enclosure and soil treatments encouraged improved husbandry. By the 1740s, grain exports accounted for 10 per cent of England's export earnings, and the old fear of starvation had been banished.

Such techniques gradually spread as the growth of towns encouraged more specialization in food production. Holland concentrated on dairy products and was exporting 90 per cent of her cheese by 1700. The Danes were sending 80,000 head of cattle a year to Germany, and the Dutch, German and Italian cloth industries were sustained by massive imports of Spanish wool. The exchange of northern Europe's cereals and timber for the fruits, wines and oils of the Mediterranean grew apace.

PEASANTS AND FEUDALISM

All improvements in productivity depended on breaking the old feudal relationships which oppressed the peasants, however, and here there was a sharp east-west cleavage. Before 1500 feudalism had been stronger in the older settled areas of western Europe than in the sparsely peopled lands of eastern Europe and Russia. After 1500 this changed completely: peasants in northwest Europe exchanged the traditional labour services on their lords' land for a money rent (especially in England and the Netherlands) or, in France and farther south, for share-cropping tenancies. They also gradually freed themselves from burdensome personal services and dues, though this required revolutionary action, inspired by France in 1789, before it was complete.

In total contrast, feudal power grew and spread in eastern Europe until it approached slavery. Feudal lords increased their power, halting migration to empty lands farther east (as in Russia) and increasing grain-export profits (as in eastern Germany and Poland-Lithuania). Free peasants only survived in newly conquered lands if they performed military service instead of paying rent. The peasants of western Germany occupied a middle position. They had tried to win their freedom in a great revolt in 1525, and briefly controlled most of southern Germany before the rebellion was savagely crushed. Yet the excesses of eastern Europe were averted, and the peasants gradually gained greater freedom by 1800. Their slow emancipation was, however, an important reason why the German industrial revolution came so late.

1550 TO 1775
THE EUROPEAN ECONOMY:
TRADE AND INDUSTRY

Population growth, expanding industry, the impact of colonial trade and changes to the banking system transformed Europe's economic performance after 1500. At the same time, there was a decisive shift in the economic centre of gravity from southern to northern Europe. The Dutch Republic and, later, Britain emerged as the new economic powerhouses.

Europe's population expanded fast in the 16th century, was retarded by famine, plague and war in the 17th century, but grew rapidly again from the mid-18th century. In 1500 only three cities – Constantinople (by far the largest), Paris and Naples – had more than 200,000 inhabitants. By 1700 this number had doubled, and London, Paris and Constantinople had passed the half-million mark.

The increased complexity of government, an acceleration of trade and finance, a growing taste for conspicuous consumption, and a feeling that survival was better assured in the cities, all helped to hasten this trend. The resulting problems, particularly the need to guarantee reliable urban food supplies, also created new opportunities. Most notably, until the mid-17th century, they generated a massive demand for eastern Europe's wheat and rye, a trade which fed the burgeoning economic strength of Holland, now nearly monopolizing the Baltic carrying trade.

The Netherlands in fact formed the hinge for a gradual but decisive shift in commercial power. In 1500 industry was largely concentrated in the corridor running north–south from Antwerp and Bruges to Florence and Milan. By 1700 this axis had swung through almost 90 degrees. At one end stood Britain and the Dutch Republic, increasingly the most dynamic commercial centres in Europe; eastward the line extended through the metal and woollen districts of the Rhine to the great industrial concentrations of Saxony, Bohemia and Silesia.

INDUSTRY, TRADE AND FINANCE

At the same time, however, technology advanced only in patches and much industrial expansion was chiefly achieved by increasing the number of workers while still using the old methods. But even this helped improve industrial organization, by splitting up production processes, developing production in rural areas free of urban restriction, and drawing on the cheap part-time labour of peasant families. Much industry was controlled by traders who organized a scattered cottage labour force. By the 18th century this had become the typical form of all but local and luxury industry.

More impressive than the erratic spread of industry was the increase in international trade. The maritime powers, with their colonies and ports in Asia and the Americas, imported a fast-growing stream of new products: tea, coffee, sugar, chocolate, tobacco. They were purchased with European manufactures and with the shipping, insurance and merchandising services that built up the wealth of ports such as Bordeaux, London, Amsterdam and Marseilles.

Governments assisted those sectors of economic activity that they favoured. Holland and England waged wars to protect and expand their shipping and trading interests, but did not consistently aid industry. The governments of France and the central European states, by contrast, established new industries and subsidized old ones. Increasingly costly wars, however, had an even more powerful influence. They called for heavy taxation and large borrowings that undermined the precarious stability of Europe's gradually evolving monetary systems. The wars were ruinous to Spain and damaging to France and many smaller states; only Britain and the Dutch Republic coped succesfully thanks to their expanding economies and new credit systems.

Trade and war also generated an unprecedented demand for money. Gold and silver were amply provided from Spanish Mexico and Peru after 1545, supported from the 1690s by Brazilian gold. This bullion was redistributed across Europe by merchants and by Spanish government transactions, much of it financing Europe's trade deficits with the East Indies and the Levant. The money supply was also supplemented by the growth of banking. In contrast to the established German and Italian banks, which were heavily engaged in government lending, Dutch and English banks served private interests with giro and foreign-exchange facilities and short-term credits. In the century after its opening in 1609, the Amsterdam Exchange Bank was the undisputed focus of continental trade; Britain could compete only after 1694, when the Bank of England provided a focus for older private banking firms. With low interest rates, free capital movement, secure international payments and an assured savings flow, the foundations of modern finance were firmly laid.

1517 TO 1670

REFORMATION AND CATHOLIC REFORMATION

The shattering of the unity of Latin Christendom altered the course of European history. The rise of assertive Protestant Churches and the reaction of the Catholic Church stimulated a battle for the consciences of ordinary Europeans which disrupted traditional loyalties and political arrangements. It was 150 years before an uneasy religious balance was restored.

In 1500 the Catholic Church seemed stronger than ever. Paganism was vanquished; the Iberian Reconquista had destroyed the last Islamic state in western Europe and the overthrow of the Byzantine empire in 1453 had weakened the Orthodox Church. Lay piety was booming, as was popular interest in the Church's promise of salvation. Yet this very success brought profound problems. The moral and spiritual quality of many clergy left much to be desired. There was widespread concern at the state of the Church and of popular religious belief which, although often enthusiastic, was frequently characterized by ignorance or heterodoxy. Attempts at reform, however, were often undermined by the unresolved problem of authority within the Church, while the invention of the printing press, by dramatically quickening the pace of debate, facilitated the questioning of established truth by clergy and laity alike.

THE REFORMATION

The Reformation began as a revolt of the clergy, as Martin Luther (1483–1546), Huldrych Zwingli (1484–1531), Martin Bucer (1491–1551) and many others rejected the authority of the Catholic Church, attacking the Papacy and basing their challenge on the authority of scripture, increasingly available in vernacular translations. These ideas proved attractive to many princes, who embraced

185

reform. With the emergence of a second wave of Protestant reform spearheaded by the followers of the French reformer John Calvin (1509–64), an increasing number turned Protestant. Protestantism was already the official religion in large parts of northern Germany, Sweden, Denmark, Scotland and England, and Calvinism, which developed sophisticated theories justifying resistance to political authority, was spreading rapidly in the Netherlands, Poland-Lithuania, Hungary and France, where there were perhaps 1200 Calvinist churches by 1570.

CHALLENGES TO PROTESTANTISM

Yet confessional divisions were by no means fixed, and Protestantism faced growing problems. The Catholic Church began a vigorous recovery after the Council of Trent reaffirmed its doctrine in response to the Protestant challenge and launched an ambitious programme of reform. Protestantism, by rejecting Catholic mechanisms for sustaining orthodoxy, could not establish the universal Church to which the early reformers had aspired while discipline was always a problem, with radical sects such as Anabaptists and Antitrinitarians surviving vigorous persecution.

The second half of the 16th century was a period of adjustment, as rulers switched between brands of Protestantism, or even considered reunification with Rome, as in England under Mary Tudor (1552–8) or, more ambiguously, in Sweden under John III (1568–92). In eastern Europe, Catholicism outflanked Protestantism by negotiating the 1596 Union of Brest, in which most of the Orthodox hierarchy in Poland-Lithuania accepted papal authority in return for keeping the Orthodox rite. Orthodox resistance to this Uniate (Greek Catholic) Church was powerful, and it was only after 1650 that it began to flourish; similar Unions were established with the Ruthenians of northeast Hungary (1646) and the Romanian Orthodox Church (1697). In such unstable circumstances, it took time for new religious convictions to take root among the ordinary people and Protestant rulers found that old beliefs died hard even where people welcomed the destruction of the power of the Catholic clergy. Nevertheless, the religious differentiation of Europe proceeded apace and was accompanied by vicious civil wars and widespread persecution. It was only after 1660 that the religious map took on a more permanent shape, as the success of evangelization made it difficult for rulers to challenge the religious beliefs of their subjects. Only now were the religious divisions of the continent accepted, if not welcomed.

1500 TO 1688
EUROPE: THE STATE AND ITS OPPONENTS

Before 1688 European rulers struggled to impose their authority. Nobles, townspeople and peasants fought to protect privileges and to resist the fiscal demands of the state. The Dutch and Portuguese revolts led to independence while in France and Spain monarchs could only increase their power by working with the elites. In England cooperation with Parliament was essential, as Charles I discovered.

Despite their apparent strength, the monarchies of Europe continued to govern through the personal ties of clientage which had characterized monarchy in the feudal period. The state still relied on the goodwill of its nobles for the enforcement of its policies, and failure to retain the support of the landed classes could provoke major revolts. The French aristocracy staged several rebellions against the crown, culminating in the Fronde (1648–53); a section of the English aristocracy rebelled against Elizabeth I in 1569–70 (the "Northern Rising") and many English peers supported Parliament's stand against Charles I after 1640. Similarly, nobles in the Netherlands opposed their "natural prince", Philip II of Spain, in 1566, 1572 and 1576 while those in Portugal rose against Philip IV in 1640.

These were only the most important rebellions of the period. Uprisings against the state were a continuing fact of life throughout the 16th and 17th centuries. Some revolts arose from attacks on the privileges of the "estates"; others were caused by economic hardship – from taxes imposed at a time of high prices and widespread unemployment, as was the case in most French popular revolts, or from the enclosing of common land, which caused the revolts of 1549 and 1607 in England. Other uprisings – the Pilgrimage of Grace in England in 1536 and the Covenanting Movement in Scotland in 1638 – were triggered by unpopular religious policies. In all cases the revolts were a response to attempts at innovation. Governments everywhere were endeavouring to create what James I of England described as: "one worship to God, one kingdom entirely governed, one uniformity of laws". The problem, however, was one of means, not ends. Neither James nor any of his fellow sovereigns had the resources to enforce such ambitions. They simply lacked the revenues and the officials required.

THE AGE OF REVOLT

The barriers to centralization in Early Modern Europe were formidable. Many subjects did not speak the same language as their government (Breton and Provençal in France, Catalan and Basque in Spain, Cornish in England, Frisian in the Netherlands); certain "corporations", notably the Church, possessed privileges which protected them against state interference; and many provinces possessed charters guaranteeing their traditional way of life.

Serious political upheavals occurred when the state tried to undermine these rights: the Dutch rebelled largely because they believed that the central government, controlled from Madrid, threatened their traditional liberties. They continued their armed opposition until 1609, when Spain, in effect, recognized the independence of the seven provinces still in rebellion. In England, Parliament began a civil war against Charles I in 1642 because it believed that he intended to destroy the established rights of "free-born Englishmen". They, too, maintained their armed resistance until the power of the king was shattered in battle, and Charles himself was tried and executed in 1649. Although Charles's son was restored in 1660 with full powers and even a small standing army, another revolt, in 1688, supported by the Dutch, drove James II into exile.

While opposition in France did not go to such lengths, the absolutist policies and fiscal exactions of Cardinal Mazarin, chief minister of the boy king Louis XIV, so alienated the crown's officials, the nobles and the people of Paris that in 1649 they drove Louis from his capital and forced him to make major concessions. Royal control was not fully restored until 1655. Philip IV of Spain pushed the Portuguese aristocracy to revolt in support of the House of Braganza and by 1668 Portugal was independent. The Spanish king was fortunate not to lose Catalonia in a similar fashion during the revolt of 1640 to 1652.

THE STRUCTURE OF THE STATE

Despite these upheavals, however, the structure of the state survived. None of the rebels seriously questioned the need for strong government, only the location of it. After 1660, and even more after 1688, power in England was shared between Parliament, representing merchants and landowners, and the crown. The last major effort to resist the rise of central power and defend local autonomy had failed. In France, the Fronde was a frightening lesson for Louis XIV whose re-establishment of royal authority was based upon a policy of compromise with aristocratic and office-owning elites (*see* p. 196). A more sensitive government, combined with a rapidly expanding standing army after 1661, ensured that France saw no repetition of the Fronde before 1789.

The Dutch Revolt, on the other hand, achieved its primary goal of protecting local independence against central encroachment. Despite the preponderance of Holland within the Republic, the other six provinces retained a large measure of autonomy within a decentralized political system reminiscent of the 15th century. It was to leave the Dutch at a permanent disadvantage in a world which permitted no profit without power and no security without war. The 18th century and its profits – particularly in the colonial world – would belong to their rivals, France and Britain.

1494 TO 1797

THE MEDITERRANEAN WORLD

The Ottoman conquest of the eastern Mediterranean and the French invasion of Italy in 1494 opened a new phase in Mediterranean history. Both the sea and the Italian peninsula became the focus for power-struggles between states whose interests were only partly Mediterranean. Meanwhile, Europe's economic centre of gravity shifted northwest.

After 1500, even as the civilization of the Italian Renaissance was spreading round Europe, Italy and the Mediterranean were losing their dominant position within the cultural and economic worlds of Europe. The invasion of Italy by Charles VIII of France in 1494 initiated over 60 years of warfare between the Habsburgs and the French Valois for control of Italy which undermined the political primacy of the Italian cities, just as the Ottoman drive into the eastern Mediterranean threatened their economic dominance. The loss of Italian primacy was precipitated in part, too, by the creation of the Habsburg empire. Charles V, elected Holy Roman Emperor in 1519, ruled not only the Habsburg lands in Austria, south Germany and the Netherlands, but also the realms bequeathed by his maternal grandparents, Ferdinand and Isabella, in Spain,

Italy and north Africa. His inheritance was soon expanded: in 1526 his brother and close ally Ferdinand succeeded to the crowns of Bohemia and Hungary, creating a huge Habsburg power block running from the Adriatic almost to the Baltic. In 1535 Charles himself acquired both Milan and Tunis.

By the peace of Câteau-Cambrésis (1559), France was excluded from Italy, which now came under the domination of the Habsburgs. Although Charles V divided his empire on his death, his son Philip II of Spain retained Milan and the kingdoms of Naples and Sicily. Henceforth, Spanish viceroys ruled in Naples, Sicily and Sardinia, with a Spanish governor in Lombardy.

THE OTTOMAN THREAT

Even Italy's largest states lacked room for manoeuvre in the face of Spain's over-whelming dominance. 80 per cent of Genoese seaborne trade was conducted with Spain, and Venice, whose eastern Mediterranean empire was falling gradually into Ottoman hands, was surrounded by Habsburg territory. Papal attempts to oppose the Habsburgs ended in catastrophe: the sack of Rome itself in 1527 and a humiliating invasion in 1556-7. Yet the Spaniards at least provided effective defence against the Ottomans who, despite their successful advance along the north African coast with the capture of Algiers (1529), Tripoli (1551) and Bugia (1555), were unable to secure a foothold in Italy. The climactic moment came with the unsuccessful siege of Malta in 1565, although the Spanish victory at Lepanto (1571) could not prevent the fall of Cyprus the same year.

ITALY AND THE HOLY ROMAN EMPIRE

The fading of the Turkish threat after the Ottoman-Spanish truce of 1577 ensured that the new status quo lasted until the 1790s. Southern Italy and Sardinia were ruled by Spain, the Papal States dominated central Italy, while the north, apart from Venice, was still part of the Holy Roman Empire, and was a complex network of imperial and papal fiefs and semi-independent territories: in the 16th century, there were some 250–300 imperial fiefs held by 50–70 families, and some 296 papal fiefs with some 223,000 inhabitants. Although the last appearance of an Italian delegation to the Imperial Diet was in 1496, the duchy of Savoy was part of the Upper Rhenish Circle, and its dukes maintained a theoretical right to speak and vote in the Diet until 1806. Many important north Italian families, such as the Doria or the Spinola, were imperial princes, and the Imperial Aulic Council heard 1500 cases involving Italians between 1555 and 1806 (400 in the 16th century; 490 in the 17th; and 540 in the 18th). Northern Italy was strategically vital to Spain during the Dutch Revolt and the Thirty Years' War: with the sea-route to the Netherlands through the English Channel dominated by the Dutch and the English, Milan was the mustering-ground for Spanish troops sent overland down the "Spanish Road" through the Valtellina, Alsace and the Rhineland to the Netherlands. Thus Italy was vital to Spain's long war against the Dutch rebels; this led to a renewal of Franco-Spanish war in Italy during the War of the Mantuan Succession (1629–31), which saw the victory of the French-backed candidate, Charles Gonzaga, Duke of Nevers.

Even when the Spanish Habsburgs died out in 1700, and the grandson of Louis XIV secured the Spanish throne as Philip V after the War of the Spanish Succession (1702–13), the status quo altered little. Austria acquired Milan, but only held Naples and Sicily between 1720 and 1735, when they reverted to a branch of the Spanish Bourbons after a series of territorial exchanges. Lesser principalities were similarly shared out. Only the republics of Venice, Genoa and Lucca remained relatively undisturbed.

BRITAIN IN THE MEDITERRANEAN

The principal guardian of this stability was Great Britain, attracted to the Mediterranean by trading opportunities in the late 16th century, when the Levant Company established a base in Istanbul (1581). In the 1650s, British fleets entered to pursue royalist vessels and punish the Barbary pirates. From 1662 to 1683, Britain held Tangier, guarding the entrance to the Mediterranean; in 1704 it took Gibraltar on the other side of the straits. Sardinia was a British base between 1708 and 1714, as was Minorca from 1708 to 1783. On the whole, though, Britain preferred diplomacy to force; it was only when Napoleon's invasion of Italy and annexation of Egypt and Malta in the late 1790s destroyed the status quo and convulsed the eastern and western Mediterranean alike that British naval power came to dominate both.

THE STRUGGLE FOR THE BALTIC

The growing economic importance of the Baltic after 1500 coincided with the decay of the political status quo as the powers which had dominated the sea in the medieval period entered terminal decline or were seriously weakened. The resultant struggle for control of the Baltic Sea lasted two centuries before Russia emerged as the most significant Baltic power.

From 1500 the Baltic provided most of the timber, tar, pitch, hemp and flax for the ships with which European powers built their world empires, as well as copper and huge supplies of cheap grain. This increasingly lucrative trade provoked serious rivalry, as neighbouring powers sought to control ports at the mouths of the great rivers which bore goods from the interior, while Denmark's control of both sides of the Sound, the narrow entrance to the Baltic, enabled it to impose the hotly contested Sound Tolls on most of the commerce passing through. After 1500, no power was strong enough to dominate the Baltic or its trade; the resultant conflicts constantly interlocked with wider European affairs.

In 1523 Sweden under Gustav Vasa broke away from the Scandinavian Union of Kalmar. Meanwhile, the Hanseatic League of Baltic trading towns began to unravel, while the Teutonic Order, which controlled the southern Baltic shore from Pomerania to Estonia, slowly decayed. A rebellion led by the burghers of Thorn, Danzig and Elbing in alliance with Poland had already seen the Order lose much of Prussia by the Peace of Thorn (1466); in 1525, Grand Master Albrecht of Hohenzollern then secularized the Order, creating the Duchy of Prussia as a Lutheran fief of the Polish crown. The decaying rump of the Order held on in Livonia, but ancient claims and a desire to profit from Baltic trade led Ivan IV of Muscovy to invade in 1558.

SWEDEN'S BALTIC EMPIRE
Ivan failed to establish Muscovite power on the Baltic. The early beneficiaries of the Order's collapse were Poland-Lithuania and Sweden. Poland accepted the overlordship of Livonia in 1561 and granted Courland to Gotthard Kettler, Grand Master of the Order, as a fief of the Polish crown. Sweden, meanwhile, seized Reval and Estonia and became involved in the Nordic Seven Years' War

with Denmark (1563–70), in which Denmark struggled to re-establish the Union of Kalmar and Sweden sought to expand its foothold on the North Sea at Älvsborg, on the site of the future city of Gothenburg. The Muscovite armies could terrorize but not conquer; they were driven back by determined resistance from the Poles and the Swedes under John III (1568–92), who then married a Polish princess and had his son Sigismund elected king of Poland in 1587. Muscovy gradually subsided into anarchy after Ivan's death in 1584; by 1619, it was cut off from the Baltic, as Sweden secured Karelia, Ingria (Ingermanland) and Estonia, and Poland-Lithuania took Livonia and regained Smolensk. Denmark, despite seizing Älvsborg in the War of Kalmar (1611–13), was unable to secure a decisive advantage, and had to remain content with control of The Sound, returning Älvsborg for a large ransom.

But the Polish-Swedish alliance was short-lived. Sigismund, raised a Catholic, was driven off the Swedish throne in 1599; for 60 years, Poland-Lithuania and Sweden were locked in a dynastic struggle which gave Muscovy time to recover.

Under the brilliant Gustavus Adolphus (1611–32) Sweden seized Livonia in the 1620s, while the powerful military system which matured in his reign enabled Sweden to play a leading role in the Thirty Years' War (*see* p. 195) after his brilliant victory at Breitenfeld (Sep. 1631). By 1648, despite Gustavus Adolphus's death in the battle of Lützen (Nov. 1632), Sweden had gained substantial territories in northern Germany and, after a devastating war with Denmark (1643–5), had widened its bridgehead on the North Sea.

Under Charles X (1654–60) Swedish power reached its zenith. Charles invaded Poland-Lithuania in 1655 and pushed the Muscovites back from Riga. Denmark, keen for revenge, attacked Sweden in 1657, but was defeated and made peace at Roskilde (Feb. 1658). Charles's decision to attack Denmark again in the summer of 1658 proved rash, however: he lost the chance to secure concessions from Poland-Lithuania or Russia, while England, the United Provinces and France, fearing Swedish domination of the Baltic, supported Denmark. After the Peace of Copenhagen (1660), though Denmark's grip on the Sound was broken, Sweden had failed to find security.

THE DECLINE OF SWEDISH POWER

Sweden's success brought it many enemies. Swedish support of the house of Holstein-Gottorp, a junior branch of the Danish royal family which shared control of the duchy of Holstein, ensured that relations with Denmark remained tense. Attacked by Brandenburg and Denmark in the Scanian War (1676–9), Sweden's precarious control of its scattered Baltic empire was revealed: it only preserved its southern Baltic holdings thanks to the intervention of Louis XIV of France.

Charles XI (1660–97) adopted a pacific policy after 1679 and revived the army, but when he was succeeded by his teenage son Charles XII (1697–1718), Denmark, Saxony-Poland and Russia formed an alliance which attacked Sweden in 1700, launching the Great Northern War (1700–21). Although Charles immediately knocked Denmark out of the war, smashed the Russian army at Narva (1700) and forced Saxony to make peace at Altranstädt (1706), he became bogged down in Poland. Peter I, given breathing-space after Narva, built a formidable army and fleet; by 1704, Ingermanland and much of Livonia was in his hands. After Charles's crushing defeat at Poltava (1709), Brandenburg-Prussia, Hanover and Denmark joined Russia in a struggle for Sweden's Baltic empire. By 1721, Sweden was once more a second-rank power, and Russia was the dominant force in the region.

1493 TO 1806

THE HOLY ROMAN EMPIRE

The Holy Roman Empire was a decentralized confederal system. While undoubtedly complex, it was effective enough to maintain a common currency and robust enough to survive religious division and the Thirty Years' War. After 1648, its institutions revived and it was regarded as the natural political framework for Germany until, undermined from outside, it collapsed in 1806.

At first sight, the Holy Roman Empire appears incoherent, with a high degree of political fragmentation and competing jurisdictions. In fact, considerable institutional consolidation took place after 1493 within what was a confederal system, with varying levels of authority which kept political control close to those affected by it. The Empire's division into ten "Circles" improved its administration, with the Circles organizing taxation, regulating disputes and supervising the common currency, the Imperial thaler. The revival of the Imperial Cameral Tribunal and the Imperial Diet and the introduction of a common criminal code provided the empire with a complex but not un-workable constitution. From the election of Maximilian I (1493), the position of emperor became all but hereditary in the Habsburg dynasty, with a brief interlude in the reign of the Wittelsbach Charles VII (1742–5) during the War of the Austrian Succession.

THE WARS OF RELIGION

After 1517 two factors put the Empire under immense strain: the Reformation and the dramatic increase in Habsburg power following the election of Charles V (1519). Religion became a central issue, as princes sought to limit the Emperor's power while the secularization of Church property in much of north-ern and western Germany sparked bitter disputes. Although the formation of the Protestant Schmalkaldic League in the 1530s brought a series of brief civil wars, all sides recoiled from all-out confrontation. At the peace of Augsburg (1555), a compromise was reached based on the principle that princes should determine the religion of their subjects.

Augsburg kept the peace for 60 years, but bitter disputes arose over its interpretation. Further instability was caused by conflict between the Habsburgs and their Austrian and Bohemian subjects, who by 1600 were largely Protestant. In 1618, the Bohemians rebelled, deposing Ferdinand II as their king in 1619. The rebels were defeated, but the war spread into the Empire after 1620. The Thirty Years' War devastated the empire, reducing a population in 1618 of between 20 and 25 million by a third.

The Peace of Westphalia (1648), which ended it, brought religious com-promise and established a new political framework. The power of the Emperor and the princes was better defined, and the Diet sat in permanent session at Regensburg from 1663; the way was opened for political and economic recovery. Nevertheless, Westphalia brought new problems. The more powerful princes soon created standing armies and played a more prominent role in European relations. The electors of Brandenburg built a new power-base in Prussia, while in 1697 the elector of Saxony turned Catholic to secure election to the Polish throne as Augustus II. In 1714, the elector of Hanover became king of England as George I.

ECONOMIC GROWTH

Despite its problems, most Germans still saw the empire as their natural political framework, and the 18th century saw economic expansion in many areas, particularly Silesia, where major landowners combined with government to invest in mining, iron and textiles, and the lower Rhineland and Saxony, which was probably the most advanced of all. But farming remained dominant, with three-quarters of Germany's population still rural in 1815, and towns and cities small compared with those of England and France: Berlin's 140,000 inhabitants in 1777 compared with 260,000 in Vienna, 670,000 in Paris and over 850,000 in London. Nevertheless, this reflected the empire's decentralized constitution, and in cities such as Weimar, Karlsruhe, Mannheim and Stuttgart attempts were made to implement Enlightenment ideas in ambitious reform programmes, often strikingly successful precisely because the principalities were so small. Germany experienced a literary revival in which Goethe and Schiller were figures of international significance. Yet with the import of French revolutionary ideas after 1789, the empire's institutions proved incapable of absorbing new ideas or adjusting to meet the challenge of Napoleon. In 1806, Francis II's abdication as Holy Roman Emperor ended a line which had begun 850 years earlier.

1648 TO 1715

THE ASCENDANCY OF FRANCE

Louis XIV's France was the most powerful state in Europe. By 1680 the king was acclaimed as "Louis the Great" and military victories were matched by a flowering of the arts and economic and colonial expansion. Yet French success pushed the other great powers, England, the Dutch Republic and the Austrian Habsburgs, into a coalition which, by 1709, had brought France close to invasion and defeat.

During the reign of Louis XIV France became so powerful that other states feared her ascendancy, regarding her as a danger to the balance of power on the

Continent. Louis was suspected of plans to oust the Austrian Habsburgs from their traditional position as elected Holy Roman Emperor and of spearheading a second Catholic counter-reformation. He was generally held to be seeking French hegemony in Europe.

Such fears rested upon solid ground. After a century of foreign war and internal strife, Louis XIV and his able ministers took advantage of the peaceful years between 1659 and 1672 to make great progress in manufacturing, in trade, in overseas expansion and in ship-building. At the same time the French army was greatly expanded. The richness of French resources, including a population estimated at 20 million (Great Britain, in comparison, had a population of less than 8 million), played a significant part in these developments, but so did conscious effort and directives from the centre.

TERRITORIAL CONSOLIDATION

Louis' objectives were at first quite limited and concerned the security of France's frontiers. Habsburg encirclement, forged by the family compacts of the Austrian and Spanish Habsburgs, was still felt to be pressing round France though the Peace of Westphalia (1648) brought sovereignty over Metz, Toul and Verdun and possession of the landgravates of Upper and Lower Alsace. The Peace of the Pyrenees (1659) plugged the gap in the southern frontier with Spain ceding Roussillon and northern Cerdagne. Yet France was still vulnerable from the Spanish Netherlands and Franche-Comté as well as through Lorraine and the Belfort Gap. This helps to explain the two aggressive wars of Louis' reign: the War of Devolution, fought to lay claim to part of the Spanish Netherlands in 1667–8; and the attack on the Dutch Republic in 1672. The latter, much to Louis' discomfiture, escalated into a European-wide war not settled until 1678–9.

FAMINE AND WAR

Louis tried to avoid large-scale war after 1679 by resort to arbitration and treaties to settle European problems, but the memories of his early wars and the enormous power of France made the rest of Europe suspicious. He caused further unease by his "reunion" policy to expand his control of German border areas and he lost the sympathy of all Protestant powers for his persecution of the Huguenots. The deleterious economic effects of the exodus of over 200,000

French Calvinists in the 1670s and 1680s have been greatly exaggerated, but the international consequences of Louis' revocation of the Edict of Nantes (1685) were far-reaching, and contributed to the outbreak of the Nine Years' War (1688–97) and the War of the Spanish Succession (1701–14).

The defensive element in Louis' foreign policy is still disputed among historians, but can be demonstrated by the construction of a *barrière de fer* of fortresses around the whole of France and by his willingness to promote a peaceful partition of the Spanish empire before the death of Carlos II. When that policy failed and the dying Spanish king offered the crown to his grandson, the future Philip V, Louis had no alternative but to accept. While understandable, it was a fateful decision for his subjects. Over a million had starved during the terrible famine of 1693–4 and nearly as many would perish as war combined with natural disaster to exact a terrible toll.

CULTURAL ASCENDANCY

French ascendancy between 1648 and 1715 was not apparent only in the fields of politics, diplomacy and war. Louis' work for French architecture, learning, and for science and the arts in general, and his pensions paid to a great number of European poets, artists and scholars, whether they studied in France or not, may seem more important than his wars. His court at Versailles and his support for academies became models for other princes. French became the language of the educated classes all over Europe and helped to create the the country's cosmopolitan civilization of the late 17th and the early 18th centuries. France also made progress during his reign in the number of colleges and hospitals; in the codification of laws; in administrative practices and efficiencies; and in a range of practical improvements from street lighting and policing in Paris to the digging of the Canal Royal (completed by 1684), which provided cheap and efficient communication between the Atlantic and the Mediterranean. Taken as a whole, the reign fixed the French frontiers in Europe (though colonial cessions had to be made to Great Britain) and in the history of French civilization, the period is deservedly honoured with the title *Le Grand Siècle*.

THE STRUGGLE FOR EMPIRE

From 1713 until 1815 Great Britain and France fought for global supremacy in India, North America and the Caribbean. Britain, with her great naval strength, was always at an advantage because France was first and foremost a continental power. Control of the seas allowed the British to defeat her enemy in North America and India.

European territorial expansion overseas continued throughout the 18th century and led to serious clashes between Portugal and Spain in the Banda Oriental (Uruguay), between Spain and Great Britain in Georgia and between Great Britain and France elsewhere in North America. Trading monopolies proved an even greater source of friction. Spanish attempts to suppress British and Dutch smugglers reduced the Caribbean to a state of undeclared war. Further north, British efforts to enforce similar restrictions upon its American colonists provoked resistance and finally, from 1775, open revolt.

THE ANGLO-FRENCH STRUGGLE

During 1739–40 the fragile peace brought about by the Treaty of Utrecht in 1713 collapsed as Great Britain and Spain went to war in defence of their trading rights, while Frederick the Great's invasion of Silesia began the struggle for supremacy in eastern Europe (*see* p. 201). The outbreak of hostilities between Great Britain and France in 1744 brought the colonial conflict and the war for Silesia together into a single conflict that extended from North America to India and from the West Indies to Russia. This struggle, which lasted intermittently until 1815, rapidly became a duel between Great Britain and France for global supremacy. European states, American settlers, Native American chiefs and Indian princes all fought as subsidized and dependent allies of these two great powers.

CONFLICT IN NORTH AMERICA

The Treaty of Aix-la-Chapelle (1748) settled none of the outstanding questions, and fighting began again in North America in 1754. France quickly achieved local military superiority with its strategically sited forts preventing further

British expansion. The outbreak of the Seven Years' War in Europe (1756–63) transformed the situation. France was handicapped by its continental commitments and Britain took control of the Atlantic, decisively defeating the French fleet at Quiberon Bay and Lagos in 1759. With French forces in Canada cut off from reinforcements Louisbourg fell in 1758, Quebec in 1759 and Montreal in 1760.

The British triumph was short-lived. Between 1763 and the American War of Independence (1776–83: *see* p. 208), France rebuilt both its navy and its alliances in pursuit of revenge. By 1781, confronted in home waters by a hostile coalition of France, Spain and the Dutch Republic and overstrained by the need to defend an empire stretching from Canada to India, Great Britain was forced to surrender control of North American waters. The French blockade of Yorktown forced a major British army to surrender, and in 1783 Great Britain was obliged to recognize American independence.

RIVALRY IN INDIA

During these same years the British founded a new empire in India. The emergence of independent princes from the ruins of the Mughal empire in the early 18th century gave the English and the French East India companies opportunities to intervene in local politics. Here again sea power was decisive. Thus, after early French successes, Great Britain's ability to reinforce its position by sea enabled it to check France's ambitious designs in the Carnatic. But the real foundation of the British empire in India followed Clive's victory at Plassey (1757) which gave the British control of the rich province of Bengal. Reinforcements from Bengal enabled the British to eliminate French influence in the Carnatic and become the predominant European power in India.

The French revolution of 1789 shattered the French navy and left British naval power preeminent. This ruined Napoleon's plans for the invasion of Great Britain. By 1815, the French, Spanish, Dutch and Danish fleets were defeated, their colonies mostly in British hands. With the acquisition of the Cape, Ceylon and Mauritius, Great Britain secured the route to India, and laid the foundations for the second British empire.

1648 TO 1795
THE AGE OF PARTITION:
EASTERN EUROPE

After 1648, a new balance of power in eastern Europe was brought about by the decline of both Poland-Lithuania and the Ottoman empire. Turkish resilience preserved the Ottoman empire from collapse, but Poland's internal weakness was cynically exploited by its neighbours to block reform and to destroy and partition the state.

Poland's failure to crush the revolt of the Zaporozhian Cossacks after 1648 opened a new chapter in east European history. Poland-Lithuania was torn by foreign invasion in the Second Northern War (1655–60) and although it recovered it could not prevent the loss of Kiev and the left-bank Ukraine to Muscovy at the treaty of Andrusovo (1667) or rebuild its military system, with the result that the Ukraine remained a battleground for Poland, Russia and the Ottomans. The Cossacks divided into pro-Polish, pro-Russian and pro-Ottoman factions in the period known in Ukraine as "the Ruin".

OTTOMAN REVIVAL AND DECLINE

The renewed opportunities in Ukraine tempted the Ottoman empire, which pursued an expansionist policy under a succession of Grand Viziers from the Köprülü family. It reconquered Tenedos and Lemnos from Venice (1657) and seized Crete (1669). At the peace of Buczacz (1672) Podolia was then taken from Poland, before Grand Vizier Kara Mustafa led a huge army to besiege Vienna (1683). A combined Imperial and Polish army led by King John III Sobieski of Poland-Lithuania (1674–96) drove the Ottomans from the city wall. Thereafter the establishment in 1684 of the Holy League of Venice, Austria and Poland-Lithuania, supported by the Papacy, marked the start of a long campaign to push the Ottomans back. In 1686 Russia, too, joined the alliance.

The Ottomans could not combat the new military sophistication of European armies. At the peace of Carlowitz (1699), Podolia was returned to Poland, and Austrian possession of Hungary was confirmed. Yet division and distractions among the allies ensured that until 1739 the Ottoman empire, far from collapsing, was able to reverse some of its defeats. Azov, seized by Russia in

1696, was returned in 1711 after Peter I's army was surrounded on the river Prut, while Serbia and parts of Wallachia, ceded to Austria at Passarowitz in 1718, were regained in 1739 at the Peace of Belgrade. It was only after 1770 that Russian expansion to the Black Sea and the Caucasus was triumphantly resumed. Nonetheless Ottoman resilience was still enough to ensure that retreat was gradual. Only after 1815 did the balance tip decisively against the Ottomans and their final decline begin.

Sobieski's triumph at Vienna, however, marked the Commonwealth of Poland-Lithuania's last major victory as a significant European power, as the political problems which increasingly paralysed its institutions became clear to its neighbours. The Commonwealth's diet (the *Sejm*) was composed of delegates from provincial dietines (*sejmiki*). Decisions were consensual; in 1652, this saw the first acceptance of the *liberum veto*, by which a sole delegate had the right to block *Sejm* decisions. Henceforth, *Sejm* sessions regularly broke up without deciding anything, including the levying of taxes with which to pay the army.

THE PARTITIONS OF POLAND

The first plans to partition Poland-Lithuania were drawn up in 1656–7, but after 1660 its neighbours recognized that there were advantages to be drawn from preserving it politically divided and weak. The *liberum veto* proved the perfect instrument: deputies could always be bribed to break the *Sejm*. Hopes of revival after the election of King Augustus II, elector of Saxony, (1697–1733) were dashed during the Great Northern War (1700–21), when Peter I's political acumen enabled him to establish a virtual Russian protectorate over the Commonwealth from 1717, when its army was limited to 24,000, tiny by 18th-century standards.

This situation suited Austria and Prussia, fighting for control of Silesia after the Prussian invasion of 1740. The War of Austrian Succession (1740–8) and the Seven Years' War (1756–63) left Prussia with Silesia; the two powers soon found common ground in the east where the election of Stanislaw Poniatowski as king of Poland in 1764 heralded the breakdown of the Russian protectorate over Poland as Poniatowski, inspired by Enlightenment teaching, sought to reform the unworkable Polish constitution. This provoked dangerous opposition: after the anti-Russian Confederation of Bar (1768–72) reduced the Commonwealth to political anarchy, Austria's seizure of the small territory of Zips (Spiz) stimulated Prussia and Russia to join in the First Partition.

Taking advantage of Russian distraction in the Turkish war of 1788–92 Poniatowski summoned the Four-Year *Sejm* (1788–92) which passed the Constitution of 3rd May 1791. This abolished the *liberum veto* and radically restructured the Commonwealth. The prospect of a revived Poland was too much for Russia and Prussia, who in 1793 agreed the Second Partition, in which Prussia secured Danzig. When the following year Tadeusz Kosciuszko led a rising in protest, Russia, Austria and Prussia combined to wipe Poland-Lithuania from the map in the Third Partition.

c. 1775
THE EMERGING GLOBAL ECONOMY

During the 18th century international trade made rapid strides, fuelled by the demand for luxury goods and foodstuffs from a Europe growing in wealth. The core of the trading system was the Atlantic triangle, dominated by Britain and France, which was based on the sale of slaves from Africa and the export of sugar and tobacco from the New World.

During the course of the 18th century, European and American merchants developed an extensive system of intercontinental trade routes which laid the foundation for the evolution of a sophisticated global economy in the next century. Trade on such a scale encouraged the development of large ocean-going merchant fleets, and the gradual development of modern commercial practices, particularly in the supply of insurance and trade credits. Nonetheless most trade in Europe and in the rest of the world remained local. In 1800 extra-European trade contributed an estimated 4 per cent to Europe's aggregate gross national product.

MERCANTILISM
For much of the century trade was still governed by mercantilist principles: trade should always be in surplus to provide a stream of bullion, and trade was always a war between states for a fixed quantity of commerce. In reality European merchants could see that trade was growing rapidly over the century, and

bullion increasingly being replaced by bills of exchange. Nevertheless states still played an important part in inhibiting trade by pursuing mercantilist policies. British tariffs rose sharply over the 18th century, averaging 30 per cent, while British colonies were banned from producing industrial products that competed with domestic manufactures. Britain's Navigation Acts prevented any other power from engaging in trade in Britain's empire. Bullion was also essential for western European trade with the Baltic, Turkey and Asia, which supplied goods much in demand in Europe but had little market for European products.

There were other factors that made trade difficult. Piracy was widespread, and not until the defeat of the Mediterranean corsairs after 1815 and the elimination of Caribbean pirates by 1830 was trade in these seas secure. Piracy remained endemic in the Indian Ocean and the China Sea. War also interrupted trade development, for states permitted official piracy in time of war. Trade security could only be guaranteed by those states that possessed large navies, which meant that Britain, France and the Netherlands profited most from the growth of world commerce.

THE SLAVE ECONOMY

Trade growth owed a great deal to the emergence of the Atlantic economy, where most trans-oceanic trade was conducted. Much of this was based on the Spanish and Portuguese empires which still played an important part in the 18th century, chiefly through the mining of gold and silver and its shipment exclusively to the Iberian peninsula. But the growth of the American colonies, the Caribbean and Canada promoted a new trade. The most important commodity was slaves, and more than 8 million Africans were shipped to the New World between the 17th and 19th centuries. Although outlawed by the United States and Britain in 1807, the slave trade continued until the 1860s.

The rise of the Atlantic slave economy was based on the growing demand in Europe for tobacco, sugar and cotton, all of which were produced in plantations in the New World. British trade in sugar grew six-fold over the 18th century, and the supply of tobacco, much of which was re-exported to Europe, grew from 14,500,000kg (32,000,000lb) to 22,700,000kg (50,000,000lb). Europeans brought manufactured goods to the west African coast to trade for slaves which were then taken to the New World and sold. Plantation products were then exported to Europe. Half of the slaves died before shipping, perhaps a quarter more on board ship, another fifth in the first year of work. It was a brutal and inefficient trade, but it kept Europe supplied with cheap luxury products which it could not afford from Asia.

TRADE WITH ASIA

Trade with the rest of the world was small. Asian and African traders kept to inland routes, or engaged in coastal trade. Europeans bought silk, spices, coffee and china, but often paid with gold or silver. Trade was conducted through local chartered companies such as the East India Company, which enjoyed a monopoly of Britain's south Asia trade until 1813. The consolidation of British power in Bengal opened the way in the late 1700s to the opening up of Asian trade. In 1700 Britain imported 32,000kg (70,000lb) of teas; by 1800 the figure had risen to 6,800,000kg (15,000,000lb). The development of Britain's cotton textile industry in the last third of the century produced a trading revolution. By then, the rapid pace of industrialization was poised to open the way for the domination of world markets by European traders in the 19th century and the development of a global system of communication, finance and production.

1760 TO 1820
THE INDUSTRIAL REVOLUTION BEGINS: GREAT BRITAIN

During the 18th century, Britain experienced the world's first industrial revolution as new technologies and overseas markets developed. British industry began to meet a growing demand for cheap consumer goods. It was a revolution that ushered in the mass market and paved the way for the economic trans-formation of the globe.

During the second half of the 18th century, the British economy was slowly transformed by the development of new industrial technologies that permitted cheaper production on a larger scale to meet the demands of a growing mass market. In fact the term "industrial revolution" is misleading. The British economy had been growing steadily since the late 17th century, while much of the success of the new industries depended on changes in agriculture, transport and financial services and on the accelerated growth of the population.

Nonetheless, at the heart of Britain's late 18th-century industrial transformation lay changes in the production of iron, textiles and machinery and a shift from wood to coal as the primary source of energy.

THE NEW TECHNOLOGIES

The key lay in steam power. Steam engines had existed since the beginning of the century, but when the Scottish scientist James Watt developed a more reliable and powerful version in the 1760s it was rapidly applied in mining, then in the iron industry. The invention of a rotative motion engine in 1781 opened the way for steam power to drive machinery. By 1800 the cotton and brewing industries were regular users of steam power. When Watt's patents lapsed in 1800, steam power spread throughout the industrial economy and the transport system. In 1825 the first steam railway was opened, ushering in another new period of economic development.

Innovation was also important in manufacturing. In the cotton textile industry, production was slowly mechanized from the 1760s to the 1790s, though hand-loom weaving was not challenged by machines until the 1820s. Mechanization permitted the shift from small-scale craft output to factory production: by 1816, for example, Arkwright's mill at Cromford in northwest England employed over 700 people. In the iron industry the inventions of Henry Cort in 1784 permitted coal to be used as the main refining fuel for iron, while the steam engine was used to produce rolled and bar-iron for working. Large production units developed which both smelted the ore and produced the finished iron products. Better quality iron could be used in all forms of construction work. Innovation became a continuous process, producing a stream of cheaper and better products.

THE CONDITIONS FOR GROWTH

Britain was by no means the only country to produce industrial inventions, but it enjoyed a number of advantages which explain its rapid industrial development. In the first place agriculture experienced its own "revolution", making it more prosperous and more productive. Improvements in patterns of land cultivation, greater use of fertilizers and improved stock breeding all contributed to raising farm incomes. The enclosure of common land accelerated after 1760 with Parliamentary Enclosure Acts, and had the effect of creating large integrated farms where modern practices could be introduced and yields and incomes raised. Farming generated growing demand for industrial goods and encouraged the creation of a wider market for farm products.

Agrarian change also encouraged the development of better transport and a more sophisticated capital market to meet the costs of farm improvement and canal-building. Both helped the emergence of early industry. Many business-men came from humble social backgrounds with little access to finance. Landlord and merchant capital, derived largely from Britain's prosperous over-seas and colonial trade, was mobilized for investment in expanding industries and in the building of canals, roads, ports and, from 1825, railways. The rapid growth of a largely unregulated capital market brought a serious bank crisis in 1825 which prompted bank reform in 1826 and, in 1844, the creation of a central bank and clearing-bank system. Without the emergence of this modern credit structure, the pace of industrial change might well have been much slower.

THE SOCIAL REVOLUTION

By 1820 Britain was in the throes of rapid social and economic transformation. Population growth produced a flow of cheap labour to the new cities and provided a large new market for mass-produced consumer goods. There were few social barriers to labour mobility or a business career, while governments favoured legislation that encouraged economic growth. It was between 1820 and 1851, when Britain hosted the Great Exhibition to trumpet its economic triumphs, that the industrialization of Britain finally overturned the agrarian social structure and traditional landlord rule. The new business class became an important political force, while the new urban workforce, toiling in appalling conditions with little security, laid the foundations for organized labour protest. "Class" in its modern sense was the direct offspring of industrial change.

1773 TO 1814
THE AGE OF REVOLT

A wave of revolutions swept over Europe and the Americas in the late 18th century, inspired in part by ideas of freedom promoted in the Enlightenment. New social forces challenged the old royal regimes and traditional privileges.

Revolutions in France and America symbolized the struggle against despotism and the triumph of a new ideal of citizenship.

In the *Social Contract* (1762), the French philosopher Rousseau claimed "Man is born free, but everywhere he is in chains". He was writing at the height of the European Enlightenment, an intellectual revolt against tradition and superstition. The spirit of the Enlightenment was the emancipation of the individual and the rational organization of society. Both ideas had deep political implications. Over the next 30 years much of the political order of Europe and America was overturned by revolutionaries who drew inspiration from the idea of political liberty and civil rights embodied in Enlightenment political philosophy.

The pattern of revolt was unpredictable and diverse. It owed something to early stirrings of nationalism, evident in Corsica, Poland and Ireland. But the chief revolutions in the American colonies and in France were responses to royal authority which came to be regarded as arbitrary, inefficient and unjust. In 1775 Britain's American colonies rebelled against the existing tax regime and under George Washington fought a six-year war against British-led forces, finally winning independence in 1783. The "founding fathers" of American liberty established a modern constitutional republic based on ideas on human rights culled from Enlightenment Europe.

THE SPREAD OF REVOLUTION

The American revolution had a great impact in Europe and many of those involved in it subsequently played a part in the many European revolts. Benjamin Franklin was an important influence in France, while the Polish nationalist Tadeusz Kosciuszko, who fought in the American revolution, returned to lead the Polish revolt against the two powers – Russia and Prussia – which had partitioned Poland in 1792. The revolution in Poland was typical of the popular reaction to the ideal of liberty and independence expressed in the newly-created USA. In the spring of 1794 thousands of Poles, drawn mainly from the educated and gentry classes, under the military leadership of Kosciuszko, drove the Russian army from Warsaw. Many of those involved were "Jacobins" who modelled themselves on the more radical social reformers and democrats of the French Revolution. The Polish revolution was destroyed by Russian and Prussian forces late in 1794. Attempts to spread the revolution further into eastern Europe failed. Small groups of Jacobins in Budapest were organized by Ignaz Martinovics in 1794 to imitate the Polish revolt, but the leaders were arrested and imprisoned. Only in the Netherlands and northern Italy did the revolutionary example have greater success, not only because ideas of "democracy" were more widely understood and broadcast, but because revolutionary groups there enjoyed the protection of the French.

The French example inspired hope of liberty around the world. In India Tipu Sultan planted a symbolic "Tree of Liberty" and declared himself an ally of revolutionary France against the British. In Haiti a slave revolt in 1791 freed the island from colonial rule. In Latin America the growing local hostility to Spanish rule was fuelled by news of the French revolution. Jacobin conspirators were discovered by the authorities in Quito and Buenos Aires. In Bogotá in 1793, 100 copies of the *Rights of Man* were printed, copied from the French declaration of 1789. In eastern Europe Jacobin activity was stamped out in Vienna and Budapest, while the 1794 Polish revolt, though led by the Polish nobility, used the French cry of "liberty and equality" against its Russian and Prussian oppressors.

COUNTER-REVOLUTION

The wave of political revolt produced a strong counter-revolutionary reaction. Many of the revolutionaries in America and France were themselves conservative in outlook and worked to eliminate more radical or utopian revolutionary movements. Slave revolts in America were brutally suppressed in the 1790s. The revolutionary Directory unleashed a "white terror" against the Jacobins in France, and Napoleon restored a strong centralist and authoritarian state after 1800. In eastern and central Europe reform introduced by so-called Enlightened despots was reversed or suspended and revolt in Poland, Hungary, Bohemia and the Ukraine violently quashed. Though Britain possessed the most liberal political system, the regime stamped hard on Irish nationalism and on any domestic threat of republicanism or domestic agitation.

In 1815 the Vienna Congress, summoned after the defeat of Napoleon, restored much of pre-1789 Europe by adopting the principle of "legitimism". But although monarchy was returned in France, the new ideas of liberty and nationhood were to find fertile ground throughout Europe and the Americas over the following century.

1789 TO 1797
THE FRENCH REVOLUTION

In the summer of 1789 the most powerful monarchy in Europe was overthrown by a popular revolution in favour of constitutional rule. There followed ten years of political turmoil as moderate parliamentarians and radical republicans fought over the political future of France. The many different ideals represented by the revolution were impossible to reconcile, and in 1799 a new era of authoritarian rule began under the dashing revolutionary general, Napoleon Bonaparte.

The French Revolution had many causes, some long-term, some more immediate. For 30 years there had been growing peasant hostility to rising rents and declining common rights as gentry and bourgeois landowners tried to cope with inflation and falling incomes by tightening the screw. For much of the century France was the hub of new ideas about liberty, citizenship and patriotism, and a powerful intellectual demolition of royal authority and clerical influence. By the 1780s the language of liberty had permeated much of the educated elite, gentry and bourgeois, and had filtered down into popular politics. Craftsmen and shopkeepers came to articulate their social and economic grievances in terms of civil rights and economic justice.

The actual events that came to be known as the French Revolution were precipitated by a crisis of state. For much of the century the monarchy had increased levels of central control and fiscal demands, undermining local privilege and raising taxes. The moral authority of the old order was eroded by the rising tide of political criticism and the spread of scurrilous libels of the monarchy and court life. Faced with severe financial crisis, failure in war and poor harvests, Louis XVI tried to stave off criticism by calling the Estates General. This assembly, representing the clergy (known as the First Estate), the gentry (Second Estate) and commoners (Third Estate), had not been summoned since 1614. However, in the summer of 1789 a group of deputies representing the Third Estate (the overwhelming majority of Frenchmen) declared themselves to be a National Assembly and overturned centuries of royal absolutism. On 14 July the royal prison at the Bastille was stormed. In August feudal privilege was abolished throughout France, and the *Declaration of the Rights of Man*, which promised individual liberty in place of royal despotism, was published. Louis was forced to accept a parliamentary constitution and the abolition of much of the structure of privilege that sustained the monarchy and the aristocratic elite.

FROM REFORM TO TERROR

A new constitution, finally accepted by the king in September 1791, established a constitutional, parliamentary monarchy. The Catholic Church lost many of its privileges, and priests were compelled in November 1790 to swear allegiance to the new order. Thousands refused, and were forced from office, or led local resistance to the Paris-based revolutionary regime in Brittany and large parts of southern France. The revolutionary assembly also reformed local administration into "departments" in 1791, and began a programme of legal reform and land redistribution.

The revolutionary leadership was never unitary. Divisions emerged over the utopian ideals of some revolutionaries, who wanted to create a new social and moral order and develop a "new man" on the enlightenment model. The more moderate Girondin faction launched a revolutionary war in April 1792 against Austria and other counter-revolutionary forces. The ensuing economic crisis, the rhetoric of patriotic mobilization and fear of conspiracy in France, produced a radical transformation of French politics. Under the leadership of the Jacobin faction, any pretence at representative government vanished. The constitutional monarchy was abolished in September 1792 and a republic declared. A Committee of Public Safety was set up in April 1793, and a little later a Committee of General Security, which launched a nationwide hunt for traitors to the revolution. Thousands of nobles, clergymen, merchants, as well as numbers of peasants and workers, were executed in 1793 and 1794 on the strength of often trumped-up charges. Growing popular revulsion against terrorism led to the execution in July 1794 of leading Jacobins, including their chief spokesman, Maximilien Robespierre. A reaction against the utopianism of the revolutionary elite produced a more moderate revolutionary Directorate in November 1795, which savagely crushed radical political circles while consolidating the reforms of the revolution.

THE LEGACY OF THE REVOLUTION

The French Revolution failed to turn France into a democratic state, and the civil rights enshrined in its opening declaration were subject to constant abuse; but the programme of legal, administrative and educational reform was enduring. The revolution provided an inspiration to political opposition, and the symbols of the new French order were widely imitated. The French parliamentary system established in 1791 gave rise to new political terms: left and right (derived from the physical make-up of the new French assembly building) came to define the battle-lines of European politics, while the term communism was coined by popular radicals in the mid-1790s. For conservatives, the revolution represented for decades to come the unbridled political appetites of the mob.

1799 TO 1815
NAPOLEON AND THE RESHAPING OF EUROPE

Between 1799 and 1815 Napoleon blazed across Europe, plunging the continent into near permanent war and ruthlessly imposing on it French revolutionary institutions and his own tirelessly cultivated image as a latter-day Julius Caesar. Though he was ultimately defeated and exiled, the world of the *ancien régime* was swept aside for ever.

Napoleon, born in 1769 to minor gentry in Corsica, was barely 30 years old when, in November 1799, he became First Consul and de facto ruler of the French First Republic. He had made his name as a revolutionary general in northern Italy in 1796–7, where his defeat of Austria allowed him to create a new state, the Cisalpine Republic, run on French lines by pro-French Italian notables, a pattern reproduced throughout the areas later conquered by him.

Though Napoleon as First Consul inherited a system with an element of popular participation, within three years the revolution's democratic aspirations had been smothered and France had been ruthlessly centralized. This concentration of power in his own hands reached its logical conclusion in 1804 with the creation of a French empire over which Napoleon presided as self-appointed emperor.

THE PRIMACY OF THE MILITARY

Napoleon's centralization of power took many forms – notably the *Code Napoléon* of 1804 which, in codifying and rationalizing French law, swept away *ancien régime* privilege and increased the power of the French state; the agreement with the Pope in 1802, which ended the dispute for primacy between state and church, again very much in the former's favour; and the creation of a paramilitary police force, the gendarmerie, which mercilessly suppressed opposition to the revolution. But its overriding characteristic was the mobilization of France on an unprecedented scale in support of the army. With more than 1.5 million Frenchmen under arms, the French economy came to be dominated by the needs of the military.

This was not yet "total war", but the demands of more than 20 years of conflict turned the Napoleonic empire into a militarized society. The military priorities explain the long string of military triumphs. In 1800 Italy was reconquered and French power extended in Germany. In 1805 Russia and Austria were defeated at Austerlitz and in 1806 Prussia humiliated at Jena. At Eylau in 1807 Russia was again defeated. Under the terms of the subsequent Treaty of Tilsit, French power was extended as far as Poland, where Napoleon established yet another puppet regime, the Grand Duchy of Warsaw.

Napoleon appointed kings, princes and dukes to enforce French rule throughout his empire. In the Kingdom of Westphalia he installed his youngest brother, Jerome. In Naples his brother Joseph was made king. When Joseph was transferred to Spain as its monarch in 1808, Naples was placed under the rule of Napoleon's brother-in-law, Joachim Murat. Holland was ruled by another brother, Louis, from 1806 to 1810. In all these areas, French officials introduced conscription and new taxes, helping finance the almost permanent state of war Napoleon faced.

By 1807 only Britain, at war with France almost continuously since 1792, remained undefeated. Britain's chief weapon was its navy, largely unchallenged by Napoleon after its defeat of the combined French and Spanish fleets at Trafalgar in 1805. But unable to defeat Napoleon on land, Britain then blockaded French ports. Napoleon responded by forbidding trade with Britain in any of the territories of his empire. But though this, the Continental System, brought hardship to Britain, its effects on France were hardly less severe. The political crisis that followed was made all the more serious when in 1809 Spain revolted against French rule. The "Spanish Ulcer" drained France of 70 million francs a year. In 1810, Tsar Alexander refused to exclude British trade. In June 1812 Napoleon invaded Russia.

DEFEAT AND EXILE

It was a fatal miscalculation. With widespread unrest against French rule in much of northern Europe as well as in Spain, Napoleon had over-reached himself. As his troops retreated from Moscow, ravaged by hunger, disease and cold, they were harried relentlessly by the Russians. About 450,000 began the campaign; only 40,000 survived.

The cost broke the empire. Steep tax rises and conscription caused bitter popular protest. At the same time, Napoleon's enemies, realizing that he could after all be defeated, reformed the coalition against him. At Leipzig in October 1813, the French army was overwhelmed. The following year Napoleon was exiled and the Bourbon monarchy restored. Though Napoleon contrived a final throw, escaping from exile in 1815 and regrouping his army, this time his defeat, at Waterloo, was decisive and he was exiled to St Helena in the South Atlantic, where in 1821 he died.

The treaty drawn up by the Great Powers to decide the fate of Napoleon's empire – the Vienna Settlement of 1815 – aimed not just to overthrow his legacy but to make any further revolutionary upsurge impossible. In the longer term, it failed. Napoleon's reforms had shaken Europe's traditional structures to their foundations, creating the conditions for the emergence of recognizably modern states across Europe.

SIX

THE AGE OF EUROPEAN DOMINANCE

Between 1815 and 1914 Europe thrust out into the world, impelled by the force of its own industrialization. Millions of Europeans poured overseas and into Asiatic Russia, seeking and finding new opportunities in the wider world. Between 1880 and 1900 Africa, a continent four times the size of Europe, was parcelled out among the European powers. And when in 1898 the United States of America, following Europe's lead, annexed Puerto Rico, the Philippines and other islands of the Pacific, and asserted a controlling voice in Latin American affairs, it seemed as though Western expansion had secured the domination of the white race over the non-white majority. But expansion carried with it the seeds of its own destruction. Even before European rivalries plunged the continent into the war of 1914–18, the beginnings of anti-European reaction were visible in Asia and Africa, and no sooner had the USA occupied the Philippines than they were met by a nationalist uprising.

Today, in retrospect, we can see that the age of expansive imperialism was a transient phase of history. Nevertheless, it left a lasting European imprint. The world in 1914 was utterly different from the world in 1815, the tempo of change during the preceding century greater than in the entire millennium before it. Though industry in 1914 was only beginning to spread beyond Europe and North America, and life in Asia and Africa was still regulated by age-old traditions, the 19th century inaugurated the process of transformation which dethroned agricultural society as it had existed for thousands of years, replacing it with the urban, industrialized, technocratic society, which continues to spread into even the most remote parts of the globe – for good or ill – more than a century later.

1815 TO 1914

POPULATION GROWTH AND MOVEMENTS

The 19th century witnessed the beginning of the remarkable population explosion which has continued ever since. Europe was at the centre of the surge, sending millions overseas to America, Africa and Australasia. Millions more left the land to work in the bustling cities whose populations grew faster than at any point in their history.

When Thomas Malthus wrote his *Essay on the Principle of Population* at the end of the 18th century the population of Europe, and of much of the rest of the world, had been stagnant for two centuries. Yet Malthus's belief that populations were always restricted – by famine, war and disease – was destroyed by the sudden explosion of world population in the century that followed.

THE POPULATION EXPLOSION

It is estimated that the world's population grew in the 19th century from 900 million to 1,600 million. Much of the increase came from the expansion of the population of Europe, from 123 million to 267 million (excluding Russia). Europe also provided emigrants whose descendants populated the huge areas of the Americas, Australasia, southern Africa and Siberia. The population of these areas increased from 5.7 million to over 200 million between 1810 and 1910. The most heavily industrialized states grew fastest: the populations of the United States, Germany and Britain multiplied five-fold across the century.

Part of the explanation for this sudden burst of population growth lay in the decline of Malthusian checks. There were few major wars in the century after 1815; the spread of cultivation worldwide gradually overcame the regular incidence of famine or poor nutrition; above all, the effects of epidemic disease, particularly in Europe and America, declined significantly.

Smallpox, one of the major killers, was successfully combated by the introduction of Jenner's vaccination. Bubonic plague, still endemic in the Ottoman empire and in Asia, almost disappeared from Europe after 1816. The poor state of urban living produced a new cluster of epidemics – typhus and tuberculosis chiefly – but over the century better public-health measures and quarantine methods, and a general rise in living-standards in Europe and areas of European settlement reduced the general impact of disease. The crisis death-rates of the previous century receded. In France in 1801 only 5,800 out of every 10,000 lived to the age of 20; by 1901 7,300 reached that age.

The rapid growth of cities in Europe and America saw them overtake the greatest cities of India and China in size. In 1800 5.5 million Europeans lived in cities of more than 100,000; by 1900 the figure was 46 million. In cities people tended to marry younger and have more children. Legal controls over the age of marriage disappeared, while larger families provided a stream of young workers and a kinship group which could support the interests of the family as a whole. The rising birth-rate and the slowly falling death-rate produced a "demographic gap", an excess of births over deaths that created a favourable cycle for further high growth.

THE MOVEMENT OF POPULATION

High population growth produced many pressures to migrate. In rural areas migration increased rapidly as peasants left their villages to find city work. In Russia and Spain migrant workers were a traditional source of labour throughout the century. Elsewhere, workers flocked to where mines and factories were springing up. Polish workers moved to the Ruhr mines; Irish workers travelled to Scotland and Lancashire; Italians worked in France and Germany. By 1914 there were an estimated 3 million migrant workers in Europe.

The promise of economic opportunity also lured millions overseas. Between 1801 and 1840 only 1.5 million left Europe, mainly for the United States; between 1841 and 1880 the figure leapt to 13 million; and between 1880 and 1910 it leapt again to 25 million. Some migrants returned (estimates suggest as many as 25 per cent), but those who stayed in the vast expanses of America or Australia or southern Africa became buoyant population groups with high growth rates, better diets and more opportunities than Europe could provide. Some migrants were the victims of coercion – the threat of famine took millions from Ireland; political or racial persecution pushed out thousands more, particularly from eastern Europe – but most were lured by the promise of wealth, freedom or adventure. Between 1800 and 1930 the white proportion of the world's population expanded from 22 to 35 per cent.

Europeans were not the only ones on the move. Chinese and Indian emigrants reached the Caribbean and Africa in search of work and business openings. Japanese workers crossed the Pacific to west-coast America. Until the 1820s slaves were still shipped from Africa to the plantations of the New World, and continued to be shipped to the Middle East until the major slave markets of Zanzibar and Madagascar were closed in the 1870s. Gradually the movement of populations became regulated by governments as local labour forces, once migrants themselves, began to protest at the further flow of fresh recruits.

1815 TO 1870
THE INDUSTRIAL REVOLUTION
IN EUROPE

The 19th century witnessed a fundamental transformation of the European economy with the spread of modern forms of industrial organization and production. Industrial regions grew up around major ore- and coalfields, drawing in millions of workers from the villages to form a new class of labouring poor. Marx called them the proletariat and defined the new era as the age of capitalism.

Industrialization in Europe was a slow and uneven process over the course of the 19th century. Europe had a rich commercial heritage and was far from an undeveloped region in 1800, but most production was still small-scale and craft-based, and most workers were on the land. Poor communications and shortages of capital allowed the traditional economy to survive until mechanized production, the coming of the railways and a modern banking system created the conditions for the rapid industrial growth of the late century.

PROTO-INDUSTRIALIZATION

The early stages of industrial change have been described as "proto-industrialization". The term reflects an economy in transition, with traditional production methods and marketing existing alongside large merchants and new experimental factories borrowing the technology of early industrial development in Britain. The textile industry was typical. The mechanization of spinning and weaving developed very slowly: in Saxony British engineers introduced mechanical spinning in 1807 and the first steam machinery in 1831, yet hand-loom weaving survived until long into the century in much of Europe. Only by 1900 was the bulk of textile production mechanized.

Heavy industry also developed slowly. Coke-fired iron production had revolutionized British industry, but as late as the 1850s charcoal furnaces supplied 70 per cent of German iron production. The first coke furnace appeared in France in 1823, yet by 1850 only two-fifths of iron was smelted by coke. Only in Belgium was the new technology embraced, and the Belgian coalfield became the second major industrial region of Europe until the 1860s. After 1850 the situation changed sharply: a long boom based on coal, iron and steel and modern engineering turned much of Europe within 25 years into industrial states.

THE MID-CENTURY BOOM

Industrial development crucially depended on changes in the wider economic framework. The transport revolution was vital. Railways and steam-shipping meant fast and reliable delivery, and cheaper food from the major food producers outside Europe. In 1850 there were 24,150km (15,000 miles) of railway, most of it in Britain and Belgium; by 1870 another 80,450km (50,000 miles) had been added. By 1914 railways smothered the European area. Russia had less than 2000km (1240 miles) of rail track in 1860; more than 65,000km (40,000 miles) 50 years later. The reform of the banking system in the 1850s and 1860s stabilized national currencies and created credit and mortgage banks that invested heavily in new technologies in industry and agriculture. The creation of the Gold Standard in the 1870s made trade and currency conversion easy; the subsequent boom in international trade encouraged another wave of industrial growth.

THE "SECOND INDUSTRIAL REVOLUTION"

By the 1870s Europe had been transformed as Britain had been from the late 18th century. Over the next 40 years there began what has been called the "second industrial revolution" based on the application of modern science in electricity, chemicals and motor vehicles. Iron gave way to high quality steel: in 1861 steel output in Europe was 125,000 tons; by 1913 it had reached 38 million. Germany became the heart of the new industrial boom, producing half of the world's trade in electrical goods and 80 per cent of the world's dyestuffs. The motor-car was pioneered in Germany by the engineers Gottlieb Daimler and Karl Benz.

Alongside the technical and scientific breakthroughs came a revolution in commerce. Department stores, chains of high-street shops and popular advertising made goods available to all and created global markets for the new products. Rising productivity produced a long boom in real wages down to 1914, freeing many workers from primary poverty and creating a culture of popular consumption. Only in the countryside, where over half of Europeans worked in 1914, was progress slower and poverty widespread.

1800 TO 1914
THE RISE OF NATIONALISM IN EUROPE

The French Revolution paved the way for the modern nation-state. Across Europe radical intellectuals questioned the old monarchical order and encouraged the development of a popular nationalism committed to re-drawing the political map of the continent. By 1914 the days of the old multi-national empires were numbered.

The French Revolution, by destroying the traditional structures of power in France and territories conquered by Napoleon, was the instrument for the political transformation of Europe. Revolutionary armies carried the slogan of "liberty, equality and fraternity" and ideas of liberalism and national self-determinism. National awakening also grew out of an intellectual reaction to the Enlightenment that emphasized national identity and developed a romantic view of cultural self-expression through nationhood. The key exponent of the modern idea of the nation-state was the German Georg Hegel (1770–1831). He argued that a sense of nationality was the cement that held modern societies together in an age when dynastic and religious allegiance was in decline.

In 1815, at the end of the Napoleonic wars, the major powers of Europe tried to restore the old dynastic system as far as possible, ignoring the principle of nationality in favour of "legitimism", the assertion of traditional claims to royal authority. With most of Europe's peoples still loyal to their local province or city, nationalism was confined to small groups of intellectuals and political radicals. Furthermore, political repression, symbolized by the Carlsbad Decrees published in Austria in 1819, pushed nationalist agitation underground.

THE STRUGGLE FOR INDEPENDENCE
Nevertheless there began to develop a strong resentment of what came to be regarded as foreign rule. In Ireland, Italy, Belgium, Greece, Poland, Hungary and Norway local hostility to alien dynastic authority started to take the form of

nationalist agitation. Nationalism came to be seen as the most effective way to create the symbols of resistance and to unite in a common cause.

Success came first in Greece where an eight-year civil war (1822–30) against Ottoman rule led to an independent Greek state; in 1831 Belgium obtained independence from the Netherlands. Over the next two decades nationalism developed a more powerful voice, spurred by nationalist writers championing the cause of national self-determination. In 1848 revolutions broke out across Europe, sparked by a severe famine and economic crisis and mounting popular demands for political change. In Italy Giuseppe Mazzini used the opportunity to encourage a war for national unification; in Hungary Lajos Kossuth led a national revolt against Austrian rule; in the German Confederation a National Assembly was elected at Frankfurt and debated the creation of a German nation.

None of the nationalist revolts in 1848 was successful, any more than the two attempts to win Polish independence from Russian rule in 1831 and 1846 had been. Conservative forces proved too strong, while the majority of the populations little understood the meaning of national struggle. But the 1848 crisis had given nationalism its first full public airing, and in the 30 years that followed no fewer than seven new national states were created in Europe. This was partly the result of the recognition by conservative forces that the old order could not continue in its existing form. Conservative reformers such as Cavour and Bismarck (see pp. 224–5) made common cause with liberal political modernizers to create a consensus for the creation of conservative nation-states in Italy and Germany. In the Habsburg empire a compromise was reached with Hungarian nationalists in 1867 granting them a virtually independent state. In the Balkans the Greek example had inspired other national awakenings. Native history and culture were rediscovered and appropriated for the national struggle. Following a conflict between Russia and Turkey, the Great Powers met at Berlin in 1878 and granted independence to Romania, Serbia and Montenegro.

NATIONALISM EXPORTED

The invention of a symbolic national identity became the concern of racial or linguistic groups throughout Europe as they struggled to come to terms with the rise of mass politics, popular xenophobia and the decline of traditional social elites. Within the Habsburg empire the different races developed a more mass-based, violent and exclusive nationalism, even among the Germans and

Magyars, who actually benefited from the power-structure of the empire. The Jewish population of eastern and central Europe began to develop radical demands for their own national state in Palestine. In 1897, inspired by the Hungarian-born nationalist Theodor Herzl (1860–1904), the First Zionist Congress was held in Basle. On the European periphery, especially in Ireland and Norway, campaigns for national independence became more strident. In 1905 Norway won independence from Sweden, but attempts to grant Ireland the kind of autonomy enjoyed by Hungary foundered on the national divisions in the island between the ethnic Irish and British migrants.

By this time the ideals of European nationalism had been exported worldwide and were now beginning to threaten the colonial empires still ruled by European nation-states.

1815 TO 1871

GERMANY AND ITALY: THE STRUGGLES FOR UNIFICATION

The French Revolution laid the foundation for a romantic nationalism in Italy and Germany that was harshly suppressed after 1815. The two regions were united in the end not by popular nationalism but by the ambitions of the major powers and the machinations of statesmen who preferred to unify from above rather than risk revolutionary demands.

The roots of Italian and German nationalism lay in the reaction to French domination under the Napoleonic empire. In both regions the experience of French revolutionary rule stimulated the emergence of a nationalist intelligentsia committed to the development of a native culture and language. National development was seen as the key to political freedom and economic success.

THE STRUGGLE FOR NATIONHOOD

In 1815 the Vienna Settlement restored the conservative order in Germany and Italy. Secret societies kept nationalist aspirations alive – the *carbonari* in Italy, the student *Burschenschaften* in Germany – but the Habsburg empire, guided by Chancellor Metternich, smothered demands for national unification. What protest there was, for example in Italy in 1820–1 and 1830–1, was more anti-Austrian than actively nationalist in character. Most German and Italian liberals looked for constitutional reform, civil rights and economic freedoms rather than for unity.

The revolutionary upheavals of the 1840s gave impetus to the infant nationalist movements. Economic crisis combined with increasing resentment at the absence of political reform to produce growing demands for nationhood. In Italy Mazzini, who founded the Young Italy movement in 1831, inspired a generation of young nationalists. When revolt broke out in 1848, Mazzini was among the revolutionaries demanding a new national Italian state. Austrian forces crushed the revolutions and defeated the army of Charles Albert of Piedmont-Sardinia, who had briefly placed himself at the forefront of Italian revival, the *risorgimento*.

In Germany the 1848 crisis gave nationalist circles, drawn largely from the educated bourgeoisie, the opportunity to overturn the Habsburg-dominated German Confederation, which had been revived in 1815, and to replace it with a united German nation. Though a national assembly met at Frankfurt, it found itself split between those who wanted a Germany which included Austria (*Grossdeutschland*) and those who wanted a smaller Germany free of Habsburg interference (*Kleindeutschland*). The debate proved academic: in 1849 Prussian troops disbanded the parliament and reimposed the old order.

The failure of 1848 pushed nationalism to the margins again. Mazzini launched nationalist revolts in the 1850s, but with no success. It took ten years before a National Society was founded in Germany, and its numbers never exceeded 25,000. In the event the unification of Italy and Germany was made possible not through nationalist agitation but as a result of the changing character of the conservative order, both at home and abroad. In Germany and Italy conservative reformers emerged who were hostile to the continuation of Austrian dominance but fearful of mass politics and revolution. A programme of "reform from above" was initiated, led by the major regional states, Prussia in Germany, Piedmont-Sardinia in Italy.

UNIFICATION FROM ABOVE

In Italy the lead was taken by Count Cavour, who became Piedmontese prime minister in 1852. He introduced economic, military and constitutional reforms that made Piedmont the most advanced state in the peninsula. When Austria found itself isolated internationally after the Crimean War (1853–5), Cavour opportunistically allied with Napoleon III of France to drive Austria out of northern Italy. Defeated at Magenta and Solferino, Austria signed the Treaty of Villafranca with France, giving up Lombardy but keeping Venetia. Lombardy then joined with Piedmont, and was followed by Tuscany, Parma, Romagna and Modena, where plebiscites overwhelmingly favoured a union with Piedmont. When Garibaldi, a flamboyant nationalist, lent his support to a peasant revolt against the Bourbon Kingdom of Naples, nationalists flocked to join him. Fearful that Garibaldi's success would result in popular uprisings throughout Italy, Cavour skilfully imposed Piedmontese control over Garibaldi, and in 1861 the Kingdom of Italy was declared with the Piedmont-Sardinian monarch, Victor Emmanuel II, its first king. Venetia was added in 1866, when Austria was defeated by Prussia, while in 1870 Rome was taken over from papal rule to become the new capital.

GERMAN UNIFICATION

A similar process occurred in Germany, where Prussia embarked on a programme of conservative modernization, building up a strong industrial economy and reforming the army. With Bismarck as minister-president from 1862, Prussia began to dominate northern Germany. Following war with Denmark in 1864 over the duchies of Schleswig and Holstein, Prussian-Austrian relations deteriorated sharply. In 1866 Austria declared war on Prussia to prevent a repeat of her loss of influence in Italy. Defeated at Sadowa, Austria was effectively excluded from northern Germany and in 1867 Prussia established a North German Confederation. Napoleon III's ambition to revive French influence in the Rhineland then led to a crisis in Franco-Prussian relations which resulted in war in 1870 in which Germany decisively defeated the French, in the process occupying Paris. The southern German states, Bavaria, Baden and Württemberg, then allied with Prussia, and in 1871 agreed to join a larger federal structure, a German empire, rather than remain isolated and economically dependent on their much more powerful northern neighbour.

Nationalists in both Italy and Germany welcomed the new states, but in neither case had mass nationalism brought about unification. The old orders took the initiative to avoid popular revolution. When, later in the century, mass nationalism did develop in Italy and Germany it eventually led to fascism and the collapse of the conservative order that had ushered in the new nation states.

1783 TO 1890
THE MAKING OF THE UNITED STATES: WESTWARD EXPANSION

At independence in 1783 most Americans lived on the eastern seaboard of the new country. Over the next 100 years there was a vast movement of population westwards into new lands acquired through treaty and exploration. It was a century of frontier towns, gold rushes and Indian wars. By 1890 railroads crossed the USA and the "frontier" was closed.

When in 1783 the independence of the USA was at last recognized, most Americans – apart from a small settlement in Kentucky – lived between the eastern seaboard and the Appalachian mountains. Soon after independence, however, a vast westward movement of population began. This was assisted by improvements in communications – first roads, later canals, and finally railroads. It was also encouraged by a series of political decisions through which, between the Louisiana Purchase of 1803 and the Gadsden Purchase of 1853, the new republic acquired vast new territories in the west and pushed its continental boundary as far as the Pacific Ocean.

After the political acquisition of new territory, 19th-century explorers – following in the footsteps of colonial predecessors such as Louis Joliet, James Marquette and Daniel Boone – visited and mapped the vast new lands. Many of these men, including William Clark, Meriwether Lewis, John C. Frémont and Zebulon Pike, were army officers. In their wake flowed pioneering settlers.

By 1820, the frontier of western settlement had reached the Mississippi River. It carried on shifting until by the 1840s it had reached the 100th meridian (bisecting present-day North Dakota and passing down through the middle of Texas). There, for a time, expansion faltered: the Great Plains to the west had too little rainfall to support mixed farming. It was only in the generation after the civil war and with the assistance of new technology – the railroads, barbed wire and steel ploughs – that this part of the west was finally settled and the region became the heart of American wheat production.

THE MOVE WESTWARDS

Beginning in the 1840s, sizeable wagon trains set out from Missouri and Midwestern states such as Illinois in order to cross the Rocky Mountains and settle near the Pacific coast. There were two basic routes: the Oregon Trail and, diverging away from it after the junction with the Snake River, the California Trail. It took most migrants about six months to complete the journey in ox-drawn, canvas-covered wagons. Often, they were under constant pressure from Indian attack or infectious disease. Some turned back. Others failed to reach the Far West – the notorious Donner party of 1846–7 experienced many fatalities when trapped by snow in the Rocky Mountains.

There were many different motives for western migration. The desire for cheap land was clearly a major one – especially in the wake of the Homestead Act of 1862 (which offered 160 acres (65ha) of land free to anyone settling it). But not just farmers moved west. There were also professional folk interested in a new career in booming towns. Some of those booming towns went on to become great cities: Chicago, a small community on the shore of Lake Michigan when first incorporated as a city in 1837, had become a huge metropolis with a population of a million by 1890. Miners also moved west – especially during the California "Gold Rush" of 1849. Some groups, such as the Mormons, who migrated to the Utah Territory in the 1840s, were in search of not simply economic opportunity but religious freedom as well. Others who moved west did so involuntarily, like the Cherokee Indians compelled to trek to Oklahoma in 1838. There were also large ethnic minorities, including blacks and Asians, in the west.

THE DEVELOPMENT OF COMMUNICATIONS

The story of the west was also one of faster communications. In 1851, a stagecoach service started between Independence, Missouri, and Salt Lake City. It was buttressed in 1857 by the Overland Mail between St Louis and San Francisco. In 1860, the Pony Express mail service was introduced – only to become immediately obsolete when the telegraph service between Kansas and

California began just 18 months later. In 1869, the stagecoach suffered the same fate with the completion of the first transcontinental railroad. Abraham Lincoln thought that the settlement of the whole west would take 100 years. It was the railroads that proved him wrong. In 1890, only 21 years after the opening of the first transcontinental service, the US Census Bureau announced that it could no longer locate a continuous area of free land for settlement in the west. With the final disappearance of the frontier line, the western stage of American development effectively came to an end.

1800 TO 1880

THE MARKET REVOLUTION IN THE UNITED STATES

The century between 1800 and 1900 witnessed a "market revolution" in the USA. Small farms and workshops gave way to a national economy where manfacturers produced for a distant marketplace. Better transportation, vast resources and favourable government policies were all crucial in creating, by 1900, the world's most productive economy.

In 1800, the USA had been internationally recognized as a nation for only 17 years. Most of its estimated population of 5,298,000 dwelt in small communities or on farms: there were only 73 towns and cities with a population of over 2500, of which just one – New York – had over 50,000 inhabitants. By 1900, the nation had been transformed. The estimated population of the USA had grown to 76,094,000 (an increase of 1337 per cent). There were now 827 settlements with a population between 2500 and 50,000, and 75 cities of more than 50,000 people (including three of more than 1,000,000). The statistics of economic growth during the century show equally large increases: the net tonnage entering US ports grew by 3400 per cent; total imports by 922 per cent; and exports by 2011 per cent.

In 1800, not only was the USA primarily an agricultural nation, but most farm crops were grown for local consumption. Farming families produced either for themselves, or for their neighbours. There was little chance, because of the high cost of internal transportation, of moving towards a more national market-oriented type of economy. According to one estimate of 1816, shipping a ton of goods from Europe to America cost approximately $9; the same amount would enable it to be transported only 14.5km (9 miles) by land.

Better transportation made possible a "market revolution". After 1800, there were many improvements in communications. The building of the Cumberland Road (1811–18) between Cumberland, Maryland, and Vandalia on the Ohio river, symbolized the drive to build turnpike roads that, by the time the road construction boom collapsed in 1821, had seen 6400km (4,000 miles) of such roads constructed. Return voyages by the Clermond between New York and Albany in 1807 and the Washington between Louisville and New Orleans in 1817 inaugurated an era of steamship navigation on rivers and inland lakes. The successful completion of the Erie Canal in 1825 also prompted a major boom in canal-building in subsequent years.

THE ARRIVAL OF THE RAILROAD

Most crucial of all was the arrival of the railroad. By 1840, the USA had 5355km (3328 miles) of railroad track (compared to 2896km/1800 miles for the whole of Europe). A further 46,660km (29,000 miles) were built during the next 20 years. The last four decades of the 19th century saw a great expansion in railroad construction and the completion of five new transcontinental railroads. By 1900, the USA had 311,094km (193,346 miles) of rail track carrying about 142 billion ton-miles of freight (compared to 39 billion in 1866). The railroads, which had played so significant a part in creating a national market, both recognized it and regularized it with the introduction of standard time zones (1883) and a common track gauge.

INDUSTRIALIZATION

During the 19th century, smaller-scale manufacturing gave place to industrial production in ever larger economic units. This process began during the war of 1812–14 between the USA and Britain, which saw considerable capital transferred from foreign trade into manufacturing. The organization of the first path-breaking cotton factory at Waltham, Massachusetts, was followed by the spread of the factory system throughout cotton manufacturing and then to other industries. The USA had a large pool of labour drawn from mass immigration, seemingly endless natural resources (for example, the huge iron-ore fields around Lake Superior, the vast coal reserves of Appalachia, and the oil-fields of

Pennsylvania), and great native inventiveness and ingenuity. It also had a class of entrepreneurs who, particularly towards the end of the century, organized themselves into larger and larger business corporations.

For most of the 19th century, Federal and state governments – while often paying lip service to laissez-faire principles – actively promoted the growth of industry and a market economy. The Erie Canal was built by the state of New York. The Federal government, which had financed the Cumberland Road, later took over the policy begun by the state of Illinois in the 1850s of promoting railroad construction through grants of land.

In 1800, the USA was a largely provincial and non-market economy. As the 19th century progressed, it not only developed a national marketplace, but also became part of the international economy. In terms of industrial production, by the end of the 19th century it was leading the world, with the most rapid developments coming in the last decades of the 19th century. In 1880, the USA produced less steel than Britain. By 1900, it was producing more than the combined total of Britain and Germany, its nearest rivals. As the 20th century dawned, the USA was well on the way to developing into an economic colossus.

1820 TO 1877
SLAVERY, CIVIL WAR AND RECONSTRUCTION

The civil war was the most dramatic event in American history. It caused the deaths of 620,000 men – more casualties than in all other American wars combined. The roots of the conflict lay in slavery. Where the North sought to abolish it, the South was determined on its preservation, as well as on protecting its rights in the Union as a whole.

Slavery was an embarrassment to many of the early leaders of the American republic. Although they launched their new nation on the basis that everyone had a right to "life, liberty, and the pursuit of happiness", many of them – including Thomas Jefferson – themselves owned slaves. In the northern states, slavery did begin to disappear at the start of the 19th century. In the South, however, the invention of the cotton gin by Eli Whitney in 1793 made cotton, grown principally by black slaves, a lucrative crop. Far from declining, slavery consolidated in the South.

THE SOUTH AND SLAVERY

During the early 19th century, Southern slavery became intimately bound up with the issues raised by westward expansion. Southerners felt politically disadvantaged if new states were forbidden to enter the Union with slaves. In 1819 Missouri applied for admission to the Union as a slave state and the North refused. The problem was solved by the Compromise of 1820, which sought to balance the two interests by admitting Missouri as a slave state at the same time as Maine as a free one. It also drew a line at the latitude of 36 degrees 30 minutes across the Louisiana territory purchased in 1803 (see p. 226): future states entering the Union north of that line would be free, whereas south of it they could be slave states.

The Compromise of 1820 was finally brought down by a rising abolitionist clamour in the North and by the territories gained by the USA as a result of the war with Mexico (1846–8). California threatened to upset the sectional balance by applying to enter the Union in 1849 as a free state. This was opposed by the South, which feared Northern political dominance. Another compromise resulted: California was allowed into the Federal Union as a free state, but the territories of Utah and New Mexico were organized on a new principle: popular or squatter sovereignty. The decision on whether or not to have slavery was left to the settlers themselves. But this Compromise lasted less than four years: in 1854 an attempt was made to extend the same principle of popular sovereignty to the territories of Kansas and Nebraska. These lay north of the line of 36 degrees 30 minutes, so the possibility arose that they might decide to have slavery in an area from which it was banned by the Missouri Compromise of 1820.

The consequences of the Kansas-Nebraska Act were disastrous for the Union. Armed conflict broke out in Kansas between pro- and anti-slavery forces. A new political party, the Republicans, was born to resist any further expansion of slavery into the territories. Relations between the North and the South deteriorated rapidly. Finally, in 1860, when Abraham Lincoln, as the Republican candidate, was elected president solely on the basis of northern votes, the South began to secede from the Union. In spring 1861, war broke out between the 11 seceded Southern states, which formed a new collective government known as the Confederacy, and the Federal Union, which refused to accept the legality of secession. Eighteen months later, Lincoln added another war aim to the salvation of the Union when he issued his provisional proclamation emancipating the slaves, to become effective on 1 January 1863.

THE CIVIL WAR

During the first months of the war, volunteer armies on both sides were neither very disciplined nor very effective. Serious military operations really began in spring 1862. The North's strategy was based on denying the South vital resources by a naval blockade, controlling key river routes and capturing the Confederate capital of Richmond. Despite overwhelming superiority in manpower and resources, however, the Union took four years to win the war. There were two principal reasons: first, the South had superior generalship during the war's first two years; second, the North's goals demanded the occupation of the South and the destruction of its armies, while the South fought on home ground to defend its own territories. General Robert E. Lee thwarted two invasions of Virginia in 1862, and carried the war into the North, only to be stopped at Antietam, Maryland, in September 1862 and defeated at Gettysburg, Pennsylvania, in July 1863. By then, in the west, the Union had gained control of the Mississippi and Tennessee rivers and opened the way for an invasion of the lower South. In 1864, with the Union blockade increasingly effective, General Ulysses S. Grant began his invasion of Virginia which, combined with General Philip T. Sherman's march through Georgia and South Carolina, had destroyed the South's armies by the spring of 1865.

RECONSTRUCTION

With Lincoln's assassination and the end of the war, a political conflict arose between Congress and the new president, Andrew Johnson, over "Reconstruction" – the process of re-admitting the South to the Union. Johnson wanted to be as lenient to the South as possible. Many Republicans, however, dismayed by the continuing intransigence of the Southern states, wished to follow a more radical policy centred around the enfranchisement of blacks in the South. In 1867, the Republicans imposed their version of Reconstruction on the South. But attempts to promote real equality for blacks were hampered by Southern resistance, through organizations such as the Ku Klux Klan, and the failure to provide land for the freed slaves. One by one, the Republican regimes supported by black voters in the South were overthrown. By 1876, only three states – South Carolina, Florida and Louisiana – were still undergoing Reconstruction. The withdrawal of Federal troops from these states, in the wake of the elections of 1876, caused the Republican regimes there to fall and Reconstruction finally came to an end.

1776 TO 1924

THE UNITED STATES:
A NATION OF IMMIGRANTS

Although the USA is not the only country to have been founded – and to have had much of its subsequent history shaped by – immigrants and their descendants, it is the most powerful, populous and ethnically diverse of such countries. Between 1820 and 1920 the USA received a total of over 34 million immigrants.

Until around 1700, the great majority of immigrants to the British American colonies were English, Welsh or Scottish. Thereafter, as British governments discouraged voluntary emigration, the ethnic composition of the population changed, as growing numbers of German, Swiss, French, Dutch, Swedish and, above all, Ulster Scotch-Irish migrants arrived. Britain continued to transport involuntary emigrants to the American colonies, including around 200,000 slaves from Africa and 30,000 British convicted felons. As ethnic groups tended to settle in particular areas and (outside towns) there was comparatively little intermingling between them, the population of late colonial America very much resembled a mosaic.

THE EARLY 19TH CENTURY

In the early years following independence, immigration was on a comparatively small scale. But, after the Napoleonic Wars in 1815, more Europeans started to emigrate to the USA, thereby beginning a mass migration that would last for more than a century. Between 1820 and 1880, largely unaffected by the Civil War of 1861–5, over 10 million immigrants entered the USA. Most came from northern and western Europe – mainly Germany, Ireland, Britain and

Scandinavia. They sailed for America to better themselves economically, to escape (in the case of the Irish) the famine of the 1840s, or – more rarely – as political refugees (German "Forty-Eighters", for example). Scandinavian immigrants often became farmers in Minnesota and Wisconsin, Germans in Illinois, Wisconsin, Iowa and Ohio. The Irish were the most urban of all immigrant groups: less than one in ten took up farming and New York, Philadelphia and Boston soon contained large Irish populations.

From the 1830s many native-born Americans were becoming increasingly disturbed by the extent of immigration. An anti-immigrant movement culminated in the 1850s in the emergence of a short-lived but, for a time, relatively successful "nativist" party: the Know Nothings. But anti-immigrant feeling dissipated during the Civil War and in the years following it, when immigrants were welcomed as contributing to the American economy. It revived in the 1880s and '90s, in part in response to economic stresses and the huge increase in the numbers of immigrants (from 2.8 million in 1871–80 to 5.2 million in 1881–90), in part because of a perceived change in the origins of immigrants themselves.

THE "NEW" IMMIGRANTS

The bulk of immigrants after 1880 came from southern and eastern Europe. These areas had suffered the collapse of the old agricultural order, huge population increases and anti-semitic pogroms. The immigrants, taking advantage of the easier and cheaper travel offered by steamships, arrived in a growing flood in the USA. Total immigration soared to 8.8 million in 1901–10 and 5.7 million in the subsequent decade. "New" immigrants – to a far greater extent than the "old" (other than the Irish) – tended to settle in cities. Cities like New York and Chicago developed a mosaic of ethnic neighbourhoods. Many Americans, between the 1880s and 1914, became increasingly uneasy over whether such groups could be assimilated and began to support demands for immigration restriction. The First World War, making Americans newly aware of their ethnic disunity, and the reaction against Europe that followed the war and the postwar recession, drove Congress, in 1921 and 1924, to impose ceilings on total immigrant numbers and introduce a "quota" system that was heavily biased against the nations that had produced most of the "new" immigration.

CONTROLS AND CONTINUITY

The legislation of the 1920s banned immigration from most Asian countries, but exempted the western hemisphere from its provisions since many southwestern employers regarded Mexican labour as essential. In 1943, the US government introduced the *braceros* system, allowing large numbers of Mexican agricultural labourers to enter the country. Meanwhile, immigration laws were relaxed to allow successive waves of refugees to enter: fugitives from communism in eastern Europe; Cubans after the revolution of 1959; and Vietnamese after the collapse of South Vietnam in 1975. The law was liberalized in 1965, allowing increased immigration from Asia. Indeed, throughout the 1970s, Asia (especially the Philippines and Korea) contributed more immigrants than Europe.

The poet Walt Whitman, writing in the 1850s, described America as "not merely a nation but a teeming of nations". Immigrants have made a massive contribution to American finance, society, politics and culture. American society today is recognizably and irreversibly multi-cultural. Yet anxieties persist among some Americans towards immigration both legal and illegal (the so-called "wetbacks") from Mexico that has transformed much of the South-West and Far West into predominantly Spanish-speaking areas.

SINCE 1810

CANADA

In 1867 Canada became the first self-governing former British colony. Like other "New World" countries, it relied on immigration for most of its population growth. Many migrants came from western and northern Europe, but in the early 20th century – and especially since the 1960s – sources of immigrants have become much more diversified. Canada is now one of the few countries to declare itself as officially multicultural.

For a short time – beginning with the British conquest of New France (1759–60) – all of eastern North America formed part of the British empire, while through the Hudson's Bay Company's claim to the vast area of Rupert's Land, British influence was felt, via the fur trade, in much of central North America. Aboriginal peoples continued to dominate the population of the west through the 19th century, but their lands were gradually taken away from them, often, but not always, through treaty negotiations.

TERRITORY

Québec, Nova Scotia and Newfoundland did not take part in the War of 1812, and the influx of loyalist refugees in the aftermath of the conflict reinforced pro-British sentiment in these colonies. At the time of the war, British troops, local volunteers and aboriginal warriors repulsed the American threat. The separate British colonies of eastern North America maintained strong local identities. On a number of occasions, proposals to unite the various colonies met with failure. In 1867, Nova Scotia, New Brunswick and the Canadas (present-day southern Ontario and southern Québec) were brought together as the self-governing Dominion of Canada, still under formal British control. Over the next 80 years, Canada subsumed the rest of the British territories in North America. The Rupert's Land territory was acquired from the Hudson's Bay Company in 1867, the Arctic Islands were transferred from British control to Canadian in 1880, and other colonies joined the new country. Newfoundland, whose decision to become a Canadian province in 1949 was determined in a close-run referendum, was the last to join.

POPULATION

Through much of its history, this region had difficulty attracting immigrants, and much of the population growth depended on natural increase. The size of the aboriginal population, beset by epidemic diseases against which it had no immunity, declined through the 19th century. British and Irish immigration transformed many parts of eastern North America between the 1810s and the 1850s. Economic difficulties during the first decades of Canada's dominion status reduced the flow of migrants. But at the very end of the 19th century, immigration to Canada expanded tremendously, at a pace that was sustained until just before the First World War. This population influx derived from Britain and northwest Europe as well as from southern and eastern Europe. Immigration of black Americans and Asians was generally discouraged by the Canadian government, although sizeable Chinese, Japanese and Sikh communities developed in British Columbia. Despite the hostility they faced, black populations continued to live in Nova Scotia and southern Ontario.

After the disruption of the Second World War, immigration levels once again rose as old migration patterns were re-established. Many people that had become displaced during the war years also made their way to Canada in this period. With the abolition of the colour bar in immigration policy – achieved through a series of revisions in the 1960s – the nature of contemporary Canada shifted more fundamentally. New sources for immigrants included the Caribbean, Africa, east Asia, the Middle East and Latin America. By the year 2000, Toronto was the most ethnically diverse city in the world, with over 40 per cent of its population born outside the country.

MULTICULTURALISM

These shifts in population composition were reflected in policy changes. In 1971, the Canadian government issued the Multiculturalism Proclamation, which recognized the extent of ethnic diversity and emphasized the bilingual nature of the country. In Québec, there are fears that the proportion of French-speakers in the country as a whole is declining, and this has galvanized the separatist movement in that province. However, two referenda (in 1980 and 1995) have rejected Québec's proposed independence from the rest of Canada.

Canada continues annually to accept immigrants in numbers that are large relative to its size. Nonetheless, the largest growing ethnic group today is the aboriginal population, which has a very high birth-rate.

1810 TO 1910

LATIN AMERICA: INDEPENDENCE AND NATIONAL GROWTH

The early 19th century saw the Portuguese and Spanish colonies break away from their mother countries, in the latter case after a bitter military struggle. The new states that emerged were at first unstable; initial confederations soon broke up and military dictatorships flourished. By the early 20th century comparative stability had returned.

By the late 18th century, demands for political freedom, administrative autonomy and economic self-determination were growing throughout Latin America. Yet, while they were encouraged by the American and French revolutions, it was the Napoleonic invasion of Spain and Portugal in 1808 that enabled them to develop into successful movements for independence. Having fled from Lisbon to Rio de Janeiro, which then became the centre of their empire, the Portuguese royal family presided over the relatively peaceful transition of Brazil from colony to independent nation. After his father had returned to Portugal, Pedro I, renouncing his claims to the Portuguese throne and assuming the title emperor, declared the independence of Brazil. This, together with the fact that the planter elite were too fearful of slave revolts to split into factions, made for considerable political and institutional continuity.

THE REVOLT AGAINST SPAIN

Spain, on the other hand, tried to crush revolts in her own Latin American colonies, and several years of conflict were necessary before her government acknowledged defeat. A southern revolution was carried by San Martín's Army of the Andes from Buenos Aires to Chile and beyond. A northern revolution, more vigorously opposed by Spain, was led by Bolívar from Venezuela to the battlefield of Boyacá in Colombia (then called New Granada). Both, by 1822, had converged on Peru, the fortress of Spain in South America. In the north, insurgency in Mexico followed a course of its own – frustrated social revolution, then prolonged counter-revolution and finally the seizure of power by Iturbide, an army officer, who proclaimed himself Emperor Agustín I.

The independence movement as a whole was essentially political. It involved a transfer of authority, but little social or economic change. Its leaders were mostly drawn from the Creole population, Iberians born in America. They were mainly politically inexperienced and, in many of the new Latin American republics, the decades between independence and mid-century were characterized by violent political conflicts. With the masses excluded from political decision-making, politics became a matter of rivalries amongst oligarchic families and military cliques. *Caudillos* – military leaders – fought with one another for political power without greatly affecting the mainly rural and traditional societies surrounding them.

POLITICAL STABILITY

From the mid-19th century there was greater stability, marked by the emergence of new institutional arrangements, "oligarchic republics", essentially based on alliances of regional elites. (Brazil remained an Empire until the monarchy fell in 1889.) The consolidation of nation-states at this point was driven by export-led growth. Politics was no longer the zero-sum game of the immediate post-Independence period. Rapid growth in the world economy meant an increasing demand for Latin American exports and an inflow of foreign investment, notably from Britain. Foreign capital helped rejuvenate the mining sector, and financed railway construction, the modernization of ports and domestic market consolidation. Associated with greater political stability and economic opportunity, mass migration from southern Europe transformed agriculture in temperate zones, such as southern Brazil, the Argentinian pampas, Uruguay, and central Chile and Colombia. Cuba, Spanish until 1898, also received large numbers of immigrants. Commodity booms – Peruvian guano, Chilean nitrates, Brazilian coffee and rubber, River Plate cereals and meat – underwrote the new political order.

THE EARLY 20TH CENTURY

By the beginning of the 20th century, the socio-political fabric of many republics was radically different from a century earlier. Economic growth, urbanization and, less so, industrial growth in countries like Argentina, Chile, Brazil and Mexico fostered the consolidation of a fairly large middle class clamouring for greater political representation, and the appearance of vocal working-class organizations. These groups sought political change at about the time when volatility in the world economy limited the capacity of oligarchic regimes to accommodate those demands. The result, in Mexico, was violent social protest involving disaffected segments of the oligarchy, middle-class intellectuals, small farmers and peasant communities whose land had been alienated during the dictatorship of Porfirio Díaz (1876–1910). Elsewhere (eg Uruguay, Argentina and Chile), electoral reform enabled newer social constellations to obtain political power via the ballot box.

1800 TO 1923
THE DISINTEGRATION OF THE OTTOMAN EMPIRE

During the 19th century, the Ottoman empire – "the sick man of Europe" – slowly disintegrated under the impact of foreign encroachment, popular anti-Turkish nationalism and a powerful reform movement. Defeat in the First World War brought complete collapse and the emergence of a modern Turkish national state under Kemal Atatürk.

By the end of the 18th century, the Ottoman empire was no longer the military and cultural force it had once been. In 1798, the Ottoman province of Egypt was invaded and occupied by Napoleon. This was the first time since the Crusades that a European power had encroached directly on the Ottoman heartlands. Although Napoleon was ousted by the British, Egypt was seized by the Albanian general Muhammad Ali, who had been sent to attack the French by the Ottoman sultan, Selim III. From 1805, Egypt became independent of the empire, beginning a century-long process of territorial decline and persistent intervention by the European powers.

THE TANZIMAT REFORMS

Defeat at the hands of the Greeks and their European allies in 1827–9 forced the Ottoman empire to modernize. The failure of the traditional janissary warriors during the war led to far-reaching military reforms based on European models. In 1839 a young generation of liberal officers and bureaucrats launched the Tanzimat reform movement, culminating in 1876 with the granting of a parliamentary constitution. Following Turkish defeat in war with Russia in 1877, which led a year later to the independence of Serbia, Montenegro and Romania, the new sultan, Abdulhamid II, suspended the constitution and ruled for 30 years as a modern authoritarian monarch.

Abdulhamid introduced further reforms and tried to modernize the economy while suppressing popular politics. The chronic financial instability of the sultanate was helped by granting European powers tax-raising privileges within the empire in 1881. Any popular nationalism was brutally repressed. When Armenian nationalists, representative of the large Christian community living in Anatolia, developed their own national awakening, the Zartonk, it sparked the revival of popular Islam. In 1895–6 the state orchestrated a series of massacres of 200,000 Armenians at the hands of Muslim Turks.

THE CREATION OF MODERN TURKEY

Abdulhamid was overthrown in 1908 by a revolution of "Young Turks" drawn from among the new liberal intelligentsia and nationalist army officers organized through the Paris-based Committee of Union and Progress, founded in 1889. The sultanate was suspended and a modernizing regime installed. In 1913 the moderate liberals were overthrown by a military coup and hardline nationalists and Islamicists under Enver Pasha came to dominate Ottoman politics.

In October 1914 Enver Pasha brought Turkey in on Germany's side in the First World War and in November 1914 a *jihad*, or Holy War, was declared. On the grounds that Armenians in eastern Anatolia were a threat to the Turkish war effort, the regime unleashed a wave of savage violence against the Christian community. An estimated 1.5 million Armenians died, others were forced into slavery or made to convert to Islam. A fraction of the population arrived in deportation centres in Mesopotamia after enduring long "death marches".

Following Turkish defeat in 1918, the Young Turk regime was overthrown and the sultan briefly restored as an Allied puppet. But in 1920, Turkish nationalists led a war of liberation against the Allied occupying forces. Under the army officer Kemal Atatürk, and with the support of the emerging Turkish middle classes, the Turkish army re-conquered Anatolia. The rest of the former empire was divided up between France and Britain by the League of Nations as mandated territories. In the Treaty of Lausanne in 1923, Turkish independence was recognized, and Atatürk began the process of building a modern nation-state based on secular rule, mass education and economic reform.

1815 TO 1917
THE RUSSIAN EMPIRE: EXPANSION AND MODERNIZATION

Though Russia emerged in the 19th century as one of the European Great Powers, her international status was compromised by economic backwardness and military failure. Efforts to modernize created demands for revolutionary change, and when Russia failed again on the battlefield in the First World War the monarchy collapsed in revolution.

In 1815 Russia was widely regarded as the foremost power in Europe. Its role in the defeat of revolutionary France had left it the largest military power on the continent and greatly reinforced the prestige of the ruling elite, which was able to reassert its own power while stifling liberal reform and modernization.

Under the tsars Alexander I (1801–25) and Nicholas I (1825–55) Russia remained a predominantly rural society, dominated by the crown, the nobility and corrupt bureaucrats and gendarmes. Attempts at political liberalization were ruthlessly suppressed. In December 1825, opponents of the autocracy, strongly influenced by Western models, tried to overthrow the tsar and install a modernizing regime. The "Decembrists", drawn mainly from the army, were easily crushed, and Nicholas I, whose one-day-old reign they had tried to destroy, imposed a harsh regime of censorship and political oppression. The instrument of control, a forerunner of the secret police empires of the 20th century, was the notorious Third Department, set up in 1826 to suppress threats to the crown and any flirtation with Western ideas.

Abroad, Russia was seen as a force for conservatism in international affairs. Under Nicholas Russia tried to increase its influence in the Balkans and the Middle East, while opposing revolutionary and nationalist threats. In 1849 Russian troops put down revolution in Hungary, and in 1853 Russia seized the provinces of Moldavia and Wallachia from Ottoman Turkey and destroyed the Turkish Black Sea Fleet at Sinop. Alarmed by Russian ambitions in the Holy Land, France and Britain declared war and invaded the Crimean peninsula. In a campaign notable for military ineptitude on both sides, Russia was nonetheless defeated. Rebuffed in Europe, Russia thereafter turned her attentions more to expansion in Asia. But the humiliation of defeat on her own soil had exposed Russian backwardness. The new tsar, Alexander II (1855–81), embarked on a widespread programme of reform.

THE REFORMING TSARS

Alexander's intention was not to liberalize Russia but to make it more efficient. Both he and his successor, Alexander III, were wedded to the idea of royal autocracy and saw reform as necessary to strengthen it rather than to alter its essential nature. Nonetheless, in 1861, following growing unrest, the serfs were emancipated while in 1864 new institutions of local government, the *zemstvo*, were introduced to stem the demand for liberal constitutional reform. In the same year Russia's legal system was overhauled on Western lines. Army reforms created a more effective fighting force. But Alexander set his face against political concessions or widespread industrialization. Radical groups turned to violent terrorism and in 1881, after three attempts, the "People's Will" group succeeded in assassinating the tsar.

Regicide produced a backlash. Alexander III introduced industrialization schemes and encouraged modern banking and transport in order to build a strong Russia capable of resisting internal demands for change or pressure from the West. A conservative nationalism was whipped up against Westernizers and Jews, while reform groups were savagely repressed. In 1881 the Okhrana secret police was established. In 1889 Land Captains were instituted in the countryside to restore the influence of the gentry. In the new industrial centres trade unions were outlawed and socialist movements persecuted. Russia in 1900 was more modern and militarily stronger, but its political system remained reactionary and unreformed.

REVOLUTION AND WAR

Under the last tsar, Nicholas II (1894–1917), the tension between the unreformed system and the new social forces thrown up by modernization reached a climax. Defeat in the Far East by Japan in 1905 saw protest reach a crisis-point. Revolt broke out across Russia. Sergei Witte, the leading architect of modernization, persuaded the tsar to grant a constitution. The October Manifesto of 1905 instituted a parliament, or *Duma*, a restricted franchise and the promise of civil rights.

Nicholas soon reverted to type. The *Duma* was prorogued twice until he got deputies he could work with; civil rights were never fully granted; the franchise became ever more narrow. The tsar still ruled by decree and through the vast police and bureaucratic apparatus. By 1914, when Russia entered the First World War, there was wide expectation of revolution. Defeat in battle, hunger in the cities and corrupt management of the home front produced irresistible pressure for a radical break. In February 1917 Nicholas abdicated, and the tsarist empire collapsed.

1839 TO 1911

THE COLLAPSE OF THE CHINESE EMPIRE

During the 19th century China experienced a systemic crisis, with rebellions and humiliations by foreign powers. The Chinese leadership was slow to grasp how much internal change was needed. Realization came in the 1890s leading to sweeping reforms along Western lines and the overthrow of a dynastic system which had lasted over 2000 years.

For much of the 19th century the Chinese failed to understand the challenge presented by Western powers. After a peak of prosperity under the Ch'ing in the 18th century, they regarded themselves as the centre of world civilization and were slow to realize that Western power, with its superior technology, productivity and wealth, had overtaken them. Such attitudes informed their negative responses to British attempts to develop diplomatic relations from 1793. Matters came to a head when the Chinese tried to end the illicit trade in opium with its damaging economic effects. They were defeated by the British in the First Opium War and in 1842 forced to cede Hong Kong and five treaty ports in which foreigners were permitted to trade free from Chinese jurisdiction.

Defeat in the Opium War weakened imperial authority and exacerbated the systemic crisis which had been developing since the 18th century (*see* p. 172). Major rebellions broke out all over China, the most important of which was the T'ai-p'ing in which, together with the Nien rebellion, 25 million died. Nevertheless, imperial support for traditional attitudes and institutions continued.

FOREIGN PENETRATION

These serious disorders allowed further foreign penetration of China and her satellites. From 1858 the Russians pressed forward their interests in northern China, and in 1860 Peking was occupied by the British and French. In 1884–5 the French defeated the Chinese over Indo-China. In 1894–5 the Japanese, having already intervened in Taiwan, the Ryukyu islands and Korea, overwhelmed China in a full-scale war.

Although this last defeat led in 1898 to an attempt at comprehensive reform headed by the Emperor, it was foiled by a reactionary coup. Meanwhile, foreign powers, believing China was about to collapse, scrambled for further concessions. This in turn produced a wave of local xenophobia, leading to the Boxer uprising and finally to the siege of foreign legations in Peking. The uprising was suppressed by foreign armies at the cost of further concessions and a huge indemnity.

After 1901 it was at last accepted that modernization was required throughout China's state and society. When the reformers, now including many foreign-educated young Chinese, realised the Manchu were still determined to cling on to power, they turned to revolution. A small army revolt at Wu-ch'ang in 1911 won support throughout China. The 2000-year-old imperial system came to an end, and the leader of the revolutionary alliance, Sun Yat-sen, was proclaimed provisional president on 1 January 1912.

1805 TO 1935

INDIA UNDER BRITISH RULE

In the early 19th century, Britain consolidated its rule in south Asia as India became the focus of its imperial system. The authoritarian style of British rule encouraged many different types of anti-imperial political organization. By 1935 anti-imperial forces had seriously weakened British power.

In the 50 years after 1805 the supremacy of the English East India Company on the subcontinent was steadily consolidated. The third Anglo-Maratha War, ending in 1818, eliminated the most serious threat to Company rule. The conquest of the Gurkhas (1816), the Sindhis (1843) and the Sikhs (1849) then saw the empire become coterminous with its natural frontiers in the north and west.

To the east the British clashed with the Burmese kingdom and from 1824 began the process of annexing all its territories. In addition, within the subcontinent dependent states such as Awadh and some Maratha kingdoms were brought under direct rule.

However, British policy was seen by many in south Asia as a serious challenge to Indian ways of life. Growing resentment resulted in the uprising of 1857. Beginning as a mutiny of the Company's army, the rebellion soon involved princes, landlords and peasants in north and central India. The insurrection was bloody; its suppression, during 14 months of bitter fighting, as brutal. From 1858, the administration of India was taken over by the British Crown.

India then became the focus of the British imperial system, the source of rivalries with Russia in central Asia and France in southeast Asia, and a factor, too, in British involvement in the partition of Africa. From Abyssinia to China the Indian army protected British interests. Simultaneously India was absorbed into the world economy as a dependant of Britain. Indian communications, largely in the form of railways, were developed to facilitate the import of British manufactures and the export of raw materials.

EXPLOITATION AND DEPENDENCY

As a result of this development and the opening of the Suez canal, India's foreign trade increased sevenfold from 1869 to 1929 and, despite severe British competition, some modern industries developed. But by 1853 India had lost her worldwide market for textiles and was actually importing cloth from Britain. GNP per capita increased only slowly and, with sustained population growth, from 1921 even declined. India increasingly took on the typical characteristics of an underdeveloped economy while at the same time contributing substantially to Britain's balance of payments.

Administrative developments also contributed to India's absorption into a world order dominated by Europe. Britain's colonial administrators set out to refashion Indian society along European lines. The net results are still debated. Probably the rural propertied classes benefited, but at the cost of the mass of producers who were subjected, while commercial agriculture flourished, to deadly famines. The beneficiaries of the new order – landlords, civil servants and professional men – formed the new elite of colonial India, and sought Western-style education. The bridges this elite built between Western knowledge and indigenous cultural resources inspired a host of religious, social and intellectual movements. Among them was the Brahmo Samaj founded by Ram Mohan Roy in the 1820s, which aimed at restoring Hindu monotheism, and the Aligarh movement founded by Saiyid Ahmad Khan in the 1870s, which aimed to reconcile India's Muslims to modernity.

ANTI-IMPERIAL POLITICS

Many different forms of anti-imperial politics flourished in the late 19th and early 20th centuries, as Indians attempted to assert their identity against British racism in many different ways. The Indian National Congress was founded in 1885 to lobby for Indians to have greater involvement within the imperial administration. It soon developed a vociferously anti-imperial wing that asserted the superiority of Indian culture and questioned Britain's right to rule. In 1905, nationalists resisted the decision to partition the province of Bengal. Many techniques adopted by them later on were first used in the swadeshi ("our country") agitation of that year. By 1917, Congress demanded Home Rule. British politicians promised eventual self-government and allowed some expansion of Indian involvement in local and provincial government. But repressive legislation after the First World War led many to question British intentions.

Congress was perceived by many Muslims as a purely Hindu organization, as many Congress politicians defined "India" to be an exclusively Hindu nation. The years after the First World War saw both the rise of mass, popular nationalist campaigning and the emergence of Hindu and Muslim separatist politics. Fuelled by Muslim fury at the destruction of the Ottoman sultan's power in the Middle East, Muslims and Hindus worked together in the Khilafat and Non-Cooperation Movements (1920–2), in which Gandhi deployed his weapon of *satyagraha* or non-violent direct action. As Congress retreated from direct action, the mid-1920s saw the rise of Hindu–Muslim riots. Gandhi led a civil disobedience movement in 1930–4, which forced the British to concede full autonomy to Indians at a provincial level with the 1935 Government of India Act.

SINCE 1770
AUSTRALIA

European settlement of Australia began in the late 18th century. Soon, settlers pushed the Aborigines by force from the most productive land. By 1900 a rich economy had emerged, still, however, dependent on British capital. Only in the late 20th century did new economic and immigration policies and circumstances signal a complete sense of independence.

Australia came into intermittent contact with Europeans from the 16th century, but neither the Portuguese nor the Dutch had any use for what they found there. The Englishman James Cook mapped the east coast extensively in 1770, though it was only in 1788 when Britain wanted to make use of the overflow from its prisons to establish a naval base on an alternative trade route to China, that European settlement in Australia began. New South Wales and Van Diemen's Land (Tasmania) were essentially convict colonies until the 1850s, though by then there were "respectable free settlements" in Western Australia and South Australia. The search for staple products produced whaling and sealing, and later wool, in great quantity. Graziers succeeded gaolers and traders as the elite in the eastern colonies. Wool came to the fore in Australia and it continues today to be a major export.

THE ABORIGINES

Highly successful in the arts of survival off the land, there were about 750,000 Aborigines in Australia in 1788. But in the face of European invasion, they retreated, their numbers decimated by a falling birthrate, disease, dispossession and the bullet. The Australian pastoral frontier witnessed much violence and bloodshed, most of it in guerrilla-type skirmishes, as it swept inland, not coming to a final halt until it reached the north of Western Australia and the Northern Territory in the 1930s. By then the Aboriginal population had been reduced to 10 per cent of its original size.

ECONOMIC DEVELOPMENT

Gold rushes in eastern Australia in the 1850s led to a huge population influx and a vast expansion of wealth. On this basis, self-government was assured. Grain, frozen beef, sugar, dairy products and a range of minerals were also exported, as rail and steam "tethered the mighty bush to the world". By 1900 Australia was labelled a "working man's paradise", boasting the highest living standards in the world. Despite the wealth of agricultural produce, most Australians then, as now, were living in cities.

The separate Australian colonies federated into the commonwealth of Australia in 1901. Australia still, however, depended on Britain for "men, money and markets". It was only after the Second World War, and especially after Britain joined the European Community in 1973, that this cycle of dependence was broken. Now Australia traded much more with the Pacific Rim and the Middle East than with Europe. Significant mineral discoveries in Australia in the 1960s and 1970s – notably oil, gas, iron, bauxite and uranium – gave the economy a boost; and a globally competitive edge.

MIGRATION AND NATIONAL CONSCIOUSNESS

Large-scale migration programmes after 1945 drew millions to Australia from Europe, more than half from countries other than Britain, notably Italy and Greece. Since the dismantling of the White Australia policy in 1974 (which had been in place for over a century), several hundred thousand immigrants have arrived from Asia. A new consciousness has emerged among the indigenous peoples, and land rights and compensation for the "stolen generations" of Aboriginal children forcibly taken from their parents before the early 1970s are key political issues. These questions will almost certainly be resolved equitably in polities that still pride themselves on being advanced social democracies where citizens can count on a "fair go".

SINCE 1800

NEW ZEALAND

European settlement of New Zealand from the 1840s led to two major wars with the Maoris over the next quarter century. Thereafter New Zealand became a rural "Britain of the South", supplying the mother country with primary produce. An advanced social and political laboratory, it was among the first to extend votes to its indigenous population and to women. Recently, it has introduced a native title tribunal and liberalized and internationalized its economy.

New Zealand had its first European visitors in the 17th century and attracted itinerant whalers and sealers in the wake of James Cook's visit in 1769. Missions to the Maoris started in 1814, but European colonization did not start there in earnest until the 1840s. A number of distinct Wakefieldian "scientifically planned" colonies of free settlers were established in Wellington, New Plymouth, Nelson and Christchurch. These settlements were injected into a seething cauldron of internecine Maori warfare, exacerbated by the introduction of the musket in the 1820s. With the new European element in the equation, competition for land and other resources soon became even more intense.

THE NEW ZEALAND WARS

The Maoris were doughty warriors with a sophisticated military tradition. Though apparently guaranteed possession and use of their lands by the Treaty of Waitangi, signed with the British Crown in 1840, they were soon fighting bloody campaigns against regular British forces in defence of their land. The first phase of the wars was the Flagstaff War around Kororareka and the Bay of Islands in 1844–6, then in the Hutt Valley near Wellington soon afterwards. A second phase came in the 1860s in the Taranaki and Waikato areas. Ultimately, the Maoris were successful in keeping title to some of their land and in making headway in European society.

ECONOMIC AND POLITICAL DEVELOPMENT

As in Australia, wool became a staple export early on in New Zealand's colonization. Then gold-rushes in the South Island in the 1860s led to huge population influxes and vast expansion of wealth. Grain, frozen beef, dairy products and a range of minerals were added to the export list. By 1900 New Zealand was a social laboratory, with high wages and state-of-the-art social welfare provision. Despite the wealth of agricultural produce, however, most New Zealanders then, as now, were living in cities.

Self-government was achieved in 1856, Maori representation in 1867, and in 1893 New Zealand women (including Maoris) bacame the first in the British Empire to win the vote. New Zealand changed its name from colony to dominion in 1907. It still depended on Britain on the one hand for migrants, investment and imported manufactures and on the other as the main market for its pastoral and agricultural exports. In both world wars New Zealanders fought and died in considerable numbers in Europe and north Africa to protect their mother country. Similarly to Australia, Britain's joining the EC gave the country full independence, and it also now trades much more with the Pacific Rim and the Middle East than with Europe. New Zealand's government reforms in the 1980s again gave its economy a globally competitive edge.

MIGRATION AND NATIONAL CONSCIOUSNESS

New Zealand's prime source of recent immigration has been the Pacific Islands, making Auckland the world's largest Polynesian city with over 77,000 Polynesians in its population of 367,000 in 2001. A new consciousness has emerged among the Maoris, and land rights and compensation are key political issues. These questions are being resolved carefully by the Waitangi Tribunal, which is a world model for its kind. Recently, New Zealand has defined itself against its larger allies, the USA and Australia, by banning nuclear warship visits and refusing to participate with them in the War in Iraq in 2003, although it has participated internationally elsewhere, notably in Rwanda, East Timor, Afghanistan, and the Solomons.

1800 TO 1880
AFRICA BEFORE THE PARTITION BY THE EUROPEAN POWERS

Africa between 1800 and 1880 was shaped by indigenous societies and their rulers, intent as ever on pursuing their own ambitions. Europeans occupied little more than the tiniest of coastal footholds, and the commercial and political developments of the period represented more than the prelude to an inevitable European partition.

In the early 19th century much of west Africa was profoundly affected by an Islamic religious revival manifested in Holy Wars (*jihads*) waged mainly against backsliding Muslim or partly-Islamicized communities. The great warriors of the *jihad* were the widely scattered Fulani cattle-keepers of the Sudanic region. In the 18th century they had established theocracies in Futa Toro, Futa Jallon and in Masina on the upper Niger. Much larger, however, was the 19th-century Fulani state set up in Hausaland. In 1804 a Fulani religious leader, Usuman dan Fodio, was proclaimed Commander of the Faithful, and declared a *jihad* against the infidel. His formidable army of horsemen soon conquered the Hausa city states, and struck out into Adamawa, Nupe and Yorubaland. His son became the sultan of Sokoto, an empire still in existence in the 1890s.

An even fiercer *jihad* was conducted by al-Hajj Umar from Futa Jallon. Conquering the Bambara kingdoms and Masina, he was only kept from the Atlantic by the French on the Senegal river. In fact, Islam increasingly became a counterforce to European advance, especially in the case of the Mandinka leader Samory who carved out another empire south of the Niger; he was finally defeated by the French only in 1898.

NEW TRADE

In the forest states further south, the slave trade had long flourished but the British in particular began to try to replace it with "legitimate trade". Although a government-sponsored mission in 1841–2 to establish "Christianity, commerce and civilization" inland failed, African responses to Europe's new commercial demands for palm oil and other products encouraged change.

Likewise in east and west central Africa new commercial patterns brought disruption. There the Western world's almost insatiable appetite for ivory (for billiard balls and piano keys) caused the hunting and trading of elephant tusks to become a major economic activity, enriching many states and peoples – the Cokwe and King Msiri in central Africa, for instance, and Buganda and the Nyamwezi in east Africa. Foreign traders in central Africa were frequently Portuguese from Angola and Mozambique, and in east Africa Swahili-Arabs from Zanzibar, who often brought their Islamic religion with them. Some peoples, particularly around lakes Nyasa and Tanganyika, suffered severely from the Arab slave trade, which went hand-in-hand with that in ivory.

In northeast Africa, the expansion of Egypt, ruled by Khedives, nominally viceroys of the Ottoman sultan, brought a foretaste of the later European conquest. Muhammad Ali's armies conquered the northern Nilotic Sudan, founding the provincial capital at Khartoum in 1821, and his grandson, Ismail, consolidated Egyptian control over much of the Red Sea coast and Horn of

Africa, as well as pushing south up the Nile towards the Great Lakes. Partly in response to this Egyptian activity, Ethiopian political power revived.

EUROPEAN COLONIZATION

Only two areas of Africa were colonized by European powers during this period. In 1830 France invaded Algeria and in a long and bitter struggle conquered and settled the territory. The British took the Cape from the Dutch during the Napoleonic wars and the south saw the presence of increasing numbers of Europeans, including the Boers – white farmers who left Cape Colony in the "Great Trek" of 1836 to avoid British rule. In the 1850s Britain recognized the Transvaal and Orange Free State republics which the Boers founded, but by the 1870s were again in dispute with them.

1880 TO 1913
THE PARTITION OF AFRICA

Once Europe's partition of Africa began in the 1880s, the continent was carved up remarkably rapidly: 30 years later only Abyssinia and Liberia remained wholly independent. The scramble was completed with the redistribution of Germany's colonies after the First World War, when, for the first time, colonial administration began to be imposed effectively.

Little of Africa was directly ruled by Europeans in 1880: the French had been subjugating Algeria since 1830; there were small French and British colonies in west Africa; and there were moribund Portuguese settlements in Angola and Mozambique. Only in the south, where the British Cape colonists were in competition with the Afrikaners of the Transvaal and Orange Free State, did political control extend far inland. Yet within two decades the continent had been seized and partitioned. Of the 40 political units to which it was reduced by 1913, 36 were completely under European control. France was the largest beneficiary, ruling nearly one-third of Africa's 30.3 million sq. km (11.7 million sq. miles).

THE SCRAMBLE BEGINS

Many ingredients contributed to this imperial explosion, among them the search for raw materials and new markets for Europe's rapidly expanding industries. At the same time, rivalries between European states were partly played out outside Europe, especially in Africa. As a result, often trivial incidents in Africa between competing European traders precipitated major international crises, accelerating the undignified scramble for the continent. Yet ironically, few European powers actively sought partition. At the Berlin West Africa Conference in 1884 the powers had agreed to avert partition and maintain access for all. Yet whatever their official hesitations, the process had acquired a momentum of its own.

In west Africa, French army officers, eager to recover their honour after their humiliating defeat by Germany in 1870, sought glory advancing inland from Senegal in the late 1870s. This created conflict with the British in Gambia and Sierra Leone, and with African rulers such as al-Hajj Umar and Samory. Intense British-French rivalry developed in the Gold Coast, Togo, Dahomey and Yorubaland and hardened after Britain's unilateral occupation of Egypt in 1882.

King Leopold of the Belgians' determination to become involved in Africa led him to recruit the explorer H. M. Stanley after his epic journey down the Congo River in 1877. In 1879 Stanley returned to the lower Congo to lay the foundations of the huge private domain the king eventually acquired in the Congo basin. His activities stimulated others in the region. The French naval officer de Brazza concluded vital protection treaties with African chiefs, which the government in Paris readily took up. Germany also entered the race, grabbing territory in Togoland, the Cameroons, southwest and east Africa. French and German commercial and political initiatives in west Africa provoked British intervention, especially in securing the lands which became Nigeria. The far interior was left to the French, who by 1900 had swept right across the western Sudan.

Germany's presence in southern Africa revived Portuguese ambitions, and threats of Afrikaner expansion led to British thrusts into central Africa, aided decisively by the Cape politician Cecil Rhodes. Likewise, German colonization in Tanganyika prompted British claims to what became Uganda and Kenya. French conquest of Dahomey (1893) and her drive towards Lake

Chad drew Britain and the Royal Niger Company into protecting its trading sphere, which in turn led to armed clashes with African states. Multiple tensions reached their height in 1898 at Fashoda on the White Nile where the two countries narrowly avoided war.

CONFLICT AND WAR

Partition caused increasing bloodshed. Abyssinia routed the Italians at Adowa in 1896; some 120,000 Sudanese died in Britain's reconquest of the Mahdist state; and Rhodes' settlers fought bitterly with Ndebele and Shona as they moved north. Conflicts climaxed with the South African War (1899–1902) in which Britain with difficulty won the Transvaal gold fields and absorbed the Afrikaner republics. Elsewhere black Africans, although bitterly opposing the European powers, could never offer concerted resistance and for the most part were easily overcome.

1868 TO 1922

THE EXPANSION AND MODERNIZATION OF JAPAN

Between the 1850s and the 1920s Japan emerged from isolation to become a major world power. Western pressure was the spur which led to the destruction of the feudal system and the unleashing of her great potential for rapid modernization. But by 1920 there were signs that her rapid growth was causing dangerous internal stresses.

Japan avoided excessive interference by expansionist Western powers during the latter half of the 19th century by implementing successful policies for rapid modernization. The very countries that had threatened her independence became models for her own development and hence fuelled her own imperialist ambitions. The process began in the 1850s and by 1920 the Japanese empire was firmly established.

The spur to modernization was the demand from Western powers, led by the USA, for access to Japan's ports. The "unequal treaties" concluded under threat in 1858 prompted the restoration of direct imperial rule in 1868 in the name of the Meiji emperor (*see* p. 176). Already the country had considerable strengths: an extensive network of commerce and credit; an agricultural sector capable of feeding the nation and providing exports of tea and raw silk; reserves of copper, coal and iron; and scholars who, in spite of Japan's enforced isolation, had studied Western science and technology.

It was crucial to Japan's rapid modernization to bring these strengths into play. The abolition of feudalism, and the replacement in 1873 of feudal dues with cash payments based on the value of land, enabled wealth to be redirected to the purposes of central government. To encourage the transfer of technology and to stimulate investment, the government used this land tax to build model factories in strategic and import-saving industries, such as steel and textiles, and became directly involved in the development of transport and communications. There was also indirect encouragement in the form of subsidies and tax privileges.

The new leaders introduced complementary administrative reforms: feudal domains were replaced by modern bureaucracy (1871); the feudal army was replaced by a conscript one (1873); a bicameral legislature provided the basis for political unity and stability (1889); a national education system was instituted (1872); and legal codes based on those of France and Germany were introduced (1882).

INDUSTRIALIZATION AND TRADE

Within this framework capitalism advanced rapidly; Japan became the outstanding example of large-scale industrialization in the non-Western world. By 1918, when she had achieved major penetration of markets in China, the USA and elsewhere, she had become a major importer of raw materials and exporter of finished goods. Such developments meant considerable changes for Japanese society: by 1918 the population had risen to 55 million (from 35 million in 1873) and nearly one-third lived in towns of 10,000 or more.

National strength brought expansion overseas, motives being both strategic and economic. Japan began by claiming neighbouring islands such as the Ryukyus and Kuriles. The "unequal treaties" were revoked in 1894. Then concerns that China was too weak to keep Russia out of Korea led to war (1894–5) in which Japan destroyed the Chinese forces and acquired Formosa (Taiwan). The Russian threat, however, was only resolved by Japan's overwhelming defeat of Russia on land and sea in 1904–5, which led to Japanese control over the Liaotung peninsula, extensive rights in southern Manchuria and the acquisition of southern Sakhalin. There followed the annexation of Korea (1910), the acquisition of former German territories in China (1914), and the "Twenty-one Demands" (1915), which made sweeping, though not wholly successful, claims over China. In 1919 the Paris Peace Conference confirmed most of these gains and granted Japan mandates to German colonies in the Pacific.

THE COST OF SUCCESS

There was, however, another side to the story: the army was beginning to act independently of civil control, politicians were becoming too beholden to business, traditionalists objected to the sacrifice of Japanese values to the West, and the farmer and the labourer began to resent the subjection of their well-being to capital. The end of the war brought economic disruption, major disturbances in town and countryside, and the assassination in 1921 of the prime minister by a fanatic. These events presaged turbulent years ahead.

1815 TO 1914

EUROPEAN COLONIAL EMPIRES

In the first 50 years after 1815, there was a gradual extension of the European colonial empires as exploration opened up new regions to European traders and missionaries. But the late 19th century saw a heightening of imperial ambitions and rivalries that resulted in the partition of almost all of Africa, southeast Asia and the Pacific.

In 1815 Britain alone remained a great overseas power: France, Spain and the Netherlands had all lost colonial territories to the British. The decade after 1815 even saw a contraction of European colonial empires as South and Central American Spanish and Portuguese colonies broke free. With Britain holding undisputed naval preeminence and discarding mercantilism (the theoretical underpinning of imperialism) in favour of free trade, the first half of the 19th century seemed unlikely to witness further British expansion.

Yet European colonial empires grew almost continuously between 1815 and 1914. The West Indies, with the decline of the Atlantic slave trade and failing economically, lost their 18th-century importance, but in India further British conquests and, in Australia and New Zealand, emigration, pushed forward the boundaries of British imperialism. Britain also acquired Singapore (1819), Malacca (1824), Hong Kong (1842), Natal (1843), Lower Burma (1852) and Lagos (1861), and claimed sovereignty over Australia (1829) and New Zealand (1840). Many of these were to secure British commercial interests and to protect Britain's position in India; others were defensive reactions against France or necessitated by settler activity. Other European countries also steadily expanded. Russia sold Alaska to the United States in 1867, but continued its continental expansion: between 1801 and 1914 over 7 million Russians emigrated to Asiatic Russia. France, determined to replace the empire lost in 1815, conquered Algeria in the 1830s, annexed Tahiti and the Marquesas in the 1840s, expanded its colony in Senegal in the 1850s and began the conquest of Indo-China in 1858–9. Over and beyond the extension of formal empires, European technology and industrialization opened up other areas of the world – from Turkey and Egypt, to Persia and China, South America and even Japan – to European, particularly British, trade and finance. As Europe continued to disgorge missionaries, explorers and settlers overseas, relations with, and knowledge of the wider world was transformed.

THE SCRAMBLE FOR EMPIRE

After 1880, the pace of imperial expansion, fuelled by commercial competition, rivalries between imperial powers and changing conditions in Asia and Africa, quickened hugely. By 1914, Europe had engrossed nine-tenths of Africa and a large part of Asia. Between 1871 and 1914 the French empire grew by nearly 10 million sq. km (4 million sq. miles) and 47 million people. Defeat in Europe by Germany in 1870 redoubled French efforts to regain prestige through overseas conquests. Germany herself acquired 2.6 million sq. km (1 million sq. miles) and 14 million subjects in southwest Africa, the Cameroons, east Africa and the Pacific islands. Italy, eager for reasons of prestige to enter the colonial race, obtained Tripoli and Libya, Eritrea and Italian Somaliland, though in 1896 failed to conquer Abyssinia. But the greatest gains of all were made by Britain, who, partly to secure areas for free trade, established control over Nigeria, Kenya, Uganda, Rhodesia, Egypt and the Sudan, Fiji and parts of Borneo and New Guinea. Nonetheless, India remained the keystone of the British empire and many of these acquisitions were made with a view to bolstering British control over and access to India.

Imperialism was not confined to Europe. The United States and Japan joined the race as well, the former acquiring the Philippines (from Spain) in 1898, the latter taking Formosa in 1895 and Korea in 1910. Of the great European trading nations, the Netherlands almost alone remained content with its existing rich possessions in the East Indies.

1881 TO 1917
THE ANTI-WESTERN REACTION

From 1881 the European scramble for global power provoked new and widespread resistance throughout Asia and Africa. Elsewhere, in China and the Ottoman empire, intense European commercial and political penetration was undermining the old order. By 1917 modern nationalist movements were emerging in many European colonies.

Resistance to European colonialism existed well before 1881. Furthermore, patterns of resistance were shaped just as much by struggles for economic advantage and by local and inter-state rivalries as by the imposition of European political control. Resistance took many forms, from mass migrations to, among African Christian converts, the establishment of indigenous Christian Churches. Nevertheless, the unprecedented scale of the annexations of the "new imperialism" after 1881 unleashed an anti-colonial wave that was bigger and more significant than anything that had preceded it. Nowhere was independence surrendered passively. Throughout Africa and Asia, Europeans met prolonged and often bitter armed resistance.

In Annam the emperor, Ham Nghi, took to the mountains and resisted French occupation; Russia encountered Muslim resistance when it invaded central Asia; the USA became embroiled in a costly war with nationalist forces under Emilio Aguinaldo after it occupied the Philippines in 1898; and the Italians were defeated by the Abyssinians at Adowa in 1896. In Africa, Europeans faced resistance movements of varying strength. In many cases local groups alternated between diplomacy and armed opposition. Before and after mounting military resistance against the French, a west African leader, Samory, unsuccessfully sought British protection. Meanwhile oppressive German rule in South-West Africa and Tanganyika provoked the Herero and Maji-Maji revolts. In the Philippines resistance to the USA continued among the Islamic population of Mindanao while in Indo-China the "Black Flags" and later De Tham took up the struggle after the emperor Ham Nghi was captured in 1888.

Even in areas not under colonial rule, European commercial and political penetration created local instability and provoked anti-Western resistance. In China the disastrous wars with Japan in 1894–5, and the subsequent threat of partition, led to the abortive Hundred Days' Reform of 1898 and, after its failure, the anti-foreign Boxer Rebellion. In Turkey the Russian assault in 1877 and the dismemberment of the Ottoman empire's Balkan territories by the European powers at the Congress of Berlin fanned the patriotism of the Young Turks, who rose in revolution in 1908. In Egypt a revolt led by Arabi against the Western-influenced Khedive provoked British occupation in 1882.

Many of these movements were strongly religious in character. Religion offered a powerful language of resistance. The Mahdiyya, which effectively controlled the Sudan from 1881 to 1898, was a Muslim revivalist movement, directed against Egyptians and Europeans alike. Hinduism played a similar role in articulating resistance in India, as did Confucianism in China. Other movements were "proto-nationalist" rather than nationalist in character: the disparate elements they brought together lacked unity and clearly defined objectives.

THE CONSEQUENCES OF RESISTANCE

But if African and Asian armed resistance was ultimately no match for European weaponry, technology and communications, its significance cannot be measured only in terms of its immediate military outcome. For the participants it often had important local political and economic consequences, and there were considerable continuities in rural resistance and in the ideologies of protest between the movements of this period and later anti-colonial opposition.

Even before 1914, "modern" nationalist movements, characterized by the formation of nationalist associations and political parties, were emerging. Many of these were little more than small groups of disaffected intelligentsia whose impact was negligible, but a few, such as the Indonesian Sarekat Islam, quickly gained a mass following. In the First World War, with the European colonial powers simultaneously preoccupied with the war and forced to demand more from their colonies, new impetus was given to this incipient nationalism.

1878 TO 1914

EUROPEAN RIVALRIES AND ALLIANCES

Under the impact of mass nationalism and economic rivalry, relations between the Great Powers of Europe moved away from the balance-of-power politics practised since 1815 to a system based on rival alliance blocs. Rapid rearmament fuelled a growing tension in Europe which finally exploded in 1914 with the outbreak of the First World War.

In the forty years before 1914 the major European powers dominated the international order as never before. With military superiority assured, the search for security and economic expansion was expressed through a wave of imperialism and conquest. This sharpened rivalries between the powers and reduced the spirit of collaboration and collective settlement of disputes which had characterized the period since 1815.

Within Europe the traditions of "concert diplomacy" were undermined by the sharp changes in the relative strength of the major players. The rise of Germany and Italy as major powers coincided with the decline of the Habsburg empire and the fatal weakening of the Ottomans. Under Bismarck Germany had played a cautious, even conservative role in Europe. After Bismarck's dismissal in 1890 German leaders began to pursue *Weltpolitik*, a global foreign policy, which brought them into conflict with the established colonial powers.

From the 1890s both Britain and France began a steady rearmament in response to the German threat. Russia, which since 1879 had been party to the League of the Three Emperors with Germany and Austria-Hungary, abandoned its traditional conservatism for an alliance with republican, democratic France, which was signed in 1894. By 1907 Britain had sealed a Triple Entente with them both to resolve colonial tensions.

The weakness of some countries was as much a source of instability as the growing strength of others. The Ottoman empire had been shored up by the Great Powers since 1815 in preference to their allowing any one of them to achieve a dominant position in the Middle East. But from the 1870s Ottoman influence declined sharply. Defeated by Russia in 1876–7 and then forced to grant independence to Romania, Serbia and Bulgaria, Ottoman Turkey found itself threatened all across the Middle East and north Africa.

THE BALKAN CRISIS

As Ottoman strength declined the Powers sought to reach agreement to prevent the "Eastern Question" from precipitating a wider crisis. In 1887 Britain, Italy and Austria combined to limit French and Russian encroachments on Turkish territory. In 1897 Russia and Austria agreed to limit their ambitions in the Balkan region and this fragile collaboration lasted until 1908.

No other issue so divided the Powers in the years immediately before 1914 as the future of the Balkan peninsula. It was the one area of Europe where territorial and political advantage was still to be won as Ottoman imperialism waned. For Russia it had been an axis of advance since at least the 18th century; for Austria-Hungary it was the one region where Habsburg ascendancy could be maintained after defeat in Germany and Italy. When in 1908 Austria moved to annex Bosnia, an Ottoman territory under Austrian administration since the 1878 Berlin Conference, Europe came to the brink of war. Russia pulled back after Germany promised assistance to its Austrian ally, but Austro-Russian collaboration was over.

Under Foreign Minister Aerenthal, Austria pursued a new course in the Balkans in an effort to exercise political and economic influence over the new states. Russia countered by appealing to traditions of pan-Slavism, and seeking her own client states in Bulgaria and Serbia. The situation reached boiling point when the Ottoman empire was attacked, first by Italy in 1911, which seized Libya, and then by a Russian-sponsored Balkan League in 1912–3. The Ottomans were all but expelled from Europe and Austria found herself faced by a network of national states in the Balkans which posed a growing threat to the multi-ethnic character of the Habsburg empire.

THE SLIDE INTO WAR

The crisis unleashed by the Balkan Wars was the immediate cause of the slide to European war in 1914, but it was not the only one. When on 28 June 1914 a Serb nationalist, Gavrilo Princip, assassinated the heir to the Habsburg throne,

Vienna was determined to punish Serbia. Russia was not prepared to stand by and watch Serbia taken under Austria's wing; Germany was not willing to risk her alliance with Austria by standing aside.

The pattern of European rearmament and imperial rivalry now came home to roost. Germany believed herself encircled by the French, Russians and the British; Russia and France feared German pre-eminence in Europe; Britain wanted to maintain the old balance of power and saw support for France as the key. No one state wanted a general European conflict. Yet the Powers reacted with fear and uncertainty to the unexpected crisis in the Balkans, instead of displaying the collective crisis-management which they had brought to bear so often over the previous century.

1870 TO 1914

THE FORMATION OF A WORLD ECONOMY

In the last third of the 19th century international trade, migration and capital flows expanded rapidly. Food and raw materials were now produced worldwide using European wealth. In return came a flow of industrial goods. This market operated informally, without state regulation. The 40 years before 1914 marked the zenith of economic liberalism.

The 40 years before the First World War witnessed a remarkable flowering of worldwide commerce, which in turn led to the establishment of an integrated and interdependent global economy. The creation of this world market derived from the economic expansion of Europe and North America, the wealthiest and most technically advanced areas of the world by 1870. Their search for markets and for new sources of raw materials and cheap food produced a restless economic imperialism at the expense of traditional native economies.

THE TRANSPORT REVOLUTION
To a large extent this growth was governed by the spread of modern communications. The most significant development was the expansion of world shipping following the development of steamships. In 1850 most of the world's tonnage consisted of sailing ships; by 1914 only 8 per cent was still powered by

sail. Between 1870 and 1910 European steam tonnage expanded from 1.5 million tons to over 19 million. Steam travel was faster, safer and allowed for much larger ships and cargoes. The average British steamship in 1914 was ten times the size of the average sailing ship in 1850.

There was also a remarkable expansion of the world rail network after 1870. While Europe possessed 97,200km (60,400 miles) of track in 1870 and the USA and Canada 90,600 (56,300), the rest of the world had only 14,650 (9100). By 1911 this had grown to 281,500km (175,000 miles). The American continent was first crossed by rail in 1869 and Canada in 1886, while the Russian empire completed the Trans-Siberian railway in 1904. Railways were essential in providing Europe with easy access to new sources of materials and food in the wider world.

The railway and the steamship also revolutionized commerce throughout the southern hemisphere. The development of effective means of refrigeration allowed meat, fruit and dairy produce to be sent across the equator to European customers. The first refrigerated cargo reached London from Australia in 1880. By the 1890s ships capable of carrying 150,000 frozen carcasses had been developed.

WORLD COMMERCE AND BANKING

This revolution in transport produced an exceptional expansion of world trade. Between 1880 and 1913 the value of the world's imports and exports increased almost six-fold, from $7 billion to $40 billion. Europe dominated foreign trade, accounting for 57 per cent in 1913, of which Britain provided over one-quarter. But Europe's trade was overwhelmingly with other European states. The significant change since 1870 was the rising share of wider global trade, particularly inter-American trade and Japanese trade with Asia.

Trade expansion was closely linked with the development of foreign investment from Europe and America. The lead was taken by the world's wealthiest states, Britain and France. By 1914 they had invested the equivalent of 25 per cent and 15 per cent respectively of their national wealth abroad. Much of this money went to the USA and the settler colonies where it was used to promote railway building, farming and mining.

The rapid expansion of trade also raised issues of payment. From the 1860s, encouraged by the British example, most major states came to adopt the common Gold Standard against which their currencies could be valued. This

Above: The Copernican System, 'Planisphaerium Copernicanum', c.1543, devised by Nicolaus Copernicus (1473-1543) from *The Celestial Atlas, or the Harmony of the Universe.* Copernicus was the first astronomer to formulate a theory that showed the Earth was not at the centre of the universe. It became a landmark in the history of modern science.

Left: The siege of Rhodes in 1522, depicting the Ottoman army storming the walls of the city. The Ottoman state became an astonishingly dynamic imperial and military power from the late 13th century, and was not dissolved until the early 20th century.

Top: The Taj Mahal in Agra, India, is the domed mausoleum of Mumtaz Mahal. It is said to have needed 20,000 workers to complete, and attracts over 3 million visitors each year. It was constructed between 1631 and 1653, and is one of the most famous buildings in the world.

Bottom: A pepper harvest in Malabar. Pepper accounted for over 70 per cent by volume of the world spice trade in the 16th century. This was made possible by the incredible extent of the European voyages of discovery that were made in the 15th to 18th centuries.

Left: James Watt's prototype steam engine. During the 18th century, Britain experienced the world's first industrial revolution as new technologies and overseas markets developed.

Below: In the summer of 1789 the most powerful monarchy in Europe was overthrown by a popular revolution. This illustration shows the execution of Louis XVI in January 1793.

Above: The 19th century witnessed the beginning of a remarkable population explosion which has continued ever since. Europe was at its heart, sending millions overseas to America. The Statue of Liberty symbolized to immigrants the promise of a better life in the New World.

Right: The First World War became a global conflict by 1918, and was to claim over 40 million casualties. On most fighting fronts soldiers' lives were dominated by trench warfare. Conditions were at their worst on the Western Front.

Above: Mahatma Gandhi became the most famous figure in the Indian independence movement, which he led from 1918.

Left: In 1929 the world was plunged into the worst slump in modern history. Trade and prices collapsed and millions were thrown out of work. The crisis provoked extreme nationalism, paving the way to dictatorship. By 1932 17 million Americans were on public relief – for many the only source of food was to queue for meals and handouts organised by charities.

Above: The devastation inflicted by the first atomic bomb, which was dropped on the city of Hiroshima by the United States on 6 August 1945. The immediate death toll was over 200,000. The world had entered the atomic age.

Right: The establishment of the People's Republic of China in 1949 marked a fundamental turning point in China's modern history. The world's most populous nation, China then experienced strong and repressive centralized government under Mao. After his death, its internal politics remained repressive – in 1989 massive student pro-democracy protests ended in a massacre in Tiananmen Square on 4 June.

p: On 13 September 1993 the Israeli prime
nister, Yitzhak Rabin, met President Clinton
d PLO leader Yasser Arafat to sign the Oslo
cords. However significant this breakthrough,
e differences between Israel and the Palestinians
main acute.

Bottom: It is likely that the island nation of
Tuvalu will be the first country to disappear
as a result of climate change. Rising sea
levels in Funafuti Atoll are already putting
the population of 10,000 at risk.

Terrorism has been experienced worldwide since the 1960s. On September 11 2001 two aircraft were deliberately flown into the two towers of the World Trade Center in New York, destroying them both and killing over 2000 people.

was made possible by a great increase in gold production following discoveries in the USA in 1848, Australia in 1851 and South Africa in 1886. During the 1870s most European states adopted a Gold Standard. Japan followed in 1886, India in 1892, Russia in 1895–7 and the USA in 1900. The core measurement became the British pound, fixed at 113 grains of gold. The result was long-term stability in exchange rates and prices.

The regulation of commerce relied largely on the City of London, which became the world's financial and commercial centre in the half century before 1914, confidently exporting the virtues of free enterprise and economic liberalism. The growth of world trade and investment benefited the developed economies very substantially. Their share of world income in 1860 was 44 per cent; by 1913 it was 60.4 per cent. Though earnings in the developed world grew steadily, in the areas opened up by Europe and America they remained low, while native industries were often undermined by foreign imports. Only Japan succeeded in adopting modern technology and enterprise without becoming an economic satellite of the richer economies. Elsewhere local elites largely came to depend for their wealth and power on their links with the new world market, a relationship which in time provoked popular political resistance.

1914 TO 1918
THE FIRST WORLD WAR

In 1914, for the first time since the Napoleonic wars, most of Europe was convulsed by warfare. Expected to be short, the conflict became a long and bloody "total war", mobilizing civilians as well as soldiers and killing millions. By 1918, the war had become a global conflict. Its legacy was economic dislocation, political violence and heightened nationalism.

When Archduke Franz Ferdinand, heir to the Habsburg throne, and his wife were shot by Serb nationalists in Sarajevo on 28 June 1914, few Europeans expected the major powers to be locked in war within five weeks. Yet deeper fears for the balance of power and the preservation of national interest turned a minor incident into a diplomatic crisis. Once Austria-Hungary had decided to punish Serbia for the outrage it proved impossible to contain the conflict. German support for Austria and Russian support for Serbia created an explosive confrontation in which neither side would give way. When Austria invaded Serbia in late July, the two European blocs found themselves within a week fighting the first major European war since 1815.

STALEMATE

Neither side thought the war would last more than six months. Germany expected to be able to quickly conquer Belgium and France – the Schlieffen Plan – by sweeping round Paris and encircling French troops before swinging its forces east to confront the more slowly mobilizing Russian army. But the decision to hold forces in reserve in the industrial regions of Alsace-Lorraine and the Saar reduced the number of troops available and the weakened German offensive was blunted by Anglo-French forces on the Marne between 5 and 8 September. By November both sides had dug in along a 650km (400-mile) front from the English Channel to Switzerland. Behind a tangle of barbed wire, machine-guns and artillery each side confronted the other for almost four years of attritional warfare.

THE WAR IN THE EAST

In the east the war was at first more mobile. The Russians pushed back German and Austro-Hungarian armies at Gumbinnen and Lemberg. Then, at the end of August, German forces defeated the Russians at Tannenberg and the Masurian Lakes. But trapped in a two-front war, Germany never had sufficient resources to consolidate its victories in the east. Elsewhere, the Central Powers found a decisive breakthrough similarly elusive. When Italy opened up a front against the Central Powers in 1915, Austro-Hungarian forces were stretched to the limit until German intervention helped crush the Italians at Caporetto in 1917. The conquest, with Bulgarian help, of Romania and Serbia by Austrian and German forces in 1916 was balanced by the Russian Brusilov offensive in June. The real breakthrough in the east for the Central Powers came with the overthrow of Russia's tsarist regime in February 1917, precipitating Russia's withdrawal from the war. In March 1918 the Treaty of Brest-Litovsk ended the war against Russia, allowing Germany to concentrate its efforts in the west.

Both sides had repeatedly tried to break the stalemate on the Western Front, launching offensives at terrible cost. In February 1916 German forces tried to seize the French fortress of Verdun with no greater strategic object than to bleed the enemy white. More than 600,000 died. Verdun was saved in July 1916 by a British offensive on the Somme but at the cost of over 400,000 British casualties. By 1917, the constant blood-letting had produced protests. French units mutinied until concessions were granted; the German parliament passed a Peace Resolution to force the military to seek an honourable settlement. But by then Germany was under the virtual military dictatorship of Field Marshal Hindenburg and General Ludendorff, both determined on victory in what was now seen as a "total war". In February 1917 the German government authorized unrestricted submarine warfare to combat the Allied naval blockade. Outraged, in April the USA joined the war on the Allied side.

VICTORY IN THE WEST

The US decision to fight not only created a real world war, it tipped the balance against the Central Powers. America loaned over $10 billion to its allies and sent much equipment and food. In March 1918 Ludendorff gambled on a last offensive. German forces broke through towards Paris until, exhausted and short of weapons, they ground to a halt. With clear superiority in arms, the Allies pushed German and Austrian forces back in France and Italy. In September, Ludendorff sued for peace. When granted, on 11 November, Austria, Turkey and Bulgaria were already beaten. A prostrate Germany and revolution in Russia transformed Europe and led to an age of violent social unrest.

SEVEN

THE AGE OF GLOBAL CIVILIZATION

The date at which the European age gave way to the age of global civilization is a matter of debate. Some historians have picked out 1917 as a year of destiny. Others have seen 1947, the year of Indian independence, and 1949, the year of the Chinese revolution, as the decisive turning points. Certainly, America's declaration of war in 1917 turned a European conflict into a world war while the Bolshevik revolution in Russia split the world into two conflicting ideological camps. Similarly, the independence of India and the revolution in China symbolized the resurgence of Asia and the gathering revolt against the West.

Today it is obvious that we live in a post-European age. By

making the world one, the European powers stirred up forces which spelled their own eclipse. The world wars between 1914 and 1945 whittled away the resources of the European powers, and only the healing of the wounds, in acts such as the formation of the European Economic Community in 1957, restored their fortunes. Europe's exhaustion after 1945 benefitted the Soviet Union and the USA, the two superpowers on the eastern and western flanks, whose rivalry produced an age of bipolarity. But bipolarity, too, proved to be a temporary phenomenon. The recovery of Europe, the emancipation of Asia and Africa, the rise of Japan and finally the collapse of the Soviet empire brought a new constellation into being, and with it the threat of confrontation between rich and poor nations and of the exhaustion of global resources through over-population. The world is now dominated by a single major power – the USA – whose massive economic and military strength is challenged by a new wave of anti-Western violence not unlike the reaction that eventually undermined the age of European empire.

1917 TO 1929

THE RUSSIAN REVOLUTION

In 1917 the Russian monarchy collapsed. For eight months liberals and moderate social democrats tried to set up a parliamentary regime, but in October radical communists under Lenin seized power and established a dictatorship which survived military intervention, civil war and economic crisis to forge the world's first communist state, the Soviet Union.

The Tsarist system in Russia was faced with intolerable strains by the First

World War. While Nicholas II did little to dispel hostility to his regime, the war effort went from bad to worse. Land was left untilled, the cities went hungry. The railway system threatened to collapse, towns were swamped with new workers who could not be adequately paid or housed. In February 1917 there were strikes and demonstrations in Petrograd. The army withdrew support from the tsar, and the Duma (parliament) called for a new order. In the face of the revolution, Nicholas abdicated. He was succeeded by a Provisional Government under the liberal Prince Lvov.

THE SECOND REVOLUTION

The first revolution in February solved none of Russia's problems. The Provisional Government had to work with a system of "Dual Power", which it exercised with the Petrograd Soviet, an elected assembly representing workers and soldiers in the capital. A constitution was promised but constantly delayed and the economic situation deteriorated sharply. Soviets sprang up all over Russia, claiming to be the authentic voice of the people. When the war could not be continued effectively, the clamour for change pushed the population towards a more radical solution.

The main beneficiaries were the Social Revolutionaries and the Bolsheviks (Marxist Social-Democrats). In May a mainly socialist government was appointed under the leadership of a Social Revolutionary, Kerensky, but he was unable to stem the radical tide. By October land had been seized by the peasantry, the cities were in chaos, the authority of the government a hollow sham. The Bolshevik leader, Lenin, called for a second, communist revolution, and when Bolsheviks stormed the government building on 25 October 1917, resistance crumbled. The Bolsheviks seized power and established an emergency dictatorship.

CIVIL WAR

Bolshevik power extended only over the heartland of Russia; the rest of the empire broke into a series of smaller national states. On the fringes anti-Bolshevik forces gathered to destroy Russian socialism. After the new regime had agreed to end Russian participation in the First World War at Brest-Litovsk in March 1918, the Bolsheviks fought a three-year civil war against the "White" counter-revolutionary armies, foreign forces sent to crush the revolution, and armed nationalist movements in the Ukraine, the Baltic states and the Caucasus.

A period of extraordinary confusion followed. By organizing a war effort on lines even more authoritarian than the tsar's, the Bolsheviks defeated one enemy after another. By 1920 the civil war was over, and by 1922, when the new state of the USSR was established, its power extended over the Ukraine, the far eastern territories and the Caucasus. In 1921 the regime allowed private trade and farming under the New Economic Policy, but the political system stayed a tight Party dictatorship. During the 1920s an uneasy social peace reigned, but the issue of how to establish an industrial state in a peasant-based society had only been postponed. Under Stalin, General Secretary from 1922, the problem of modernizing Russia was addressed in 1928 in a savage "revolution from above".

1919 TO 1941
IMPERIALISM AND NATIONALISM

Though the First World War destroyed the German and Ottoman empires, the British and French empires reached their greatest territorial extent after 1919. Nevertheless, the war had eroded the foundations of imperialism in Asia and the Middle East while by the 1930s the stability of Europe's empires was being shaken by the Depression.

The imperial contribution to the Allied cause during the First World War led Lloyd George to reflect that "the British empire was not an abstraction but a living force to be reckoned with". Britain, like France, then consolidated the strategic underpinning of its empire by the acquisition of new Middle East territories and expansion in Africa. This was possible because the new League of Nations distributed former Ottoman and German dependencies in the form of "mandates" among the victorious powers. Britain gained trustee-ships for Palestine, Iraq and Transjordan, as well as former German colonies in Tanganyika and, with France, Togoland and German Cameroon. France also gained Syria and Lebanon. Germany's Pacific islands and New Guinea went to New Zealand and Australia respectively and German South West Africa went to South Africa.

Ironically, by 1919 the British faced significant challenges. National identities had been consolidated in the white self-governing colonies, and after the war these countries, termed "dominions" since 1907, pressed for a definition of their status as independent countries within the British Commonwealth. At the same time, there was growing criticism of colonialism from the United States and the Soviet Union, while, despite the real economic rewards they brought with them, the empires were increasingly expensive to maintain.

NATIONALIST OPPOSITION

Above all the European empires faced growing opposition from within their territories, led by educated elites who sought a role in local administration or even national autonomy. The war lubricated the existing nationalist movements in India and Egypt, and intensified opposition in Ireland. Between 1920–2 and again in the early 1930s Mahatma Gandhi led the first nationalist Congress All-India campaigns for self rule. Confronted by mass opposition, in 1919 and 1935 Britain greatly extended Indian participation in government. Egypt, although Britain retained great influence and military rights, was given independence in 1922, while, after violently suppressing guerrilla warfare, Britain conceded "dominion status" in 1921 to a new state created in southern Ireland. Meanwhile post-war uprisings in the newly acquired territories of the Middle East presaged problems to come. In Palestine, where Britain had committed itself to supporting the creation of a Jewish homeland, Jewish immigration after Hitler came to power in Germany led to a widespread Arab uprising after 1936. Iraq meanwhile had secured independence by 1932.

In other European colonies the 1920s were less troubled. In tropical Africa, a "thin white line" of officials administered the colonies acquired in the late 19th century, and African chiefs were incorporated into colonial structures of local governance. Large settler communities developed in east and central Africa, especially in Kenya and southern Rhodesia.

IMPERIALISM IN THE 1930S

The 1930s saw a last burst of imperialism as Japan invaded Manchuria in 1931 and Italy conquered Abyssinia in 1935–6. The League of Nations, however ineffective in practice at dealing with such aggression, had nonetheless, through its mandate system, introduced the idea of international accountability in colonial affairs. Together with the British idea of progress towards "dominion status", it gave rise to a new conception of colonial rule as something temporary and limited. Other colonial powers also faced mounting opposition. In north Africa, Italy experienced continuous resistance while nationalist movements mushroomed in the French territories of Tunisia, Algeria and Morocco. In the Dutch East Indies, a phase of revolutionary movements, beginning with the communist revolt of 1926, was seen off with only limited changes in provincial government, but in Indo-China the preservation of firm French control led to unrest in the 1930s and the creation of a nationalist guerrilla organization, the Viet Minh, by Ho Chi Minh in 1941.

Differing political and social conditions meant that there were fewer challenges in sub-Saharan Africa; nonetheless, discontent with colonial rule took a variety of forms, and the Depression in particular, hitting colonial economies vulnerable to changes in world trade, saw widespread unrest. Cocoa farmers in the Gold Coast were stirred to protest. In the West Indies, meanwhile, unemployment and falling export prices led to a series of strikes and riots between 1935 and 1938.

By 1939 the development of nationalism in Asia and north Africa and the rise of new, more radical nationalist leaders – Sukarno in Indonesia, Nehru in India, Bourguiba in Tunisia – was placing strains on the European colonial empires. It was the Second World War, however, which was to deliver the fatal blow to European colonialism.

1912 TO 1949

THE CHINESE REVOLUTION

China from 1912 entered a phase of brutal internal anarchy. With no effective central government, warlords, Nationalists and Communists struggled for control while imperialist Japan occupied increasingly large areas of the north. Japan's defeat in 1945 saw a further civil war from which the Communists emerged victorious in 1949.

The foundation of the republic in 1912 (see p. 245) failed to produce a lasting solution to China's problems. Within weeks Sun Yat-sen, the revolutionary who had been elected China's provisional first president, was replaced by Yüan Shih-k'ai, the most powerful general of the imperial era. China's continuing weakness was clear: the government had to borrow huge sums abroad to offset the lack of a modern revenue system; the satellite states of Tibet and Mongolia fell under British and Russian dominance respectively; and Japan expanded her influence on Chinese territory. At the outbreak of the First World War Japan seized the German-leased territory in Shantung and presented "Twenty-one Demands" which would have reduced China to a Japanese dependency. Though Yüan was able to resist most, he was forced to acknowledge Japanese dominance in Shantung, Manchuria and Inner Mongolia.

After Yüan died in 1916 power passed increasingly into the hands of provincial generals. For the next decade, although the Peking government claimed to rule China, it was the puppet of one group of generals or another. Some of these warlords established stable and reforming regimes, as in Shansi, Kwangsi and Manchuria, others, as in Szechwan, presided over anarchy. In the 1920s warlord coalitions fought devastating campaigns against each other. Only the treaty ports, under foreign protection, remained secure.

NATIONALIST REACTION

After the First World War there was an upsurge of revolutionary activity driven by widespread popular reaction against foreign interference and economic exploitation, as well as disgust at the terms of the Paris Peace Conference, which reinforced Japan's position in Shantung. In 1919 the reaction erupted into the nationalist "May 4th Movement" in which a new generation of Western-oriented students and intellectuals, joined by urban workers, became a force in politics for the first time. The Movement even succeeded in preventing the government from signing the Treaty of Versailles. There followed the transformation in 1923 of Sun Yat-sen's revolutionary party into the Nationalist (Kuomintang) Party.

With Sun's death in 1925, the Nationalists were headed by Chiang Kai-shek, who in 1926 led the "Northern Expedition" from the Nationalist base in Canton to eliminate the warlords and unify the nation. By 1928 Chiang's armies had taken Peking. For much of this period the Nationalists operated in alliance with the Communist Party, which had been founded in 1920. The Communists showed themselves most effective at organizing support in the industrial cities until Chiang, in April 1927, decided he was strong enough to do without them, and they were ruthlessly purged.

Although the Nationalists now dominated China, serious competitors for power remained. With warlords still flourishing, Chiang's government had firm centralized control over only the rich provinces of the lower Yangtze. There it modernized the administration and the army, built a road and railway system and established new industries.

The Japanese, meanwhile, remained full of imperial ambition: in 1931 they occupied Manchuria, which they industrialized to great effect; in 1933 they occupied the neighbouring province of Jehol; and in 1935 they attempted, without success, to turn the whole of northern China into a puppet state. At the same time, the Communists were beginning to establish themselves effectively in the countryside. From 1929–34 they had made a great success of the Kiangsi Soviet at Jui-chin, where they pioneered a revolution in Marxist theory, developing reform programmes as a peasant-based party rather than as one of the urban proletariat. After the Nationalists forced them to leave the region in 1934, the Communists embarked on what they later saw as the achievement which established their national reputation, the "Long March" to Yenan in northern China. During the march, Mao Zedong, who had pioneered the peasant-based theory, came to dominate the Party.

JAPANESE ADVANCE

From 1936 a three-cornered struggle for power developed between the Nationalists, the Communists and the Japanese. In that year the Nationalists and Communists formed a united front against the Japanese, who responded by invading in force. By the end of 1938 the Japanese controlled most of north and central China, the main coastal ports and all the centres of modern industry. The Nationalist retreat to the far west of China provided the Communists with their opportunity. Using their reform policies they won support in the countryside of occupied China, and with this new peasant base they waged guerrilla warfare against the Japanese. By the end of the Second World War they controlled numerous "liberated" areas.

After the Japanese surrender the Nationalists and Communists raced to take control of former Japanese-held territories with the Communists gaining control of much of the north and most of Manchuria. In 1946 civil war broke out, ending in a Communist victory after bitter fighting involving on occasions hundreds of thousands of troops on both sides. On 1 October 1949 the People's

Republic of China was founded. By May 1950 the Nationalist government had fled to Taiwan (Formosa).

FORTY YEARS OF DESTRUCTION

The civil war ended four of the most destructive decades of Chinese history. As well as hundreds of thousands killed or maimed, it left industry in ruins, railways wrecked and business and finance destroyed by years of hyperinflation. But for the first time for over a century a strong regime controlled the Chinese mainland, with plans, already tested in limited areas, for the regeneration of the economy and the transformation of the country.

1919 TO 1934
EUROPEAN POLITICAL PROBLEMS

The end of the Great War was supposed to usher in an age of peace and disarmament, but the conflict had undermined economic stability, opened up the threat of communist revolt and left a generation of veterans alienated from parliamentary politics. The slump of 1929 left European capitalism in deep crisis and opened the way to political extremism.

In 1919 the political map of Europe was transformed. The defeat of the German and Austro-Hungarian empires in 1918 (and the collapse of the Tsarist system in Russia the year before) brought to an end the long period of dynastic empires that had dominated central and eastern Europe. The victorious Allies met at Versailles in January 1919 to try to replace the imperial regimes with a system of independent states.

The Allies brought with them conflicting ambitions: the American president, Woodrow Wilson, hoped to broker a peace that would end war for ever and establish a liberal, democratic Europe of national states; the French wanted to punish Germany and prevent her revival; Italy, Serbia and Romania sought territorial concessions. The outcome was a messy compromise. Weak new democratic states were created, based loosely on the principle of national self-determination, but the defeated countries were heavily penalized and their national territories dismembered. The political instability of the post-war years can be traced back to the bitter legacy imposed by the peace settlement.

The settlement itself took four years to complete. New states were created: Finland, Estonia, Latvia and Lithuania freed themselves from Russian rule; a Polish state was reconstituted after a bitter conflict with the new Soviet armies in the east and with German nationalist militia in the west; Czechoslovakia was carved out of the northern territories of the Habsburg empire, and Yugoslavia was created. The defeated powers were forced to relinquish territory, to pay substantial reparations and to disarm. The German army was reduced to a mere 100,000 men, the Austrian forces to 30,000 and the Hungarian to 35,000.

THE LEAGUE OF NATIONS

Europe was now dominated by France, the most heavily armed state in the world in the 1920s. She played a key role with Britain in running the League of Nations, which was established in 1920 as a forum for the conduct of international politics on peaceful lines. The French aim was to find a system of "collective security" which could protect her from any revival of German power. In 1926 Germany was admitted to the League and in 1928 the Kellogg-Briand Pact was signed in Paris by all the powers, committing them to the settlement of disputes without resort to war.

The collective system was a superficial one. The League had no agreed procedures for enforcing settlement and no military back-up. The Soviet Union did not join until 1934, and the United States refused to join at all. The expectation that Europe would embrace democracy as a foundation for collaboration soon evaporated. Economic crisis and bitter social conflict, engendered by the rise of socialism and the revolutionary activity of European communists, could not be contained within weak parliamentary systems by liberal politicians often quite out of touch with popular social and nationalist agitation. Between 1922 and 1926 democracy was torn up in Italy by Mussolini and the Fascist party; Spain had military rule imposed in 1923 by Primo de Rivera and, after a brief republican interlude between 1931 and 1936, the army imposed Franco's dictatorship. In Poland, Austria, the Baltic states, Yugoslavia, Hungary, Romania, Greece and Bulgaria, democracy was eventually suspended and nationalist regimes installed based on royal dictatorship, military coup or single-party rule.

Even in the victor powers democracy was challenged. In Ireland a bloody civil war led to the creation of an independent Irish state and the break up of the Anglo-Irish Union. In 1926 a General Strike provoked sharp social conflict in Britain. In France conflicts between right and left led to growing violence, which culminated in the storming of the French parliament in 1934 and the overthrow of the government. Yet democracy survived in both states despite the noisy agitation of right and left.

THE RISE OF HITLER

In Germany democracy was overcome by extremism. Despite efforts to make the new system work through coalition rule, the slump of 1929, which hit Germany harder than anywhere else, created an economic catastrophe that the government was powerless to ameliorate. German society was politically polarized. Communist support doubled, but millions of Germans turned to Adolf Hitler's Nazi Party with its promise of a New Order, neither socialist nor parliamentary. Hitler was committed to overturning Versailles, and his appointment as German chancellor in January 1933 challenged not only the German peace settlement but the whole system set up across Europe in 1919–20. Hitler emboldened radical nationalists and irredentists everywhere who rejected liberalism and collective security in favour of dictatorship and the violent revision of the peace treaties.

1929 TO 1939

THE GREAT DEPRESSION

In 1929 the world was plunged into the worst slump in modern history. Trade and prices collapsed, millions were thrown out of work. As governments took responsibility for economic revival, the old economic order was replaced by state intervention. At the same time, the crisis provoked extreme nationalism, paving the way to dictatorship.

The great inter-war slump is usually dated from 29 October 1929 when the New York stock market crashed. When in July 1933 the index at last stopped falling, shares stood at 15 per cent of their 1929 value. Thousands of Americans were bankrupt, millions unemployed and impoverished. In the developed world alone over 23 million were out of work by 1932. At its peak, unemployment affected one in four of the American workforce; in Germany almost 9 million were thrown out of work in a workforce of 20 million.

THE CAUSES OF THE CRISIS

The crash of 1929 was a symptom as much as a cause of the worldwide slump that followed. The world economy had been weakened by the First World War and the massive debts it generated. It proved impossible to re-introduce the Gold Standard (see p. 265) system fully, or to revive an effective multilateral trading system. Over-production led to falling prices and declining profits. Despite the boom in America, business confidence elsewhere had been low and investment sluggish. When the US stock market crashed, it was against the background of an already declining and fragile world economy.

THE EFFECTS OF THE SLUMP

The effects unfolded slowly. Protective tariffs were set up worldwide to save domestic industry. Even laissez-faire Britain adopted Imperial Preference in 1932, a protected trading bloc within the empire. World trade in the 1930s never recovered its 1929 level, and bilateral trade agreements came to replace the liberal system of multilateral trade and exchange. Germany in 1934 adopted a "New Plan" for state-regulated trade, and in 1936 a programme of "autarky", or self-sufficiency.

Declining trade encouraged domestic sources of economic revival. In Britain, Sweden, Germany and the USA, experiments in state work-creation projects soaked up some of the millions of unemployed. In 1933 Roosevelt introduced a package of recovery policies known as the "New Deal", which extended state regulation of the economy in a country with little tradition of such government activity. In Britain and Germany state regulation by the late 1930s had produced what was called a "managed economy", a forerunner of the mixed economies of the post-1945 era.

THE POLITICAL COST

The severity of the slump produced a political backlash. In more vulnerable economies such as Germany or Japan, radical nationalist groups argued for economic empire-building and an end to the old liberal capitalist order. In France and Spain economic crisis stimulated communism or anarchism, sparking prolonged social conflict. Only in Britain, with its large empire markets, did democracy survive and a modest prosperity set in during the 1930s. In much of Europe and Latin America various forms of dictatorship came to replace parliamentary systems now irrevocably associated with economic disaster.

1931 TO 1941

THE OUTBREAK OF THE SECOND WORLD WAR

In the 1930s the world order was violently challenged by states committed to establishing a "New Order" based on military conquest and brutal imperial rule. As the post-war system dissolved, bitter political conflicts between democrats, communists and fascists tore Europe apart and sent the world spiralling once again to war.

In the 1930s the international order constructed after the First World War, based upon the League of Nations and "collective security", collapsed under the violent impact of major revisionist powers bent on building a "New Order" in their favour.

The crisis of the international system owed much to the effects of the worldwide slump, which encouraged strident nationalism and militarism in the weaker economies. In Japan the economic crisis provoked the military into seizing economic resources and markets by force to compensate for their declining trade. In 1931 the Chinese province of Manchuria was conquered and soon turned into a Japanese satellite state, Manchukuo, ruled by the last Manchu emperor, Pu Yi. Japan left the League and declared a "New Order" in East Asia. With the League of Nations powerless in the face of this aggression, Japan continued to encroach on Chinese sovereignty until full-scale war broke out in 1937, bringing much of northern China under direct Japanese rule.

In Europe Mussolini's Italy also looked for a new economic empire. In 1935, expecting little reaction from the other major powers, Italy invaded Ethiopia. Though sanctions were half-heartedly applied by the League, by 1936 the conquest was complete. Italy, too, pulled out of the League.

GERMAN EXPANSION

In 1935 Hitler began the process of overturning the Versailles settlement, declaring German rearmament in defiance of the Treaty. In March the following year, he ordered German troops back into the Rhineland. When the expected protest from Britain and France failed to materialize, his ambitions widened. In March 1938 Austria was occupied and united into a Greater Germany. In May Hitler's plans for the conquest of Czechoslovakia were frustrated only by belated protests from Britain and France. At the Munich conference in September that year, called to discuss the crisis, Britain and France nonetheless agreed to the incorporation of the Sudetenland, the German-speaking areas of Czechoslovakia, into Germany.

Far from marking an end to "legitimate" German territorial aspirations, the Munich Pact encouraged Hitler further. In March 1939, in clear defiance of the Pact, Germany occupied Bohemia and Moravia. Slovakia, all that remained of Czechoslovakia, became a German puppet state. At the same time, Hitler forced Lithuania to agree the return of Memel on the Baltic coast to Germany. Hitler then formally demanded the return of Danzig, which had been made a Free City under League jurisdiction after the war.

The failure of Britain and France to respond to Hitler's aggression was largely the result of their horror of a further European conflict, a dilemma heightened by the events of the Spanish Civil War and the crisis in eastern Europe. Nonetheless, despite political resistance at home they both in 1936 began a programme of large-scale rearmament, which they hoped would deter Hitler from further aggression. By the time Hitler threatened Poland in 1939 both Western powers had reached the point where they could no longer postpone confronting the threat to the European balance of power. Hitler reacted to growing Western firmness by concluding a non-aggression pact with the ideological enemy, the Soviet Union, in August 1939. Hitler was convinced that Western resistance would crumble, but instead Britain signed a military alliance with Poland on 26 August, and when Germany invaded Poland on 1 September Britain and France declared war two days later.

WAR IN EUROPE

Poland was defeated within two weeks and was divided between Germany and the Soviet Union in a second agreement signed in Moscow in September 1939.

The western Allies sat behind the Maginot Line in eastern France waiting for a German attack. In April, Germany occupied Norway to secure the northern flank, and on 10 May 1940 invaded the Netherlands, Luxembourg, Belgium and France. In six weeks all were defeated and British forces humiliatingly expelled from continental Europe. Emboldened by Hitler's success, Italy invaded France in June and Egypt in September 1940, and then attacked Greece in October.

Hitler wanted Britain to sue for peace. When Churchill, Britain's new prime minister, refused, German air forces tried to force a surrender. The ensuing Battle of Britain in the air was Hitler's first defeat. In November 1940, he confirmed a decision made in July to attack the Soviet Union. Delayed by a campaign in the Balkans in April 1941 against Yugoslavia and Greece, the invasion began on 22 June 1941. After a series of spectacular victories German forces approached Leningrad and Moscow. The Axis seemed poised to remake the world order.

1941 TO 1945

THE WAR IN ASIA AND THE PACIFIC

In 1941 Japan embarked on an ambitious programme of expansion in the Pacific and southeast Asia. War with the USA and Britain, together with the ongoing war with China, proved more than Japanese resources could cope with. In 1945, after the US air force had reduced many of her cities to ruin, two by atomic weapons, Japan capitulated.

The German victories in the Soviet Union in 1941 prompted Japanese leaders to establish a new order in southeast Asia and the Pacific while the colonial powers were weakened and before the United States began serious rearmament. The object was to create a southern zone which could be defended by the formidable Japanese navy while resources, particularly oil, were seized and shipped north to help the Japanese war economy and stiffen the Japanese army in its war with China.

The decision for war with the United States was taken in November 1941 and on 7 December Japanese aircraft attacked the Pearl Harbor naval base in the Hawaiian islands, crippling part of the US Pacific Fleet. Japan then occupied European colonial territories to the south – Burma, Malaya, Singapore, the East

Indies – and captured a string of Pacific Islands stretching to the Solomons north of Australia. Though Japanese warships threatened Ceylon and Madagascar, there were no plans to occupy any larger region despite the rapid and comprehensive success of the original campaign.

The Japanese attack on Pearl Harbor brought the United States fully into the war. Within a year the USA was turning out more vehicles, ships and aircraft than all the other combatant powers together. Japan could not hope to compete with American industrial might on this scale and planned instead to inflict a crippling defeat on what was left of the US Pacific Fleet, severing American communications across the Pacific and forcing a compromise peace. The naval battle sought by Admiral Yamamoto was fought off Midway Island between 3 and 6 June and resulted in a major Japanese defeat. In August 1942 US forces, commanded by General MacArthur, invaded Tulagi and Guadalcanal in the Solomons.

THE ALLIED BUILD-UP

Though the Allies could not afford to allow the Pacific campaign to divert resources from the European theatre, sufficient supplies were made available to push the Japanese back island by island, using a combination of massive air power, fast carriers and submarines. The Japanese merchant fleet, on which the whole southern campaign relied, was reduced from over 5 million tons in 1942 to 670,000 tons in 1945. Communications were cut when US forces reoccupied the Philippines in 1944 and seized the Marianas. Japan threw its final air and naval reserves into these battles. Defeated in the Philippine Sea in June 1944 and at Leyte Gulf in October, the remaining Japanese forces were stranded in what was left of the southern empire. Only fanatical resistance held up the Allied advance. By the spring of 1945, with the fall of Iwo Jima and Okinawa, America was in a position to attack mainland Japan.

THE FINAL DEFEAT

The war in Asia made slower progress. In March 1944 Japan's forces in Burma attacked India, but were decisively defeated at Imphal with the loss of 53,000 men out of 85,000. In China, Japanese forces in the north fought both the Chinese Nationalists and the Communists under Mao Zedong. A million men were tied down in the Chinese war, which soaked up far more resources than the southern campaign. In 1944 Japan launched its last major offensive, Ichi-Go, which brought a large area of south-central China under Japanese rule, opened up a land-link with Indo-China and destroyed the Nationalist armies.

But victory in China came just as Allied forces in the Pacific could bring mainland Japan into their sights. Between March and June 1945, a series of devastating air raids were launched in which heavy B-29 bombers destroyed 58 Japanese cities, killing more than 393,000 Japanese civilians. Within the Japanese government arguments continued through the summer about surrendering, but the military refused to countenance such a dishonour. Suicide pilots (*kamikaze*) were sent out to attack Allied shipping, sinking or damaging 402 ships. America planned Operation Downfall for the invasion of the Japanese home islands, using 14,000 aircraft and 100 aircraft carriers, but the decision to drop atomic bombs on Hiroshima and Nagasaki in August 1945 ended Japanese resistance. On 15 August, with her cities in ruins and her economy devastated, Japan surrendered unconditionally to the Allies.

1941 TO 1945
THE EUROPEAN WAR

The Second World War was the largest and bloodiest conflict in human history, bringing the deaths of more than 55 million people and transforming the international order. In Europe, the main land battle was won in the east but the bombing offensive in the west destroyed German air power, paving the way for the invasion of German-held western Europe.

By the autumn of 1941 Hitler's empire in Europe had reached its zenith. German forces, buttressed by the industrial resources of a whole continent, seemed unconquerable. Yet within a year the balance began to tilt towards the Allies. Despite his failure to defeat the USSR in 1941, in December that year Hitler nonetheless declared war on the USA. Germany now faced not only a two-front war but enemies who were rapidly learning from their earlier mistakes and, above all in the shape of the USA, could claim immense and increasing military and industrial potential.

THE TURN OF THE TIDE

But in early 1942, the prospects for the Allies looked bleak. The Soviet Union had suffered catastrophic losses, American rearmament was in its infancy and the U-Boat war in the Atlantic was strangling British trade. The Allied cause was saved by a remarkable resurgence of Soviet fighting power and morale in the face of the most barbarous conflict of the war and by the prodigious manufacturing record of American industry. In 1944 Allied aircraft production reached 168,000 against only 39,000 German.

Allied victory was also aided by German treatment of the conquered areas. Instead of winning the conquered peoples over to Hitler's European "New Order" and to his crusade against communism, German rule was terroristic and exploitative. More than seven million Europeans, from France to Russia, were taken as forced labour to Germany. One-third of Germany's war costs was met by tribute extracted from occupied Europe. Thousands were executed or imprisoned for their ideological beliefs. Nazi racism was directed at the so-called lower races in the east, who were to be enslaved, and against Jews, Gypsies and the disabled. Around 6 million Jews were murdered in a state-sponsored campaign of genocide.

At the end of 1942 German forces suffered their first reverses, at El Alamein in north Africa and at Stalingrad. Anglo-American forces landed in Morocco and Algeria in November 1942, and in the same month the Red Army began an offensive on the Don river which initiated almost three years of continuous Soviet victories. The following spring the submarine offensive in the Atlantic was ended by the use of combined air and sea power, allowing American assistance to pour into Europe on a massive scale. In July 1943 the western Allies invaded Sicily, opening up a major southern front which drained German resources, while at Kursk on the Russian steppe the largest pitched battle in history was won by an increasingly well-organized Red Army.

THE DEFEAT OF GERMANY

In June 1943 Anglo-American forces in Britain and the Mediterranean began the Combined Bombing Offensive, which by the spring of 1944 had imposed crippling destruction on the German urban population, undermined further expansion of German war production and almost destroyed the German air force. The campaign also paved the way for the massive Allied seaborne invasion of northern France in June 1944. France was liberated in four months, while Soviet forces continued their push into eastern Europe.

Soviet victories raised the issue of the post-war order. As the likelihood of German defeat increased, the western powers found themselves facing a second authoritarian system in the form of their Soviet ally. Conferences at Teheran in 1943 and Yalta in 1945 exposed these growing divisions over the future of Europe. Yet this potential split, though it would come to dominate the post-war world, was never great enough to break up the alliance and in the last bitter months of fighting the Allies remained united in their determination to defeat Hitler. In 1945 a final assault on Germany brought western and Soviet forces face to face across central Germany. On 2 May Berlin fell, two days after Hitler had committed suicide. By 7 May German forces had surrendered.

The war was enormously costly. Worldwide, at least 55 million lost their lives, including an estimated 17 million Soviet citizens. Some 10 million Germans fled eastern Europe in 1944–5; millions of Soviet citizens were forced into internal exile or sent to Soviet labour camps. After four years of destruction, Europe lay in ruins, its economy shattered. The Second World War had exceeded by far the terrible cost of the First.

1919 TO 1953
RACISM AND DEPORTATIONS

For almost 40 years Europe witnessed an exceptional period of forced population transfers, mass asylum-seeking, savage racial discrimination and genocide. Millions were forced from their homeland through political revolution, irredentism or social exclusion; millions more were murdered in the name of narrow nationalist ideologies or scientific racism.

One of the direct causes of the First World War was an upsurge in extreme forms of nationalism and xenophobia. The post-war peace settlements not only failed to stem the tide, but in many cases encouraged it by leaving ethnic enclaves in states dominated by a different nationality. Millions of Germans ended up living in the newly created states of Czechoslovakia and Poland. Hundreds of thousands of Hungarians ended up under Romanian rule. Germans in the South Tyrol were ruled by Italians. In the Near East a war between Greece and Turkey ended in 1921 with the transfer of thousands of Greeks and Turks living on alien territory.

The new nationalism had a strong racial basis to it. Theories of scientific racism common before 1914 were adopted to justify policies of racial exclusion and to encourage a process of biological selection to ensure that racial stock remained pure and uncontaminated. The target of much of this racism was Europe's Jewish population. Popular anti-Semitism in the 1920s developed the idea of a world Jewish conspiracy to weaken the nation and pollute its gene pool. In many states in central and eastern Europe popular hostility was followed by legislation to restrict Jewish rights and economic opportunities.

DEPORTATION AND EXILE

The Bolshevik Revolution of 1917 provoked a bitter civil war inside the new Soviet state, which resulted in a mass exodus of almost one million former Russians to Europe and overseas. The deep ideological divisions inspired by communism and anti-communism led to further waves of exile, voluntary and otherwise. In the 1920s thousands of Italian opponents of Mussolini's fascism fled abroad; after 1933 hundreds of thousands of Germans fled from Hitler's Third Reich, including more than half Germany's Jewish population.

In the 1930s the Soviet regime began to deport sections of its own population, at first removing nationalities from the borderlands who were thought to be sympathetic to the Soviet Union's enemies – Koreans, Finns, Poles, Greeks. Then in 1939–41, millions were deported from the new lands acquired under the terms of the German-Soviet agreements of August and September 1939. From 1941, when Axis forces invaded, millions more were deported to Siberia and central Asia, including almost one million Soviet Germans, because their loyalty to the Soviet war effort was in doubt. At the end of the war more deportations removed potential anti-communist resistance in the states of eastern Europe and nationalists in the Ukraine or Belarus who had used German occupation to extend their influence.

THE MURDER OF EUROPEAN JEWS

The Hitler regime regarded the Soviet state as a haven for "Jewish-Bolshevism" and linked its anti-Marxism and anti-Semitism together. In the 1930s German Jews were encouraged to emigrate, stripped of their citizenship, and subjected to economic discrimination and social exclusion. As German power spread into the states of central Europe, so the anti-Semitism became more strident. With the conquest of Poland in 1939 there began a deliberate programme of isolation and ghettoization of the Jews in the east.

In 1941 with the invasion of the USSR, the German regime began a systematic programme of murder directed at certain categories of Soviet Jews, then at whole Jewish populations. In reaction to the coming of global war in late 1941, Hitler ordered the murder of all Europe's Jews in revenge for their alleged efforts to destroy the new Germany. A system of extermination camps was set up and more than three million Jews from all over occupied and Axis Europe were murdered in gas chambers. Some countries resisted German demands; in Bulgaria, Denmark and Italy large numbers of Jews were saved. Elsewhere local anti-Semites encouraged the programme of deportation and murder. At the end of the war the populations in the East turned on the Germans still living in their midst and around 13 million were driven westward, many ending up in America or Britain. This marked the end of a short and savage period of ethnic cleansing in Europe which resulted in the death of well over ten million people and the uprooting of millions more.

1945 TO 1973
EUROPE

War-devastated Europe after 1945 was a continent on an ideological fault-line: capitalist and democratic in the west, communist and authoritarian in the east. The division was clear, too, in the west's superior economic performance. Despite the confrontation, the continent also experienced a growing stability and prosperity.

Europe was a region of extraordinary desolation in 1945. More than 30 million people had been killed and 16 million permanently displaced from their homes. Many of Europe's greatest cities lay in ruins. Industrial production had sunk to one-third of the pre-war level, agricultural production to half. The war also left a legacy of bitterness. Collaborators with fascism were ostracized, imprisoned or murdered while the revival of communism brought real fears of social collapse in the areas of Europe not under Soviet rule.

NEW FRONTIERS

The first task was to dismantle Hitler's New Order in Europe (*see* p. 285). The new frontiers of Germany were agreed by the Allied powers at Yalta (February 1945) and Potsdam (July 1945). Germany lost its eastern territories to Poland and was separated from Austria. Czech and Yugoslav sovereignty was restored. In the east, however, the German New Order was replaced by a Soviet one. The USSR moved westward to absorb most of the territories of the former Tsarist empire – eastern Poland, the Baltic States, Bessarabia. Czech democracy, briefly restored in 1945, was overturned in 1948. Only Yugoslavia, under the rule of Tito's communists, retained real independence from Moscow. The other states of eastern Europe had traded one dictatorship for another.

ECONOMIC REVIVAL

The economic and social revival of Europe depended on the two super-powers: the USA and the Soviet Union. In western Europe revival was linked to American economic strength. Through the UN and the International Bank for Reconstruction and Development the USA pumped $17 billion into Europe's economy. In 1947 a European Recovery Programme was set up which released another $11.8 billion. In 1948 the 16 nations qualifying for aid set up the Organization for European Economic Cooperation to coordinate the aid programme, the harbinger of much closer economic collaboration over the following decades. In 1952, France, Germany, Italy and the Benelux countries set up the European Coal and Steel Community to coordinate industry in their countries. In 1957 they moved to a full customs union, the European Economic Community.

Western Europe underwent the greatest economic boom in its history. By 1950 output of goods was 35 per cent higher than in 1938; by 1964 it was 250 per cent higher. Even in eastern Europe's command economy there was sustained economic growth though the price was high: low living standards, pollution and police oppression. The gap between the two economic systems widened greatly in the 1950s and 1960s, fuelling popular unrest in the East. There were strikes and political protests in East Germany and Poland in 1953, in Hungary in 1956 and Czechoslovakia in 1968, all violently suppressed by the USSR.

In the west, the EEC made another war between France and Germany virtually unthinkable and the two countries' relationship lay at the heart of the continent's new political alignment from the 1950s onwards. Economic growth encouraged political stability, too. Democracy was restored in Italy in 1946, in West Germany in 1949, in Austria in 1955. Authoritarianism survived in Portugal and Spain, and emerged briefly in Greece after 1967, but it remained the exception. Local independence movements in Northern Ireland, the Basque region of Spain and in Corsica produced sporadic violence, but the nationalist tensions that brought war twice since 1914 finally evaporated.

1945 TO 1991
THE COLD WAR

At the end of the Second World War, the world was dominated by the USA and the USSR. Their ideological differences produced a complete polarization between the capitalist west and the communist bloc. Both sides developed nuclear arsenals but the fear of nuclear destruction led to a "Cold War", a confrontation short of armed conflict.

After 1945 the international order was dominated by the division between the capitalist west and communist east, each side grouped around the two new "superpowers" that emerged from the defeat of Hitler: the United States in the west, the Soviet Union in the east. Yet though their hostility produced persistent confrontation, open conflict was avoided, a state described by the American journalist Walter Lippmann as "Cold War".

THE SOURCE OF THE CONFLICT

The roots of the Cold War lay in the Russian Revolution of 1917. Communism, with its belief in its own inevitable domination of the world, was seen as a profound threat to the world capitalist system, of which the USA was taking the leadership. The United States and the other western allies had found themselves allied to the Soviet Union in the Second World War through force of circumstance: the imperatives of defeating Hitler overrode all other considerations, though this did not prevent persistently strained relations throughout the war. But with Hitler beaten, the underlying tensions resurfaced. The west saw in Soviet communism the spectre of a second expansionist authoritarian system, while for its part the USSR believed it had helped defeat one form of capitalist imperialism only to be confronted with an even more powerful one in the form of the USA.

THE HEIGHT OF THE COLD WAR

With both sides eager to avoid open conflict, the Cold War was fought out in a world of spies and secrets, political threat and subversion. In large measure it was a war fought by proxy. Both camps exploited or entered local conflicts in which they armed, equipped and trained the opposing sides, each seeking to extend their spheres of influence without coming to blows directly.

Tension was most acute in the period between 1947 and 1963, as the new political order in Europe and Asia was being fashioned, above all in central and eastern Europe where the USSR sought to impose itself on those territories it had liberated in the war. The consolidation of communist regimes in the region combined with the success of the communist revolution in China in 1949 under Mao Zedong created an apparently solid communist bloc from Europe to the Pacific, though by 1960 an open rift developed in Sino-Soviet relations.

America in 1947 committed itself to "containing" communism (the Truman Doctrine) and lent support to countries fighting wars against the communist threat, in Greece (1947), in Korea (1950–3) and then in the long and draining conflict in Vietnam (1961–73). At the same time, the United States tried to bolster these efforts by creating security blocs – NATO in Europe in 1949, SEATO in southeast Asia in 1954 and CENTO in the Middle East in 1959. The Soviet Union and China retaliated by giving military aid and political support to anti-colonial or nationalist struggles against "world imperialism" throughout Asia, Latin America and Africa. In 1955 the Soviet Union also sponsored a military alliance of its own, the Warsaw Pact.

THE SHADOW OF THE BOMB

The most important factor preventing the shift to "hot war" was the existence of nuclear weapons. First used in 1945 against Japan, America's monopoly of the weapon was broken by the Soviet Union in 1949. In 1952 the USA developed thermonuclear weapons, with still more destructive power, and by 1953 the Soviet Union had them, too. By 1958 the American arsenal of warheads was estimated to be able to kill 200 million on a first strike. The development of intercontinental ballistic missiles and submarine-launched missiles in the 1950s then gave both sides the ability to destroy the other almost entirely, indeed to obliterate much of the globe. By the 1960s, Britain, France and China had also developed a nuclear capability. The prospect of mutual destruction on a horrific scale acted as a deterrent to conflict. The closest the world came to war was the Cuban missile crisis of 1962. The experience so alarmed the two sides that from 1963 a slow thaw set in with the signing of a partial test-ban treaty.

It was followed in 1969 with the opening of strategic arms limitation talks (SALT) and, in 1970, by a nuclear non-proliferation treaty (though France, China, India, Pakistan and Israel refused to sign). Although relations improved again in the early 1970s with the advent of détente, tensions increased with the communist victory in Vietnam and the Soviet military intervention in Afghanistan in 1979. The USA responded in the early 1980s with renewed anti-Soviet rhetoric and a massive rearmament programme, calculating that the cost of matching it would be more than the already impoverished Soviet economy could bear.

The expense of maintaining their unwinnable war in Afghanistan coupled with the costs of this renewed arms race was to prove too great a burden for the USSR. In 1985 President Gorbachev announced Soviet willingness to disarm and between 1985 and 1987 negotiations proceeded for the progressive reduction of nuclear arsenals. The collapse of the Soviet communist bloc in 1989–91 and reform in Asian communist states brought the Cold War to an end.

SINCE 1939

RETREAT FROM EMPIRE

In 1939 European colonial powers still controlled much of Asia, the Caribbean and the Pacific and almost all of Africa. The dissolution of their empires after 1945, frequently accompanied by violence, was one of the most remarkable transformations of the modern world. By the 1990s only a handful of European dependencies remained.

By 1939 there were already significant nationalist movements in some European colonies. Britain, France and the Netherlands were also, to varying degrees, committed to the evolution of their colonial territories towards self-government, and this commitment was reinforced, in the case of Great Britain and France, by the terms under which they had been granted mandates by the League of Nations over territories formerly part of the German and Ottoman empires.

The Second World War accelerated these developments. The Italian empire was dismembered entirely, while after the war the remaining European colonial powers no longer had the economic muscle to enforce imperial rule. Furthermore, international politics were dominated by the two avowedly anti-colonial superpowers, the United States and the USSR. In addition, in east Asia, where the British, French and Dutch set about attempting to restore control of colonies overrun by the Japanese in the war, nationalists were unwilling to return to dependence. Similarly, in north Africa, Anglo-American occupation of French colonies during the war revitalized the independence movements there, while in British India independence had already been promised during the war in an unsuccessful attempt to secure the cooperation of the nationalist Congress.

ASIA

It was in Asia that nationalists and, in some colonies, communists, presented the greatest challenges to European colonialism. The British, knowing they could not hold India on pre-war terms, advanced the sub-continent rapidly towards independence in 1947. Neither Britain nor Congress was able to resist the Muslim campaign for a separate state of Pakistan, and India was partitioned in circumstances of great violence. The following year Britain abandoned its mandate in Palestine, and withdrew from Ceylon and Burma. In Malaya a long struggle against communist insurgents culminated in Britain granting independence in 1957. The Dutch never regained control of the Dutch East Indies after the Japanese left and independence was finally achieved in 1949. In Vietnam communists and nationalists opposed the restored French administrations. After prolonged conflict and military defeat at Dien Bien Phu, the French abandoned their Far Eastern empire.

The French were also engulfed in violent anti-colonial conflict in north Africa. Tunisia and Morocco were given independence in 1956. The French withdrew from Algeria in 1962 after eight years of brutal war – between French settlers, Algerian nationalists, Islamic insurgents and the French army – had threatened civil war at home. In the Middle East, French and British credibility was damaged by the Suez invasion in 1956. British influence in the region and her world status were further diminished by retreat from Cyprus and Aden in 1960 and 1967 and the announcement in 1968 that British forces east of Suez would be withdrawn.

In sub-Saharan Africa, where nationalist movements were initially less developed, Britain and France sought relief from their domestic economic problems by vigorous exploitation of African resources. Economic concerns, as well as a desire to obstruct a possible extension of South African influence, also led to the establishment of a short-lived federation of Britain's central African territories. However, Britain, facing mounting nationalism and keen to avoid wholesale rupture of British-African relations which might encourage the spread of Cold War rivalries to Africa, withdrew from west Africa, beginning with the Gold Coast (Ghana) in 1957. Though settlers resisted a transition to African majority rule in east and central Africa, independence nonetheless came after 1960, precipitated when France under de Gaulle suddenly withdrew from all its tropical African colonies and Belgium retreated from the Congo, in the process provoking a bloody civil war. Italy's African colonies, Libya and Somalia, placed under UN control in 1945, became independent in 1951 and 1960. Portugal alone still clung to its colonies, Angola and Mozambique, but both had broken free by 1975 after bitter guerrilla wars.

THE COLONIAL LEGACY

Though the winding up of colonial empires continued through the 1970s and 1980s in the Caribbean and the South Pacific and into the 1990s – Hong Kong was returned to China by the British in 1997 – by the beginning of the 1970s the age of European overseas empires was effectively past. In the process of decolonization, not only had many former dependencies faced rapid, some-times violent, political change, a number then had to reconcile the demands of rival ethnic or religious divisions within their new borders. In varying degrees, most also confronted economic problems that for some would prove all but insuperable.

SINCE 1945
JAPAN AND EAST ASIA

In the years after 1945 east Asia struggled to throw off the legacy of the Second World War. After 1948, United States support for Japan, South Korea and Taiwan, perceived as its first line of defence in east Asia, transformed their economies. Until the late 1990s they seemed to form the core of one of the world's most dynamic economic regions.

In the autumn of 1945 the future for Japan looked grim. The economy was in ruins; most of the towns and industrial plant had been destroyed; the navy had been sunk; nearly all foreign assets had been lost; domestic capital was run down; the victorious enemy demanded large reparations; all the necessities of life were short.

THE RECONSTRUCTION OF JAPAN

The rebuilding of the country was led by the American occupation administration. Japan had to accept a new constitution which ended the divinity of the emperor and gave sovereignty to the people. An independent judiciary was established, free labour unions were permitted and war was renounced as a means of settling disputes. From 1948, with the advance of the Chinese communists, the USA increasingly came to see Japan not only as the key bulwark of Western power in east Asia but also as one whose effectiveness depended on the reconstruction of its economic power. In September 1951 the American occupation was ended.

For Korea Japan's defeat ended the harsh Japanese colonial regime imposed in 1910. But it also brought a division of the country between a communist state in the north backed by the Soviet Union and an anti-communist state in the south backed by the USA. In June 1950 war broke out and, when it came to an end in 1953, Korea was divided along the armistice line.

The Korean War provided the first boost to the Japanese recovery. There followed a period of exceptionally high economic growth – well over 10 per cent a year throughout the 1960s – which turned her into an economic superpower. In the years 1974–85 her economy grew at 4.3 per cent per annum, faster than that of any other OECD country. A key feature of Japan's growth was her flexibility in pursuing economic objectives: in the 1950s she emphasized heavy industry, ship-building and iron and steel; in the 1960s she moved into high-technology consumer manufactures largely for export; from the 1970s she concentrated on technological innovation and higher value-added products while transferring the production of lower value-added goods overseas. There began an era of massive Japanese investment in Asia, Europe and North America. In the early 1990s Japan had the world's strongest economy with the largest per capita GNP and the largest holding of foreign assets and debt. Amongst the causes of this remarkable success were: Japan's surplus labour in the 1950s–60s which kept prices down; the role of government intervention (and support); the high levels of domestic saving; and the distinctive character of employee-company relations which emphasized extensive consultation and group loyalty.

KOREA AND TAIWAN

Korea epitomized the relative success of the communist and capitalist projects. Until 1970 North Korea had the higher GNP per capita. By the 1990s GNP was declining at 5 per cent and the state, still communist, was close to economic and humanitarian disaster. From the mid-1960s South Korea embarked on rapid industrialization under Park Chung Hee and emerged as one of the "little tigers" amongst the Asian economies. By the 1990s it was the world's 13th largest economy with great strengths in car manufacture, shipbuilding and semi-conductors. For much of this period of rapid economic growth, however, its regime showed little tolerance of political dissent: open protest was forcefully crushed.

Taiwan, where the Chinese Nationalists established their government in 1949 after the Communist takeover on the mainland, experienced economic success similar to that of South Korea. A one-party state to 1986, it subsequently become a fully-functioning multi-party democracy. The growing diplomatic recognition from the 1970s of communist China, which saw Taiwan as a province, has left it isolated. Since 1990, however, Taiwan has been responsible for more than 60 per cent of inward investment into China.

The economic turmoil which hit the east Asian economies in 1997 exposed serious structural weaknesses, particularly in the inefficient and debt-laden finance and banking sectors. Yet the vast underlying strength of Japan suggests that the region, together with China and southeast Asia, will continue to play a critical role in the world economy in the early 21st century.

CHINA UNDER COMMUNISM

The establishment of the People's Republic of China launched China's economic modernization. Under Mao Zedong continuing revolutionary turmoil did as much to retard as to advance economic progress. From the late 1970s, however, China pursued economic liberalization with outstanding success. Its internal politics, however, remained repressive.

The establishment of the People's Republic of China in 1949 marked a fundamental turning point in China's modern history. After a century of internal conflict and disintegration, exacerbated by external aggressors, China now experienced strong centralized government. Despite the excesses and failures since 1949, not least the systematic repression of much of the population, this is a fundamental achievement.

CHINA UNDER MAO

The central concern of the new regime was the economy, crucially the raising of agricultural production and the creation of a heavy industrial base. But by the late 1950s Mao Zedong was impatient with the slowness of progress. In February 1958 he launched the "Great Leap Forward" which aimed to modernize China in three years. Rural China was divided into 26,000 communes which were required to abolish private property and to meet huge targets in agricultural and industrial production. 600,000 backyard furnaces sprang up across the countryside. The experiment was an unmitigated disaster: production declined sharply and 20–30 million died from starvation or malnutrition. In 1961 the project was abandoned. This failure strengthened the hands of moderates in the Chinese Communist Party (CCP) under Liu Shaoqi who preferred a more centrally planned, Soviet-style development. Mao responded by forming an alliance with the People's Liberation Army (PLA) under Lin Biao and with Chinese youth who, as "Red Guards", faithfully supported his policies.

In 1966 Mao launched the Great Proletarian Cultural Revolution. Red

Guards were set loose to prevent the development of "vested interests" and careerism in party and state by establishing permanent revolution. Chaos followed throughout China. Mao was forced to call on the PLA to restore order. On 9 September 1976 Mao died. His wife Jiang Qing with three conspirators, the "Gang of Four", tried to seize power. By this time the PLA and the elite had had enough of revolution. The "Gang of Four" were arrested, tried and expelled from the Communist Party.

From the late 1970s the dominant figure in China's politics was Deng Xiaoping. A beginning had been made in opening up China to the capitalist West with President Nixon's visit in 1972. Deng then launched a policy of economic liberalization. He created special economic zones in areas bordering Hong Kong, Macao and Taiwan and in Shanghai with inducements to encourage foreign investment. By 1992 $36 billion had been invested. Other reforms followed. Peasants were permitted to own land and by 1984, 98 per cent did so, the communes had vanished and agricultural output had increased 49 per cent in five years. Private businesses were also permitted. Their numbers grew from 100,000 in 1978 to 17 million in 1985. However, the success of liberalization brought its own problems: inflation, external deficits, migration to the cities and corruption.

REFORM AND PROTEST

Economic reforms led to demands for political liberalization. In December 1986, students demonstrated for democracy in 15 cities. Deng responded with repression: "troublemakers" were arrested; Hu Yaobang, the liberal secretary-general of the CCP, was sacked. When Hu died in April 1989, students used the occasion to demand democracy. For six weeks they gathered in Tiananmen Square, at times numbering over a million. In June the PLA was sent in and the movement ruthlessly crushed.

After the Tiananmen massacre China moved quickly to reassure the world that it was a stable economic partner; the world largely ignored human rights concerns to assure itself of a share of China's economic boom. There was further economic liberalization: most of China now operated a "socialist market economy". Growth rates which averaged 10 per cent or more for the 1980s and 1990s were only slightly affected by the economic turmoil which hit east Asia in 1997–8. The economic opening of China was sealed by its joining of the World Trade Organization in 2001 and its successful bid to host the 2008 Olympic Games. But the issue of democratic freedoms remained the unfinished business of China's 20th-century achievement.

1945 TO 1975

SOUTHEAST ASIA'S LONG WAR

For the first three decades of the post-war period, much of southeast Asia was embroiled in conflict. After the end of colonial rule, the Western powers tried to establish supportive regimes in the region. But left-wing forces with strong rural support inflicted heavy losses. The late 1960s and early 1970s saw the Cold War played out on Southeast Asian soil, with disastrous consequences.

Once Japan was defeated in 1945, the Western powers sought to return to their territories, but with differing ambitions and different consequences. At first they tried to return as colonial rulers, but a brief period of rule proved this to be unrealistic and led the way to European and American attempts to hand power to friendly, moderate nationalist regimes that could block the rise of communism. This in turn gave rise to more radical nationalism.

In July 1946, the USA left the Philippines but provided military training and financial support against peasant insurgencies between 1946 and 1954. Throughout the period the Philippines remained one of the USA's most loyal allies. The country was one of only three Asian states to join the US-dominated South-East Asian Treaty Organization in 1954.

SUKARNO AND NON-ALIGNMENT

In Indonesia and French Indo-China, the Netherlands and France sought to reimpose their direct authority forcefully. Both became embroiled in bloody wars. In Indonesia, the Dutch almost defeated the republic declared in 1945, but withdrew in December 1949 once world opinion had turned against them. Attempting to forge a non-aligned path between capitalism and communism, Sukarno's Indonesian regime initially attempted to direct a planned economy with a multi-party parliament. Sukarno called this "guided democracy". Yet by the late 1950s, Sukarno's regime was moving closer to the Soviet Union and taking a hard-line stance against internal enemies and the Indonesian Chinese population. His regime was brought down by a US-backed coup in 1966, which led to a bloody battle in the countryside. Suharto, his successor, adopted a much more pro-Western stance.

THE VIETNAM WAR

The French struggle in Vietnam was bitter. After the Japanese defeat, Ho Chi Minh established a nationalist regime in the north while the French reasserted their authority in the south. War broke out between the two in 1946. After colossal losses on both sides, the war ended in the humiliating defeat of the French at Dien Bien Phu in 1954, and Vietnam was temporarily partitioned at the 17th parallel. The communist North Vietnamese expected that the country would be reunited once elections were held in 1956; but fearing a communist victory, and guided by the USA, the South refused to hold the scheduled elections. Vietnam became a major battlefield of the Cold War. The anti-communist South received massive US support, which from 1965 took a directly military form, while the North was supplied by China and the Soviet Union. In the late 1960s, after sending half a million troops to the region, the Americans realized they could not prevent a communist victory. By 1973 the USA had negotiated a withdrawal but continued to supply the South. After almost 30 years of division and conflict, a North Vietnamese victory brought unity and peace under communist rule to the two Vietnams in 1975.

After gaining its independence from France in 1954, Cambodia initially maintained its independence from the wars raging around it. Governed by the magnetic personality of Prince Sihanouk between 1954 and 1970, Cambodia was successful at maintaining a non-aligned path. Cambodia's neutrality was undermined by Vietnamese incursions and US bombing, which led to a pro-American regime in 1970.

Throughout the post-war period, Thailand managed to retain its in-dependence by gaining US protection. Thailand joined SEATO and sent troops to support the South in the Vietnam War. Like other states in the region, it faced a rurally based communist resistance movement that was suppressed with US assistance.

The British also returned to Burma and Malaya, committed to re-establishing colonial rule. But post-war Britain could not afford to defend an empire in Asia, and accepted quickly that withdrawal was inevitable. After civil order broke down rapidly after the end of the Second World War the British quit Burma in January 1948. Throughout southeast Asia, pro-Soviet communists had allied with Britain against Japanese occupation. In the post-war period many southeast Asian communists found themselves opposing their former allies. In Malaya, between 1948 and 1960, communist insurgents based in the countryside violently opposed British rule and its Malaysian successor state. The Malayan "emergency" ended after troops were sent from Britain, and potential rebel supporters in the villages resettled. The separate peninsular states of Malaya achieved independence in 1957, uniting with Sabah, Sarawak and the city-state of Singapore to form the Federation of Malaysia in 1963. Tension between ethnic Chinese and Malays led to Singapore's breaking away to become an independent republic in 1965. The Malay-dominated regime faced risings by Chinese minority groups in 1969.

By the late 1960s, southeast Asia was divided between Indo-China, Burma and the Philippines, which were beset by internal conflict or embroiled in international war, and Malaysia, Thailand, Singapore, and even Indonesia, which had achieved a degree of political stability, had begun to reap the beneficial economic consequences of peace.

SINCE 1975
SOUTHEAST ASIA

In 1975, southeast Asia was divided between communist states allied to China and the Soviet Union, and virulently anti-communist countries allied to the USA. The late 1970s and 1980s were years of political violence – even genocide – and unrest. Poverty remained endemic in many areas, but despite instability many parts of the region have seen phenomenal rates of growth.

In 1975 communist regimes achieved political dominance in Vietnam, Cambodia and Laos. All three regimes were rooted in peasant protest against colonial and then pro-Western rule, yet the paths each state took were very different. In Cambodia, Pol Pot's anti-Vietnamese faction gained control of the Communist Party. A French-educated intellectual, Pol Pot knew little about the countryside, but his Khmer Rouge (the communist movement founded in the 1960s) attempted to create a self-sufficient rural utopia by forcibly moving people from the cities to the countryside. Estimates of the number of people who lost their lives to the resulting famine, disease and maltreatment vary, but at least a million and a half people may have died in the Cambodian genocide. The world's first war between communist states began when Vietnam invaded Cambodia and installed a pro-Vietnamese puppet government in 1979, and China's invasion of Vietnam followed. The Vietnamese announced their withdrawal from Cambodia in 1988, and elections were held in 1993, but the Khmer Rouge continued their guerrilla war until 1998, when Pol Pot died.

COMMUNIST RULE

Vietnam suffered from diplomatic isolation and from the economic impact of its war with Cambodia and China after the end of the Vietnam War. Many of the South Vietnamese middle class, including a large number of Vietnamese Chinese, fled the country in boats rather than face communist repression. These "boat people" found refuge across the globe. Since the late 1980s Vietnam has developed closer ties with Europe and, eventually, the USA. Undergoing a process of economic but not political liberalization, Vietnam's economy was, by the late 1990s, amongst the fastest growing in the region. Neighbouring Laos became increasingly dependent on Vietnam after the communists took over in 1975. Like Vietnam, Laos abandoned economic communism in the 1990s while the communist party retained control of the country's political institutions.

ASIAN "TIGERS"

Since 1975, Thailand has been governed by fervently anti-communist regimes, alternating between military rule and periods of democracy. Despite an unstable and violent political culture, Thailand appeared to have Indo-China's strongest economy for many years. But economic growth obscured the extent of corruption and unsustainable speculation. In 1997 the collapse of the Thai currency plunged the Thai economy into deep recession and started a crisis across Asia's financial markets. But, like other countries hit by Asia's economic crash, Thailand's recovery has been quicker than most people predicted.

Along with Singapore, Malaysia and Indonesia, Thailand has been described as one of Asia's "tiger economies". Each country achieved an annual growth rate well in excess of 5 per cent by creating an export-oriented industrial base. Many factors contributed: massive Japanese investment; cheap labour; and a close relationship between investors, industrialists and the state. Southeast Asia's "tigers" have developed closer ties with each other through ASEAN, an organization that promotes free trade and closer communication – but not political integration – within the region. By 1999, ASEAN had expanded to include Cambodia, Laos, Myanmar (Burma) and Vietnam. Along with Japan and Taiwan, southeast Asia offered an example of planned capitalism. This allowed high rates of growth to occur. But the close relationship between the state and business made corruption an endemic problem.

Singapore is Asia's most prosperous economy. Its economy was built upon political stability, a close relationship between business and government and a strict – some would say repressive – social order. Prime Minister Lee Kuan Yew held office continually between 1959 and 1990. Similarly, Malaysia's transformation occurred under a stable administration. In the 1960s its economy was based on agriculture and rubber production. By 2000 manufacturing and the service sector played a much greater role.

PEOPLE POWER

Throughout much of the 1970s and 1980s, both the Philippines and Indonesia were governed by stable but repressive regimes that only survived in power with US support. Each eventually succumbed to populist democratic aspirations. In the Philippines Ferdinand Marcos was overthrown by Corazan Aquino's People Power movement in 1986. Unlike other anti-communist regimes in southeast Asia, Marcos's government was not effective at developing the economy in the Phillipines. In Indonesia the premier Suharto (who had replaced Sukarno in 1967) survived until the Asian crash when he handed over power to a loyal ally, BJ Habibie. Unemployment soared, violence increased, and in the wake of the independence of the region of East Timor, Habibie's government lost support. After general elections in 1999, the Islamic reformer Abdurrah-man Wahid became president, only to be replaced less than two years later by Sukarno's daughter Megawati Sukarnoputri, amid continuing unrest. The situation only stabilised after Susilo Bambang Yudhoyono won Indonesia's first-ever direct presidential elections in September 2004. By the same year, the region's economy had largely recovered.

Years of opposition to authoritarian rule meant Islamist politicians in both Indonesia and the Philippines tended to be fervent supporters of democracy.

But since democratization, more radical Islamist organizations in southeast Asia have allied themselves to groups from outside the regime in a series of violent confrontations with Christian populations. In the wake of tsunami of 2004, a peace deal was signed by separatists in the devastated region of Aceh, but political violence continued in Mindanao, East Timor and southern Thailand. In 2006, a military coup in Thailand jeopardised the country's democratic progress, and much of Southeast Asia was still shadowed by the conflict between national states and movements for regional and religious autonomy.

SINCE 1947
SOUTH ASIA: INDEPENDENCE AND CONFLICT

The politics of south Asia since the early 1940s has been dominated by conflict between the nation-state and the demand for regional autonomy and separation. This struggle drove the partition of British India in 1947. It has influenced the course of south Asian politics between parliamentary democracy and – in Pakistan, Bangladesh and Burma (Myanmar) – military intervention since.

Independence came to British-ruled India with the creation of independent India and Pakistan in August 1947, to Burma in January 1948 and to Ceylon in February 1948.

Partition occurred as British and nationalist politicians were unable to agree to a balance of power between a united Indian government and provincial governments. Indian National Congress and Muslim League politicians reluctantly agreed to partition British India on religious lines, with Pakistan being created as the "homeland" for India's Muslims. Partition included the division of the populous provinces of Punjab in the west and Bengal in the east. Independence took place on 14 and 15 August, but the border between Pakistan and India was only announced on 17 August. As large numbers of Hindus and Muslims found themselves on the wrong side of the border, 15 million trekked from one state to the other. Law and order entirely broke down whilst political power was transferred. Over 500,000 were slaughtered in wave after wave of religious killings in an atmosphere of panic and fear.

Newly independent India and Pakistan had quickly to define the relationship between their new governments and the different communities living within their borders. The new regimes needed to determine the role of the 600 princely states, surviving from the period of British rule. Most chose to join India or Pakistan. The Muslim-ruled state of Hyderabad was forcibly integrated into India in 1948. Kashmir had a majority Muslim population but was ruled by a Hindu dynasty. India and Pakistan fought a war for control of the state between October 1947 and January 1949, before the UN imposed a ceasefire and divided the area. The solution satisfied neither side. War broke out in 1965 and a peace settlement was signed in 1966. Escalating tension almost saw war again over Kashmir in 1999, as India accused Pakistani troops of infiltrating into Indian territory. India and Pakistan's explosion of nuclear devices in 1998 made many fear nuclear catastrophe. Although tensions receded after peace talks began in 2004, Kashmir remained part of the unfinished business of Partition.

NATION OR REGION? A STRUGGLE FOR IDENTITY

Throughout south Asia, regional politicians have accused the nation-state (whether Indian, Pakistani, Bangladeshi, Burmese or Sri Lankan) of failing to accommodate regional identities. In India, early conflicts were over language, even after 1956 when prime minister Jawaharlal Nehru agreed to reorganize state boundaries on provincial lines. Tribal groups in India and Bangladesh fought with both state administrations and central governments for separate statehood and independence, leading to the division of northeast India into seven separate states in the 1970s, and the creation of the new states of Chattisgarh, Jharkhand and Uttaranchal in 2000. Serious religious conflict began to emerge from the 1970s. Sikh demands for the independent state of Khalistan led to the assassination of prime minister Indira Gandhi in 1984. In response to what was perceived as the erosion of Indian identity since 1947 by regional separatism and the rise of lower castes, many middle-class Hindu Indians asserted the Hindu-ness (*Hindutva*) of the Indian state. In 1992 the growth of Hindu nationalism saw the demolition of a 16th-century Muslim mosque built on what many believed to have been the birthplace of the Hindu god Ram. By then, India's Muslim population exceeded that of Pakistan. But the rise of Hindu nationalism meant India's Muslim minority felt ever more insecure.

Conflict between centre and region dominated the politics of other areas of south Asia. In Ceylon there was little friction until 1972, when a new constitution renamed it Sri Lanka and institutionalized the pursuit of a state dominated by the Buddhist religion and Sinhala language. The Tamil minority made up 15 per cent of the island's population, and began to demand their separate state of Eelam. Between 1983 and the 1990s Tamils fought the Sri Lankan army for control of the northeast of the island, a situation hardly helped by the intervention of an Indian peacekeeping force in 1987–90. In 1991 the LTTE (Tamil Tigers) assassinated the ex-prime minister of India, Rajiv Gandhi. Many Tamils emigrated. The LTTE stronghold of Jaffna was overrun by government troops in 1996. Despite this, Tamil resistance to the Buddhist majority continued, forcing the government to engage in peace talks in 2002 and push Sri Lanka towards a form of federalist state.

In Pakistan strife was seen between *muhajir* refugees from India and the local population in Sind, as well as between the Sunni majority and Shi'a and Ahmadi Muslim minorities. Most important, though, was the political and economic subordination of East Pakistan (eastern Bengal) by Pakistan's western wing. This led to the emergence of Bengalee separatism and the creation, with Indian military assistance, of the state of Bangladesh in 1971. However, in 2006 the violence once again intensified.

MILITARY RULE

Even after Bangladesh's independence, the construction of Pakistani nationhood has had difficulty competing with entrenched regional Sindhi, Punjabi, Pashtun, Kashmiri, Baluchi or *muhajir* identities. Only two forces have been capable of binding the nation together – Islam and the military. The Islamization of politics during the 1970s and 1980s occurred as politicians used Islam as a rallying cry to unite a fragmenting nation. Military government occurred in Pakistan – as also in Burma and Bangladesh – when soldiers believed civilian rule was incapable of maintaining the unity of the state. In Burma, despite a promise in 1990 of free multi-party elections to end 30 years of increasingly repressive rule, the military have remained in power. Ethnic tension persisted in Burma as groups such as the Karens and Shans have struggled for regional autonomy against an authoritarian state. Burma's military regime justified its rule by claiming that it alone was capable of maintaining the "sovereign and territorial integrity" of the Burmese state.

India has avoided military rule whilst its parliamentary system has been able to accommodate (often uncomfortably) tension between regional identities and the nation-state. The BJP is a party which asserts the existence of a very strong, national Hindu-Indian identity. Yet it survived in power during the early 2000s by allying with regional parties from outside its north Indian heartland. Despite a government with a strongly nationalist ideology, during the early 2000s a large number of Indian states were governed by regionalist parties.

SOUTH ASIA IN GLOBAL POLITICS

During the initial phases of the Cold War, non-alignment was a feature of the external relations of south Asian states. The Chinese invasion of India in 1962 showed the limits of that policy. For the rest of the War, India tilted towards the Soviet Union whilst Pakistan was backed by the USA. Since the Soviet occupation of Afghanistan in 1979, south Asia has been on the frontline in the Cold War and subsequent global conflict. The USA funded the Islamic opposition to the Soviet-backed communist state in Afghanistan. Soviet forces left Afghanistan in 1989, but were replaced with a power struggle between Afghani politicians from different regions. The weakness of the Afghan state allowed the Taliban, a group of Islamists supported by Pakistan's intelligence services, to win power in the mid-1990s by presenting themselves as a force for stability. The Taliban regime's support for those seen as responsible for terror attacks in the USA led to the second occupation of Afghanistan – by the USA and its allies. From 2005, NATO forces faced a large-scale Taliban insurgency against the US-backed regime of Hamid Karzai. By the early 21st century, south Asia had opened up dramatically to global trade. Although many of its 1.1 billion people still lived in poverty, India was one of the fastest growing economies in the world, and the sub-continent's role in world affairs seemed likely to increase as a consequence.

1957 TO 1989

AFRICA

Africa's development since the ending of European colonial control was anything but smooth. Poverty, corruption and ethnic rivalry dogged parts of the continent, while wars, repressive one-party governments, disease and famine meant that the lives of many Africans were a mockery of the optimistic goals proclaimed at independence.

By 1975 most African states were independent of European colonial control. Decolonization was sometimes peaceful, although there were major wars in Algeria and in the Portuguese colonies, as well as anti-colonial rebellions from Madagascar to Morocco. South Africa's policy of apartheid, introduced in 1948, legally segregated people by race and colour. African social, economic and political advance was blocked.

At independence Africa inherited weak economies and fragile political systems. After 1950 population and urbanization grew rapidly. Increased pressure on land caused ecological problems. Times of serious drought, as in the Sahelian region in 1972–3, led to famine and political instability, which in turn created refugees. Endemic tropical diseases were joined in the late 1980s by the scourge of AIDS. African states had low levels of capital accumulation, small markets, inadequate public utilities and limited welfare services. Widespread corruption discouraged foreign investment. Many educated people left the continent, and the gulf between rich and poor steadily widened.

ETHNIC AND POLITICAL CONFLICT

The new states of Africa had inherited colonial frontiers. Ethnic, religious and political rivalries resulted in secessionist movements and civil wars. Major wars of secession occurred in the southern Sudan (see p. 311), in Nigeria where the Igbo tried to secede Biafra (1967–70), and in Ethiopia against Amharic rule in the 1970s–80s. Nigeria, the most populous state in Africa, faced acute problems in nation building with over 250 languages, a Muslim north and a predominantly Christian south.

At independence most African states had hastily created systems of parliamentary government that were short-lived. In many states ruling politicians suppressed opposition parties and declared one-party rule. Arbitrary government could be removed only by force and thus, in many sub-Saharan states, the military seized power from civilians. Army officers, ill-suited to civil government, were rarely willing to surrender power, and this led to a succession of coups.

From the 1960s sub-Saharan Africa saw a rapid growth in Christianity and Islam. New Protestant heartlands developed. Islam also grew in militancy, encouraged by the creation of an Islamic Republic in Iran after the revolution of 1979 (*see* p. 316). Religious fervour led to communal tension, particularly in Nigeria where ethnic and political differences met along the religious fault line dividing the mainly Christian south and the mainly Islamic north.

ECONOMIC FAILURE

The State dominated early economic development schemes, but with limited success. Governments' economic ambitions were rarely able to match their administrative capacities. Even plans that focused on rural development, such as Tanzania's "Ujamaa" policies, introduced in 1967, were largely failures. Several countries adopted economic policies modelled on those of communist countries, a particular example being that of Ethiopia's Marxist regime (1975–91).

African states relied on the export of primary products in a global economy where prices were determined by industrial countries. They were weak players in a system dominated by Western capitalist powers that they depended on for capital and markets. The price of manufactured imports, vital for African development, rapidly increased in the 1970s and 1980s. Foreign loans and global inflation led to increased indebtedness so that the annual income of some countries amounted to less than the cost of servicing their debt.

SINCE 1989

AFRICAN DEMOCRATIZATION

The end of the Cold War brought political change to Africa. Elected governments replaced authoritarian rulers, and South Africa's system of apartheid finally fell apart. However, wars continued to ravage areas of the continent, and Africa's social and economic future was blighted by heavy debt and the scourge of HIV/AIDS.

With the end of the Cold War, Africa lost its former global strategic significance. Incompetent and corrupt military rulers and one-party states, increasingly challenged by civic groups, churches and trade unions, surrendered power in an era of democratization with multi-party elections. Elected governments gained power in more than 30 countries – for example, in Nigeria in 1999

– although the once relatively stable Ivory Coast experienced a military coup, mutiny and civil war. The collapse of the USSR also ended South Africa's weak claim that it was a bastion against communist penetration. The country's economy was weak, apartheid was crumbling under assault from confident African popular institutions and external economic pressure from the USA and the European Community. Military defeat in Angola forced South Africa to recognize Namibia's independence, and president F. W. De Klerk freed Nelson Mandela from prison and unbanned the African National Congress (ANC) – the political party that campaigned against apartheid. His hope was that power would nonetheless remain in white hands, but in democratic elections in 1994 the ANC gained a majority and Mandela headed a government of national unity.

CONFLICT AND GENOCIDE

Elsewhere in Africa, conflict – both long-running and newly erupted – meant that democratic progress remained a distant goal. The persistent war in southern Sudan between the largely Arab government in Khartoum and the Christian and animist rebels in the south continues. In Ethiopia the Marxist regime was overthrown in 1991, and Eritrea gained independence in 1993. Peace was short-lived, and the two countries fought each other over a border area. Somalia's military dictatorship collapsed and, following civil war, the country divided into several autonomous regions. US and United Nations (UN) interventions ended in failure. In 1994 a UN force also failed to prevent genocidal violence in Rwanda. Ethnic and communal hatred between the majority Hutu and the minority Tutsi people resulted in the killing of over 800,000 (mainly Tutsi) people and the flight of two million Rwandan refugees. The violence spilled into the Democratic Republic of Congo, and although this helped bring down the bankrupt Mobutu regime it also led to military and economic intervention by several African states, notably Zimbabwe and Uganda. In complex civil wars in Liberia and Sierra Leone until 2002–3, rival warlords inflicted great brutality on civilians and created many refugees. Foreign intervention eventually succeeded in ending the violence.

Across Africa in the 1990s, the rise of Islamism, fuelled by ideas from the Muslim heartlands of Asia, led to clashes with political authorities and also with growing Christian communities. In Algeria an Islamist terror campaign left over

100,000 people dead. The extension of Islamic Sharia law in the Sudan and in northern Nigeria caused violent reactions. After the al-Qaeda attack on New York in September 2001, and the bombings of US embassies in Nairobi and Dar es Salaam, the USA accused Sudan and Somalia of harbouring terrorists.

Since 1990 Africa's economies have grown weaker and foreign aid has been reduced. Sustainable development is hindered by unequal terms of trade, food shortages and heavy debts. Structural adjustment programmes imposed by the International Monetary Fund (IMF) since the 1980s to regularize African debt have made life harder for many Africans. African initiatives for economic renewal include the New Economic Partnership for African Development (NEPAD) of 2001. The problems to be tackled are many and severe, not least HIV/AIDs, which affects a large part of Africa's productive population.

SINCE 1947

PALESTINE, ZIONISM AND THE ARAB-ISRAELI CONFLICT

The Arab-Israeli conflict has proved among the most intractable of the last 60 years. Given tragic urgency by Hitler's mass extermination of the Jews, in 1948 the Zionist movement created a vibrant new state in the Middle East. While the Jews saw this as their rightful homeland, the Arabs of the region saw it as their land, taken from them and sustained by force.

The rise of Zionism was part of the general movement of ethnic and linguistic nationalism in the 19th century. In the case of the Jews, the idea was particularly audacious: they were widely dispersed; they did not speak the same language; in conventional terms they were not even a people. But at the first Zionist Congress in 1896 it was nonetheless agreed that a Jewish homeland should be created. It was subsequently agreed that this should be in Palestine, or biblical Israel, then within the Ottoman empire.

With the collapse of Ottoman rule at the end of the First World War, Palestine became a British mandated territory under the League of Nations. The Arab population of Palestine, encouraged by British promises to further Arab aspirations, sought independence. At the same time, however, in the Balfour

Declaration of 1917 Britain had committed itself to creating a Jewish homeland in Palestine. Throughout the 1920s and 1930s, Britain found itself caught between the conflicting, sometimes violent, demands of Arabs and Jews.

THE STATE OF ISRAEL

Reviled by both sides, Britain turned the problem over to the United Nations. In November 1947, it divided Palestine into separate Jewish and Arab states. The following May Britain withdrew and the State of Israel was proclaimed. It was immediately invaded by Arab armies. After fierce fighting, a ceasefire was agreed early in 1949. It left an uneasy truce. Israel had beaten off the Arab forces, though had failed to take East Jerusalem. As important, up to 750,000 Palestinians had become refugees, crowded into the Gaza Strip and the West Bank, and the Arab state of Palestine had disappeared.

The hostility which followed became a prime cause of instability within the Middle East as well as a major focus of Cold War rivalry. To Egypt, Syria and Iraq, buttressed by the Soviet Union, Israel represented not only an affront to Arab nationalism but, with its support from the USA, an extension of American imperialism in the region. Three further full-scale Arab-Israeli wars broke out after 1949: in 1956, over Suez, when Israel inflicted a humiliating defeat on Egypt; in 1967, when in the face of renewed Arab hostility Israel achieved a crushing pre-emptive strike against Egypt and then routed Jordanian, Syrian and Iraqi forces; and in 1973, when a combined Egyptian-Syrian attack was repulsed by Israel after days of desperate fighting. In all three cases, not only did Israel extend its territorial domination, occupying the West Bank, Sinai and the Golan Heights, but huge numbers of new Palestinian refugees were created in Jordan and Lebanon, increasing the Palestinian sense of injustice and giving rise to militant Arab movements dedicated to winning back the lost territories. In 1967, the Palestine Liberation Organization (PLO) assumed leadership of the struggle, using the refugee camps as bases for terrorist attacks against Israel.

THE SEARCH FOR PEACE

While defeat in 1973 had hardened the resolve of some Arab states to continue the war against Israel, Egypt under President Sadat sought to make peace. In 1978 the two sides agreed terms at Camp David in the USA, provoking outrage in the Arab world. The PLO, meanwhile, stepped up its attacks on Israel from its new bases in Lebanon sparking an Israeli invasion of southern Lebanon.

Nonetheless the peace treaty had created a framework which permitted a gradual easing of tension. In 1994 Jordan also agreed peace with Israel while the following year Syria agreed to open talks with Israel. But the most significant breakthrough had come in 1988 when the PLO agreed to recognize two states in Palestine, Jewish and Arab. In 1993 Israel and the PLO agreed a Declaration of Principles on interim self-government for the West Bank and Gaza Strip (the Oslo Accords). The following year, the Palestinian National Authority assumed responsibility for both areas with an understanding that further Israeli withdrawals and an extension of Palestinian self-rule would follow.

In the ten years since the agreement little progress has been made. Hardliners on both sides have sustained intermittent violence. The revolutionary Islamic movement HAMAS has kept up a terrorist campaign against Israeli targets while since 2001, under prime ministers Ariel Sharon and, from 2006, Ehud Olmert, the Israeli government has adopted a more aggressive approach to controlling Palestinian violent protest. In 2006 Israeli forces attacked Hezbollah bases in Lebanon causing widespread damage and loss of life and established a virtual blockade around the Gaza Strip settlements. The long conflict in the Middle East shows no sign of ending.

SINCE 1945

NATIONALISM, SECULARISM AND ISLAM IN THE MIDDLE EAST

The Middle East has been among the world's most unstable and politically sensitive regions since the end of the Second World War. Independence struggles, the Cold War, Arab-Israeli conflict, military interventions, repression, regional rivalries, Islamic revival, oil riches and extremes of wealth and poverty have created near permanent turmoil.

In the immediate post-war period, war weariness, financial pressure and local opposition led Britain and France to abandon their colonial possessions in the Middle East. Despite efforts to keep a European military presence in an area of vital strategic importance to the West, by 1956 the Arab world was largely independent of European power.

But while the Europeans retreated, the USA and the Soviet Union advanced, both anxious to increase their influence in the region. In the process, the Middle East rapidly became a key theatre of the Cold War. Fearing Soviet expansion, the USA underpinned Israel, Saudi Arabia and, until 1979, Iran, all of which became the principal surrogates of American interests. For its part, the Soviet Union, through its support for Egypt, Iraq and Syria, sought to portray itself as the champion of anti-imperialism, the Palestinian cause, revolutionary socialism and Arab nationalism.

NATIONALISM

It was nationalism that formed the keynote of Arab political goals in the period, with President Nasser of Egypt its principal standard bearer. Having led a military coup against the Egyptian monarchy in 1952, within two years he had become president of Egypt and the most charismatic Arab leader of the period even if his avowedly modernizing and secular policies alienated the more conservative Arab regimes and the cause of Arab unity, which he energetically pursued, was to prove no more than a chimera.

Nonetheless, with the active support of the Soviet Union, Nasser's influence was crucial to the development not just of Egypt but of Iraq, Sudan, Syria, South Yemen, Algeria and Libya, all of which owed much to eastern European economic and political models. In every case, the ruling regime was backed by the military while their economies were dominated by the state and all of them introduced ambitious and generally ineffectual land reforms and nationalized most of industry, banking and foreign trade. In common with most other Arab states, they all also maintained huge armies, supposedly to counter the threat posed by Israel, in reality to maintain the ruling regimes in power.

RIVALRIES AND WARS

Regional rivalries and tensions have also led to a series of Middle Eastern wars in addition to the persistent Arab-Israeli conflict. In Lebanon, divisions between Christians and Muslims, between Lebanese and Palestinians and between Sunni and Shi'a Muslims created a microcosm of the tensions in the wider Arab world. In 1975 full-scale civil war broke out in which both Israel and Syria became deeply involved. In 1980 Iraq's President Saddam Hussein launched a pre-emptive assault on Iran, then in the throes of revolutionary turmoil. The conflict turned into a lethal eight-year campaign of attrition reminiscent of the First World War. It cost an estimated 450,000 dead and 750,000 wounded. Undaunted, in 1990 Hussein invaded oil-rich Kuwait. Though Saddam Hussein survived Iraq's defeat in 1991 at the hands of a US-led United Nations coalition force, the international isolation the country endured in the ensuing decade and the chaos following his final overthrow in 2003 all only increased the brutality and misery endured by almost all Iraqis.

THE RISE OF ISLAM

If the politics of the Arab world in the 1950s and 1960s were dominated by Cold War tension between conservative and radical Arab states, in the 1970s they gave way to a new development: the rise of revolutionary Islam. The Islamic movement dated back to the foundation of the Muslim Brotherhood in 1928 but was given new life partly by the military failures against Israel in 1967 and 1973 and partly by the general sense of hopelessness and despair which pervaded the region. In such an atmosphere, militant Islamic activity seemed to give new hope, however illusory, for the future.

In 1978-9, an alliance of Islamic radicals overthrew the US-backed regime of the Shah in Iran and an Islamic republic was installed under the guidance of Ayatollah Khomeini. Islamic radicalism was extended all over the Muslim world, leading to savage civil war in Algeria and Sudan and widespread Islamic terrorism in the rest of North Africa and the Middle East. With the collapse of Saddam Hussein's regime in Iraq a new crisis appeared. The profound division between Sunni and Shi'ite Muslims was exposed and a vicious religious civil war erupted from 2003 onwards which threatened to spread beyond the borders of Iraq and to transform the nature of Islamic conflict.

SINCE 1910

SOUTH AMERICA: SEARCH FOR STABILITY AND DEVELOPMENT

Latin America since the 1930s has experienced a cycle of economic crisis, radical politics and revolutionary movements, then right-wing reaction and a gradual return to democratic politics. Vulnerable to external economic shocks and political and military intervention from outside, the stability of the region has always been fragile.

WAR AND DEPRESSION

The pre-1910 order was shattered by war and depression. Although prices of strategic exports rocketed, import scarcity and the evaporation of investment inflows in 1914 destabilized Latin America. While the world economy appeared to recover in the 1920s, the 1930 depression hit Latin America hard. Between 1929 and 1932, governments failing to cope with crisis collapsed. In Chile and Brazil, new regimes applied Keynesian-style measures to stimulate activity. Populist leaders – Getúlio Vargas, in Brazil, and Juan D. Perón, in Argentina – encouraged industrialization. Around 1948, ad hoc responses to crisis were synthesized into a strategy for development by the UN Economic Commission for Latin America: "structuralism" advocated industrialization to substitute imports, agrarian reform and regional economic integration in order to promote national, state-led capitalist development. Nevertheless, primary commodities dominated exports until around 1990.

URBANIZATION, POPULISM AND VIOLENCE

Democratic aspirations, often frustrated by violent reaction, characterized the decades from 1910 to the 1970s. The 1920s witnessed democratic openings in the Southern Cone republics (Argentina, Chile and Uruguay), although these were curtailed by crisis. The late 1940s saw another brief wave of democratization. The main political expressions were populism and nationalism, which overlaid societal tensions driven by competition for land (notably in the Andean republics and Brazil), and unemployment and poverty in burgeoning cities. Land reform was achieved in Bolivia (1952), in Peru (1968) and in Chile (1970 – reversed in 1973). The Cuban Revolution, 1959, triggered a wave of hope and fear – and the reality of Havana-directed insurgency. Christian democratic and constitutionalist left-wing parties enjoyed some success in the 1960s, culminating in the 1970 election of marxist President Salvador Allende in Chile, although the pendulum was already swinging in the other direction. Threats of terrorism and the need for "discipline" to deepen industrialization were invoked to justify military interventions. The Brazilian military regime of 1964 lasted until 1985. In Chile (1973) and Argentina (1976) military administrations applied bloody repression: "disappearances" and violation of human rights were widespread. An alliance of the military and civilian technocrats – bureaucratic-authoritarian regimes of the 1960s and 1970s – were undermined by economic mismanagement (culminating in the Debt Crisis), political miscalculation and sheer incompetence (the Argentine invasions of the Falklands in 1982), and a groundswell of civic protest. A reappraisal of the statist model of industrialization resulted.

VIOLENCE, DEMOCRACY, NEO-LIBERALISM AND GLOBALIZATION

The neo-liberal Washington Consensus promised growth with macroeconomic-based state shrinkage (privatization of government corporations and pension funds, and "pruning" of social spending), decentralization, balanced budgets, capital market deregulation, trade liberalization and labour reforms. Liberal experiment sometimes followed failed heterodox efforts at stabilization – Austral Plan (Argentina), Cruzado Plan (Brazil) and Inti Plan (Peru) – that ended in hyperinflation. In some republics, neo-liberalism was applied as a "surprise" economic reorientation after the election of candidates who had advocated populist strategies during presidential campaigns; for example, in Argentina, Peru, and Venezuela. Elsewhere, in Brazil and Uruguay, victorious candidates explicitly advanced a Washington Consensus agenda. The difference between the late 1980s and 1990s, and the earlier neo-liberal experiments in the 1970s, was that structural reform was applied in a democratic context. Electoral support for neo-liberalism was strong amongst the urban poor, who had gained least from post-Second World War industrialization. Late 20th-century liberal-ism yielded contending models of international and intra-Americas economic relations: the MERCOSUR (Argentina, Brazil, Paraguay and Uruguay) – evolving from a trade association into a common market – sought closer collaboration with the European Union and broader international engagement; the Free Trade Area of the Americas, fitfully fostered by Washington, was envisaged as a trade zone stretching from Alaska to Tierra del Fuego by 2010. Yet the long-term outcomes of neo-liberalism remain in doubt. Currency crises challenged administrations and policy: street protests triggered regime change in Argentina, Bolivia, Ecuador and Venezuela around 2001–3.

As South America approaches the bicentenary of independence, poverty and inequality remain pressing problems, along with drug-related violence, particularly in Columbia and Brazil. Following the 2002/6 electoral cycle, the political pendulum has swung to the left partly in response to forces of globalization. In Brazil, Chile and Peru reformist centre-left administrations were elected or re-elected, committed to retaining much of the liberal economic project, with an interventionist social policy designed to reduce unemployment and inequality. In Chile in 2005, Michelle Bachelet was the first woman in Latin American history to be elected president. Administrations in Bolivia and Venezuela have adopted a more radical posture. Globalization also represents a challenge to continued industrial expansion, as well as a growth opportunity, mostly associated with an export commodity boom driven by a surge in soya, maize, and oil prices.

SINCE 1910

MEXICO, CENTRAL AMERICA AND THE CARIBBEAN

The "backyard" proximity of Mexico, Central America and the Caribbean to the USA has given rise to much anxiety. Relations have been dynamic and destructive – shaped by political interventions and economic integration, by ideological conflict, by equivocal US support for dictatorships and democracy, and by Washington's preoccupation with trade, finance, revolution, insurgency, migration and drugs.

REVOLUTION AND INTERVENTION

By the early 20th century, agrarian reform was a pressing issue, featuring in the revolutionary upheavals that punctuated the period. Such upheaval culminated in the Mexican Revolution (which began in 1910) and the Cuban Revolution (1959), and frustrated reform in Guatemala in the 1950s. The aims of the Mexican Revolution, encapsulated in the 1917 Constitution, were nationalist, socially reformist and broadly pro-capitalist, promising land to peasants, workers' rights, political democracy and stability for business. The apogee of radicalism occurred under president Lázaro Cárdenas (1934–40), who embarked on massive land redistribution projects and the nationalization of British and

US oil companies. Factors that prompted protest in Mexico also existed elsewhere: before 1914, US companies had established dominant positions in plantation agriculture and mineral extraction across the Isthmus and circum-Caribbean. Corporations such as United Fruit virtually functioned as states within states – with transport systems that crossed international boundaries, and running hospitals and schools for workers and their families. Foreign corporations appeared to function with little reference to national governments. Collaborating with landed and commercial elites, international businesses – their position guaranteed by US might – seemed secure, certainly in dynastic kleptocracies run by the Somoza clan in Nicaragua, or Duvalier in Haiti.

ECONOMIC DEVELOPMENT AND VIOLENCE

The 1959 Cuban Revolution, headed by Fidel and Raúl Castro and Argentine émigré Ernesto "Ché" Guevara, sought national solidarity through social progress and economic growth. With Soviet subsidies, welfare gains were impressive until the 1990s; the record regarding political and civil rights was decidedly less so. Nevertheless, Cuba became a beacon. Peasant demand for land and student-inspired pressure for political reform generated tensions in Central America. Anxiety about communist agitation and threats to business, as well as fear of Cuban-style revolution, led to Washington-inspired *golpes* designed to pre-empt political radicalization. The action was counter-productive: uprisings occurred in every republic between Panama and Mexico, save Costa Rica. The 1970s and 1980s witnessed the operation of CIA-trained military death squads, massive human rights abuses by government forces and reprisals by guerrilla forces. There was an ethnic component to violence: elites regarded Indian communities as sources of subversion. Gradually guerrillas consolidated their position in the countryside and, in the case of Nicaragua, toppled regimes. Elsewhere, changes in attitude in Washington, and peace deals brokered by Costa Rica, Colombia, Mexico and Venezuela, led to cease-fires and reasonably fair elections. But decades of war and terrorism had resulted in massive population movements and emigration.

DEMOCRATIZATION

Central America and Mexico began a fragile process of democratization in the mid-1980s. A mixture of exhaustion, regime-collapse and external aid (and pressure) fostered stability in Central America, while in Mexico the combination was growth, followed by inflation and crisis, and a remarkable transition within the single party, the PRI, which dominated politics after the 1920s. Attempts at political liberalization in the late 1960s were thwarted by internal resistance within the governing party apprehensive at student-led demands for change that led to a crackdown in 1968. After the collapse of oil prices, inflation and default in 1982, the ground was laid for economic reorganization and democratic opening. Export-oriented manufacturing and commodity diversification were prioritized. Elected president in 1988, Carlos Salinas announced that Mexico would enter the North American Free Trade Area and the GATT. The 1994 elections, which took place at a time of armed struggle in the southern state of Chiapas and economic crisis – were possibly the freest in Mexican history. Further institutional democratization allowed Vicente Fox, from the rightist National Action Party (PAN), to take the presidency in 2000. Subject to charges of vote-rigging, the PAN narrowly retained the presidency in 2006. With high levels of poverty, and a new surge in emigration to the USA, Mexican society and politics is riven by discontent.

Another factor making for instability in the region is the problem of succession in Cuba. After his 80th birthday in 2006 Fidel Castro stepped down as president in February 2008, leaving his brother as acting president, but no clear succession plan. A regime crisis in Cuba will have profound repercussions beyond Central America and the Caribbean.

SINCE 1939

THE UNITED STATES: THE AGE OF ABUNDANCE

For much of the 20th century the USA has seen exceptional economic growth, becoming by far the world's largest economy and enjoying a remarkable age of consumer-led abundance. This prosperity brought mass migration to the cities and a new wave of immigration from Latin America, bringing new problems in its wake.

The 20th century began with the USA poised to become the most powerful economy in the world. It had vast reserves of minerals and other natural resources. It had ample labour as a result of mass immigration and large-scale rural migration to the cities. Its business corporations were steadily becoming both bigger and more powerful. It had labour unions, in contrast, that were weak and small. It had well-developed – if largely unregulated – banks and financial services.

Before the First World War, the USA was primarily a debtor nation. It emerged from the war as a creditor country, having advanced funds to the Allied nations to support their war effort. Despite a period of strikes and labour unrest attending the readjustment to a peacetime economy, the post-war years saw a "New Era" of prosperity. Successive Republican governments adopted pro-business policies on corporate regulation, taxation and labour.

The Great Depression after 1929 affected the USA more deeply than any other nation. While President Franklin D. Roosevelt's "New Deal" stabilized the economy and reformed financial and business regulation, unemployment remained high until the Second World War. The period after 1945, however, saw not a return to the economic difficulties of the 1930s but rather the start of a long economic boom. The American economy almost doubled in size between 1945 and 1960 and continued to grow sharply in the 1960s.

THE POST-WAR BOOM

A combination of consumer demand, military expenditure and technological innovation fuelled fast economic growth. The rate of personal income continued to grow and ownership of durable consumer goods increased markedly. While there were only around 7000 television sets in the entire country in 1946, by 1960 there were over 50 million. Car ownership became much more widespread. By 1956, around 75 million cars and trucks were on American roads.

In 1955, the USA, with just 6 per cent of the world's population, was producing and consuming half of all its goods. By 1970, with the same proportion of the total population, it accounted for two-thirds of the world's goods. Yet for all its vast wealth, there existed large pockets of poverty within American society itself. While much of this poverty was rural, particularly in the deep South, the increasing focus of attention of 1960s government programmes was in urban areas, where the issue of poverty became bound up with that of race.

RACE AND URBAN DEPRIVATION

Beginning in 1915–16, as a result of wartime demand for labour, African Americans began to move from the South to northern cities in search of jobs. This "Great Migration" continued for several decades. The 1960 Census showed that for the first time a majority of blacks lived outside the deep South. As a result of social, economic and discriminatory pressures, enclaves of many large cities came to contain black ghettoes, forming the home of a permanent black underclass. During the 1960s, beginning in the Watts district of Los Angeles in August 1965, many exploded into racial riots.

After the 1960s, as the political climate became less favourable to their aspirations, many blacks began to leave northern cities in search of jobs in the booming industries of the "Sunbelt" – the South and Southwest states. The black middle and professional classes expanded in size. Yet many ghettoes remained, wracked by unemployment, drugs, crime, HIV/AIDS and violence.

IMMIGRATION, TRADE AND NAFTA

By the 1990s, fresh flows of immigrants, above all from Latin America, had begun to transform American society anew. Between 1941 and 1970 approximately 800,000 legal immigrants from Mexico entered the USA, and many more did so illegally. By 1990 people of Hispanic origin made up 26 per cent of the population of California and 35 per cent of New Mexico, with the possibility of their becoming a majority in these states within a century. US relations with its Latin American neighbours had traditionally been uneasy, but by the early 1990s the need to institutionalize Mexican economic reform helped to promote the idea of a North American free-trade area. Canada had made such a pact with the USA in 1985, and on 1 January 1994 Mexico joined in the North American Free Trade Agreement (NAFTA), the largest free-trade area in the world.

SINCE 1945
THE UNITED STATES AS
A WORLD POWER

In the years following the Second World War, the USA found itself resisting the expansion of international communism. This led to American participation in two major wars – in Korea and Vietnam – and frequent military and diplomatic interventions in other areas. The break-up of the Soviet Union in 1991 left the USA as the sole surviving superpower.

In 1920, the USA declined to join the League of Nations and retreated into a period of isolationism, which was only brought to a close by the Japanese attack on the American fleet at Pearl Harbor in December 1941. When the war ended in 1945, the USA and the Soviet Union were left as the two greatest military powers. The USA found itself playing the leading role on the world scene in resisting the attempts of the Soviet Union to further the advance of international communism.

THE POLICY OF CONTAINMENT
In the spring of 1947, conscious of what appeared to be a Soviet threat in eastern Europe, Greece and Turkey, the Truman administration adopted a policy of "containing" communist expansionism. Containment remained the basis of American foreign policy until the 1980s. It had a number of successes in the late 1940s: Marshall Aid (introduced in 1948) which saved the economies of war-torn Europe; the Berlin airlift of 1948–9 which defeated a Soviet blockade of the city; and the creation of the North Atlantic Treaty Organisation (NATO) in 1949. Yet the policy also suffered reverses: the communist take-over of China in 1949 and, the same year, the Soviet Union's detonation of an atomic bomb. President Truman responded in 1950 by ordering the construction of the hydrogen bomb and accepting NSC-68, a document calling for the rearmament of America's conventional forces. In 1950, when communist North Korea invaded South Korea, Truman committed US forces against them and their Chinese allies in the Korean War (1950–3).

Under the Eisenhower administration from 1953, secretary of state John Foster Dulles talked not of containing communism but of the "liberation" of eastern Europe. The hollowness of this rhetoric was demonstrated when the Russians suppressed East German workers' food riots in 1953 and by the Hungarian uprising of 1956. On both occasions the USA proved powerless to help.

After an abortive US-backed attempt to overthrow the Castro regime in Cuba in 1961, Cuba was the site (in October 1962) of the most dangerous moment of the Cold War. When the USSR attempted to install nuclear missiles in Cuba, President Kennedy ordered a naval blockade of the island. Both sides seemed on the brink of nuclear war until the Russians agreed to withdraw their missiles in return for concessions over US missiles in Turkey. From 1962, relations between the two "superpowers" – the USA and the USSR – began slowly to improve, as symbolized by the 1963 treaty banning nuclear testing in the atmosphere and the first Strategic Arms Limitation Treaty (SALT) agreed in 1972. The Nixon Administration (1969–74) also began a process of rapprochement with Communist China.

THE VIETNAM WAR

Kennedy provided South Vietnam with military advisers, but not troops, in an attempt to shore up a South Vietnamese government threatened by North Vietnamese-backed communist insurgents. In 1965, his successor, Lyndon Johnson, committed American ground forces to the preservation of South Vietnam. US involvement in Vietnam lasted eight years, cost 58,000 American lives, and had profound repercussions on domestic politics. It also failed: in April 1975, North Vietnam successfully unified the country under communist rule.

The Vietnam War led to a period of "neo-isolationism". President Carter, elected in 1976, helped Israel and Egypt make peace (in the wake of the Yom Kippur War of 1973). But he had no answer to the Soviet invasion of Afghanistan in 1979 or the holding of American hostages by Iranian revolutionaries.

THE COLLAPSE OF COMMUNISM

Ronald Reagan was elected president in 1980 promising a firmer line in foreign policy. He followed a two-prong strategy: large-scale rearmament, directed at the Soviet Union; and intervention, either open (as in Grenada in 1983) or covert (as in Nicaragua) to overthrow left-wing regimes.

The collapse of communism in eastern Europe in 1989 and the demise of the Soviet Union itself in 1991 left the USA as the sole remaining superpower and replaced a bipolar with a multipolar world. With the ending of the Cold War, a whole series of ethnic, nationalist and separatist conflicts emerged. In many of these the USA played a crucial role – as in the 1995 bombing of Bosnian Serbs that persuaded them to join the Dayton peace negotiations. The USA also led the coalition against Iraq in the Gulf War of 1991. Despite a strong post-Vietnam dislike of involving American forces in conflicts abroad, the 1990s saw American troops deployed in many trouble-spots overseas.

Since the late 1990s the United States has become the dominant force in international affairs. Following the Al-Qaeda attacks on New York and Washington on 11 September 2001, President George W. Bush declared a "war on terror" which brought US intervention in Afghanistan in October 2001 and a US-led invasion of Iraq in March 2003 in defiance of much world opinion. The occupation of Iraq cost US forces over 33,000 casualties by 2008.

SINCE 1929

THE DEVELOPMENT OF THE SOVIET UNION AND RUSSIA

In 1929 Stalin led the drive to modernize the Soviet Union in a ten-year programme of forced industrialization and agrarian reform, generating a "second revolution" and a wave of state terror. After the defeat of the German invasion, the Communist Party consolidated its grip on power, but demands for reform led in 1991 to the break up of the Union.

A decade after the Russian Revolution, the new Soviet Union had progressed little beyond the economic achievements of the pre-war Tsarist regime. Under Stalin's leadership the decision was taken to launch a "second revolution" to modernize society and economic structure. The renewed modernization drive was necessary, Stalin believed, in order to reduce the size and economic preponderance of the peasantry – still 80 per cent of the population – and to strengthen the country against the threat of international conflict. It was also seen as the key to cementing the power of the Communist Party. The social upheaval that followed completed the social revolution only partially achieved in 1917.

The First Five-Year Plan for economic development was launched in 1928, and was followed by two more, each one setting extravagant targets for the expansion of heavy industry. The whole enterprise rested on the ability to extract a grain surplus from the countryside to feed the cities. In the second half of 1929 the Party began a programme of collectivizing peasant landholdings, and by 1935 90 per cent of land previously owned by the peasants had been taken, often by force, into large state-owned farms (*kolkhozy*). Peasant resistance resulted in the slaughter of millions of animals and the mass deportation of millions of farmers to work in the cities or to labour camps.

The consequences were mixed. Even allowing for Soviet exaggeration, industrial output expanded remarkably in the 1930s: the armed forces became the largest in the world, armed by 1941 with over 20,000 tanks and 10,000 air-craft. The social goal, too, was achieved, with the urban population expanding by 30 million between 1926 and 1939, and the peasantry falling to 52 per cent of the population.

THE COST OF MODERNIZATION

Yet the cost was high. To cope with modernization the state increased its policing of society. The regime fomented popular hatred against spies and saboteurs which turned into a nationwide witchhunt as brutal as the Terror of the French Revolution. In 1937–8 the terror reached a ghastly crescendo with the slaughter of more than 600,000 by the state security apparatus, including most of the senior officer corps (though only about one-fifth of all officers were purged, and most of these were dismissed rather than shot).

Modernization and terror also served to strengthen Stalin's personal grip on the Soviet Union. Victory over Germany in the Great Patriotic War of 1941–5 (*see* p. 285) showed how far Soviet society had come from the more feeble war effort of the Tsarist regime, and bolstered Stalin's domestic reputation even more. The war also saw Stalin order the shipment of millions from the country's smaller nationalities – including Germans, Poles, Chechens and Tatars – to the labour camps of the north and east.

After 1945 economic development continued with priority for heavy industry and armaments to compete in the Cold War arms race. The death of Stalin in 1953 was followed by a partial relaxation of the terror under Nikita Khrushchev. In the 1960s under Leonid Brezhnev greater efforts were made to help agriculture and the consumer industries. The Party, meanwhile, continued to dominate politics and dissent was relentlessly penalized. But by the 1980s the Soviet system was under pressure. Economic growth slowed, while the population became restless about the gap between the living standards of the West and those of the Communist bloc. Calls for more political openness followed, and when Mikhail Gorbachev became Soviet leader in 1985 he initiated a thorough programme of economic and political reform (*perestroika*). In 1988 he launched a limited democratization, and was elected president in 1989.

PROTEST AND REFORM

Popular demands for reform could not now be stemmed. A freer economic market and greater political and cultural freedoms (*glasnost*) opened the floodgates of popular protest. In August 1991 hard-line Communists staged a coup against Gorbachev, which was suppressed by Boris Yeltsin, head of the Russian Republic. By December the Soviet Union was fragmenting along nationalist and ethnic lines, and Gorbachev bowed to reality. On 31 December 1991 the Soviet Union was wound up and replaced by a loose Commonwealth of Independent States. Russia itself became a presidential democracy with Yeltsin as its first head of state.

Since the collapse of communism the new Russian Federation has been plagued by crisis. The economy declined and poverty became widespread again. The new capitalism was dominated by an elite of violent and corrupt businessmen and many of the welfare and educational achievements of the Soviet age were eroded. Violent repression in Chechnya provoked a wave of terrorism, first under Boris Yeltsin, then under his successor, a former security officer, Vladimir Putin, elected in 2000. Under his presidency the government has had to challenge internal corruption and the threat of terrorism, but during the process Russia has became once again a more authoritarian state, though very different from communism.

SINCE 1973
EUROPE

With the oil crisis of 1973, the post-war boom was replaced by more unstable growth and high inflation. While western Europe became more united through the EU, the Soviet bloc collapsed. Renewed economic growth after 2000 brought an enlarged union, linking east and west.

In 1973 the oil-producing states almost trebled the price of oil in a year, triggering worldwide price inflation. In Europe, the crisis coincided with a general slowdown in productivity and profit growth and mounting unemployment. The 1970s saw the onset of "stagflation" – low rates of growth and soaring inflation. Unemployment, which had been almost eradicated in the 1960s, rose sharply, producing widespread labour unrest. Oil prices in the USSR affected the Soviet bloc as well. Economic performance stagnated behind the Iron Curtain, and in some cases actually declined.

ECONOMIC INTEGRATION
Across much of western Europe, the crisis was confronted by continuing the trend to greater economic integration. By the late 1960s, the original six members of the EEC (European Economic Community) had established themselves as the economic vanguard of the continent. Fearful that they were being left behind by their more dynamic neighbours, in 1973 Britain, Ireland and Denmark joined them. They were followed in 1981 by Greece, in 1986 by Spain and Portugal and in 1995 by Austria, Finland and Sweden.

Underpinning the EEC (renamed the EU, European Union, in 1995) was the belief, first proposed in the 1950s (*see* p. 290), that integrating the nations of western Europe was the only effective means of guaranteeing continued economic success. The massive economic bloc thereby created would allow Europe to compete effectively with the world's other leading economies, the USA and Japan. Such integration should in time evolve into full political union, with the aim of creating a single state. In 1985, the EEC agreed to create a single market and free-trade zone. The subsequent Maastricht Treaty of 1991 also committed what became known in 1995 as the European Union to a single currency. The Euro was introduced into most of the EU in 2002, though Britain declined to join at that time. The EU drew up proposals for a European Constitution in 2003, but no firm commitment existed to extend economic collaboration into a political union. In 2004 a further ten states joined the EU and, in 2007, two more.

THE COMING OF DEMOCRACY

The combined effects of the economic slowdown after 1973 and the realization that by clinging to their pre-war authoritarian governments they were increasingly being pushed to the margins of Europe were sufficient to see the reintroduction of democracy to Portugal (1974) and Spain (1975). Greece also embraced democracy in 1974.

But these changes paled in comparison with events in eastern Europe in the late 1980s. These involved nothing less than the disintegration of the Soviet Union and the fall of communism in every one of its satellite states as well as in Yugoslavia and Albania. As remarkable as the collapse of this apparently permanent system was the creation in its wake of no less than 15 new countries. The reasons for this transformation were as much economic as political. Throughout the 1970s and 1980s, the economies of the communist bloc had declined to the point where the region was effectively bankrupt. Unable to guarantee the survival of its client states, the Soviet Union under President Gorbachev abandoned them. By 1991 free elections had been held in every country of the region, including the Soviet Union, and the two Germanies had been reunited. Except for a short surge of violence in Romania, the transformation had been relatively peaceful.

THE REVIVAL OF NATIONALISM

The euphoria which greeted the end of communism was followed swiftly by a fresh set of economic problems as the new regimes struggled to come to terms with democracy and economic liberalization. In the atmosphere of crisis old ethnic or religious conflicts revived. Slovakia won its independence from the Czechs in 1993. In 1991 Moldova declared independence and a brief civil war followed between the differing ethnic groups making up the new state.

But the most bloody and prolonged struggle took place in Yugoslavia, which in 1991 disintegrated under pressure from the long-suppressed rivalries of its ethnic groups, despite Serbian resistance. Between 1991 and 1995 Serbia fought first against Slovenian, then Croatian and finally Bosnian independence, declared in 1992 by its Muslim majority. Only the intervention of NATO in 1995 prevented further bloodshed in what had become the most barbarous European conflict since the Second World War. In 1998 civil war broke out in Serbia itself when ethnic Albanian separatists in Kosovo fought for independence.

Nationalist conflict continued in western Europe, too. Basque separatism in Spain and Irish nationalism in Ulster were both sustained by terrorism from the 1970s. In Ireland political agreement for closer cooperation between Nationalists and Unionists was secured in 1998. Since the millennium the greatest problem facing Europe was the increased number of political and economic refugees. Fear of "asylum seekers" fuelled radical right-wing movements in Europe and heightened racial tension. In France this exploded in 2006 in major urban riots among frustrated and impoverished immigrant communities. Terrorism and asylum has forced European governments to increase state powers and compromise civil liberties.

SINCE 1991

EUROPE'S CIVIL WARS

The collapse of communism in Russia and Eastern Europe in 1989–90 provoked serious conflict between national minorities which now sought independence or ethnic cleansing. In Armenia, Azerbaijan and Moldova there were brief ethnic wars, but in Chechnya and in Yugoslavia there developed major conflicts which resulted in wide destruction and a high death toll. Yugoslavia fragmented into five separate states. Chechnya was forced to stay within the Russian Federation and remains a focus of terrorist violence.

The long period of peace in Europe after 1945, a product of the Cold War divisions and Soviet domination of the eastern bloc, came to an end with the collapse of the Soviet system and the eclipse of European communism. In the former Soviet Union there were violent clashes in Moldova which led to the establishment of an autonomous region in Transnistria. The new states established in the Caucasus also provoked ethnic violence in Georgia, Armenia and Azerbaijan. The Armenian enclave of Nagorno-Karabakh in Azerbaijan rejected Azeri rule and war broke out between the two new states which ended in a ceasefire in 1994 and virtual autonomy for the contested area.

WAR OVER CHECHNYA

When the Russian province of Chechnya, whose population had returned from deportation in the 1960s, declared its right to become an independent state in 1991, the Russian army intervened. Between 1994 and 1996 a bitter civil war was waged, with heavy losses on both sides. The Chechen capital Grozny was destroyed. A ceasefire in 1996 granted virtual autonomy, but in 1999 Russia again sent in troops to occupy the whole region which had descended into rival warlord provinces and was host to a rising tide of Islamic fundamentalism. The war ended officially in 2001, but Chechen guerrillas loyal to the idea of an independent state continued to fight against Russian occupation and spread a terror campaign into the Russian capital which provoked harsh Russian reprisals. A new constitution in 2003 gave limited autonomy, and Chechnya is now ruled by a Russian backed militia leader, Ramzan Kadyrov.

THE COLLAPSE OF YUGOSLAVIA

Although Yugoslavia was not formally a member of the Soviet bloc, the collapse of the Soviet Union hastened the collapse of Yugoslav communism. A weak economy, growing nationalist sentiment and the assertion of Serb predominance over the six federal republics that made up Yugoslavia provoked the collapse of the state in 1991. In December that year Croatia and Slovenia declared their independence. After a brief civil war Slovenia successfully seceded. Full-scale war broke out between Croatia and Serbia, which ended in 1992 with Croat independence. Serbia and Montenegro formed a new Yugoslav Federation of their own.

In between the two warring groups lay the provinces of Bosnia-Herzegovina, which were inhabited by a mixture of Croats, Christian Serbs and Muslim Bosnians. All but the Serbs wanted an independent Bosnian state, and this was formally recognized abroad in 1992. Both Croats and Serbs had ambitions to partition the region and add it to their territory. There followed a confused and savage civil war between the three groups, which left the Bosnian Serbs under Radovan Karadzic in control of 70 per cent of the region by 1993. The Bosnian Serb army surrounded the Bosnian capital of Sarajevo and laid it to siege for three years. International efforts to end the fighting proved abortive, but in 1995, as the Serbs seemed poised for victory, NATO forces compelled an end to hostilities and, under the Dayton Agreement, Bosnia was divided into three ethnically distinct republics in a federal Bosnian state. There existed thereafter a fragile truce.

In the southern Yugoslav province of Kosovo fighting broke out between Serbs and ethnic Albanians which escalated into a full civil war in 1998–9. Serb rejection of international pressure to grant autonomy to the province provoked a wave of NATO bombings between March and May 1999 which ended with Serbian agreement. Within a year the hardline Serbian president, Slobodan Milosevic, was voted out and in 2001 sent to stand trial at The Hague on charges of genocide. In 2003 Serbia and Montenegro became de facto independent states, completing the ethnic fragmentation of the region.

SINCE 1945

WARFARE

Though there has been no major war since 1945 there have been smaller regional wars throughout the past half-century. Conventional weaponry has been transformed and armed forces reorganized to meet the reality of the small war. Many of the conflicts have been asymmetrical, a major state using armed power to enforce its political will. Other regional or civil wars have been fuelled by the worldwide sale of modern armaments from developed states which have tried at the same time to limit the violence their trade stimulated.

The first half of the 20th century saw the two largest and costliest wars in history, waged by the world's most militarily powerful and economically advanced states. The First and Second World Wars were total wars, absorbing huge resources and mobilizing manpower in tens of millions. By contrast the 60 years since 1945 experienced no major war between the developed states, largely because the nuclear and missile technologies that emerged after the Second World War made war between the major states too costly and terrifying to risk.

The nuclear standoff did not prevent hundreds of smaller conflicts. The typical wars after 1945 were civil wars, or wars of insurgency or national liberation, often not limited to defined state territories. Many of these smaller wars and civil wars were asymmetrical conflicts, the imbalance widening remarkably if a major state was involved, as with the French in Algeria and Vietnam, or the USA in Korea, Vietnam and the Middle East. Asymmetry as such did not guarantee victory to the stronger power. France was forced to withdraw from Algeria; the USA withdrew from Vietnam; and the Korean conflict ended with the peninsula divided.

NEW WAYS OF WARFARE

The nature of modern warfare produced two entirely contradictory developments. The developed states created the scientific and technical means to wage a sophisticated land, air and sea war. The three services became increasingly integrated, and the technology of modern radio, satellite and electronic communication, high quality air power, rockets, chemical agents, laser guided weapons and, more recently, the extensive "electronic battlefield" to direct the massive and destructive firepower available, have all produced modern armed forces of exceptional striking power and flexibility, demonstrated fully in the two wars against Iraq in 1991 and 2003.

Yet most wars have involved forces with limited, simple and easily portable weaponry adaptable for use by poorly trained militia and proved ideal for the many guerrilla conflicts since 1945. The chief weapons for the irregular forces were the sub-machine gun, the mine, booby traps and primitive bombs, and hand-held rocket launchers. This arsenal was easily available worldwide. More sophisticated weaponry also spread to developing areas, usually to the local armies trying to maintain domestic control. This produced a further paradox. While the industrially developed states fed the growing appetite of the rest of the world for weapons of all kinds, they also promoted a more interventionist approach to conflict through the United Nations and the growth of a body of international law and the institutions to enforce it.

PEACEKEEPING AND MODERN WARFARE

Ever since its foundation in 1945 the United Nations has been involved in efforts to keep warring sides apart. In many cases intervention only occurred after the damage had been done. In others intervention has made little difference to a situation of perennial conflict – for example in the Congo or Israel. Since the

1980s the United Nations has taken a larger role in policing conflict and compelling reconciliation. At the same time, the international community drew up agreements to define and proscribe a whole range of potential war crimes and crimes against humanity, beginning with the Genocide Convention of 1948. In 1977 at Geneva a set of Protocols were signed to protect the civilian population in conflicts of all kind, but its provisions have largely been ignored, even by major states. In 2001 an International Criminal Court was established where cases related to war crimes and crimes against humanity could be heard, but the failure to secure American agreement to the court weakened its influence. The gap between the efforts to outlaw and control war and the reality of worldwide military conflict remains as wide as ever.

SINCE 1945
WORLD TERRORISM

The use of indiscriminate violence against military and civilian targets to achieve defined political objectives, generally described as "terrorism", has become a characteristic feature of politics worldwide since 1945. Employed on the right as well as the left of the political spectrum, terrorism has been used as an instrument for national liberation, or to challenge conventional politics or to sustain religious conflict. In 2001 the American President George W. Bush declared a worldwide "war on terror".

Terrorism existed long before 1945, but only in the past 40 years has it become a major element in world politics. Since Bush's declaration the USA has been in a permanent "state of war". In reality terror is not a movement or a defined political concept. Terrorism describes the means by which, usually small, groups of political dissidents or criminals fight against a potentially stronger political or military opponent. The aims of those who have used terror tactics are extraordinarily diverse. They share only the tactics, using methods of irregular or guerrilla warfare – ambushes, bombings, kidnapping, suicide attacks, assassination – and targeting either representatives of the "enemy" system or ordinary civilians.

TERRORISM AND NATION-BUILDING

Many of the longest-running and most violent terrorist campaigns were launched by groups demanding national liberation. In Ireland the Irish Republican Army (IRA) fought a terror campaign against the British authorities from the 1920s, demanding a united Ireland that included the province of Ulster. In Spain, demands for an independent Basque homeland led in 1966 to the onset of a long wave of violence which in 40 years claimed over 800 deaths, more than half of them army or police targets. The organization Euskadi Ta Askatasuna (ETA), founded in 1959, drew on Marxism-Leninism for its inspiration. It has remained uncompromisingly committed to armed struggle.

Terrorism was used as a deliberate tactic in the struggle to create a Jewish homeland in Israel under British rule in 1945. In 1947 Britain abandoned the effort to maintain control and many former Jewish terrorists became prominent Israeli politicians, facing their own terrorist threat in demands for a Palestinian homeland. In the 1970s and 1980s the Palestine Liberation Organisation (PLO) carried out prominent terrorist attacks, and in the 1990s radical Islamic groups, including Hamas and Hezbollah, added a religious dimension to the terror campaigns. Since the late 1990s the al-Qaeda ("The Base") network led by Osama bin Laden, first founded in 1985, added to the conflict, which broadened out into a general campaign of terror by Islamic militants to drive Jews and Westernizers out of Islamic territory and to establish fundamentalist Islamic states. In Algeria those very politicians who had used terrorism to free Algeria from French rule found themselves facing savage terrorism from the Islamic Salvation Front, founded in 1989. These many Islamic groups form the core target for the current "war on terror".

TERRORISM AND SOCIAL REVOLUTION

Many of the terrorist movements since 1945 have been linked with ideas of social revolution and radical Marxism. In the aftermath of the 1968 youth movement in Europe, there developed small cells of committed revolutionary terrorists, in France the Action Directe movement, in Germany the Baader-Meinhof group and in Italy the Red Brigades. In the 1970s these urban guerrilla movements kidnapped businessmen and politicians, robbed banks and murdered policemen. The Italian interior minister was kidnapped and killed in 1978. The extreme right also used terrorist tactics in Europe and America, where a massive bomb in Oklahoma City was eventually traced to a militant white supremacist group.

The European urban terrorists modelled their campaigns on the guerrilla wars in Latin America, where left-wing rebels, inspired by Leninism or Maoism, ran long campaigns of violence against the military and authoritarian regimes that dominated the continent from the 1950s to the 1980s. In Peru, Abimael Guzman, a philosophy professor, founded the Shining Path movement in 1980, a terrorist organization that launched a wave of savage violence against the state and the peasantry it sought to liberate, until Guzman's arrest and imprisonment in 1992. Terrorist activity in Colombia has lasted for more than 40 years, practised by all sides in the many disputes about Colombia's political future and the massive trade in narcotics. Here the divide between political dissidence and crime has been eroded and terrorism has become a way of life.

1979 TO 2007
IRAQ AND AFGHANISTAN: THE ARC OF INSTABILITY

From the early 1980s Afghanistan and Iraq were at the centre of two separate areas of crisis which produced more than 20 years of civil or guerrilla war in and around Afghanistan and involved Iraq in three wars against Iran, a UN-led coalition and a USA-UK invasion force. Western efforts to stabilize the two states has proved costly and produced at best a fragile stability.

Since the late 1970s two states have been at the hub of much of the world's violence. Iraq and Afghanistan, both for differing reasons were involved in a series of civil wars, guerrilla wars or inter-state wars which provoked the intervention of the world's major powers on at least four occasions, the last, in March 2003, leading to the occupation of Iraq by an invading Western force and the attempt to impose a political system more sympathetic to Western interests.

During the 1980s Afghanistan and Iraq were united by a common conflict with the revival of fundamentalist Islam. Both were secular states, Afghanistan a pro-Soviet regime, Iraq dominated by Saddam Hussein's Ba'ath Party. In 1980 Iraq launched a war against the new Islamic state set up under Ayatollah Khomeini which lasted for eight years and cost more than 400,000 lives. In

Afghanistan the pro-communist presidents Babrak Karmal, followed in 1986 by Mohammed Najibullah (responsible for an estimated 80,000 deaths during his period as security chief in the state), led a savage civil war against Islamic "muhajeddin" rebels, with the support of Soviet troops and equipment. The civil war cost 1.5 million lives and produced some 5 million refugees from the conflict.

AFGHANISTAN AFTER COMMUNISM

The collapse of communism and the withdrawal of Soviet aid produced political chaos in Afghanistan, with fighting between rival warlords, some former communists, some hard-line Muslims. In October 1994 the southern city of Kandahar was captured by a religious militia or "Taliban" led by Mullah Omar. With increased support and armed from outside, the Taliban captured Kabul in September 1996 where they declared Afghanistan a completely Islamic state and imposed a harsh regime of Islamic law. The region remained in a state of turmoil as anti-Taliban tribal forces continued to fight against radical Islam. In 1998 the USA, which during the Soviet intervention had armed the Islamic guerrilla war, turned against their former allies as American military bases and embassies became the target of militant Islamic terrorism. By October 2000, with the region still plunged in civil war, the USA was preparing to attack Afghanistan as the home to al-Qaeda, the most dangerous of the new terrorist groups. After the September 11 attacks in 2001 on New York and Washington, American and British forces began a heavy bombardment of Afghanistan to support an offensive by a Northern Alliance of anti-Taliban warlords. In 2002 a new regime was in power in Kabul, but within a year Taliban irregulars began fighting again in the south and by 2006 had extended their influence in much of the area.

THE IRAQI WARS

In the aftermath of the Iraq-Iran war Saddam Hussein ordered the invasion of Kuwait in August 1990. The response not only of the Western states, but also of many Arab countries, was to condemn the invasion and organize a coalition force to expel Iraq. "Operation Desert Storm" in January and February 1991 forced the expulsion of Iraqi forces and inflicted enormous damage on Iraq's already impoverished economy. For the following 12 years harsh sanctions and military restrictions were imposed on Iraq, which had also been the victim of a sharp change in American attitudes. From distant support for Iraq's war to contain Islamic fundamentalism, American policy in the 1990s penalised Iraq as a potential threat to peace despite its secular outlook and more westernized society. Sanctions were followed from December 1998 by five years of persistent and heavy bombing of Iraq by US and British aircraft to force Saddam to comply with the terms of his defeat in 1991.

In the spring of 2003, without the sanction of a UN resolution, and in the face of international condemnation, Britain and the USA launched an attack on Iraq in the belief that Saddam had "Weapons of Mass Destruction" under development. Saddam was deposed, and the USA and Britain occupied Iraq, secured its large oil supplies and engaged in brutal acts of pacification against radical Muslim militia and Iraqis hostile to Western intervention. The aim was to turn Iraq into a functioning parliamentary state. A violent wave of anti-occupation insurgency coincided with a mounting religious civil war between the rival Sunni and Shia Moslems. Although a constitution was popularly ratified in October 2005, the new Iraqi government was unable to prevent a slide into further instability. Religious conflict in both Iraq and Afghanistan continues to make this the most unstable region in the world.

THE WORLD IN THE 21ST CENTURY

In 2000 the world turned its back on an ambiguous century torn by violence and conflict, but capable of extraordinary technical and economic progress. The new century has inherited that same ambiguity. Wars in Afghanistan and Iraq, civil wars in Africa and bitter religious conflict in the Middle East have already shown that the new century will be no less violent. The nuclear threat did not disappear with the Cold War. Bitter divisions still exist between the secular western world and the revival of popular religion.

The 20th century bequeathed to its successor a variety of issues and problems. Some are long-term issues about global development which first alerted public concern in the 1960s and 1970s. Population growth has slowed down but is still high, and will mean by the year 2050 that the world will have to sustain 50 per cent more people than it does today. There has already been severe pressure on natural resources, which will worsen as the new populations demand food and basic living standards. Oil, which is essential to the motorized populations of the developed world, is a shrinking commodity, and most of it is located in the Middle East, the least stable area in world politics. High consumption has also helped to fuel environmental damage. Despite agreements reached at the Kyoto Summit in 1997, a number of major industrial powers have refused to ratify or implement those agreements to the full.

RELIGION AND THE RISE OF TERROR

One of the factors encouraging instability in the Middle East is the long-running tension between Western capitalism and its Westernizing allies and the rise of radical Islam. In the first four years of the new century this tension has produced a growing train of violence and terrorism. A number of spectacular attacks by Islamic militants, on the World Trade Center and the Pentagon in 2001, on a Bali nightclub in 2002 and on Madrid railway targets in 2004, have been accompanied by regular killings, bomb attacks and other atrocities. The militant groups, particularly al-Qaeda, led by Osama bin Laden, have declared holy war against the West and are committed to reducing Western influence in the Islamic world. Hundreds of young Muslims have died in suicide attacks or in battles with security and military forces from Afghanistan to Egypt.

The religious revival has also affected Christianity. In the USA religious fundamentalism has also become an important political force both in foreign policy and in domestic politics, where popular Christianity has challenged the accepted orthodoxies of secular, rationalist science. In the former Yugoslavia an uneasy peace reigns, but tensions between Catholics, Muslims and Orthodox Christians played a part in the civil war of the 1990s, and remain an issue that divides not only the Balkans but the Caucasus and southern Russia. Religious conflicts have become the major force for destabilizing world politics, and will remain so among the youthful and disillusioned populations of the Islamic world.

WEAPONS OF MASS DESTRUCTION

The great fear in the West has been the distribution of weapons capable of producing a high destructive yield for relatively little terrorist effort, including toxic biological and chemical agents, radioactive material for making so-called "dirty bombs", or small nuclear devices produced by states with the scientific potential to do so. Much of this technology was first made available during the Cold War confrontation with world communism, but the overwhelming bulk of such weapons still lies in the hands of the most powerful and militarily sophisticated states.

Nuclear capability is still restricted to no more than eight or nine states, but the danger of a nuclear confrontation cannot be ruled out. In 2002 Pakistan and India came close to the brink of military crisis and both possess nuclear warheads and missile delivery systems. Nuclear programmes in North Korea and Iran provoked strong UN pressure in 2006 and 2007 to compel disarmament. The most heavily armed state remains the USA, which not only has sophisticated nuclear weapons and delivery systems and tactical nuclear weapons for the battlefield, but also a variety of armament for high-technology warfare whose effects have yet to be fully assessed. US military power has been used twice already this century. The uni-polar world system produced by the collapse of communism has become a reality; the United States spends more on defence than the rest of the world together.

THE GLOBAL ECONOMY

By the 1990s electronic communication and worldwide investment and marketing had created a genuinely global economy. Giant transnational companies dominated finance and production. Yet the gulf between rich and poor nations remained, and the developing world relied on the developed world for aid, investment and export markets.

In 1992 an American State Department official, Francis Fukuyama, published *The End of History*, in which he argued that the collapse of the Soviet bloc signalled the final worldwide triumph of modern free-market capitalism over all other systems. In the former Communist bloc capitalist free-market reforms had been introduced. Even in China, the remaining Communist superpower, the economy was liberalized and Western capital and technology introduced. By the end of the decade an integrated global economy had emerged.

However, world economic development still depended in part on the central management of key economic factors by groups of states, and on collaboration between them. Representatives of the largest industrial economies met regularly as the Group of Seven to co-ordinate financial and trade policies. Additionally, regional agreements sought to expand trade between small groups of states.

REGIONAL AND GLOBAL INTEGRATION

The most successful of these groupings was the European Union, which grew from the original six members of the EEC in 1957 to embrace 15 states by 1996. Gradual economic integration culminated on 1 January 1999 in the introduction of a single currency, the euro. Economic groups elsewhere were looser associations aiming to enhance regional economic integration. In 1994, for example, the USA, Canada and Mexico joined together in the North American Free Trade Association (NAFTA).

Integration was also encouraged by the rapid growth of multinational (or transnational) enterprises and high levels of foreign direct investment. In the early 1990s it was estimated that the 37,000 multinationals employed 73 million people. The 100 largest companies controlled one-third of all foreign investment, most of it in the developed world. The existence of multinationals, many with assets larger than the GDP of smaller states, acted to stabilize the world economy, though at the cost of lack of supervision by sovereign states.

GLOBAL INEQUALITY

The fruits of the global economic success were spread very unevenly. Sustained expansion in Asia, Europe and the USA was accompanied by economic decline in Africa, Latin America and the former Soviet bloc. The Russian economy in particular faced serious crisis by 1998 as the rush for capitalism failed to generate the wealth to sustain employment and welfare at the level achieved under communism. Even in east Asia, which grew faster than anywhere else in the world from the 1960s to the mid-1990s, the boom turned sour in 1997. Burdened with debt, high population growth and excessive dependence on a cluster of manufacturing exports, the new Asian economies generated a financial crisis which threatened the health of the whole global economy.

Outside the growth areas there was persistent reliance on aid and investment from the developed world, much of it supplied by the International Monetary Fund or the Organization for Economic Co-operation and Development (OECD). The per capita GDP of the poorest states in 2005 was around

$600–700; for the richest states the figure is over $30,000. For many sub-Saharan African states aid represented more than half of the value of total GDP. This pattern of aid-dependence has altered little in recent decades, and the gulf between the poverty of the developing world and the vast wealth of the developed industrial core remains one of the unresolved issues of global economics.

COMMUNICATIONS IN THE MODERN AGE

The past century has witnessed a profound revolution in communication of every kind. Motor vehicles and aeroplanes have made the whole globe accessible, moulding the modern high-growth economy and transforming social life and leisure. The age of mass electronic communications has opened up possibilities undreamed of a century ago.

The 20th century witnessed a revolution in communication that transformed practically every aspect of daily life. The changes were the fruit of a remarkable cluster of scientific breakthroughs in the 40 years before the First World War: the telephone, invented by Alexander Bell in 1876; the first automobiles powered by the internal combustion engine, pioneered by Karl Benz and Gottlieb Daimler in the 1880s; the radio transmitter, developed by Guglielmo Marconi in 1896; the discovery of the electron in 1897 by Joseph Thomson; and the development of powered flight, begun by the Wright brothers in 1903. The development of the silicon microchip in the late 1950s completed this scientific foundation.

THE INTERNAL COMBUSTION ENGINE

The development of motorized transport on land and in the air was dependent on the development of a sufficiently powerful and efficient engine. The internal combustion engine, fuelled by refined oil, provided the key. Improvements in engine technology then made possible the evolution of mass-motoring and high-performance aircraft. Motor vehicles and aeroplanes gave transport a flexibility and speed unattainable by railways and horses.

Motorization began before the First World War in Europe and America.

Henry Ford established his motor company in 1903, and within a decade had become the world's most successful mass producer of motor cars. The greater spread of wealth in the USA encouraged high levels of car ownership and by 1939 the majority of the world's motor vehicles were produced there. Rising incomes after 1945 fuelled growing demand worldwide. By 1959 there were 119 million vehicles in use; by 1974 the figure was 303 million. Motor transport transformed industry and commerce, produced a sharp change in social patterns and broke down the isolation of rural areas. Motorization also made possible mass leisure and mass tourism.

AIR TRAVEL AND TELECOMMUNICATIONS

In 1919 the first primitive airlines opened in Europe using the experience of the war years in producing larger and safer aircraft. The first modern multi-engined monoplane airliners were developed in the 1930s by the Boeing and Douglas companies in America, and in 1939 the first successful passenger services were opened across the Atlantic Ocean. Air travel expanded rapidly from the 1950s thanks to the development of a new generation of high-performance wide-bodied jet aircraft. The first jet airliner, the British Comet, flew in 1952, but world airliner markets were subsequently dominated by a succession of Boeing models.

Aircraft have made the world a smaller place. Journeys that took months in the 19th century now take less than a day. For the populations of the richer developed states global travel is taken for granted. Meanwhile, many poorer states now depend on tourism as their primary source of income. The shrinking of the globe has led to the emergence of a common global culture. The exotic may be within reach, but modern communication and consumerism is challenging its very survival.

Telecommunications have changed faster than any other form of communication. The use of telephones expanded rapidly from the 1880s – there were just 50 million globally in 1930, but 350 million by 1975. Meanwhile in the 1920s television was developed, and the first public broadcasts followed in the 1930s. The development of the space programme after the Second World War encouraged the search for new forms of electronic communication. The development of the microchip opened up a new world of advanced communication. It allowed the development of small and increasingly efficient computer systems, and a modern global telephone network. In 1962 the first of many telecommunications satellites entered service. By the 1990s satellite communications were widely used for computer, television and telephone communication. In the early 1990s the growth of the internet opened up a world of instant electronic information for its millions of users.

The electronic revolution has shrunk the worlds of finance, commerce and education. Billions of dollars or yen can be transferred at the press of a button. Information can be made instantly available. The pace of innovation shows no sign of slackening. The 21st century will see more changes in lifestyle and work as microchips perform work previously done by routine human labour.

THE GLOBAL ENVIRONMENT

Until the 20th century, the environment was largely determined by natural changes. Industrialization, modern communications and mass consumption have combined to produce damaging man-made environmental change. Pollution now threatens the atmosphere itself. Ecological disasters have become among the most urgent of global problems.

Ever since the onset of large-scale population growth and industrialization in the 19th century (see p. 216), there has been a parallel rapid increase in man-made damage to the world's environment. Before 1945 this damage was largely localized, though very visible. However, the spread of industry worldwide after 1945 produced new threats to the environment which, if less visible, were nonetheless more deadly. Acid rain from waste in the atmosphere destroyed forests and eroded buildings. Pollutants in rivers and seas poisoned wildlife. High levels of carbon dioxide released from the burning of fossil fuels raised global temperatures, while other chemicals began to weaken the ozone layer in the earth's atmosphere.

GLOBAL WARMING

Between 1800 and 1900 the level of carbon dioxide in the atmosphere increased by only 4 per cent; in the 20th century it increased by 23 per cent, with most of the change occurring since the 1950s. The effect of this increase was to raise world temperatures artificially. The 1990s was the warmest decade of the millennium.

Global warming was due in part to a massive increase in energy consumption, most of which consisted of fossil fuels (oil, coal and natural gas). Between 1970 and 1990 energy consumption increased by 60 per cent, despite efforts to find more efficient ways of generating power and to reduce emissions. Fossil fuels released a range of chemicals into the atmosphere which blocked the natural loss of heat and created the so-called "greenhouse effect", leading to a global rise in temperatures. Warming was also the result of extensive deforestation. The world's tropical rainforests absorb carbon dioxide and give out oxygen, but as the rise of population put pressure on the land in tropical regions it led to the spread of agriculture at the expense of forest.

From the 1960s, the developed world began to recognize the dangers. The Clean Air Act in the USA in 1970 helped reduce emissions. Motor vehicles, too, in most of the developed world have been adapted since the 1980s to reduce the release of harmful gases. At Kyoto in 1997 agreement was reached to reduce the emission of greenhouse gases by the year 2010. The main barrier in the fight against global warming, however, remains the developed world itself. The USA, Europe and Russia are still the chief sources of the gases that cause global warming.

By the 1990s, global warming threatened the delicate balance of the natural world. Climatic changes caused regular flooding and widespread droughts. The ice-caps have begun to melt, and without effective control of the greenhouse effect the sea level will rise in the 21st century. The changes also threaten the pattern of world agriculture and the distribution of animal and plant species.

Other damage to the natural world was even more avoidable. In the Soviet Union in the 1970s a decision to use the water of the Aral Sea to irrigate the surrounding area to grow cotton and rice produced an environmental disaster. By the late 1980s, two-thirds of the sea had disappeared, the fish stock had died out, the local climate had become hotter and drier and the water-table had contracted. The result was the collapse of local industries and rising levels of disease.

THE OZONE LAYER

The most notorious damage to the environment was the effect of the release of chlorofluorocarbons (CFCs) into the atmosphere. Discovered in the 1920s, CFCs were used in refrigeration, air-conditioning and in aerosol sprays. In the 1970s it was found that they were destroying the ozone layer in the atmosphere, which is responsible for reducing the harmful ultraviolet rays of the sun. International action on phasing out CFCs was agreed by the early 1990s, and the ozone layer may gradually regenerate itself in the 21st century.

Action on CFCs showed what the international community was capable of doing. Environmental issues were a central concern of the 1990s and state action did produce results. In Brazil deforestation fell from a rate of 21,000 square kilometres in 1988 to only 1000 square kilometres by 1993. At Rio de Janeiro in 1992 agreements were made to reduce harmful pollutants and emissions, a decision reinforced at Kyoto. The richer states subsidized industrial and agricultural projects in the developing world which respected environmental interests. In European states political movements developed based entirely on issues of the environment, and in 1998 the environmentalist Green Party won a share of power in Germany. Yet the future of the world ecosystem depends on the willingness of the world's richest states to accept substantial changes in consumption patterns. If this fails to happen, pessimistic forecasts suggest the collapse of that eco-system by 2100.

CHRONOLOGY
OF SIGNIFICANT
EVENTS IN WORLD
HISTORY

	ASIA (excluding the Near East)	EUROPE
c. 9000 BC		
c. 8000 BC		
c. 7000 BC	*c.* 7000 Evidence of rice cultivation in China	*c.* 7000 First farming in Greece and Aegean; reaches Iberia and Low Countries *c.* 5000; Britain and southern Scandinavia *c.* 4000
c. 6000 BC		
c. 5000 BC		
c. 4000 BC		
c. 3000 BC	*c.* 3000 First agricultural settlements in southeast Asia	*c.* 3000 Spread of copper-working. Beginning of Greek Early Bronze Age
c. 2000 BC		
	c. 1500 Bronze Age in northeast Thailand and north Vietnam	*c.* 1600 Beginnings of Mycenaean civilization in Greece
		c. 1100 Earliest fortified hilltop sites in western Europe
c. 1000 BC		
c. 700 BC		753 Traditional date for foundation of Rome
	c. 660 Jimmu, legendary first emperor of Japan	
c. 600 BC	*c.* 650 Introduction of iron technology in China	
c. 500 BC		

NEAR EAST AND NORTH AFRICA	OTHER REGIONS	CULTURE AND TECHNOLOGY
c. 9000–8000 Evidence of domesticated cereals and pulses in the Levant – the "Neolithic revolution" – in the Near East; first permanent settlements *c.* 8350–7350 Jericho founded: first walled town in the world (4ha/10acres)	*c.* 9000 Southern tip of South America colonized	
c. 6000 Earliest cereal cultivation in north Africa		*c.* 6000 First known pottery and woollen textiles (Çatal Höyük)
c. 4000 Bronze casting begins in Near East; first use of plough *c.* 4000–3000 Desiccation of Sahara begins; north African populations expand south and east		
		c. 3500 Construction of Megalithic tombs and circles in Brittany, Iberian peninsula and British Isles (Stonehenge *c.* 2000). Invention of wheel and plough (Mesopotamia) and sail (Egypt) *c.* 3200 Earliest readable documents from Mesopotamia
c. 2686 The "Old Kingdom" (pyramid age) of Egypt begins (to 2181 BC) *c.* 2296 Sargon I of Agade founds first empire in world history	*c.* 3000 Maize first cultivated in Mesoamerica. First pottery in Americas (Ecuador and Colombia)	*c.* 3100 Pictographic writing invented in Sumer *c.* 2590 Cheops builds great pyramid at Giza *c.* 2500 Domestication of horse (central Asia)
	c. 2000 First metal-working in Peru. Settlement of Melanesia by immigrants from Indonesia begins	*c.* 2000 Use of sail on sea-going vessels (Aegean) *c.* 1500 Ideographic script in use in China; "Linear B" script in Crete and Greece; Hittite cuneiform in Anatolia *c.* 1450 Development of Brahma worship; composition of Vedas (earliest Indian literature) begins
c. 1200 Collapse of Hittite empire. Jewish exodus from Egypt and settlement in Palestine 1152 Death of Ramses III, last great pharaoh of Egypt		*c.* 1200 Beginning of Jewish religion (worship of Yahweh). Teachings of Zoroaster *c.* 1100 Phoenicians develop alphabetic script (basis of all modern European script) 776 Traditional date for first Olympic Games, in Greece
671 Assyrian conquest of Egypt; introduction of iron-working		
	c. 550 Iron use begins in sub-Saharan Africa. Bantu speakers expand southwards *c.* 500 Foundation of Zapotec capital, Monte Albán, in Mexico. Iron-making techniques spead to sub-Saharan Africa	*c.* 650 First coins: Lydia (Asia Minor) and Greece (*c.* 600). Rise of Greek lyric poetry (Sappho born *c.* 612) *c.* 551 Birth of Confucius *c.* 530 Pythagoras, mathematician and mystic, active *c.* 500 Achaemenid Persians transmit food plants (rice, peach, apricot, etc.) to western Asia. Caste system established in India. First hieroglyphic writing in Mexico (Monte Albán)

ASIA (excluding the Near East)   EUROPE

475–221 "Warring States" period
in China

431-404 Peloponnesian War between
Sparta and Athens

c. 400 BC

390 Sack of Rome by Gauls

c. 300 BC

290 Rome completes conquest of
c. 200 BC   central Italy

c. 100 BC   c. 112 Opening of "Silk Road" across
central Asia linking China to West

AD

AD 43 Roman invasion of Britain

AD 100

117 Roman empire at its greatest extent

165 Smallpox epidemic ravages
Roman empire

AD 200

212 Roman citizenship conferred on
all free inhabitants of empire
238 Gothic incursions into Roman
empire begin

280 China unified under Western China
AD 300   304 Hsiungnu invade China; China
fragmented to 589
320 Chandragupta I founds Gupta
empire in northern India

AD 400

AD 500   511 Huns rule northern India

NEAR EAST AND NORTH AFRICA	OTHER REGIONS	CULTURE AND TECHNOLOGY
		c. 486 Birth of Buddha
		479–338 Period of Greek classical culture: poetry, Pindar (518–438); drama, Sophocles (496–406), Euripides (480–406), history, Herodotus (c. 486–429), medicine, Hippocrates (c. 470–406); philosophy, Socrates (469–399), Plato (c. 437–347), Aristotle (384–322); sculpture, Phidias (c. 490–417)
		479 Death of Confucius
		447 Parthenon begun in Athens
334 Alexander the Great (of Macedon) invades Asia Minor; conquers Egypt (332), Persia (330) reaches India (327); death of Alexander: empire divided between Macedon, Egypt, Syria and Pergamum (323)		**350–200** Great period of Chinese thought: formation of Daoist, Legalist and Confucian schools; early scientific discoveries
304 Ptolemy I, Macedonian governor of Egypt, founds independent dynasty (to 30)		**312/311** Start of Seleucid era; first continuous historical dating-system
149 Third Punic War (149–146): Rome destroys Carthage and founds province of Africa	**100** Camel introduced into Saharan Africa	**277** Death of Ch'u Yuan (b. 343), earliest major Chinese poet
		46 Julius Caesar reforms calendar; Julian calendar in use until 1582 (England 1752, Russia 1917)
30 BC Death of Antony and Cleopatra: Egypt a Roman province		**31–14** The Augustan Age at Rome: Virgil (70–19), Horace (65–27), Ovid (43–17), Livy (59–17)
		c. 5 BC Birth of Jesus Christ
		c. AD 33 Jesus of Nazareth, founder of Christianity, crucified in Jerusalem
	c. AD 50 Expansion of kingdom of Aksum (Ethiopia) begins	**46–57** Missionary journeys of St Paul
70 Romans destroy the Jewish Temple in Jerusalem		**65** First Buddhist missionaries arrive in China
		105 First use of paper in China
132 Jewish rebellion against Rome leads to "diaspora" (dispersal of Jews)		**150** Earliest surviving Sanskrit inscription (India). Buddhism reaches China
		c. 200 Earliest Sanskrit writing in southeast Asia
224 Foundation of Sasanid dynasty in Persia		**c. 200–250** Development of Christian theology: Tertullian (c. 160–220), Clement (c. 150–c. 215), Origen (185–254)
	c. 250 Kingdom of Aksum gains control of Red Sea trade	**271** Magnetic compass in use (China)
		274 Unconquered Sun proclaimed god of Roman empire
		285 Confucianism introduced into Japan
	c. 300 Rise of Maya civilization in Mesoamerica; large civilized states in Mexico (Teotihuacán, Monte Albán, El Tajín). Settlement of eastern Polynesia	**c. 300** Foot-stirrup invented in Asia
		404 Latin version of Bible completed
		413 Kumaragupta; great literary era in India
429 Vandal kingdom in North Africa		**497** Franks converted to Christianity
		c. 520 Rise of mathematics in India: Aryabhata and Varamihara invent decimal system

	ASIA (excluding the Near East)	EUROPE
		c. 542 Bubonic plague ravages Europe
AD 600	589 China reunified by Sui dynasty 607 Unification of Tibet 617 China in state of anarchy 618 China united under T'ang dynasty (to 907)	610 Accession of East Roman Emperor Heraclius; beginning of Hellenization of (East) Roman empire, henceforth known as Byzantine empire
AD 700	658 Maximum extension of Chinese power in central Asia; protectorates in Afghanistan, Kashmir, Sogdiana and Oxus valley 712 Arabs conquer Sind and Samarkand	711 Muslim invasion of Spain
AD 800	842 Tibetan empire disintegrates	774 Charlemagne conquers northern Italy 793 Viking raids begin 800 Charlemagne crowned emperor in Rome; beginning of new Western (later Holy Roman) empire
AD 900	907 Last T'ang emperor deposed 939 Vietnam independent of China	
AD 1000		
AD 1100		1054 Schism between Greek and Latin Christian churches begins 1066 Norman conquest of England 1071 Fall of Bari completes Norman conquest of Byzantine Italy 1073 Gregory VII elected Pope: begin- ning of conflict of Empire and Papacy
	1126 Chin overrun northern China; Sung rule restricted to south	1154 Accession of Henry II: Angevin empire in England and France

NEAR EAST AND NORTH AFRICA

622 Hegira of Mohammed; beginning of Islamic calendar
632 Death of Mohammed: Arab expansion begins
636 Arabs overrun Syria; Iraq (637); conquer Egypt and begin conquest of North Africa (641)

717 Arab siege of Constantinople repulsed

936 Caliphs of Baghdad lose effective power
969 Fatimids conquer Egypt and found Cairo

1055 Seljuk Turks take Baghdad

1096 First Crusade: Franks invade Anatolia and Syria, and found crusader states

OTHER REGIONS

c. **600** Apogee of Maya civilization

c. **700** Rise of empire of Ghana. Decline of kingdom of Aksum. Teotihuacán destroyed

c. **850** Collapse of Classic Maya culture in Mesoamerica

c. **990** Expansion of Inca empire (Peru)
c. **1000** Vikings colonize Greenland and discover America (Vinland). First Iron Age settlement at Zimbabwe

CULTURE AND TECHNOLOGY

529 Rule of St Benedict regulates Western monasticism
c. **540** Silkworms brought into Byzantine empire from China
c. **550** Buddhism introduced into Japan from Korea
607 Chinese cultural influence in Japan begins
625 Mohammed begins his prophetic mission

c. **645** Buddhism reaches Tibet (first temple 651)
692 Completion of Dome of Rock in Jerusalem; first great monument of Islamic architecture
c. **700** Buddhist temples built at Nara, Japan. Golden age of Chinese poetry: Li Po (701–62), Tu Fu (712–70), Po Chü-i (772–846)
725 Bede (673–735) introduces dating by Christian era
c. **730** Printing in China
751 Paper-making spreads from China to Muslim world and Europe (1150)
760 Arabs adopt Indian numerals and develop algebra and trigonometry
782 Alcuin of York (735–804) organizes education in Carolingian empire: "Carolingian renaissance"
802 Foundation of Angkor, Cambodia
849 Pagan (Burma) founded
853 First printed book in China
863 Creation of Cyrillic alphabet in eastern Europe
865 Bulgars and Serbs accept Christianity
c. **890** Japanese cultural renaissance: novels, landscape painting and poetry
935 Text of *Koran* finalized

988 Foundation of Russian Church

c. **1000** Great age of Chinese painting and ceramics
c. **1045** Moveable type printing invented in China

c. **1100** First universities in Europe: Salerno (medicine), Bologna (law), Paris (theology and philosophy). Omar Khayyam composes *Rubaiyyat*
c. **1150** Hindu temple of Angkor Wat (Cambodia) built
1154 Chartres Cathedral begun; Gothic architecture spreads through western Europe

ASIA (excluding the Near East)	EUROPE
1175 Muhammad Ghuri invades India and begins the establishment of a Muslim empire *c.* **1180** Angkor empire (Cambodia) at greatest extent **1185** Battle of Dannoura (Japan): first shogunate founded	**1198** Innocent III elected Pope

AD **1200**

1206 Mongols under Genghis Khan begin conquest of Asia. Sultanate of Delhi founded	**1204** Fourth Crusade: Franks conquer Constantinople and found Latin empire **1215** Magna Carta: King John makes concessions to English barons
1234 Mongols destroy Chin empire	**1237** Mongols invade and conquer Russia (1238) **1250** Death of Emperor Frederick II: collapse of imperial power in Germany and Italy **1260** Expulsion of Jews from England
1264 Kublai Khan founds Yüan dynasty in China **1279** Mongols conquer southern China	**1261** Greek empire restored in Constantinople

AD **1300**

	1314 Battle of Bannockburn: Scotland defeats England **1315–17** Great Famine in northern Europe **1337** Hundred Years' War between France and England begins (to 1453)
c. **1342** "Black Death" starts in Asia	**1347** Black Death from Asia ravages Europe (to 1351) **1354** Ottoman Turks capture Gallipoli, gain first foothold in Europe
1368 Ming dynasty founded in China **1370** Hindu state of Vijayanagar dominant in south India **1392** Korea reduced to vassal status **1398** Tamerlane invades India and sacks Delhi	**1378** Great Schism in West (to 1417) **1389** Battle of Kosovo: Ottomans gain control of Balkans **1394** Expulsion of Jews from France

AD **1400**

1405 Chinese voyages in Indian Ocean begin	
1427 Chinese expelled from Vietnam	**1415** Battle of Agincourt: Henry V of England resumes attack on France **1428** Joan of Arc: beginning of French revival **1453** England loses Continental possessions (except Calais). Ottoman Turks capture Constantinople: end of Byzantine empire
1467–77 Onin Wars: Japan plunged into civil war	**1478** Ivan III, first Russian tsar, subdues Novgorod and throws off Mongol yoke (1480) **1492** Fall of Granada: end of Muslim rule in Spain; Jews expelled from Spain
1498 Vasco da Gama: first European sea-voyage to India and back	**1499–1552** Jews expelled from many German states

NEAR EAST AND NORTH AFRICA	OTHER REGIONS	CULTURE AND TECHNOLOGY
		c. 1160 Development of European vernacular verse: *Chanson de Roland* (*c.* 1100), *El Cid* (*c.* 1150), *Parzifal*, *Tristan* (*c.* 1200)
		1193 Zen Buddhist order founded in Japan
	c. 1200 Rise of empire of Mali in west Africa *c.* 1200 Emergence of Hausa city states (Nigeria). Aztecs occupy valley of Mexico 1200–1400 Buildings of Great Zimbabwe	*c.* 1215 Islamic architecture spreads to India
1258 Mongols sack Baghdad; end of Abbasid caliphate		
		1275 Marco Polo (1254–1324) arrives in China 1290 Spectacles invented (Italy)
1299 Ottoman Turks begin expansion in Anatolia		
		c. 1320 Cultural revival in Italy: Dante (1265–1321), Giotto (1276–1337), Petrarch (1304–71) 1339 Building of Kremlin (Moscow)
		c. 1350 Japanese cultural revival
	1375 Chimú conquest of central Andes begins	
1402 Battle of Ankara: Tamerlane defeats Ottomans in Anatolia		1400 Death of Chaucer, first great poet in English 1406 Death of Ibn Khaldun, Muslim historian
1415 Portuguese capture Ceuta: beginning of Portugal's African empire		
		1455 Johannes Gutenberg (1397–1468) prints first book in Europe using moveable type
	1470 Incas conquer Chimú kingdom	
	1487 Bartolomeu Dias rounds Cape of Good Hope 1492 Columbus reaches America: discovery of New World 1493 First Spanish settlement in New World (Hispaniola). Treaty of Tordesillas divides New World between Portugal and Spain 1497 Cabot reaches Newfoundland 1498 Columbus discovers South America	
1492 Spaniards begin conquest of north Africa coast		

	ASIA	EUROPE
AD **1500**	**1500** Shah Ismail founds Safavid dynasty in Persia	
		1519 Charles V, ruler of Spain and Netherlands, elected Holy Roman Emperor **1521** Martin Luther outlawed: beginning of Protestant Reformation. Suleiman the Magnificent, Ottoman sultan, conquers Belgrade **1534** Henry VIII of England breaks with Rome **1541** John Calvin founds reformed church at Geneva
		1562 Wars of Religion in France (to 1598)
		1588 Spanish Armada defeated by English **1598** "Time of Troubles" in Russia
AD **1600**	**1603** Beginning of Tokugawa shogunate in Japan	**1600** Foundation of English and Dutch (1602) East India Companies
		1609 Dutch Republic becomes independent
	1619 Foundation of Batavia (Jakarta) by Dutch: start of Dutch colonial empire in East Indies	**1618** Outbreak of Thirty Years' War
	1638 Russians reach Pacific **1644** Ming dynasty toppled; Manchus found new dynasty (Ch'ing)	**1642** English Civil War begins **1648** Peace of Westphalia ends Thirty Years' War **1667** Beginning of French expansion under Louis XIV
		1683 Turkish siege of Vienna
	1690 Foundation of Calcutta by English **1697** Chinese occupy Outer Mongolia	
AD **1700**		**1702** War of the Spanish Succession (to 1713) **1703** Foundation of St Petersburg, capital of Russian empire (1712)
	1707 Death of Aurangzeb: decline of Mughal power in India	**1707** Union of England and Scotland **1713** Treaty of Utrecht ends War of the Spanish Succession

AFRICA	AMERICAS AND AUSTRALASIA	CULTURE AND TECHNOLOGY
		c. **1500** Italian Renaissance: Leonardo da Vinci (1452–1519), Michelangelo (1475–1564), Raphael (1483–1520), Botticelli (1444–1510), Machiavelli (1469–1527), Ficino (1433–99)
1505 Portuguese establish trading posts in east Africa		
		1509 Watch invented by Peter Henle (Nuremberg)
	c. **1510** First African slaves to America **1519** Cortés begins conquest of Aztec empire (to 1520)	
	1520–1 Magellan crosses Pacific	
	1531 Pizarro begins conquest of Inca empire for Spain (to 1533)	**1539** Death of Kabir Nanak, founder of Sikh religion **1543** Copernicus publishes *Of the Revolution of Celestial Bodies* **1559** Tobacco first introduced into Europe *c.* **1565** Introduction of potato from South America to Europe
1571 Portuguese colony established in Angola **1578** Battle of Al-Kasr al-Kebir: Moroccans destroy Portuguese power in northwest Africa		
		1598 Shah Abbas I creates imperial capital at Isfahan
	1607 First permanent English settlement in America (Jamestown, Virginia) **1608** French colonists found Quebec	**1609** Telescope invented (Holland) *c.* **1610** Scientific revolution in Europe begins: Kepler (1571–1610), Bacon (1561–1626), Galileo (1564–1642), Descartes (1596–1650) **1616** Death of Shakespeare (*b.* 1564) and Cervantes (*b.* 1547)
	1620 Puritans land in New England (*Mayflower*) **1625** Dutch settle New Amsterdam	**1620** First weekly newspapers in Europe (Amsterdam)
		c. **1630** Apogee of Netherlands art: Hals (1580–1666), Rembrandt (1606–69), Vermeer (1632–75), Rubens (1577–1640) **1636** Foundation of Harvard College, first university in north America
	1645 Tasman circumnavigates Australia and discovers New Zealand	
1652 Foundation of Cape Colony by Dutch	**1664** New Amsterdam taken by English from Dutch (later renamed New York)	**1653** Taj Mahal, Agra, India, completed *c.* **1660** Classical period of French culture: drama, Molière (1622–73), Racine (1639–99), Corneille (1606–84); painting, Poussin (1594–1665), Claude (1600–82); music, Lully (1632–87), Couperin (1668–1733)
	1693 Gold discovered in Brazil	**1687** Isaac Newton's *Principia* **1690** John Locke's *Essay Concerning Human Understanding*
c. **1700** Rise of Ashanti power (Gold Coast)		*c.* **1700** Great age of German baroque music: Buxtehude (1637–1707), Handel (1685–1759), Bach (1685–1750)
	1718 New Orleans founded by France	

ASIA	EUROPE
	1740 War of the Austrian Succession (to 1748): Prussia annexes Silesia
1747 Ahmad Khan Abdali founds kingdom of Afghanistan	
1755 Alaungpaya founds Rangoon and reunites Burma (to 1824)	**1756** Seven Years War begins
1757 Battle of Plassey: British defeat French	
1761 Capture of Pondicherry; British destroy French power in India	
	1772 First Partition of Poland (Second and Third Partitions 1793, 1795)
	1774 Treaty of Kuchuk Kainarji: beginning of Ottoman decline
	1783 Russia annexes Crimea
	1789 French revolution begins; abolition of feudal system and proclamation of Rights of Man
1796 British conquer Ceylon	
	1799 Napoleon becomes First Consul and (1804) Emperor of France
	1805 Battle of Trafalgar: Britain defeats French and Spanish fleets
	1806 Abdication of Emperor Francis I; end of the Holy Roman Empire
	1807 Abolition of serfdom in Prussia
1813 British defeat the Marathas and become the effective rulers of India	**1812** Napoleon invades Russia; suffers catastrophic defeat. Last major outbreak of bubonic plague in Europe (to 1815)
1819 British found Singapore as free trade port	**1815** Napoleon defeated at Waterloo, exiled to St Helena. Congress of Vienna
	1821 Greek declaration of independence
1824 Treaty of London formalizes British control of Malaya and Dutch control of East Indies. British begin conquest of Burma and Assam	
1825–30 Java war: revolt of Indonesians against Dutch	
1830 Russia begins conquest of Kazakhstan (to 1854)	**1830** Revolutionary movements in France, Germany, Poland and Italy; Belgium wins independence. Greece independent
	1833 Slavery abolished in British empire.
	1834 Formation of German customs union, Zollverein

AD **1800**

AD **1825**

AFRICA	AMERICAS AND AUSTRALASIA	CULTURE AND TECHNOLOGY
c. **1730** Revival of ancient empire of Bornu (central Sudan)		*c.* **1735** Wahabite movement to purify Islam begins in Arabia
	1754 Renewed war between Britain and France for control of North America	
	1768 Cook begins exploration of Pacific	**1760** European enlightenment: Voltaire (1694–1778), Diderot (1713–84), Hume (1711–76) *c.* **1770** Advance of science and technology in Europe: J. Priestley (1733–1804), A. Lavoisier (1743–94), A. Volta (1745–1827), Harrison's chronometer (1762), Watt's steam engine (1765), Arkwright's water-powered spinning-frame (1769)
	1775 American revolution begins **1776** American Declaration of Independence **1778** France enters American War of Independence **1783** Treaty of Paris: Britain recognizes American independence **1788** British colony of Australia founded **1789** George Washington becomes first president of United States of America	**1776** Publication of *The Wealth of Nations* by Adam Smith (1723–90) and *Common Sense* by Tom Paine (1737–1809) **1781** Immanuel Kant's *Critique of Pure Reason*
1798 Napoleon attacks Egypt	**1803** Louisiana Purchase nearly doubles size of USA	**1792** Cartwright invents steam-powered weaving loom **1793** Decimal system introduced (France). **1796** Jenner discovers smallpox vaccine (UK) **1798** Malthus publishes *Essay on the Principle of Population*
1807 Slave trade abolished within British empire **1811** Mohammed Ali takes control in Egypt		
1818 Shaka forms Zulu kingdom in southeast Africa **1822** Liberia founded as colony for freed slaves	**1820** Missouri Compromise bans slavery north of 36 degrees 30 minutes	**1817** Foundation of Hindu college, Calcutta, first major centre of Western influence in India **1821** Electric motor and generator invented by M. Faraday (UK) **1822** First photographic image produced, by J.-N. Niepce (France) **1825** First passenger steam railway: Stockton and Darlington (UK) **1828** Foundation of Brahmo-samaj, Hindu revivalist movement
1830 French begin conquest of Algeria		**1832** Death of Goethe (born 1749) **1833** First regulation of industrial working conditions (UK)

	ASIA	EUROPE
	1839–42 First Opium War: Britain annexes Hong Kong	**1845** Irish famine (to 1849) stimulates hostility to Britain and emigration to USA **1846–7** Last major famine in Europe
AD **1850**	**1850** T'ai-p'ing rebellion in China (to 1846), with immense loss of life **1853** First railway and telegraph lines in India **1856–60** Second Opium War **1857** Indian Mutiny	**1852** Fall of French republic; Louis Napoleon (Napoleon III, 1803–73) becomes French emperor **1853** Crimean War (to 1855)
	1863 France establishes protectorate over Cambodia, Cochin China (1865), Annam (1874), Tonkin (1885) and Laos (1893)	
		1861 Emancipation of Russian serfs
		1864 Prussia defeats Denmark: annexes Schleswig-Holstein (1866). Russia suppresses Polish revolt
	1868 End of Tokugawa shogunate; Meiji restoration in Japan	
AD **1875**	**1877** Start of Tanzimat reform era in Ottoman empire. Queen Victoria proclaimed Empress of India **1879** Second Afghan War gives Britain control of Afghanistan	**1870** Franco-Prussian war **1871** Proclamation of German empire, beginning of Third French Republic: suppression of Paris commune **1875** Growth of labour/socialist parties: Germany (1875), Holland (1877), Belgium (1885), Britain (1893), Russia (1898) **1878** Congress of Berlin held; leads to the Treaty of Berlin: Romania, Montenegro and Serbia become independent and Bulgaria autonomous. **1879** Dual alliance between Germany and Austria-Hungary
	1885 Foundation of Indian National Congress	
		1890 Dismissal of Bismarck; Wilhelm II begins new policy
	1894–5 Russo-Japanese War: Japan occupies Formosa	**1894** Franco-Russian alliance

AFRICA	AMERICAS AND AUSTRALASIA	CULTURE AND TECHNOLOGY
		1838 First electric telegraph (UK)
	1840 Britain annexes New Zealand	**1840** First postage stamp (UK)
		1848 *Communist Manifesto* issued by Marx (1818–83) and Engels (1820–95)
		1849 Death of Chopin (*b.* 1810); apogee
1852 South African Republic (Transvaal) established by agreement between Britain and Boers	**1850** Australian colonies and (1856) New Zealand granted responsible government	of Romantic music with Berlioz (1803–69), Liszt (1811–86), Wagner (1813–83), Brahms (1833–97), Verdi (1813–1901)
1853 Livingstone's explorations begin		**1855** Bessemer process permits mass-production of steel
		1859 Darwin publishes *The Origin of Species*
1860 French expansion in west Africa from Senegal	**1860** Abraham Lincoln US president; South secedes	*c.* **1860** Great age of European novel: Dickens (1812–70), Dumas (1802–70), Flaubert (1821–80), Turgenev (1818–83), Dostoyevsky (1821–81), Tolstoy (1828–1910)
	1861 Outbreak of American Civil War	**1861** Pasteur evolves germ theory of disease. Women first given vote (Australia)
	1863 Slavery abolished in USA	**1863** First underground railway (London)
	1864 War of Paraguay against Argentina, Brazil and Uruguay (to 1870)	
	1865 End of American Civil War	**1867** Marx publishes *Das Kapital* (vol. 1)
1869 Suez canal opens		**1869** First trans-continental railroad completed (USA)
		1870 Declaration of Papal infallibility
		1874 First electric tram (New York); telephone patented by Bell (USA 1876); first electric streetlighting (London 1878)
1875 Disraeli buys Suez Canal Company shares to ensure British control of sea route to India		
		1878 First oil tanker built (Russia)
	1879 War of the Pacific (Chile, Bolivia, Peru)	
1881 French establish protectorate over Tunisia		
1882 Revolt in Egypt leading to British occupation		
1884 Berlin Conference on the partition of Africa. Germany acquires SW Africa, Togoland, Cameroons		*c.* **1885** Daimler and Benz pioneer the automobile (Germany)
1886 Germany and Britain partition east Africa	**1888** Brazil becomes last Latin American country to abolish slavery	**1888** Dunlop invents pneumatic tyre
		c. **1890** Beginnings of modern literature in Japan on Western models. Europe – realistic drama: Ibsen (1828–1906), Strindberg (1849–1912), Chekhov (1860–1904), Shaw (1856–1950)
		1891–1905 Trans-Siberian railway built
		1895 Röntgen discovers X-rays (Germany); first public showing of motion picture (France)
		1896 Marconi builds first radio transmitter. Herzl publishes The *Jewish State* calling for Jewish National Home

	ASIA	EUROPE
AD 1900	1898 Abortive "Hundred Days" reform in China	1898 Germany embarks on naval building programme: beginning of German "world policy"
	1904 Partition of Bengal: nationalist agitation in India 1904–5 Russo-Japanese War; Japanese success stimulates Asian nationalism	1904 Anglo-French entente 1905 Revolution in Russia, followed by tsarist concessions. Norway independent of Sweden 1907 Anglo-Russian entente
	1910 Japan annexes Korea 1915–16 Armenian massacres in Turkey	1912–13 Balkan wars: Turkey loses bulk of remaining European territory 1914 Outbreak of First World War 1915 Italy enters war on the side of the Allies 1917 Revolution in Russia: tsar abdicates (February), Bolsheviks take over (October); first socialist state established 1918 Treaty of Brest-Litovsk; Russia withdraws from First World War. Germany and Austria-Hungary sue for armistice (November): end of First World War. Civil war and foreign intervention in Russia
	1919 Amritsar incident; upsurge of Indian nationalism 1920 Mustafa Kemal (Atatürk) leads resistance to partition of Turkey; Turkey Nationalist Movement 1920–2 Gandhi leads Indian non-cooperation movement 1922 Greek army expelled from Turkey; last Ottoman sultan deposed; republic proclaimed (1923) 1926 Chiang Kai-shek begins reunification of China	1919 Paris treaties redraw map of Europe 1920 League of Nations established (headquarters Geneva) 1921 Lenin introduces New Economic Policy 1922 Mussolini takes power in Italy 1924 Death of Lenin; Stalin eventually emerges as Soviet leader (1929) 1925 Locarno treaties stabilize frontiers in west 1928 First Five-Year Plan and (1929) collectivization of agriculture in USSR
AD 1925	1930–1 Civil disobedience campaign in India (and in 1932–4) 1932 Iraq independent. Kingdom of Saudi Arabia formed by Ibn Saud 1934 "Long March" of Chinese communists begins 1935 Government of India Act: Indians gain provincial autonomy	1931 Collapse of central European banks begins major recession 1933 Hitler made Chancellor in Germany; beginning of Nazi revolution
	1936 Japan signs anti-Comintern pact with Germany. Arab revolt in Palestine against Jewish immigration 1937 Beginning of full-scale war between Japan and China	1936 German reoccupation of Rhineland. Spanish Civil War begins (to 1939). "Great Terror" launched by Stalin in Russia 1938 Germany occupies Austria. Munich conference: Czechoslovakia dismembered

AFRICA

1899 The South African ("Boer War") begins (to 1902): Britain conquers Boer republics, Transvaal and Orange Free State
1900 Copper mining begins in Katanga

1905 First Moroccan crisis

1908 Belgian state takes over Congo from King Leopold
1911 Italy conquers Libya

1914–15 French and British conquer German colonies except German East Africa

1922 Egypt independent

1935–6 Italy conquers Abyssinia

1936 Anglo-Egyptian alliance; British garrison Suez Canal Zone

AMERICAS AND AUSTRALASIA

1898 Spanish-American war: USA annexes Guam, Puerto Rico and Philippines

1901 Commonwealth of Australia created

1907 Peak year for immigration into USA. New Zealand acquires dominion status
1910 Mexican revolution begins

1914 Panama canal opens

1917 USA declares war on Central Powers

1918 President Wilson announces "Fourteen Points"

1921 USA restricts immigration

1923 General Motors established: world's largest manufacturing company

1929 Wall Street crash precipitates Great Depression
1930 Military revolution in Brazil; Vargas becomes president

1933 US President Franklin D. Roosevelt introduces New Deal

1935 Cárdenas president of Mexico: land redistribution and (1938) nationalization of oil
1936 Pan-American congress; USA proclaims "good neighbour" policy

CULTURE AND TECHNOLOGY

1898 Pierre and Marie Curie observe radioactivity and isolate radium (France)

1900 Planck evolves quantum theory (Germany). Freud's *Interpretation of Dreams*, beginning of psychoanalysis (Austria)
1901 First wireless message sent across Atlantic
1903 First successful flight of petrol-powered aircraft (Wright Brothers, USA)

1910 Development of abstract painting: Kandinsky (1866–1944), Mondrian (1872–1944). Development of plastics

1917 First use of massed tanks (Battle of Cambrai)

1919 Rutherford (1871–1973) splits atom (UK). Bauhaus school of design at Weimar (Germany). First crossing of Atlantic by air (Alcock and Brown)

1923 Development of tuberculosis vaccine (France)
1927 Emergence of talking pictures. Rise of great film makers: D. W. Griffith (1874–1948), Chaplin (1889–1977), John Ford (1895–1973), Eisenstein (1896–1948), Clair (1898–1981), Hitchcock (1899–1980), Disney (1901–66)

1936 First regular public television transmissions (UK)

1937 Jet engine first tested (UK); invention of nylon (USA)

	ASIA	EUROPE
	1939 Russian forces defeat Japan at Khalkin Gol (Manchuria); Russo-Japanese neutrality pact (1941)	**1939** Germany occupies Czechoslovakia; Germany-Soviet non-aggression pact; Germany invades Poland; Britain and France declare war on Germany
		1940 Germany overruns Norway, Denmark, Belgium, Netherlands, France; Italy invades Greece but is repulsed; Battle of Britain
	1941 Japan attacks USA at Pearl Harbor; USA declares war	**1941** Germany invades Russia; declares war on USA. "Final solution" initiated by Nazis
	1942 Japan overruns SE Asia. Battle of Midway: USA halts Japanese expansion. Gandhi and Indian Congress leaders arrested	**1943** German VI army surrenders at Stalingrad; Italian capitulation
		1944 Anglo-American landing in Normany; Russian advance in E Europe
	1945 USA drops atom bombs on Japan, forcing surrender	**1945** Yalta Conference; defeat of Germany and suicide of Hitler
	1946 Civil war in China (to 1949). Creation of Philippine Republic. Beginning of Vietnamese struggle against France (to 1954)	
	1947 India and Pakistan partitioned and granted independence	**1947** Development of Cold War; Truman Doctrine enunciated. Marshall Plan for economic reconstruction in Europe
		1948 Communist takeover in Czechoslovakia and Hungary; Berlin airlift (to 1949). Split between Yugoslavia under Tito and USSR
	1949 Communist victory in China; Chiang Kai-shek retreats to Formosa (Taiwan). Indonesia independent	**1949** USSR tests its first atomic bomb. Formation of NATO alliance and of COMECON
AD 1950	**1950** China invades Tibet. Korean War begins (to 1953)	
	1951 USA ends occupation of Japan	
		1953 Death of Stalin; East Berlin revolt crushed
	1954 Geneva conference: Laos, Cambodia and Vietnam become independent states	**1955** Warsaw Pact signed
		1956 Soviet leader Khrushchev denounces Stalin at Party Congress. Polish revolt, Gomulka in power. Hungarian revolt crushed by Russians
		1957 Treaty of Rome: Formation of EEC and (1959) of European Free Trade Association
		1958 Fifth Republic in France: de Gaulle first president
	1961 Increasing US involvement in Vietnam	**1961** East Germans build Berlin Wall
	1962 Sino-Indian war	
	1964 China tests first atomic bomb	**1964** Khrushchev ousted as Soviet leader; succeeded by Leonid Brezhnev

AFRICA	AMERICAS AND AUSTRALASIA	CULTURE AND TECHNOLOGY
		1939 Development of penicillin (UK). Development of DDT (Switzerland)
1940–1 Italians expelled from Somalia, Eritrea and Ethiopia		
1941 Germans conquer Cyrenaica and advance into Egypt (1942) **1942** Battle of El-Alamein; German defeat and retreat. Anglo-American landings in Morocco and Algeria. Apartheid programme inaugurated in S Africa	**1941** USA enters war against Germany and Japan	**1942** Fermi builds first nuclear reactor (USA)
	1945 Death of Roosevelt; Harry Truman US president. United Nations established (headquarters New York) **1946** Perón comes to power in Argentina	**1945** Atom bomb first exploded (USA) **1946** First electronic computer built (USA)
		1947 First supersonic flight (USA)
		1948 Transistor invented (USA)
1952 Beginning of Mau Mau rebellion in Kenya.	**1951** Australia, New Zealand and USA sign ANZUS pact	**1951** First nuclear power stations **1952** Hydrogen bomb first exploded (USA). Contraceptive pill developed (USA) **1953** Crick and Watson explain structure of DNA (UK)
1954 Beginnings of nationalist revolt in Algeria (to 1962) **1956** Suez crisis: Anglo-French invasion of Canal Zone	**1955** Overthrow of Perón regime in Argentina	**1956** Beginning of rock and roll music (USA): Elvis Presley (1935–77)
1957 Beginning of decolonization in sub-Saharan Africa: Gold Coast (Ghana) becomes independent		**1957** First space satellite launched (USSR)
1960 "Africa's year"; many states become independent; outbreak of civil war in former Belgian Congo. Sharpeville massacre in South Africa **1961** South Africa becomes independent republic **1962** Algeria becomes independent **1963** Nationalist uprising against Portuguese rule in Angola	**1959** Fidel Castro takes power after Cuban insurgency	**1961** First man in space: Gagarin (USSR)
	1962 Cuban missile crisis **1963** Kennedy assassinated; Lyndon Johnson succeeds (to 1968) **1964** US Civil Rights Act inaugurates President Johnson's "Great Society" programme	

ASIA	EUROPE
1966 Cultural Revolution in China (to 1976) **1967** Third Arab-Israeli war (Six-Day War) **1968** Vietcong launch Tet offensive in Vietnam	
1971 Indo-Pakistan war leads to break-away of East Pakistan (Bangladesh)	
1973 US forces withdraw from South Vietnam. Fourth Arab-Israeli war; OPEC countries triple oil price	**1973** Oil crisis ends post-war economic boom. Britain, Ireland and Denmark join EEC
1975 Civil war in Lebanon: Syria invades (1976). Communists take over Vietnam, Laos and Cambodia **1976** Death of Mao Zedong; paves way for economic re-orientation and modernization under Deng Xiaoping **1977** Egypt/Israeli peace talks (Camp David Peace Treaty, 1978). Military coup ends democratic rule in Pakistan **1978** Vietnam invades Cambodia **1979** Fall of shah of Iran, establishment of Islamic Republic under Ayatollah Khomeini (*d.* 1989). Afghanistan invaded by USSR (to 1989). Sino-Vietnamese War. Vietnam expels Khmer Rouge government from Cambodia **1980** Outbreak of Iran/Iraq War (to 1988)	**1975** Death of Franco; end of dictatorship in Spain **1980** Death of Marshal Tito. Creation of independent Polish trade union Solidarity; martial law (1981) **1981** Greece joins EEC **1982** Death of USSR president, Brezhnev, succession of Yuri Andropov (*d.* 1984), then Konstantin Chernenko (*d.* 1985)
1984 Indira Gandhi assassinated **1985** Israel withdraws from Lebanon **1986** Fall of Marcos in the Phillipines; Cory Aquino succeeds **1988** Benazir Bhutto restores civilian rule in Pakistan. Palestine uprising (*intifada*) against Israeli occupied territories. PLO recognizes State of Israel **1989** Death of Ayatollah Khomeini. Student pro-democracy demonstration crushed in Beijing **1990** Iraq invades Kuwait **1991** Gulf War: UN Coalition forces led by USA attack Iraq and liberate Kuwait; Rajiv Gandhi assassinated	**1985** Mikhail Gorbachev leader of USSR (to 1991) **1986** Spain and Portugal join EEC **1988** Gorbachev introduces glasnost and perestroika in USSR **1989** Communist bloc in E Europe disintegrates; Berlin Wall demolished **1990** Reunification of Germany **1991** Boris Yeltsin elected president of Russian Federation; USSR disintegrates; Disintegration of Yugoslavia; Slovenia and Croatia declare independence

AD **1975**

AFRICA	AMERICAS AND AUSTRALASIA	CULTURE AND TECHNOLOGY
	1966 Eruption of Black American discontent; growth of Black Power	
	1968 Assassinations of Martin Luther King and Robert Kennedy; R.M. Nixon elected US president	**1968** World-wide student protest movement
	1970 Allende elected president of Chile (killed 1973)	**1969** First man lands on moon: Armstrong (USA)
	1971 USA initiates policy of detente with China and USSR. USA abandons Gold Standard and depreciates dollar	
	1972 President Nixon visits China	
	1973 Overthrow of Allende regime in Chile. Major recession in USA triggered by oil crisis	
1974 Emperor Haile Selassie of Ethiopia deposed by Marxist junta	**1974** President Nixon resigns after Watergate scandal; Gerald Ford succeeds	
1975 Portugal grants independence to Mozambique and Angola		
1976 Morocco and Mauritania partition Spanish Sahara. Unrest in Soweto, South Africa, suppressed	**1976** Jimmy Carter elected US president	**1976** First supersonic trans-Atlantic passenger service begins with Concorde
1979 Tanzanian forces invade Uganda and expel President Amin	**1979** Civil war in Nicaragua (to 1990). Civil war in El Salvador (to 1992)	
1980 Black majority rule established in Zimbabwe (Rhodesia)	**1980** Ronald Reagan elected US president	**1980s** Computer revolution: spread of computers in offices and homes in Western world
1981 President Sadat of Egypt assassinated		**1981** First re-usable shuttle space flight (USA)
	1982 Argentina occupies South Georgia and Falkland Islands; surrenders to UK forces	
	1983 Democracy restored in Argentina. USA invades Grenada	
1984 Famine in Sahel and Ethiopia; continuing war against secession	**1985** Democracy restored in Brazil, Bolivia and Uruguay	
1986 USA bombs Libya in retaliation for terrorist activities	**1987** INF treaty between USSR and USA: phased elimination of intermediate-range nuclear weapons. US stock market crash	**1986** Launch of world's first permanently manned space station (USSR). Major nuclear disaster at Chernobyl power reactor (Ukraine). US space shuttle *Challenger* explodes
	1989 Democracy restored in Chile	**1987** World population reaches 5 billion
	1989–90 US military intervention in Panama; arrest and extradition of Manuel Noriega	**1988** Global recognition that ozone layer is being depleted; global ban on CFCs (chlorofluorocarbons) (1990)
1990 Namibia independent; S African government moves towards accommodation with ANC, frees Nelson Mandela, and (1991) announces intention to dismantle apartheid		**1990** Voyager space probe mission completed

ASIA

EUROPE

1993 Israel and PLO sign Palestinian autonomy agreement for limited Palestinian self-rule

1992 Civil War in Bosnia-Herzegovina; Czech Republic and Slovakia emerge as separate states

AD **2000**

1997 Hong Kong returned to China;
1998 India and Pakistan carry out nuclear tests
1999 Civil war in East Timor ends in independence from Indonesia

1999 European single currency (euro) launched; NATO campaign against Serbia over Kosovo

2001 Taliban regime overthrown in Afghanistan
2002 India and Pakistan near war over Kashmir; Sri Lankan civil war ended; Terrorist bombing in Bali

2002 NATO enlargement includes states from former communist bloc

2003 SARS virus outbreak; US-led coalition attacks Iraq and topples Saddam Hussein
2004 Religious civil war in Iraq
2004 Tsunami kills 150,000 in Indian Ocean area
2005 Iraq granted limited sovereignty
2006 Israel attacks Lebanon
2006 Trial and execution of Saddam Hussein
2006–7 Confrontation with Iran over nuclear programme

2003 European Constitution drafted

2004 EU enlargement takes in ten new states; terrorist bombing in Madrid; Vladimir Putin re-elected Russian president

2007 Bulgaria and Romania join European Union

2008 Earthquake kills more than 55,000 in Sichuan province, China; cyclone kills more than 80,000 in Burma

2008 Former Bosnian Serb leader Radovan Karadzic arrested for war crimes

AFRICA

1992 US forces intervene to end Somalia's famine and civil war; Prolonged terrorism in Algeria after elections are cancelled
1994 Nelson Mandela elected as South Africa's first black president; up to one million Tutsis and moderate Hutus massacred by Hutu extremists in Rwanda

1999 Thabo Mbeki elected President of South Africa; seizure of white-owned farms in Zimbabwe

2002 End of Angolan civil war; Sierra Leone civil war ended by UK intervention; civil war in Côte d'Ivoire
2003– continuing civil war in Darfur

2004 ANC wins landslide victory in South Africa; Libya agrees to abandon weapons of mass destruction

2007 Refugee crisis in Chad
2007 Islamic regime in Mogadishu overthrown
2007– Political crisis in Zimbabwe

AMERICAS AND AUSTRALASIA

1992 Bill Clinton elected US president

1994 US military intervention in Haiti

1998 USA bombs Afghanistan and Sudan after terrorist attacks on US embassies in Kenya and Tanzania
2000 George W. Bush elected US President
2001 Al Qaeda attacks on World Trade Center and Pentagon

2003 Bush declares global "War on Terror"; USA intervenes in Haiti coup

2007 Washington Declaration on global environment

2008 Raul Castro succeeds his brother Fidel as Cuban president

CULTURE AND TECHNOLOGY

1994 Cross-Channel rail link between Britain and France inaugurated
mid-1990s Growth of world-wide web

1997 Kyoto global warming agreement

2000 First successful animal cloning; entire human genome sequenced

2003 Space probe finds water on Mars
2003 First video-phone

2004 Olympic Games return to Greece

2005 Death of Pope John Paul II
2005 *Harry Potter and the Half-Blood Prince* becomes the world's fastest-selling book – over 9 million copies in 24 hours
2007 Scientists create first image of the 'dark matter' of the universe
2007 First artificial sperm cells created

2008 China host Olympics

BIBLIOGRAPHY

HISTORY ATLASES

Atlas zur Geschichte, 2 vols, Leipzig 1976

Bazilevsky, K V, Golubtsov, A & Zinoviev, M A *Atlas Istorii SSR*, Moscow 1952

Beckingham, C F *Atlas of the Arab World and the Middle East*, London 1960

Bertin, J (*et al.*) *Atlas of Food Crops*, Paris 1971

Bjørklund, O, Holmboe, H & Røhr *A Historical Atlas of the World*, Edinburgh 1970

Cappon, L (*et al.*) *Atlas of Early American History*, Chicago 1976

Channon, J *The Penguin Historical Atlas of Russia*, London 1995

Darby, H C, Fullard, H (eds) *The New Cambridge Modern History*, vol. XIV: *Atlas*,
   Cambridge 1970

Davies, C C *An Historical Atlas of the Indian Peninsula*, London 1959

Engel, J (ed.) *Grosser Historischer Weltatlas*, 3 vols, Munich 1953–70

Fage, J D *An Atlas of African History*, London 1958

Fernández-Armesto, F (ed.) *The Times Atlas of World Exploration*, London 1991

Gilbert, M *Russian History Atlas*, London 1972

Gilbert, M *Recent History Atlas 1860–1960*, London 1966

Gilbert, M *First World War Atlas*, London 1970

Gilbert, M *Jewish History Atlas*, London 1969

Haywood, J (ed.) *The Cassell Atlas of World History*, London 1997

Hazard, H W *Atlas of Islamic History*, Princeton 1952

Herrmann, *A Historical and Commercial Atlas of China*, Harvard 1935

Herrmann, A *An Historical Atlas of China*, Edinburgh 1966

Jedin, H, Latourette, K S & Martin, J *Atlas zur Kirchengeschichte*, Freiburg 1970

Kinder, H & Hilgemann, W *Atlas zur Weltgeschichte* 2 vols, Stuttgart 1964 (published in English as *The Penguin Atlas of World History*, London 1974 & 1978)

Magosci, P R *Historical Atlas of East Central Europe*, Toronto, revised edn 1995

Matsui & Mori *Ajiarekishi chizu*, Tokyo 1965

May, H G (ed.) *Oxford Bible Atlas*, Oxford 1974

Mackay, A & Ditchburn, D (eds) *Atlas of Medieval Europe*, London 1997

McNeill, W H, Buske, M R & Roehm, A W *The World . . . its History in Maps*, Chicago 1969

Nelson's Atlas of the Early Christian World, London 1959

Nelson's Atlas of the Classical World, London 1959

Nelson's Atlas of World History, London 1965

Nihon rekishi jiten Atlas vol., Tokyo 1959

Palmer, R R (ed.) *Atlas of World History*, Chicago 1965

Paullin, C O *Atlas of the Historical Geography of the United States*, Washington 1932

Ragi al Faruqi, I (ed.) *Historical Atlas of the Religions of the World*, New York 1974

Roolvink, R *Historical Atlas of the Muslim Peoples*, London 1957

Scarre, C (ed.) *Past Worlds: The Times Archaeology of the World*, London 1999

Schwartzberg, J E (ed.) *A Historical Atlas of South Asia*, Chicago 1978

The Times Atlas of European History, 2nd edn, London 1997

Toynbee, A J & Mers, E D *A Study of History, Historical Atlas and Gazetteer*, Oxford 1959

Treharne, R F & Fullard, H (eds) *Muir's Historical Atlas*, London 1966

Tubinger Atlas der Vorderen Orients, Wiesbaden (various vols) since 1972

Van der Heyden, A M & Scullard, H H *Atlas of the Classical World*, London 1959

Wesley, E B *Our United States . . . its History in Maps*, Chicago 1977

Westermann Grosser Atlas zur Weltgeschichte, Brunswick 1976

Whitehouse, D & R *Archaeological Atlas of the World*, London 1975

Wilgus, A C *Latin America in Maps*, New York 1943

GENERAL WORKS

Abu-Lughod, J L *Before European Hegemony: The World System AD 1250–1350*, Oxford 1991

Ajayi, J F A & Crowder, M *History of West Africa*, 2 vols, 3rd edn. 1988

Allchin, B & R *The Birth of Indian Civilization*, London 1968

Atkinson, A *The Europeans and Australia*, vol. 1, Melbourne 1997

Australia, Commonwealth of, Department of National Development, *Atlas of Australian Resources*, 3rd series 1980

Bakewell, P J *A History of Latin America: Empires and Sequels, 1450–1930*, Malden Mass. 1997

Bartlett, R *The Making of Europe: Conquest, Colonization and Cultural Change 950–1350*, London 1993

Basham, A L *The Wonder That Was India*, 2 vols, 3rd revised, London 1987

Belich, J *Making Peoples*, Allen Lane, Auckland 1996

Belich, J *Paradise Reforged*, Allen Lane, Auckland 2001

Bellwood, P *Prehistory of the Indo-Malay Archipelago*, Ryde, NSW 1985

Berdan, F F & Anawalt, P R *The Codex Mendoz* (4 vols), University of California Press, Berkeley 1992

Bethel, L (ed.) *The Cambridge History of Latin America*, 11 vols, Cambridge 1984–95

Beresford, M *New Towns of the Middle Ages*, London 1967

Boardman, J (ed.) *The Oxford History of the Classical World*, Oxford 1989

Bolton, G (ed.) *The Oxford History of Australia*, vol. V, 2nd edn, Melbourne 1996

Bonney, R *The European Dynastic States 1494–1660*, Oxford 1991

Braudel, F *The Mediterranean and the Mediterranean World in the Age of Philip II*, 2 vols, London 1972–3

Brown, C (ed.) *Illustrated History of Canada*, Key Porter, Toronto 2002

Brown, P *The Rise of Western Christendom: Triumph and Diversity 200–1000*, Oxford 1996

Burkholder, M A & Johnson, L L *Colonial Latin America* (4th edn), Oxford University Press 2001

Bury, J B, Cook, S A & Adcock, F E (eds) *The Cambridge Ancient History*, Cambridge 1923–; 2nd edn 1982

Cameron, A M *The Mediterranean World in Late Antiquity AD 395–600*, London 1993

Campbell, P R *Louis XIV*, London 1994

Chang, K C *The Archaeology of Ancient China*, 4th edn, New Haven 1986

Chaudhuri, K N *Trade and Civilization in the Indian Ocean: An Economic History From the Rise of Islam to 1750*, Cambridge 1985

Chaudhuri, K N *Asia Before Europe: Economy and Civilization of the Indian Ocean from the Rise of Islam to 1750*, Cambridge 1991

Chungse Omunsŏn (ed.) *"Hunmin chŏngŏm Onhae"*. In *Han'gukŏ munhakho*, Hyŏngsŏl ch'ulp'ansa, Seoul 1988

Cook, M A (ed.) *A History of the Ottoman Empire to 1730*, Cambridge 1976

Coward, B *The Stuart Age*, London, 2nd edn 1996

Crowder, M *West Africa Under Colonial Rule*, London 1968

Cunliffe, B (ed.) *The Oxford Illustrated Prehistory of Europe*, Oxford 1994

Curtin, P D *The Atlantic Slave Trade*, Madison 1972

Curtin, P D *Cross-cultural Trade in World History*, Cambridge 1984

Dalton, B J *War and Politics in New Zealand, 1855–1870*, Sydney 1967

D'Altroy, T N *The Incas*, Blackwell, Oxford 2002

Darby, H C (ed.) *An Historical Geography of England Before AD 1800*, Cambridge 1936 & 1960

Daniels, P & Lever, W *The Global Economy in Transition*, London 1996

Davis, R W *The Industrialization of Soviet Russia*, 3 vols, Cambridge 1989

Demand, N *A History of Ancient Greece*, New York 1996

Denoon, D, (*et al.*) *The Cambridge History of the Pacific Islanders*, Cambridge University Press 1997

East, W G *The Geography Behind History*, London 1965

East, W G *An Historical Geography of Europe*, 5th edn. London 1967

Eckert, C J, (*et al.*) *Korea old and new: a history*, Ilchokak Publishers (for the Korea Institute, Harvard University), Seoul 1990

Edwardes, M *A History of India*, London 1961

Ettinghausen, R. & Grabar, O *The Art and Architecture of Islam, 650–1250*, Pelican Books 1987

Fage, J D & Oliver, R (eds) *Cambridge History of Africa*, Cambridge 1975–86

Ferguson, J *The Heritage of Hellenism*, London 1973

Ferrier, R W *A Journey to Persia: Jean Chardin's Portrait of a Seventeenth Century Empire*, London 1996

Fisher, C A *South-East Asia*, London 1964

Flannery, T *The Future Eaters: An Ecological History of the Australasian Lands and People*, Reed Books, Sydney 1995

Fletcher, A *Tudor Rebellions*, 3rd edn, London 1983

Flood, J *Archaeology of the Dreamtime*, Angus & Robertson, Sydney 1994

Floor, W *Safavid Government Institutions*, Costa Mesa C., 2001

Frye, R N *The Golden Age of Persia*, Weidenfeld 1993

Geelan, P J M & Twitchett, D C (eds) *The Times Atlas of China*, London 1974

Gernet, J *Le Monde Chinois*, Paris 1969; English translation 1982

Goodman, J & Honeyman, K *Gainful Pursuits: The Making of Industrial Europe 1600–1914*, London 1988

Goodwin, G *A History of Ottoman Architecture*, Thames and Hudson 1971

Graff, E & Hammond, H E *Southeast Asia: History, Culture, People*, 5th revised edn, Cambridge 1980

Grousset, R *The Empire of the Steppes: A History of Central Asia*, New Brunswick NJ 1970

Guillermaz, J *Histoire du Parti Communiste Chinois*, Paris 1968; English translation 1972

Hall, D G E *A History of South-East Asia*, 4th edn, London 1981

Hallam, E *Capetian France 987–1328*, London 1980

Harlan, J R "The Plants and Animals that Nourish Man", *Scientific American* 1976

Harlan, J R & Zohary, D "The Distribution of Wild Wheats and Barleys", *Science* 1966

Harley, J B & Woodward, D *The History of Cartography*, 2 vols, Chicago 1987–

Hatton, R M *Europe in the Age of Louis XIV*, London 1969

Hawke, G R *The Making of New Zealand: An Economic History*, Cambridge 1985

Henderson, W O *Britain and Industrial Europe, 1750–1870*, Liverpool 1965

Higham, C F W *The Archaeology of Mainland Southeast Asia from 10000 BC to the Fall of Angkor*, Cambridge 1989

Higham, C F W & Thosarat, R *Prehistoric Thailand from Early Settlement to Sukhothai*, Bangkok 1999

Hillenbrand, C *The Crusades: Islamic Perspectives*, Edinburgh 1999

Historical Atlas of Canada, Vols 1–3, University of Toronto Press, Toronto 1987–93

Holt, P M *The Age of the Crusades*, Longman 1986

Hopkins, A G *Economic History of West Africa*, London 1973

Hørai, S *DNA jinrui shinkagaku, Iwanami shoten*, Tokyo 1997

Hornung, E *History of Ancient Egypt*, Edinburgh University Press 1999

Horton, D (ed.) *Encyclopedia of Aboriginal Australia*, Aboriginal Studies Press, Canberra 1994

Hourani, A *A History of the Arab People*, Harvard 1991

Howe, K *Where the Waves Fall: A New South Sea Islands History from First Settlement to Colonial Rule*, Allen & Unwin, Sydney 1984

Inalcik, H *The Ottoman Empire: The Classical Age, 1300–1600*, reprint, London 1989

Inikori, J E & Engerman, S L *The Atlantic Slave Trade: Effects on Economy, Society, and Population in Africa, America, and Europe*, Durham, NC 1992

Jeans, D N *An Historical Geography of New South Wales to 1901*, Sydney 1972

Jennings, J D *Prehistory of North America*, 3rd edn, Mountain View, CAS 1989

Johnson, G (ed.) *New Cambridge History of India*, Cambridge 1989–

Jones, G *The Evolution of International Business*, London 1996

Josephy, A M (ed.) *America in 1492: the World of the Indian Peoples before the Arrival of Columbus*, New York 1992

Kahan, A *Russian Economic History*, Chicago 1991

Kelly, P *The End of Certainty*, Sydney 1992

Kennedy, H *Muslim Spain and Portugal*, Longman 1996

Kennedy, H *The Prophet and the Age of the Caliphates*, Longman 2004

Kennedy, J A *History of Malaya, 1400–1959*, London 1967

Kinross, Lord P *The Ottoman Centuries*, Jonathan Cape 1977

Koeningsberger, H G, Mosse, G L & Bowler, G Q *Europe in the 16th Century*, 2nd edn, London 1989

Kuhrt, A T L *The Ancient Near East* c. *3000–330 BC*, London 1995

Laird, C E *Language in America*, New York 1970

Lambton, K S *A History of Qajar Persia*, London 1987

Landes, D *The Wealth and Poverty of Nations*, London 1998

Langer, W L (ed.) *An Encyclopedia of World History*, revised edn, London 1987

Lapidus, I M *A History of Islamic Societies*, Cambridge 1988

Lattimore, O *Inner Asian Frontiers of China*, New York 1951

Lossky, A *Louis XIV and the French Monarchy*, London 1995

Lyashchenko, P I *History of the National Economy of Russia to the 1917 Revolution*, New York 1949

Macintyre, S *A Concise History of Australia*, Melbourne 1999

Macmillan's *Atlas of South-East Asia*, London 1988

Majumdar, R C *The Vedic Age*, Bombay 1951

Majumdar, R C *History and Culture of the Indian People, Age of Imperial Unity*, Bombay 1954

Mantran, R *Histoire de l'Empire Ottoman*, Paris 1989

McCarthy, J *The Ottoman Turks: an Introductory History to 1923*, London 1994

McKitterick, R *The Frankish Kingdoms under the Carolingians 751–987*, London 1983

McKitterick, R (*et al.*) *The New Cambridge Medieval History*, Cambridge 1995

McNeill, W H *The Rise of the West: A History of the Human Community*, Chicago 1991

McNeill, W H *Plagues and Peoples*, New York 1992

McPherson, J M *Battle Cry of Freedom: the Civil War Era*, Oxford 1988

Meining, D W *On the Margins of the Good Earth*, New York 1962, London 1963

Mellaart, J *The Neolithic of the Near East*, London 1975

Milner, C A (*et al.*) *The Oxford History of the American West*, New York 1994

Morgan, D *The Mongols*, Blackwell 1986

Morgan, D *Medieval Persia 1040–1797*, London 1988

Morrell, W P & Hall, D O W *A History of New Zealand Life*, Christchurch 1962

Mulvaney, D J *The Prehistory of Australia*, London 1975

Mulvaney, J & Kamminga, J *Prehistory of Australia*, Allen & Unwin, Sydney 1999

Nahm, A C *Korea: Tradition & Transformation, A History of the Korean People*, Hollym
    International, Seoul 1988

The National Atlas of the United States of America, Washington DC 1970

Neatby, H *Quebec: The Revolutionary Age 1760–1791*, London 1966

Ogot, B A (ed.) *Zamani: A Survey of West African History*, London 1974–1976

O'Hagan, J *Conceptualizing the West in International Relations: From Spengler to Said*, Palgrave,
    London 2000

Oliver, R & Fagan, B *Africa in the Iron Age* c. *500 BC–AD 1400*, Cambridge 1975

Oliver, R & Atmore, A *Africa Since 1800*, 3rd edn, Cambridge 1981

Oliver, W H & Williams, R R *Oxford History of New Zealand*, Oxford 1981

Osbourne, M E *Southeast Asia: An Introductory History*, 2nd edn. Sydney 1983

Osborne, R *Civilization: A New History of the Western World*, Pimlico, London 2007

Ostrogorsky, G *History of the Byzantine State*, Oxford 1969

Overy, R *Why the Allies Won*, London 1995

Parker, W H *An Historical Geography of Russia*, London 1968

Phillips, J R S *The Medieval Expansion of Europe*, Oxford 1988

Pierce, L *The Imperial Harem*, Oxford University Press 1993

Piggott, S *Prehistoric India to 1000 BC*, London 1962

Pitcher, D E *An Historical Geography of the Ottoman Empire*, Leiden 1973

Porter, R *Blood and Guts: A Short History of Medicine*, Allen Lane, London 2002

Postan, M M *Medieval Trade and Finance*, Cambridge 1973

Pounds, N J G *An Historical Geography of Europe 1800–1914*, Cambridge 1985

Powell, J M *An Historical Geography of Modern Australia: the Restive Fringe*, Cambridge 1988

Ragozin, Z *A History of Vedic India*, Delhi 1980

Reuter, T *Germany in the early Middle Ages, 800–1056*, London 1991

Rice,G W (ed.) *The Oxford History of New Zealand*, 2nd edn, Oxford University Press, Auckland 1992

Rizvi, A A *The Wonder That Was India: 1200–1700*, 2 vols, London 1987

Roberts, J M *The Hutchinson History of the World*, revised edn, London 1987

Rouse, I *The Tainos: Rise and Decline of the People who Greeted Columbus*, Yale University Press, New Haven 1992

Sanders, W T & Marino, J *New World Prehistory: Archaeology of the American Indian*, Englewood Cliffs, NJ 1970

Saum, L O *The Fur Trader and the Indian*, London 1965

Sawyer, P (ed.) *The Oxford Illustrated History of the Vikings*, Oxford 1997

Scammell, G V *The First Imperial Age: European Overseas Expansion, c.1400–1715*, London 1992

Seltzer, L E (ed.) *The Columbia Lippincott Gazetteer of the World*, New York 1952

Shaw, I & Nicholson, P *British Museum Dictionary of Europe*, Oxford 1994

Shaw, S *History of the Ottoman Empire*, Cambridge University Press 1976

Shepherd, J & Franklin, S *The Emergence of the Rus*, London 1996

Simkin, C F *The Traditional Trade of Asia*, Oxford 1968

Sinclair, K (ed.) The *Oxford Illustrated History of New Zealand*, Oxford University Press, Auckland 1990

Smith, C D *Palestine and the Arab-Israeli Conflict*, Oxford 1994

Smith, C T *An Historical Geography of Western Europe before 1800*, revised edn, London & New York 1978

Smith, W S *The Art and Architecture of Ancient Egypt*, revised edn. London 1981

Snow, D *The American Indians: Their Archaeology and Prehistory*, London 1976

Sonyel, S R *The Ottoman Armenians*, London 1987

Spate, O *The Spanish Lake*, ANU Press, Canberra 1979

Stark, R *The Rise of Christianity: A Sociologist Reconsiders History*, Princeton 1996

Stavrianos, L S *The World Since 1500: A Global History*, 7th edn, Englewood Cliffs, NJ 1995

Stavrianos, L S *The World to 1500: A Global History*, 7th edn, Englewood Cliffs, NJ 1998

Stokes, M & Conway, S (eds) *The Market Revolution in America: Social, Political and Religious Expressions, 1800–1880*, Charlottesville 1996

Stoye, J *The Siege of Vienna*, London 1964

Tate, D J M *The Making of South-East Asia*, Kuala Lumpur 1971

Thapar, R *A History of India*, London 1967

The Times Atlas of the World, 9th Comprehensive Edition, London 1992

Thompson, E A *The Huns*, Oxford, 1996

Toynbee, A J *Cities of Destiny*, London 1967

Toynbee, A J *Mankind and Mother Earth*, Oxford 1976

Twitchett, D & Loewe, M (eds) *The Cambridge History of China*, Cambridge 1979–

Van Alstyne, R W *The Rising American Empire*, reprint, Oxford 1974

Van Heekeren, H R *The Stone Age of Indonesia*, 2nd revised edn, The Hague 1972

Wadham, S, Wilson, R K & Wood, J *Land Utilization in Australia*, Melbourne 1964

Ward-Perkins, B *The Fall of Rome and the End of Civilization*, Oxford University Press 2005

Webster, L & Brown, M (eds) *The Transformation of the Roman World 400–900*, London 1997

Wheatley, P *The Golden Khersonese*, Kuala Lumpur 1966

Wheeler, M *Early India and Pakistan to Ashoka*, London 1968

White, D W *The American Century: the Rise and Decline of the United States as a World Power*, New Haven 1996

Wickins, P L *An Economic History of Africa From Earliest Times to Partition*, New York 1981

Willey, G An *Introduction to American Archaeology*, vols 1 & 2, Englewood Cliffs, NJ 1970

Williams, M *The Making of the South Australian Landscape*, London 1974

Williamson, E *The Penguin History of Latin America*, London 1992

Wilson, M & Thompson, L *Oxford History of South Africa*, vols 1 & 2, Oxford 1969, 1971

Wood, I N *The Merovingian Kingdoms 450–751*, London 1994

Yarshater, E (ed.) *The Cambridge History of Iran*, vol. 3, Cambridge 1983

PICTURE CREDITS

Credits are by page, and in order from left to right, top to bottom

1 – Yoel Rak; e.t. archive; 2 – Janet & Colin Bord/Fortean Picture Library; Robert Estall Photo Agency/David Coulson; 3 – Ancient Art and Architecture Collection Ltd/Ronald Sheridan; Ancient Art and Architecture Collection Ltd/J Lynch; 4 – South American Pictures; e.t. archive; Robert Harding Picture Library; 5 – AKG Photo London; Ancient Art and rchitecture/Barry Crisp; 6 – C M Dixon; 7 – Stapleton Collection/Corbis; Hugh Kennedy; National Palace Museum, Taiwan; 8 – Werner Forman Archive, University Library, Prague; South American Pictures; 9 – British Library Board/The Bridgeman Art Library; Sonia Halliday Photographs; 10 – Corbis; e.t. archive; 11 – The Print Collector/Alamy; Corbis; 12 – Times Books; Imperial War Museum; 13 – Hulton Getty; Aldus Archive; 14 – e.t. archive; Sygma/J Langevin; 15 – Gamma; Ashley Cooper/Corbis; 16 – STR/Reuters/Popperfoto

INDEX

'B. of' denotes 'Battle of'.

Aachen 96
Abbas I (the Great), Shah (1588–1629) 169
Abbasid Caliphate 120, 131, 133
Abbasid dynasty (750–1258) 89
Abd al-Malik (685–705) 89
Abd ar-Rahman III (912–61) 93
Abdulhamid II, sultan 240, 241
Abdurrah-man Wahid 304
Aboriginal society 22–23, 248, 249
Aborigines, Australian 248, 249
Abu Bakr, caliph 88–89
Abu Hureyra 11
Abu Khamis, Persian Gulf 12–13
Abyssinia 255, 259; Italy conquers (1935–6)
    273, 274, 281; see also Ethiopia
Acapulco, Mexico 154
Aceh, Sumatra 131, 305
Achaemenid family 56, 57, 58
Achaia 106
Acre 104, 133
Action Directe movement 336
Actium, B. of (31 BC) 63, 75, 76
Adad-nirai I (1295–1264 BC) 35
Adal coastal state 136
Adamawa 252
Aden 295

Adowa, B. of (1896) 255, 259
Adrianople (Edirne) 136; B. of (378) 78, 85
Aegean region 13, 29, 47; Latin states around
    104, 106
Aerenthal, Foreign Minister 262
Aeschylus 60
Aethelred "the Unready" 99
Afar region, Ethiopia 2
Afghanistan 120
    independence 169–170
    Soviet occupation (1979) 293, 308, 325
    1979 to 2007 308, 326, 337–338; after
        communism 338
Afghans of Bihar 170
Africa
    900 BC to AD 700 72–73; iron-working and
        farming 73
    1000 to 1500, emergence of states 134–136;
        east and central states 136; western states
        135
    1500 to 1800, trade and empire in 151,
        163–165; Europeans and slave trade
        164–165; Islam, spread of 164
    1800 to 1880, before partition by European
        powers 251–253
    1880 to 1913, partition of 253–255; conflict
        and war 255; the scramble begins 254–255
    1920s administration of 273

Africa – *cont.*
  1957–89: 308–310; economic failures 310;
    ethnic and political conflict 309–310
  1989, democratization since 310–312;
    conflict and genocide 311–312
  Britain and France withdraw from 295
  coast, exploration of 153
  early man in and migration from 3–4, 5
  European colonization 253
  new trade 252
  parcelled out among European powers
    214
  peoples and cultures, early 15–17
  resistance movements in 252, 254,
    259–260
  transcontinental railways 152
African Americans 323
African National Congress (ANC) 311
Afrikaners 253, 254
Agade empire 31
Agha Muhammad Khan 169
Agni, fire god 47
agricultural villages, early European 13–14
agriculturalists, early, in China 41–42
agriculture, origins of 9–11
Aguinaldo, Emilio 259
Agustin I, Emperor of Mexico 238
Ahmad Gran, Sultan of Adal 164
Ahmet II, Sultan (1703–30) 168
Ai Khanoum, Afghanistan 62
AIDS 232, 309, 310, 312 *see also* HIV
Ain Ghazal, Jordan 12
'Ain Jalut, B. of (1260) 123, 133
Ain Mallaha, Jordan 11
air travel 344
Aix-la-Chapelle, Treaty of (1748) 199
Akbar (1556–1605) 170, 171
Akhenaten (Amenophis IV) (*c* 1364–1347 BC)
  33, 34–35
Akkad 31
Akkadian language 31, 34
Akkerman 137
Aksum 72, 73
al-Din Zengi 103
al-Hajj Umar 252, 254
Al Qadisiyya, B. of (637 BC) 58
al-Qaeda 312, 326, 336, 338, 340

Alans 85–86
Alaska 258
Alauddin Khalji (1296–1316) 127
Alaungpaya (1735–60) 179
Albigensian Crusade (1208) 110
Albigensian heretics 102, 111
Albrecht, Grand Master of Hohenzollern
  192
Albuquerque, Alfonso de 178
Aleppo 34, 138
Aleuts, ancestors of 17
Alexander I, Tsar (1801–25) 214, 242
Alexander II, Tsar (1855–81) 243
Alexander III, Pope (1154–81) 109, 110
Alexander III, Tsar 243
Alexander Nevsky, prince 108
Alexander the Great 57, 61, 63, 68
Alexandria, Egypt 62, 89, 92, 132
Alexis Mikhailovich, Tsar (1645–76) 158–159
Alexius I of Byzantium (1081–1118) 105
Alfonso VIII of Castile 133
Algeria: Anglo-American forces land in 286;
  cattle-herding in 16; France invades
  (1830) 253, 258; French withdraw from
  (1962) 294, 334; Islamist terror campaign
  in 311–312, 316, 336; nationalist
  movements 274
Algiers 164, 167, 190
Aligarh movement 247
Allende, Salvador 317
Almohads 133
Alp Arslan, sultan 132
Alpine passes 114
Alsace, Upper and Lower 197
Altranstädt, peace of (1706) 194
Älvsborg (Gothenburg), Sweden 193
Amarna, Egypt 33
"Amarna letters" 34
Amazonia, tribal groups 143, 144
"Amboina, Massacre of" (1623) 179
Amenophis III 34
Amenophis IV (Akhenaten) (*c* 1364–1347 BC)
  33, 34–35
American Civil War (1861–5) 230, 232, 234
American Indians, Native xx, 152, 160, 226
American War of Independence (1775–83)
  xxxvi, 160, 161, 200, 208

Americas *see also* Central America; Latin America; Mesoamerica; North America; South America; *individual countries*
   discovery of (1492) 154, 161
   Christianity enforced 151
   coastal exploration 153
   domestication of animals 10
   early peoples of 17–19; civilizations, early 18–19; farming 18; settlements, first 17–18; trading, long distance 18
   man reaches 4, 6, 7
Amorites 31
Amoy, China 157
Amsterdam 94, 184
Amsterdam Exchange Bank 184–185
Amun, god of Thebes 33
Amun-Re cult 33
Amutpiel of Qatna 31
An Lu'shan 118
An-Yang, China 27, 41
Anabaptists 186
Anacreon 59
Anasazi culture 39
Anatolia 11, 12, 124, 132; advance of Ottoman empire into 106; Armenians in 240–241; Hittite empire 34; Ottoman supremacy in 137, 138; retreat of Mongols from 136; urbanization in 29; *see also* Turkey
Andalus, Umayyas ruler of 132
Andes, Army of the 238
Andes, the 142, 143, 144; complex societies develop in 36; domestication of crops in 10, 18; temples 19
Andrusovo, Treaty of (1667) 159, 201
Angevin "empire" 111
Angkor, Cambodia 130
Angkor Borei, Cambodia 129
Angles 86
Anglo-Burmese War, first (1824–6) 179–180
Anglo-Maratha War, Third 245
Angola 156, 157, 253, 295
animals, domestication of 9, 10, 14, 16, 18, 70
animals, draught, first use of 15
Anjou 111; house of 140–141
Ankara, B. of (1402) 137
Annam *see* Vietnam
Antietam, B. of (1862) 232

Antigonid Macedon 61
Antilles, Lesser 37, 146
Antioch 62, 79, 103
Antitrinitarians 186
Appalachia 229
Aquino, Corazan 304
Aquitaine 95, 111
Arab conquests 89
Arab shipping 153
Arab-Israeli conflict 312, 313–314; search for peace 313–314
Arabia 58, 86–89
Arabs 58, 72–73, 86, 105
Aragon 148; army of 103; Crown of 141–142; invaders from 140–141
Arakan 180
Aral Sea 346
Arawak language 37
Archilochus 59
Archimedes 62
Arctic 4
Arctic Islands 236
Ardabil, Azerbaijan 169
Ardashir 57
Ardavan 57
Ardipithecus ramidus 2
Argentina 239, 317–318
Argentinian pampas 239
Aristophanes 60
Arius 90
Arizona 39
Arkwright, Richard 206
Armenia 331
Armenians 123, 240–241
Arnhem Land, Australia 22
Arnulfings *see* Carolingians
Arpachiyah 12
Arpád dynasty 101
Arsaces 57
Arsacid family 56, 57
art: aboriginal 22; "Celtic" 71; Mughal 170–171
Aryans 46
Arzawa 34
ASEAN 304
Ashoka 68
Ashur, Assyria 55

Ashur-uballit I (1353–1318 BC) 35
Ashurbanipal (668–627 BC) 55
Ashurnasirpal II (883–859 BC) 54–55
Asia
    nationalism in, since 1939 294–295
    Russian expansion in (1462 to 1815)
        157–159; growth of empire 158–159
    Second World War in (1941–5) 283–285;
        Allied build-up 284; final defeat 284–285
Asia, central (600 to 1501) 119–121; Mongol
    invasion 120–121
Asia, east: 220 to 618 65–67; since 1945 296,
    297–298
Asia, south: independence and conflict (since
    1947) 305–308; in global politics 308;
    military rule 307–308; struggle for
    identity 306–307
Asia, southeast
    before civilization (to 500 BC) 19–21;
        archaeological evidence 20; Indian
        influence 21; metal technologies 20–21
    500 BC to AD 1511, early civilizations
        129–131; decline of the temple states 130;
        early kingdoms 129–130; Vietnam, rise
        of 130–131
    1511 to 1826, European powers in 178–180;
        Anglo-Dutch agreement 180; Dutch and
        English conquests 179–180
    1945 to 1975, long war in 300–302; Sukarno
        and non-alignment 300–301; Vietnam
        War 301–302
    since 1975 302–305; Asian "tigers" 303–304,
        342; communist rule 302, 303; people
        power 304–305
Asia, southwest 11–13
Asian migrants 235, 236, 237, 249
Asiatic Huns 85
Askia the Great (1493–1528) 163
Assam 180
Assyria 34, 35, 54–56
Assyrians 34, 54
Astrakhan khanate 158
"asylum seekers" 331
Aten (solar disc) worship 33
atheism xxx
Athenian empire 59–60
Athens xxii, 59, 60, 106

Atlantic trade triangle 152, 203, 204
atomic bombs, dropping of 283, 285, 292 see
    also weapons, nuclear
Attila 85
Auckland, New Zealand 251
Augsburg, Germany 139; peace of (1555) 195
Augustus (formerly Octavian) 63, 75–76
Augustus II of Poland (1697–1733) 195–196,
    202
Aurangzeb (1659–1707) 171
Austerlitz, B. of (1805) 213
Austral Plan 318
Australia
    to 1770 21–23
    in 16th century 151
    since 1770 248–249; aborigines 248, 249;
        economic development 248–249;
        migration and national consciousness
        249
    Aboriginal society 22–23, 248, 249
    agriculture introduced 10
    animals, early 22
    Britain claims sovereignty over 258
    man reaches 4, 6, 21
    mapping of coast (1770) 154, 248
    migrants in 249
    Pleistocene 21–22
    rock paintings 22
    settlement in 8
    tools 22
Australian Core/Small Tool Traditions 22
Australopithecenes 2
Austrasia 95
Austria: democracy restored in (1949) 291;
        democracy suspended in 278; German
        occupation of (1938) 282; and the
        Habsburgs 195; holds Italian lands 191;
        moves to annex Bosnia (1908) 262; and
        Napoleon 213; possession of Hungary
        201; and Serbia 262–263, 265–266; and
        struggle for unification 224, 225
Austrian Habsburgs 197
Austrian Succession, War of (1743–8) 161, 195,
    202
Austro-Hungary 266, 267
Austronesians 24
automobiles, first 220, 343–344

Ava, Myanmar 130
Avars 96
Avignon, France 110, 141
Awadh state 246
Ayutthaya, Thailand 130
Azerbaijan 120, 170, 331–332
Azov 159, 201–202
Aztec empire 84, 143, 144, 145–146, 151, 161,
    162

Baader-Meinhof group 336
Ba'ath Party 337
Babrak Karmal 338
Babur 128, 170
Babylon 31, 32, 34, 35, 55, 56
Babylonians 34, 54, 56
Bachelet, Michelle 319
Bactria 57, 58, 68
Baden 225
Baghdad 120, 131, 132, 133; capture of 123, 168,
    169
Bahia (later Salvador), Brazil 162
Bahmani sultanate 127, 128
Balfour Declaration (1917) 312–313
Bali 21, 340
Balkan crisis (1887 to 1914) 262, 263
Balkan League 262
Balkans 13, 15, 137, 167 see also individual
    countries
Balkh 89, 120
Baltic, struggle for the (1523 to 1721) 192–194;
    Sweden's Baltic empire 192–193; Swedish
    power, decline of 194
Baltic Sound 192, 193
Baltic states 278
Baltic trade 192
Bambara kingdoms 252
Ban Chiang, Thailand 20
Ban Chieng Hian, Thailand 21
Ban Don Ta Phet, Thailand 21
Ban Lum Khao, Thailand 21
Ban Na Di, Thailand 20
Ban Prasat, Thailand 21
Banda Oriental (Uruguay) 199, 239
Bangladesh 307
banking, world (1870 to 1914) 264–265
banking houses, collapse of (13th-14th C.) 139

banking system, European, reform of 219, 220
banks, Dutch and English 184–185
Bannockburn, B. of (1314) 112
Bar, Confederation of (1768–72) 202–203
Barbaricum, India 69
Barcelona, Spain 139
Bardi banking house 139
Bari, Italy 97
Barygaza, India 69
Basil II (976–1025) 105
Basle, First Zionist Congress (1897) 223
Basque independence movement 291, 331, 336
Basra, Iraq 167
Basse-Yutz 71
Basta, Jordan 12
Bastille, storming of (1789) 210
Batavia, Java 156, 179
Batu 122
Bavaria 96, 225
Bay of Islands, New Zealand 250
Bayezid, sultan 124
Bayezid II (1481–1512) 137, 138
Beaumanoir (lawyer) 111
Bede, the Venerable xxxi
Begram, Gandhara 54
Beijing xv, xxvi, 299, 300 see also Peking
Beikthano, Myanmar 129
Belarus 288
Belgian Congo 254, 295
Belgium 219–220, 221–222, 283
Belgrade 137; Peace of (1739) 202
beliefs xxvii–xxviii
Belisarius 79, 86
Bell, Alexander 343
Bengal province, India 127, 171, 200, 205,
    247, 305
Benin 135, 163
Benz, Karl 220, 343
Berbers 72
Berenice, Red Sea 54
Bergen, Norway 139
Berlin, Germany 93, 94, 196, 287; airlift
    (1948–9) 324; Congress of 260
Berlin West Africa Conference (1884) 254
Beta, King of Aragon 102
Bhagavad-gita 126
"bhakti" devotionalism 126–127, 128–129

Biafra 309
Bible, the 54, 96
Bihar Afghans 170
bin Laden, Osama 336, 340
Birka, Sweden 113
Bismarck, Prince Otto von 222, 225, 261
BJP party 308
Black Death xxii, 138, 139, 140, 217
"Black Flags" 260
Black Sea, waterway route from Gulf of
    Finland to 106, 107
Boeing 344
Boer War (1899–1902) 255
Boers 253
Bogotá, Colombia 209
Bohemia 101, 104, 183; in 14th century 142;
    Germans occupy 282; and the
    Habsburgs 195; revolt in 209
Bolesław I, Pøemyslid prince (929–67) 101
Bolesław Chrobry (992–1025) 101
Bolívar, Simon 238
Bolivia 143, 317
Bolshevik Revolution (1917) 271, 288
Bolsheviks (Marxist Social-Democrats) 271,
    272
Bombay, India 157
Bombing Offensive, Combined 286
Bonaparte family 213 see also Napoleon III;
    Napoleon Bonaparte
Boniface VIII, Pope (1294–1303) 91, 110, 141
Boone, Daniel 226
Bordeaux, France 184
Borneo 258
Borobudur, Java 130
Boru, Brian 100
Bosnia 137, 262, 332–333
Bosnia-Herzegovina 332
Bosnian Serbs 326, 332–333
Bosnians 136–137
Boston, Massachusetts 234
Bostra, Syria 87
Bourbons 191, 214
Bourgneuf as place-name 114
Bourguiba, Habib ben Ali 274
Boxer Rebellion 245, 260
Boyacá, B. of 238
braceros system 235

Bracton (lawyer) 111
Braganza, House of 188
Brahmo Samaj movement 247
Brandenburg, electors of 195
Brandenburg-Prussia 194
Brazil: deforestation 347; independence 163,
    238; industrial growth 239; migrants in
    239; new regimes in 317, 319; Portuguese
    settlement of 156, 157, 162
Brazza, de 254
Breitenfeld, B. of (1631) 193
Brest, Union of (1596) 186
Brest-Litovsk 93; Treaty of (1918) 266, 271
Brezhnev, Leonid 327–328
Britain see also England; Ireland; Scotland,
    Wales
  agriculture in (1500 to 1815) 180–181
  alliance with France and Germany (1907)
    261
  and American War of Independence 208
  Angles occupy 86
  clashes with Spain and France 199–200
  colonialization by 258
  fight for global supremacy (1713 to 1815)
    199, 200
  in the Great Depression 280, 281
  Industrial Revolution begins 205–207;
    conditions for growth 206–207; new
    technologies 206; social revolution
    207
  joins European Community (1973) 249,
    251
  in the Mediterranean 191
  monarchy in (1154–1314) 110–111, 112; royal
    power, limits of 112
  and Napoleonic Wars 213
  population growth 217
  rearmament in (1890s) 261
  Saxons occupy 86
  stone circles 15
  surrenders control of North American
    waters 200
Britain, Battle of (1940) 283
British: colonies in Africa 254–255; migrants
    233–234, 236; in southeast Asia 178,
    179–180; voyages of discovery (1487 to
    1780) 154–155 see also English

British power, growth of, in Mughal India (1526 to 1803) 170–171; and East India Company 171; Mughal decline 171
British Columbia 236
British Empire 258–259, 272
Brittany 15, 211
Bronze Age 20, 34, 35, 41, 47, 69–70
Bruges, Belgium 139
Bruno, Giordano xxxiii
Brusilov offensive 266
Bucer, Martin (1491–1551) 185
buckwheat 181
Buczacz, peace of (1672) 201
Budapest 93, 209
Buddha 47
Buddhism 43, 44, 45, 52, 66, 67, 68–69, 115, 123, 126, 129, 130 see also Mahayana Buddhism; Theravada Buddhism
Buenos Aires, Argentina 209
buffalo, North American xx, 17
Buganda 164, 252
Bugia, capture of (1555) 190
Bukhara 169; Khanate 170
Bulgaria 86, 105, 137; advance of Ottoman empire into 106; democracy suspended in 278; independence 262; Jewish community in 94, 289
Bulgars 98, 102, 104; Volgar 107–108
Buonsignori banking house 139
Burgundians 85
Burgundy 71, 148
Burgundy, Valois dukes of 141
Burma (Myanmar): British annex 246; British withdraw from 294, 301–302; Buddhist shrines in 129; cyclone (2008) xix; new political centres 130; since 1947 307
Burma, Lower 258
Burmese empire, new 179
Burschenschaften (secret student society) 223
Bush, George W. 326, 335
Byzantine Empire (610 to 1453) 104–106; collapse of 104, 158, 185; Comeneni and the crusades 105–106; last centuries 106; renewal and retreat 104–105
Byzantines 86, 87, 89, 91, 107
Byzantium, from Rome to (AD 235 to 565) 77–79; reconquests of Justinian 79, 86; rise of Christianity 78, 80–81; see also Constantinople; Istanbul

Cabot, John 159
Caesar, Julius 71–72, 75, 76
Caffa (Kefe), Crimea 137
Cairo 92, 132, 134, 135, 138
Calatrava military order 103
Calcutta, India 157
Çaldiran, B. of (1514) 138, 167, 169
California 226, 231, 323
Caliphate, united, break up of 131
Caltyabellotta, Treaty of (1302) 141
Calvin, John (1509–64) 186
Calvinism 186
Calvinists, French 197–198
Cambodia 129, 130, 301, 302–303
Cambyses (530–522 BC) 56
Cameroons 254, 258, 272
Camp David agreement (1978) 313, 314, 325
Canada
    since 1810 235–237; multiculturalism 236, 237; population 236–237; territory 236
    French forces in 200
    migrants in 235, 236–237
    trade pact with US 323
    transcontinental railways 152, 264
Canal Royal, France 198
canals, early, construction of 28
Cannae, B. of (216 BC) 74
Canossa 109
Canton, China 157
Canute (Cnut), king 99, 100
Cape Colony/Province 73, 156, 253
Capetians 111
Caporetto, B. of (1917) 266
Caracalla (198–217) 76, 77
carbonari (secret society) 223
Cárdenas, Lázaro 319
Caribbean
    300 BC to AD 1300, peoples 37
    c. 1300 to 1520, eve of European conquest 144, 146
    1500 to 1825 161, 163, 199
    since 1910 319, 320–321; economic development and violence 320
Caribs, Island 146

Carloman 95
Carlos II of Spain 198
Carlowitz, peace of (1699) 201
Carlsbad Decrees (1819) 221
Carolina, South 232, 233
Carolingians (formerly Arnulfings) 94, 95,
    96–97, 108
cars, first 220, 343–344
Carter, Jimmy 325
Carthage 72, 74, 78
Cartier, Jacques 160
Casas Grandes, Chihuahua 40
Castile 103, 139, 142, 148
Castro, Fidel 320, 321
Castro, Raúl 320
Catalaunian Fields, B. of (451) 85
Çatalhöyük 12, 13
Catalonia, revolts in (1640 to 1652) 188
Câteau-Cambrésis, peace of (1559) 190
Cathars 91
Catherine II (the Great) 159
Catholic Church xxviii, xxxii–xxxiii, 90, 92,
    211
Catholic Reformation (1517–1670) 185–186
Catholicism xxx, xxxiv, 162
cattle farming, expansion in Europe of 139
Cau Chan, Vietnam 20
Cavour, Count Camillo di 222, 224–225
Çayönü, Anatolia 11
Celebes 20
Celts 69, 70–72
CENTO 292
Central America: since 1910 319–321;
    democratization 320–321; economic
    development and violence 320;
    revolution and intervention 319–320;
    see also Latin America; Mesoamerica
Central Powers 266, 267
Cerdagne, northern 197
cereals, domestication 9–10, 14, 16, 18
Cerro Sechín, Andes 19
Ceuta 142
Ceylon (Sri Lanka) 294, 306–307
CFCs (chlorofluorocarbons) 347
Chaeronea, B. of (338 BC) 61
Chagatai khanate 123
Chalcedon, church council (451) 81

Chalukya dynasty 125
Cham Shivite, Vietnam 130
Champagne fairs 114
Chandragupta 68
Chandragupta II 69
Ch'ang-an, Korea 44, 65
Chanson de Roland 96
Characene 58
Charlemagne, Emperor 96
Charles I, King of England 187, 188
Charles IV, Emperor 142
Charles V, Emperor (1519–56) 148, 189–190,
    195
Charles VII, Emperor (1742–5) 195
Charles VIII, King of France 189
Charles X of Sweden (1654–60) 193
Charles XI of Sweden (1660–97) 194
Charles XII of Sweden (1697–1718) 194
Charles Albert of Piedmont-Sardinia 224
Charles Martel 95
Charles of Anjou 110
Charles the Bold 148
Chattisgarh state 306
Chavín cult 19–20, 36
Chechnya 328, 331, 332
Cheng-chou, China 41
Cheops (Khufu) 32
Chernigov 158
Cherokee Indians 226
Ch'i dukedom 63
Chiang Kai-shek 275, 276
Ch'iang people 66
Chiang tribes 65
Chicago, Illinois 226, 234
Ch'ien Ch'in 66
Ch'ien-lung, emperor (1736–96) 172
Chieng Mai, Thailand 130
Chihuahua, Mexico 39, 40
Childeric 95
Chile 239, 317–318, 319
Chimú people 36
Chin empire 121
Ch'in state 63, 64
Chin-ch'uan tribal risings (1746–9, 1771–6)
    172
China xv, xvii, xviii
    475 BC to AD 220, unification 63–65; Han

empire, collapse of 65; Han expansion
64–65; the first emperor 64

220 to 618 65–67; Northern Wei 67;
Western Chin dynasty 66–67

1368 to 1644, Ming Dynasty 150, 151,
165–167; consolidation 165–166; overseas
expansion 166–167

1644 to 1839, Ch'ing dynasty 172–173; crisis
of government 173; population growth
173

since late 19th c. xvi

1839 to 1911, collapse of empire 244–245;
foreign penetration 245

1912 to 1949, Revolution 269, 274–277,
292; civil war (1946–9) 276–277;
Japanese advance 276–277; nationalist
reaction 275–276

since 1949, under Communism 298–300;
reform and protest 299–300; under Mao
Zedong 298–299

agriculture, early 10–11

Boxer Rebellion 245, 260

canals, early, construction of 28

civilization, earliest 29–30

early man in 20, 41

earthquake (2008) xix

emperors, divine status xxix

favourable conditions for human
settlement 41

Han dynasty 52, 53

influence on Japan of 115–116

invasion of India (1962) 308

inventions xxxv

Japanese expansion into (1937) 175

Mongols in 123, 165, 166

Second World War 284–285

Sino-Japanese War (1894–5) 245, 256,
260

trade with 157

urbanism begins in 29

war with Japan 281

Western influence on xxxvii

writing, early, in 29–30

China, Great Wall of 121

China, People's Republic of 276–277, 298

Chinese civilization
beginnings of (to 475 BC) 41–42;

agriculturalists, early 41–42; Chou
dynasty 42

618 to 1279 117–119; rise of the Sung
118–119; T'ang dynasty 117–118

expansion of 52

Chinese emigrants 218

Chinese medicine xxii–xxiii

Chinese shipping 153

Chinese warlords 275, 276

Ch'ing dynasty, China under (1644 to 1839)
167, 172–173, 244; crisis of government
173; population growth 173

Chingiz (Genghis) Khan 120, 121–122, 124, 133

Chionite Huns 58

Chola empire 124, 125–126

cholera xxii

Cholula 39

Choson dynasty (1392–1910) 44, 174

Chosroes II 58

Chou dynasty 42, 63

Christchurch, New Zealand 250

Christian Church 96; indigenous churches,
establishment of 259

Christian missionaries 102

Christian pilgrimages to Holy Land 101–102

Christianity 52, 72, 99
rise of (to AD 600) 78, 79–81; and
Constantine 80–81; doctrinal
development 81

600 to 1500, expansion 90–92; papacy,
power of 91–92; Rome and
Constantinople, schism between 90–91,
106

in Africa from 1960s 309, 310

and Mongols 122–123

Russia, introduction into 107

spread of 151

US religious fundamentalism 340

Christians xxviii, 89, 90

Chrobry, Boleslaw (992–1025) 101

Ch'u dukedom 63

Chu Hsi: *Family Rites of Zhu-xi, The* 174

Chu Yüan-chang 165, 166

Churchill, Winston 283

CIA 320

Ciompi rebellion (1378) 140

Cisalpine Republic 212

cities, first, in Eurasia 27–28, 29–30
civil rights xxxvi–xxxvii, xxxviii
Clark, William 226
clay for containers, use of 11–12
Clean Air Act (1970) (USA) 346
Clearchus 62
Clement IV, Pope (1265–8) 110
Cleopatra 75, 76
Cleopatra VII 63
Clermond river 229
Clermont, Council of (1095) 102
climate change xxi, 346
Clive, Robert 200
cloth industry and trade in Europe 139, 182
Clovis 85, 94, 95
Cnut, king 99, 100
Cochabamba 143
Cocom rulers 146
Code Napoléon 213
Cokwe people 252
Cold War (1945 to 1991) 291–293, 324–325,
    327–328, 341; in Asia 300, 301, 308;
    height of 292; Middle East in 315, 316;
    shadow of the bomb 292–293; source of
    the conflict 291–292
Cologne, Germany 114
Colombia 143, 239, 337
Colorado 39
Columbus, Christopher (Cristoforo
    Colombo) xxxiv, 8, 144, 154, 161
Comanche tribe 160
Comet, de Havilland 344
commerce, revolution in 220–221
commerce, world (1870 to 1914) 264–265
Committee of General Security 211
Committee of Public Safety 211
Committee of Union and Progress 241
communications in the modern age 343–345;
    air travel 343, 344; engine, internal
    combustion 343–344;
    telecommunications 344–345
communism: collapse of 325–326, 330, 338;
    revival of 289
Communist Party, Chinese 274, 275, 276,
    284, 292, 296, 298–300
Communist Party, Soviet 291, 292, 326, 327,
    328

Compagnie de Chine 157
computer systems, development of 344–345
Confederacy, US 231–232
Confucianism xxii, 63–64, 177, 260
Confucius 42
Congo, Democratic Republic of 311
Congo River 254
Congress All-India campaigns 273
Conrad 108
Constantine 78, 80–81, 101
Constantinople 77–78, 89, 91; Arab sieges
    (674–8 and 717–18) 104; capture of
    (1204) 104, 105; and expansion of
    Christianity 90–91, 106; Ottoman
    conquest of (1453) 106, 137; population
    183; St Sophia's church 79
Constantius II 78
Continental System 213
Cook, Capt James 4, 155, 248, 250
Cook Islands 24
Copenhagen, Peace of (1660) 193
Copernicus, Nicolaus xxxii
Cordoba, Spain 133
Corsica 97, 291
Cort, Henry 206
Cortés, Hernán xxxv
Cossacks 201; Zaporozhian 158, 201
Costa Rica 146
cotton 152; gin, invention of (1793) 230–231;
    textile industry 206, 229; trade 204, 205
Courland 192
Courtrai, B. of (1302) 112
Covenanting Movement (1638) 187
Covilha, de 153
Cracow, Poland 93, 122
Creoles 238
Crete: clay inscriptions 30; early farming
    villages 13; Ottoman capture of 168, 201;
    palaces in 47–48, 58; settlements in 47,
    48
Crimea, annexation of 159
Crimea Khanate 123, 137
Crimean War (1853–5) 225, 242–243
Croatia 86, 122, 332
Croesus of Lydia 56
Cromford, Derbyshire 206
crops, new European 181–182

Crusades 91, 101; Albigensian (1208) 110; First (1096–9) 93, 101, 102, 105, 109; Second (1146–8) 103; Third (1189–91) 103, 133; Fourth (1204) 106; and the Muslim world (1100 to 1350) 133–134; Crusade of Varna (1444) 104

Crusaders 103, 132

crusading in Europe (1095 to 1492) 101–104; crusaders 103, 132; first crusade 93, 101, 102, 105, 109; later crusades 103–104

Cruzado Plan 318

Cuba 37, 239, 321

Cuban migrants 235

Cuban missile crisis (1962) 293, 325

Cuban Revolution (1959) 317, 319, 320

Cumberland Road 229, 230

Cuna chiefdom 146

Cyprus 168, 190, 295

Cyrenaica 89

Cyril 91

Cyrus (559–530 BC) 56

Cyrus I (752 BC) 56

Czechoslovakia 278, 287, 290

Dahomey 254

Daimler, Gottlieb 220, 343

daimyô (feudal barons) 117, 176–177, 178

Dalmatia 142

Damascus 89, 138

Danelaw 99

Danes 98, 88

Danube, river 114, 137

Danzig 192, 203, 282

Daoism 63–64, 66

Dar al-Islam 131, 132

Dar es Salaam 312

Darius (522–486 BC) 57

Darwin, Charles: The Origin of Species (1859) xxvii

Dasas 46

Dawkins, Richard: The God Delusion (2006) xxx

Daylamite military adventurers 131

Dayton Agreement (1995) 326, 333

de Gaulle, Charles 295

De Klerk, F. W. 311

De Tham 260

"Decembrists" 242

Deccan 125, 127, 128

Decius 80

Delhi 128, 129; sacking of (1738–9) 169, 171; sultanate 127–129

Delphi 59, 62, 71

Deng Xiaoping 299

Denmark: 900 to 1050 100; agriculture in (1500 to 1815) 182; controls Baltic Sound 192, 193; Jews saved in 289; joins Russia against Sweden 194; in Seven Years' War 192–193; Swedish wars with (1643–5, 1657, 1658, 1676–9) 193, 194

deportations (1919 to 1953) 287–289

Depression, Great (1929 to 1939) 274, 279–281, 322; causes and effects 280; political cost 280–281

Deulino, Treaty of (1618/19) 158

Devolution, War of (1667–8) 197

Dhu'l-Qadr emirate 138

Dias 153

Díaz, Porfirio (1876–1910) 239

Dien Bien Phu, B. of (1954) 294, 301

Diocletian 77, 80

disasters, natural xix

disease xxi–xxii, xxiii–xxiv see also individual entries

Dnieper, river 106, 107

Doc Chua, Vietnam 21

dogs as food 18

Dominic (1172–1221) 91

Dominican republic 37

Dominicans 91, 110

Domitian (81–96) 76

Don river 286

Dong Dau, Vietnam 20

Dong Son, Vietnam 20

Donner party 226

Dorestad 98, 113

Doria family 190

Dorian invaders 49

Dosariyah, Persian Gulf 12

Dost Muhammad (1819–63) 169–170

Douglas 344

drums, bronze 20–21

Dublin 100, 113

Dulles, John Foster 324–325

Duma (parliament) 243–244, 271
Dutch: in the Americas 160, 163; migrants
    233; revolt 187, 188, 189, 191; settlers in
    southern Africa 164; in southeast Asia
    178, 179–180; trading empire, expansion
    of (1500 to 1700) 156–157; voyages of
    discovery (1487 to 1780) 154–155
Dutch East India Company 156
Dutch East Indies 259, 274, 294
Dutch Republic 183, 184, 197 *see also* Holland;
    Netherlands
Dutch West India Company 157
Duvalier family 320
Dzungaria 118

Eadgar (959–75) 99
East, Near: 1600–1000 BC 34–35; 1000–539 BC
    54–56;
East India Company, Dutch 156
East India Company, English 157, 171, 179,
    200, 205, 245
East India Company, French 200
Easter Island 24
Eastern Chin dynasty 66
economic revolution xxxvi
economy, global 341–343; global inequality
    342–343; regional and global integration
    342
Ecuador 143
Edessa 103
Edirne see Adrianople
Edo, Japan 176, 177
education xxxvi
Edward I, King of England (1272–1307) 111,
    112
Edward II, King of England 112, 141
Edward the Confessor 99
Egypt
    c. 3100–1000 BC 32–33; expansion and
        disunity 33; Middle Kingdom
        reunification 33
    Arab occupation of 89
    British occupy (1882) 254, 258, 260
    cities, first 29
    conflict with Assyrians 55
    conquests of 72–73
    dynastic, rise of 16–17

expansion of 252–253
    hostility with Hittites 34, 35
    independence (868) 131, 132
    independence after Napoleon 191
    independence (1922) 273
    invasion by Napoleon 191, 240
    irrigation in 28
    nationalist movements 273
    Ottoman conquest of 164, 167
    Ptolemaic 61, 62
    Roman annexation of 63
    seeks peace with Israel 313
    since 1945 315
    as single unified kingdom 29
    writing, early, in 30
Egyptians, ancient xx, 34; religion xxviii
Eight Trigrams rebellion (1813) 173
El Alamein, B. of (1942) 286
Elam kingdom 35, 55
Elamites 34
Elbing, burghers' rebellion 192
electron, discovery of 343
electronic revolution 345
Elizabeth I, Queen of England 187
Ellora, Kalaisanatha temple 125
Elmina fortress-factory, Africa 155
Emishi tribesmen 115
Emma of Normandy 99
empire, retreat from (since 1939) 293–295;
        Asia 294; colonial legacy 295
empire, struggle for (1713 to 1815) 199–200;
        Anglo-French struggle 199; India,
        Anglo-French rivalry in 200; North
        America, conflict in 199–200
Enclosure Acts, Parliamentary 206–207
engine, internal combustion, development of
        343–344
England: 900 to 1050 99; cloth exports
        from 139; economic strength 184;
        Normans in 111; Peasants' Revolt (1381)
        140; Tudor dynasty in 148; *see also*
        Britain
England, Bank of 185
English 112; in the Americas 160, 161, 163;
        conversion to Christianity 102; migrants
        233–234; missionaries 102; in southeast
        Asia 178, 179–180

English Channel, sea-route to Netherlands through 191

English Civil War (1642–9) 188

English East India Company 157, 171, 179, 200, 205, 245

'Enlightenment', European (18th c.) xxxiii, 207, 208, 221

Enver Pasha 241

environment, global 345–347; global warming 345–346; ozone layer 347

Ephesus, Greece 59

epidemics xxi–xxii, xxiii *see also individual entries*

Epirus, Greek enclave 106

Eratosthenes of Cyrene 62

Erh-li-t'ou, China 41

Eridu, Mesopotamia 13

Erie Canal 229, 230

Eritrea 258, 311

Esarhaddon (680–669 BC) 55

Estado de India 157

Estates-General 112, 210

Estonia 159, 192, 193, 278

ETA (Euskadi Ta Askatasuna) (Basque independence movement) 291, 331, 336

Ethelred (Aethelred) "the Unready" 99

Ethiopia 2, 3, 5; Italy invades (1935) 273, 274, 281; Marxist regime 310, 311; rivalry with Muslims 164; war in (1970s-80s) 309; *see also Abyssinia*

Ethiopians 87

Etruscans 70, 71

Euboea 58

Euclid of Alexandria 62

Euphrates valley, lower 27, 28, 30

Eurasia, commerical and cultural bonds (550 BC to AD 752) 52–54; maritime trade 53–54

Eurasian trading routes 64

Eurasian world, beginnings of civilization in (3500 to 1500 BC) 28–30; cities, first 27–28, 29–30

Euripides 60

Europe
9th and 10th century, Magyars, Saracens and Vikings in 97–99

1252 to 1381, crisis of the 14th century 84, 138–140; Black Death and economic crisis 139; peasant unrest and revolt 139–140

1450 to *c.* 1600, state consolidation 84, 147–148

1500 to 1688, the state and its opponents 187–189; age of revolt 188; state, structure of the 188–189

1799 to 1815, reshaping of, under Napoleon 212–214; defeat and exile 214; military, primacy of 213–214

1800 to 1914, rise of nationalism 221–223; independence, struggle for 221–222; nationalism exported 222–223

1945 to 1973 289–291; economic revival 290–291; new frontiers 290

since 1973 329–331; coming of democracy 330; economic integration 329–330; nationalism, revival of 330–331

civil wars in (since 1991) 331–333; Chechnya, war over 332; Yugoslavia, collapse of 332–333

crusading in (1095 to 1492) 101–104; crusaders 103; first crusade 93, 101, 102, 105, 109; later crusades 103–104

early, colonization of 13–15; agricultural villages 13–14

early modern state in (1450 to *c.* 1600) 148

economic growth in (*c.* 950 to 1150) 112–114; markets 114; new regions, opening of 113–114; Scandinavian world 113; trade 114

economy: agriculture and society (1500 to 1815) 180–182; new crops 181–182; peasants and feudalism 182

economy: trade and industry (1550 to 1775) 183–185; and finance 184–185

evolution of xxxiv–xxxv

Industrial Revolution in (1815 to 1870) 219–221; mid-century boom 220; proto-industrialization 219–220; "second" 220–221

Megalithic 14–15

migrant workers 218

Mongol conquests in 122

Europe – *cont.*
  political problems in (1919 to 1934)
    277–279; Hitler, rise of 279; League of
    Nations 278–279
  population growth 217
  Renaissance in (1450 to *c.* 1600) 147–148
  Russian expansion in (1462 to 1815)
    157–159; growth of empire 158–159
  Second World War in (1939–45) 282–283,
    285–287; Germany, defeat of 286–287;
    turn of the tide 286
  social mobility xxxvi
  voyages of discovery (1487 to 1780) xxxv,
    153–155; French, British and Dutch
    154–155; Spanish and Portuguese 153–154
  world colonisation xxxv, xxxvii
Europe, eastern
  900 to 1050 99, 100–101
  in the 14th century 142
  age of partition (1648 to 1795) 201–203;
    Ottoman revival and decline 201–202;
    Poland, partitions of 202–203
  Scandinavia and 142
Europe, northern
  900 to 1050 99–100
  peoples of (2300 to 50 BC) 69–72; Celtic
    world 70–72; Urnfield period 70
Europe, western
  Germanic settlement of (341 to 597) 84–86;
    European periphery 86; Franks 85–86;
    Ostrogothic Italy 86; Visigoths 85–86
  modern humans arrive 8
European cities, growth of 217
European Coal and Steel Community 290
European colonial empires (1815 to 1914)
    257–259; resistance, consequences of
    260–261; the scramble for empire
    258–259
European Economic Community (EEC) 249,
    251, 270, 290, 329
European expansion, world on eve of (*c.*
    1500) 150–152; global impact 152; tempo
    of change 151
European migrants to America 234, 235, 239
European power, growth of xxxvii–xxxviii
European powers and southeast Asia (1511 to
    1826) 178–180; Anglo-Dutch agreement

180; Dutch and English conquests
    179–180
European rivalries and alliances (1878 to 1914)
    261–263; Balkan crisis 262, 263; war,
    slide into 262–263
European states in the 14th century (1300 to
    1400) 140–142; rulers and subjects
    141–142
European Union 329–330, 342
European uprisings (1500 to 1688) 187
European voyages of discovery (1487 to 1780)
    153–155; French, British and Dutch
    154–155; Spanish and Portuguese 153–154
Evans, Sir Arthur 47
Eylau, B. of (1807) 213

Falklands conflict (1982) 318
Famine, Great (1315–17) 138
famines xx, 138, 198
farming 10–11, 13, 18
fascism 288, 289
Fascist party 278
Fashoda 255
Fatehpur Sikri, India 171
Fatima 132
Fatimid dynasty 131–132
fealty, chains of, Japanese (*kenmon*) 116
Federal Union, US 232, 233
Ferdinand, king of Bohemia and Hungary
    190
Ferdinand II of Austria 195
Ferdinand of Spain 189
Ferghana 118
"Fertile Crescent" 10, 16
feudalism 182
Fiji 24, 258
Finland 278
Finland, Gulf of, waterway route to Black Sea
    106, 107
fishing grounds off North America 159–160
"Five Barbarians' Disruption of China" 66
Five-Year Plans 327
Flagstaff War (1844–6) 250
Flanders 112, 114, 140
Flemings 112
flight, powered, development of 343, 344
flint mines 15

Florence, Italy 139; Ciompi rebellion (1378) 140; dedicated to republican liberty 141

Florida 160, 233

food plants, spread of 152

food supply xx–xxi

foragers 9, 14

Ford, Henry 344

Formosa (Taiwan) 256, 259, 277; early cultures in 41; since 1945 296, 297

Fox, Vicente 321

France see also French; Napoleon Bonaparte
   1648 to 1715, ascendancy 196–198; cultural ascendancy 198; famine (1693–4) 198; territorial consolidation 197; war 197–198
   1713 to 1815, fight for global supremacy 199–200
   Algeria, invasion of (1830) 253, 258
   Britain, clashes with 199–200
   cave paintings 8
   colonialization 258
   concordat with Papacy (1516) 147
   domination of Europe (1920s) 278
   English expelled from 148
   German occupation of (1940) 283
   Germany, alliance with (1894) 261
   in Great Depression 280–281
   iron production in 219
   Italian workers in 218
   Italy, invasion (1494) 189
   monarchy in (1154–1314) 110–112; consolidation 111–112
   rearmament in (1890s) 261
   riots in (2006) 331
   Spain revolts against rule by 213–214
   violence in (1930s) 279

Francis II, Emperor 196

Francis of Assisi (1181–1226) 91

Franciscans 91, 110; missionaries 162

Franco, Francisco 278

Franco-Prussian War (1870–1) 225

Frankfurt 94; National Assembly 222

Frankish kingdom, rise of (482 to 814) 94–97, 108; Carolingian government 96–97; Charlemagne 96; expansion 98; Merovingians 95

Frankish missionaries 90, 102

Franklin, Benjamin 208

Franks 79, 85–86, 89, 90, 112

Frederick I, Emperor (1152–90) 109, 110

Frederick II, Emperor of Germany 102

Franz Ferdinand, Archduke 262, 265

Frederick Barbarossa, Emperor 111

Frederick the Great 199

Free Trade Area of the Americas 318

Frémont, John C. 226

French: in the Americas 160, 161, 163; aristocracy 187; colonies in Africa 254–255, 258; empire (1919 to 1941) 272; explorers in N America 40; forces in Canada 200; Huguenot settlers in southern Africa 164; migrants 233; on the Senegal river 252, 254, 258; in southeast Asia 179; voyages of discovery (1487 to 1780) 154–155; see also France

French and Indian War (1754–60) 161, 200

French East India Company 200

French Revolution (1789 to 1797) 200, 208, 210–212, 221, 223; from reform to terror 211; legacy of 212

Freud, Sigmund xxvi, xxvii

friars 91

Frisia 98

Frisians 95, 102, 112

Fronde rebellion (1648–53) 187, 189

Fujiwara family 115, 116

Fukuyama, Francis: The End of History (1992) 341

Fulani cattle-keepers 251

Fulani state 252

Futa Jallon 251–252

Futa Toro 251–252

Gadsden Purchase (1853) 226

Gaiseric 86

Galerius 80

Galicia 85

Galileo Galilei xxxii–xxxiii

Gallipoli 136

Gallo-Romans 95

Gambia 254

Gandhara 54, 58

Gandhi, Indira 306

Gandhi, Mahatma 247, 273

Gandhi, Rajiv 307
"Gang of Four" 299
Ganges River 47; delta 29
Ganj Dareh, Zagros 11–12
Gao, Niger 135, 163
Garibaldi, Giuseppe 225
Gascony 111, 112, 141
Gasga 34
Gaul: conquest by Roman Empire 71–72;
    Franks establish kingdom in 79, 85, 94;
    Saracen pirates in 97
Gaza 87
Gaza Strip 313, 314
Geisa, Duke (972–97) 101
General Strike (1926) 279
Geneva Protocols (1977) 335
Genghis (Chingiz) Khan 120, 121–122, 124,
    133, 170
Genoa, Italy 106, 114, 137, 140, 190
Genocide Convention (1948) 335
Genpei Wars (1180–5) 116
George I of England 196
Georgia, ethnic war in 331
Georgia, USA 199, 232
German: colonies in Africa 254, 258; Jews
    (*Ashkenazim*) 93; migrants 233–234;
    threat in 1890s 261; tribes 78
German Confederation 222, 224
German empire (962 to 1250) 108–109; and
    the Papacy 109–110; imperial
    government 109
Germanic settlement of western Europe (341
    to 597) 84–86; European periphery 86;
    Franks 85–86; Ostrogothic Italy 86;
    Visigoths 85–86
Germans 108
Germany *see also* World War, First; World
    War, Second
  colonization 258, 260
  dynastic alliances 148
  economic growth 196
  extremism in (1930s) 279
  expansion of (1931 to 1941) 282, 283
  France, alliance with (1894) 261
  French power in (1800) 213
  in the Great Depression 280
  industrialization in 220

Italian workers in 218
new frontiers after Second World War 290
peasants' rebellion (1525) 182
population growth 217
princely houses 141
unification, struggle for (1815 to 1871)
    223–226; unification from above
    224–225
Germany, East 290, 325
Germany, West 291
Geta (209–12) 76
Gettysburg, B. of (1863) 232
Ghana 84, 135
Ghassanids 87–88
Ghazan Khan (1295–1304) 120, 123, 133
Ghibelline faction 141
Ghilzai Afghans 169
Ghuzz Turks 120
Gibraltar 191
Gilimanuk, Bali 21
Giong Ca Vo, Vietnam 21
Giong Phet, Vietnam 21
Girondin faction 211
Giza, Egypt, pyramids 32
glasnost 328
global economy, emerging (*c.* 1775) 203–205;
    Asia, trade with 205; mercantilism
    203–204; slave economy 204–205
'global warming' xxi, 345–346
Go-Daigo, Emperor 116–117
Go-Toba, Emperor 116
Goa 155, 156
Göbekli Tepe, Anatolia 11
Goethe, Johann von 196
Gold Coast 254, 274, 295
gold 134, 136, 156; 184; gold rushes 248, 265,
    250, 265
Gold Standard 220, 264–265, 280
Golden Horde (Kipchak Khanate) 108, 123
Gona, Ethiopia 3
Gonzaga, Charles, Duke of Nevers 191
Gorbachev, Mikhail 293, 328, 330
Gorm, king of Denmark 100
Gorze monastic houses, Lorraine 109
Gothenburg (Älvsborg), Sweden 193
Goths 78, 85 *see also* Ostrogoths; Visigoths
Government of India Act (1935) 247

governments, language differences with
 subjects 188
Granada, Spain 102, 133, 148
Grand Canal (China) 166
Grant, Gen Ulysses S. 232
grasses, wild, domestication 9–10, 14, 16, 18
Great Exhibition (1851) 207
"Great Leap Forward" 298
Great Northern War (1700–21) 194, 202
"Great Persecution" (303–12) 80
Great Proletarian Cultural Revolution
 298–299
"Great Trek" (1836) 253
Greece: clay inscriptions 30; democracy in
 (1974) 330; democracy suspended in 278;
 intellectual life xxxii; Mycenaean 48–49;
 nationalist agitation in 221–222;
 settlements in 47; war against
 communists in (1947) 292
Greek
 civil war (1822–30) 222
 civilization, spread of (800 to 336 BC)
  xv–xvi, 58–61; "age of the tyrants" 59;
  Athenian empire 59–60; expansion, age
  of 59; Macedon, rise of 60–61; polis
  (city-state) 58, 59–60
 colonies, western Mediterranean 70
 empire (13th century) 106
 influence on Roman Empire 74–75
 medicine xxiii
 migrants to Australia 249
 trading posts 53
Green Party 347
'greenhouse gases' xxi, 346
Greenland 17, 100
Gregory VII, Pope (1073–85) 90, 91, 109
Grodno 93
Grozny, Chechnya 332
Guadalcanal 284
Guadalest, Spain: Museum of Torture
 Instruments xxv
Guaymí chiefdom 146
Guelph faction 141
Guevara, Ernesto "Ché" 320
Guianas 161, 163
guinea pigs 18
Gujerat, India 127–128

Gulf War (1991) 316, 326, 338
Gumbinnen 266
Gupta empire 67, 69, 125
Gurkhas 245
Gustav Vasa of Sweden 192
Gustavus Adolphus of Sweden (1611–32) 193
Guzman, Abimael 337

Habibie, BJ 304
Habsburg dynasty 168, 195, 224; Austrian 197;
 Spanish 197
Habsburg empire 189–190, 191; and demands
 for national unification 223; decline of
 261; lands 148; nationalism in 222–223
Hadrian (117–38) 77, 92
Hafrsfjord, B. of (890s) 100
Haidar Ali 171
Haithabu, Denmark 113
Haiti 37, 144, 145, 209
Ham Nghi 259
Hamas 314, 336
Hamburg, Germany xxvi–xxvii, 93
Hamid Karzai 308
Hammurabi of Babylon 31; law code 32
Hamwic, England (later Southampton) 113
Han dynasty 52, 53, 63, 64; expansion 64–65;
 invasions 130
Han Empire 43; break up of 65–66
Hang-chou, China 119, 166
Hang Gon, Vietnam 21
Hannibal xix, 62, 74
Hanover 194
Hansa trading confederation (Hanseatic
 League) 139, 140, 192
Harald, king of Denmark 100
Harald Finehair 100
Harappa, Indus valley 27, 29, 45
Harappan culture 45
Harun al-Rashid, Caliph 131
Harvey, William xxiii
Hattin, B. of (1187) 133
Hattusa, Anatolia 34
Hattushash, Anatolia 34
Hattusili I (c. 1650–1620 BC) 34
Hau Xa, Vietnam 21
Hausa merchants 135
Hausaland 135, 252

Hawaiian Islands 24
health, public 217
Heaven and Earth Society 173
Hebrew Bible 54
Hegel, Georg (1770–1831) xviii, 221
Helena 101
Hellenism 52
Hellenistic world (336 to 30 BC) 61–63;
    centres for literary work 62; cultural life
    in successor states 61–62; growth of
    Roman power 62–63
Henry I, king of Saxony (911–36) 100, 108
Henry II, King of England 111, 112
Henry IV, emperor 109
Henry VI, Emperor (1190–7) 110
Henry VII, King of England 159
Hephthalite Huns 58
Heraclius (610–41) 104
Herat 89, 121, 169
Herero revolt 260
heretical movements 91, 102, 104, 110, 111
Herodotus 60
Herzegovina 137
Herzl, Theodor (1860–1904) 223
Hesiod 59
Heuneburg hill fort 71
Hezbollah 336
Himiko, Empress 115
Hindenburg, Field Marshal 267
Hindu cults in southeast Asia 129
Hindu nationalism 306, 308
Hindu Rajput princes 170
Hinduism 45, 47, 124, 128, 260; temple 125,
    126–127
Hindus 247, 305, 306
Hippocrates xxiii
Hira, Iraq 58, 88
Hiroshima, Japan 285
Hispaniola 37
Hitler, Adolf xx, 282, 283, 285, 287, 289, 291,
    312; rise of 273, 279
Hittite empire 34–35, 55
Hittites 32, 34, 35
HIV virus xxiv, xxxix, 232, 310, 312 see also
    AIDS
Ho Chi Minh 274, 301
Hoabinhian tradition 20

Hobbes, Thomas xxxiii; Leviathan (1651) xxxii
Hohenstaufen 109–110
Hohokam culture 39
Hôjô family 116
Holland: agriculture in (1500 to 1815) 180–181,
    182; economic strength 183, 184; Louis
    Bonaparte rules 213; see also Dutch;
    Netherlands
Holstein-Gottorp, house of 194
Holy Land 101–102
Holy League of Venice, Austria and Poland-
    Lithuania 201
Holy Roman Emperor, concordat with
    Papacy (1448) 147
Holy Roman Empire
    1493 to 1806 194–196; economic growth
    196; religious wars 195–196
    and Italy (1494 to 1797) 190–191
Holy Wars (jihads) 241, 251, 252
Homer 47, 49; Iliad 59; Odyssey 59
Homestead Act (1862) 226
hominines 2–4, 5, 6, 41
Homo erectus 3–4, 5, 6, 19, 23, 41
Homo ergaster 3–4
Homo heidelbergensis 3–4
Homo sapiens 4, 6, 23, 41
Hong Kong xxxviii, 244, 258, 295
Hopewell, Ohio 39
horses, domestication of 70
horses re-introduced into New World 8
Hosokawa family 117
Hospitallers 103
Hsi-an, China 42
Hsi-hsia kingdom 118
Hsienpei people 66
Hsin dynasty (AD 9–23) 65
Hsiungnu see Huns
Hsüan-tsang 125
Hu Yaobang 299
Huari people 36
Huayna Capac 143
Hudson's Bay Company 235, 236
Huguenots, persecution of 197
Huitzilopochtli, warrior god 145
Hülegü 120
Hülegü Khan 123
human origins 2–4

human sacrifice 145
humans, ice age 7–8
humans, modern 4; 'bottle-necking' 5; spread
 of 4–6
Humayun 170
Hundred Days' Reform (1898) 260
Hundred Years' War (1337–1453) 141, 148
Hungarian Church 98
Hungarian Plain 98
Hungary 101, 107; in 14th century 142;
 Austrian possession of 201; democracy
 suspended in 278; granted independence
 (1867) 222; Jewish community in 94;
 Mongol attack on 122; nationalist
 agitation in 221–222; and the Ottomans
 137, 167, 168, 290; revolt in 209, 242;
 ruled by Romania 287; uprising (1956)
 325
Huns (Hsiungnu) 53, 64, 65, 66, 78, 125;
 Asiatic 85; Hephthalite and Chionite 58
hunters xx, xxi, 9, 36, 40; Paleolithic 7–8
hunting 17
Hus 141
Hussein, Saddam 315, 316, 337, 338, 339
Hussites 104, 142
Hutt valley, New Zealand 250
Hutu people 311
Hyderabad province 171, 306
Hyksos people 33
Hyrcania 57

Ibalpiel of Eshnunna 31
Iberian peninsula, Muslims in 133
Ibrahim, sultan (1640–8) 168
Ice Ages 7–8, 14, 17; population movement
 8
Iceland 100
Ichi-Go offensive (1944) 285
Igbo people 309
Il-Khan dynasty 133
Il-Khanid empire 120
Ile de France 111
Ilkhans 122, 123
Illinois 227, 230, 234
Ilmert, Ehud 314
Imhotep xxxi
Imperial Aulic Council 191

Imperial Cameral Tribunal 195
Imperial Diet 190, 195
Imperial Examination System (Chinese) 117
Imperial Preference 280
imperialism (1919 to 1941) 272–274; in the
 1930s 273–274
Imphal, Burma 284
Inca empire 36, 84, 143–144, 161, 162;
 destruction of 151
Independence, Missouri 227
"Independence" cultures 17
India
 500 BC to AD 550 67–69; first empire
  67–68; the Guptas 69; Kushana empire
  67, 68–69
 550 to 1206, emergence of temple
  kingdoms 124–127; Cholas, rise of the
  125–126; dynastic struggles 125; temple
  Hinduism 125, 126–127
 1206 to 1526, Delhi sultanate 127–129;
  India and Islam 128–129; the Hindu
  south 128
 since 1947 305–306, 307–308
 Anglo-French rivalry in 200
 Anglo-French war in 179
 under British rule (1805 to 1935) 245–247;
  anti-imperial politics 247 campaign for
  self-rule 247, 273
 empire 67, 68–69
 exploitation and dependency 246–247
 British empire, as keystone of 258–259
 Chinese invasion (1962) 308
 conquest of xxxvii
 Europeans kept at arm's length 151
 independence 269, 294, 305
 influence on southeast Asia 21
 irrigation in 28
 and Islam 128–129
 military crisis (2002) 341
 Mongol attacks on 128
 Mughal, 16th-century resurgence of
  Muslim power 150
 Mughal, and growth of British power (1526
  to 1803) 170–171; and East India
  Company 171; Mughal decline 171
 nationalist movements 273
 Taj Mahal 171

India – *cont.*
  trade with 45, 157
  Turks in 124, 126, 127
  and volcano eruption 5
Indian army 246
Indian civilization, beginnings of (to 500 BC)
  45–47; post-Indus India 46; the south
  46–47; Vedic religion 47
Indian civilization, expansion of 52
Indian emigrants 218
Indian Mutiny (1857) 246
Indian National Congress 247, 305
Indian shipping 153
Indo-China 245, 258, 260, 274
Indonesia 129, 131, 300–301, 304
Indra, warrior god 47
Indus valley 27, 28, 68; culture 45, 46;
  cultivation of 45; first cities 29; writing,
  early 30
industrial production xxi
Industrial Revolution
  in Europe (1815 to 1870) 219–221; mid-
  century boom 220; proto-
  industrialization 219–220; "second"
  220–221
  in Great Britain (1760 to 1820) 205–207;
  conditions for growth 206–207; new
  technologies 206; social revolution 207
influenza, 'Spanish' xxii
Ingermanland (Ingria) 193, 194
Innocent III, Pope (1198–1216) 91, 110
Innocent IV, Pope (1243–54) 110
International Bank for Reconstruction and
  Development 290
International Criminal Court 335
International Monetary Fund (IMF) 312,
  342
Inti, sun god 143
Inti Plan 318
Inuit, ancestors of 17
Iowa 234
Ipswich, England 113
Iran: 600 to 1501 119–121; rise of Safavids 138;
  from the Safavids to the Qajars (1501 to
  1906) 168–170; *see also* Persia
Iran, Islamic Republic of 310, 316
Iran-Iraq war (1980–8) 315–316, 337

Iranian plateau 56, 57
Iraq: 1979 to 2007 337, 338–339; British
  trusteeship of 272; civil war in (2003
  onwards) 316, 339; independence (1932)
  273; invades Kuwait (1990) 316, 338;
  occupation of (2003) 326, 337, 339;
  unrest in (800 to 1100) 132; war with
  Iran (1980–8) 315–316, 337: *see also*
  Mesopotamia
Ireland; 900 to 1050 99–100; attempted
  conquest of (1171) 112; civil war in
  278–279; conflict in (since 1920s) 336;
  famine in 181, 218, 234; megalithic
  tombs 15; nationalist agitation in 209,
  221–222, 223, 273, 291, 331; political
  agreement in (1998) 331; and potato
  crop 181; under Scandinavian control
  113; southern, "dominion status"
  273
Irish church 90
Irish migrants 218, 233–234, 236
Irish missionaries 90, 102
Irish Republican Army (IRA) 336
iron industry 206, 219–220
iron-working in Africa 73
Iroquois tribe 160
Isabella of Spain 189
Isfahan, Iran 120, 169; Mosque of 120
Islam xxviii–xxix, 52, 72–73 *see also* Muslims
  in Africa 134, 164, 251, 252; from 1960s
  309–310, 311–312
  and India 127, 128–129
  in Indonesia 129, 131
  in Middle East since 1945 316
  and Mongols 122–123
  in Philippines 129, 131
  rifts xxx
  rise of 84
  spread of 88–89, 90, 118, 129, 131, 134, 164;
  culture 89; Muslim conquests 88–89;
  politics 89, 307
  terrorism xxviii–xxix, xxxviii, 336, 340
Islamic militants 336, 338
Islamic rule in Iran 119–120
Islamic Salvation Front 336
Islamist organizations in southeast Asia
  304–305

Ismail 252–253
Isma'il, Shah (1501–24) 138
Isma'il I of Iran 169
Israel: Arab-Israeli conflict 312, 313–314, 325; kingdom of 54; state created 313; terrorism in 336 *see also* Palestine
Istanbul 191; Suleimaniye mosque and tomb complex 167
Italian merchants 132
Italian migrants 218, 249
Italians routed in Abyssinia 255, 259
Italy
    Abyssinia, invasion of (1935–6) 273, 281
    colonialization 258
    democracy restored in (1949) 291
    empire dismembered 294
    Fascists in 278
    France conquers 189, 191, 213
    and Holy Roman Empire (1494 to 1797) 190–191
    invasion of (1556–7) 190
    Jews saved in 289
    Kingdom of, declared (1861) 225
    nationalist agitation in 221–222
    northern, in 14th C 141
    Ostrogoths in 86
    post-Renaissance xx
    religion in xxviii
    struggle for unification (1815 to 1871) 223–225, 226; unification from above 224–225
Iturbide, Agustin de 238
Ivan III of Muscovy (1462–1505) 158
Ivan IV of Muscovy 158, 192, 193
Ivory Coast 311
ivory trade 252
Iwo Jima 284

"Jacobins" 208, 209, 211
Jaffna, Sri Lanka 307
Jagiello, duke 142
Jahangir (1605–27) 170–171
Jainism 45, 47, 67
James I, King of England 187–188
James II, King of England 188
Jamestown, Virginia 160
janissaries, Turkish 168, 240

Japan
    to 1477, imperial 114–117; influence of China 115–116; shogun, first 116–117
    1477 to 1868, under the shogunate 176–178; the *daimyō* 176–177, 178; Tokugawa control 177–178
    1868 to 1922, expansion and modernization of xxxvii, 255–257; industrialization and trade 256–257; success, cost of 257
    since 1945 296–297
    air raids on (1945) 285
    China, war with 245, 256, 260, 281
    Chinese territory, moves into 275, 276–277
    defeat of (1945) 274, 276
    emperors, quasi-divine status xxix
    in Great Depression 280, 281
    Korea, invasion of (1592) 166, 174
    Korea annexed (1910) 175
    Manchuria, invasion of (1931) 175, 273, 275, 276, 281
    modern technology adopted 265
    Russia, war with (1904–5) 256–257
    in Second World War 283–285
    tools, early 22
Japanese emigrants 218
Japanese merchants 177
Jarrow, N.E. England xxxi
Jaunpur, India 127–128
Java: "Culture System" 180; Dutch control of 179; early man in 19, 21, 23; Hindu temples in 129, 130
Jefferson, Thomas 230
Jehol 276
Jem 137
Jena, B. of (1806) 213
Jenne, Songhay empire 135, 163
Jenne-Jeno, Africa 73
Jenner, Edward 217
Jerf al Ahmar, Anatolia 11
Jericho, Jordan 12, 13
Jerome Bonaparte, king of Westphalia 213
Jerusalem 62, 92, 101, 103, 105; in Assyrian period 54, 56; capture of (1099) 132; Dome of the Rock 89; First Temple 93; Latin kingdom of 103; True Cross of 101
Jesuit missionaries 162
Jesus Christ 80, 81

Jewish diaspora (AD 70 to 1800) 92–94;
    eastern Europe 94; Jewish life, revival of
    93–94; medieval Jewry and expulsions 93
Jewish migration to Palestine 273
Jews 79–80, 87, 92; anti-Semitism 288, 289;
    European, demand national state in
    Palestine 223; European, murder of xxvi,
    286, 288–289, 312; German (Ashkenazim)
    93; in Spain 142; see also Judaism;
    Zionism
Jharkhand state 306
Jiang Qing 299
Jochi 122
John, King of England 110, 112
John II of Byzantium (1118–43) 105
John III of Sweden (1568–92) 186, 193
John III Sobieski of Poland-Lithuania
    (1674–96) 201, 202
Johnson, Andrew 232
Johnson, Lyndon 325
Jôkyû War (1221) 116
Joliet, Louis 226
Jordan 12, 314
Joseph Bonaparte, king of Naples and Spain
    213
Judaea 92
Judah, kingdom of 54
Judaism 52, 79, 93 see also Jews; Zionism
Jui-chin 276
Julian 78, 80
Julius Caesar 71–72, 75, 76
Jurchen (Liao) people 44
Justinian 79, 86; Codex xxix

Kabir (1440–1518) 128
Kabul, Afghanistan 89, 338
Kadesh, B. of (1275 BC) 35
Kadyrov, Ramzan 332
K'ai-feng, China 119
Kalinga 68
Kalisz, Poland 93
Kalmar, Union of 142, 192, 193
Kalmar, War of (1611–13) 193
Kamakura, Japan 116
Kamakura shogunate 116
Kandahar, Afghanistan 338
Kanem city state 135

K'ang-hsi, emperor (1661–1722) 172
Kanisha 68
Kano city state 135
Kansas 231
Kansas-Nebraska Act (1854) 231
Kansu rebellion (1781–4) 172
Kant, Immanuel xxxii
Kanuri kings 135
Kara Khitai 121
Kara Mustafa, Grand Vizier 168, 201
Karadzic, Radovan 332
Karaman emirate 137
Karelia 193
Karens 307
Karim Khan Zand 169
Karlsruhe, Germany 196
Kashmir 306
Kasi mahajanapada 67
Kassites 35
Katsina city state 135
Kaupang, Norway 113
Kaveri river delta 126
Kaya, Korea 43
Kazan khanate, conquest of (1552) 158
Kefe (Caffa), Crimea 137
Kellogg-Briand Pact (1928) 278
Kemal Atatürk 240, 241
kenmon (Japanese chains of fealty) 116
Kennedy, John F. 325
Kentucky 226
Kenya 254, 258, 273; Rift valley 3
Kerensky, Alexandr 271
Kerma, Egypt 16–17
Kettler, Gotthard 192
Khalji dynasty (1290–1320) 127
Khan Batu 107
Khandesh, India 127–128
Khao Jamook, Thailand 21
Khartoum 252
Khaybar, Arabia 87
Khazars 107
Khedives 252, 260
Khilafat Movement 247
Khitan (Liao) 118, 121
Khiva Khanate 170
Khmer Rouge 302–303
Khmer rulers 130

Khoisan peoples 164
Khok Phamon Di, Thailand 20
Khomeini, Ayatollah 316, 337
Khotan 68
Khrushchev, Nikita 327
Khuan Lukpad, Thailand 21
Khufu (Cheops) 32
Khurasan 120
Khwarizm 121
Kiangsi Soviet 276
Kiden-Hutran (c. 1235–1210 BC) 35
Kiev 99, 107, 108; lost to Muscovy (1667) 159,
    201; Mongol invasion of 122; ruler of 98
Kievan Rus 157–158
Kievan Russia (882 to 1242) 106–108;
    expansion of 107; Mongol invasions
    107–108
Kilia 137
Kilwa city state 136
Kim Il Sung 175
Kim Pu-sik: Samguk sagi (c. 1145) 44
King's Lynn, England 139, 140
Kipchak Khanate (Golden Horde) 108, 123
Kisiwani city state 136
Klasies River Mouth, Africa 5
Knights of St John 167
Knossos 47, 48
Know Nothing "nativist" party 234
knowledge, human xxx–xxxi
Koch, Robert xxiii
Koguryo (northern Korea) 117, 118
Koguryo tribe 43
Kokand Khanate 170
Kongo kingdom 164
Köprülü family 168, 201
Koran 88, 89
Korea
    to 1392 43–44
    1392 to 1953 174–176; Japanese annexation
        (1910) 175, 257, 259
    Japanese invasion of 166
    Mongol invasion 44
    northern (Koguryo) 117, 118
    northern parts placed under Chinese
        administration 65
Korea, North 297
Korea, South 296, 297

Korean peninsula, unification 115
Korean War (1950–53) 175, 296, 292, 324,
    334
Kororareka, New Zealand 250
Koryo dynasty 44
Koryo era (918–1392) 174
Kosala mahajanapada 67
Kosciuszko, Tadeusz 203, 208
Kosovo 136–137, 331, 333
Kossuth, Lajos 222
Ku Bua, Thailand 129
Ku Klux Klan 232
Kublai Khan 122, 165
Kuns 107
Kurds 123
Kurile islands 256
Kursk, B. of (1943) 286
Kushan empire 52, 53, 54, 58, 67, 68–69
Kushite kingdom 72
Kuwait 316, 338
Kwangsi rebellion (1790) 172
Kweichow rebellion (1795–7) 172
Kyongju, Korea 44
Kyoto, Japan 116, 117, 177
Kyoto Summit and Agreement (1997) 340,
    346, 347

Lagos 258; B. of (1759) 200
Lakhmids 87–88
Lamongan, Java 21
Lancashire 218
Land Captains 243
land-rights, Japanese (shiki) 115–116
Lang Rongrien, Thailand 20
Lang Vac, Vietnam 20
languages: Akkadian 31, 34; early
    Mesopotamian 31; Greek 61; Indo-Aryan
    46; Latin 95; Na-Dene 17; Nahua 39;
    Quechua 143; Sumerian 31
Languedoc 111
Laos 302, 303
Lapita people 24
Las Navas de Tolosa, B. of (1212) 103
Later Chou dynasty 118
Latin 95
Latin America see also Central America;
    Mesoamerica; South America

Latin America – *cont.*
  1500 to 1825 161–163; beyond the frontiers 162–163; moves for independence 163; Portuguese in 162
  1810 to 1910, independence and national growth 237–239; commodity booms 239; early 20th century 239; political stability 238–239; revolt against Spain 238
  left-wing rebels in 337
Latin Christians 104; Crusaders 105
Latin empire in Aegean 104, 106
Latvia 278
Lausanne, Treaty of (1923) 241
Le Grand Siècle 198
"League of Corinth" (338 BC) 61
League of Nations 241, 272, 273, 278–279, 281, 294, 312, 324
League of the Three Emperors 261
Leang Burung, Celebes 20
Lebanon 272, 313–314, 315
Lechfeld, B. of (955) 98
Lee, Gen Robert E. 232
Lee Kuan Yew 304
Legalism 63–64
"legitimism", principle of 209, 221
Legnica 122
Leinstermen 100
Leipzig, B. of (1813) 214
Lelang colony, Korea 43
Lemberg 266
Lemnos 201
Lenin, V. I. 270, 271
Leopold, King of the Belgians 254
Lepanto, B. of (1571) 168, 190
Levant: as battle ground between rival empires 34; early agriculture in 9, 10; Egyptian influence in 55–56; lime plaster vessels used 12
Levant Company 191
Lewis, Meriwether 226
Leyte Gulf, B. of (1944) 284
Li Tzu-ch'eng 167, 172
Liao (Jurchen) people 44
Liao (Khitan) 118, 121
Liaotung peninsula 256–257
Liberia 311
Libya 258, 262, 295

Libyans 33
Licinius 80
Lin Biao 298
Lincoln, Abraham 228, 231, 232
Lindisfarne, Northumberland 98
Lippmann, Walter 291
Lisbon 133, 238
Lithuania 157–158; in 14th century 142; grand dukes of 158; Jewish migration to 92, 93; state created 278; struggle for control in 148; union with Poland 158
Liu Pang (256–195 BC) 64
Liu Shaoqi 298
Livonia 102, 159, 192, 193, 194
Livorno, Italy 94
llamas 18
Lloyd George, David 272
Lo-yang, China 42, 65
Locke, John xxxiii
Lodi dynasty (1451–1526) 127, 128
loess 14, 41
Lombard League 109
Lombards 79, 86, 96
Lombardy 141, 190, 225
London: coastal market in 113; Hansa trade through 139, 140; international trade 184; Jews in 94; population 183, 196
London, Anglo-Dutch Treaty of (1824) 180
London, City of 265
Long Giao, Vietnam 21
"Long March" 276
Lorraine, Gorze monastic houses 109
Los Angeles 232
Louis I 96
Louis VI of France (1108–37) 111
Louis IX of France 102
Louis XIV of France 179, 188, 189, 194; and ascendancy of France 196, 197, 198
Louis XVI of France 210, 211
Louis Bonaparte 213
Louisburg, fall of (1758) 200
Louisiana 160, 233
Louisiana Purchase (1803) 226, 231
Low Countries, agriculture in (1500 to 1815) 180–181, 182
Lualaba region, upper 136
Luanda, Angola 156

Luang Prabang, Thailand 130
Luba state 164
Lublin, Union of (1569) 158
'Lucy' (fossil skeleton) 3
Ludendorff, Gen 267
Lunda state 164
Luther, Martin (1483–1546) 185
Lützen, B. of (1632) 193
Luxembourg 148
Lvov 93
Lvov, Prince 271
Lydia 55, 56
Lynn (King's Lynn), England 139, 140

Maastricht Treaty (1991) 329
Macao 154, 155
MacArthur, Gen Douglas 284
Macassar, seizure of (1667) 179
Macedon, kingdom of 60–61, 63
Macedonia 74, 106; emperors 104; phalanx 62
Madagascar 218
Madras, India 157
Madrid 340
Magadha, India 47, 67–68
Magellan 154
Magenta, B. of 225
Maghreb (northwest Africa) 89, 134
Magyars 97, 98, 100, 101, 107, 108
Mahabharata 126
"mahajanapadas" 67
Mahavira 47
Mahayana Buddhism 68–69, 125
Mahdiyya movement 260
Mahmud of Ghazni (927–1030) 126, 127
Mainz cathedral 114
maize, American 181
Majapahit empire 84, 130, 178
Maji-Maji revolt 260
Majorca 141–142
Malabar 154
Malacca 130, 154, 155, 178, 179, 180, 258
Malatya plain 12
Malaya 294, 301, 302; "emergency" 302
Malayan archipelago 178, 179, 180
Malaysia 302, 304
Malcolm II, king of Scotland 100
male primogeniture, principle of 147

Mali empire 84, 135
Malinke merchants 135
Malta 167, 190, 191
Malthus, Thomas: *Essay on the Principle of Population* (1798) xxvii, 216–217
Mamluks 132, 133, 134, 138, 164, 167
man, early 2–3, 19; in China 41; in Melanesia and Polynesia 23–24
Manchuria 44, 118, 172, 257, 276; Japan invades (1931) 175, 273, 275, 276, 281
Manchus 167, 172, 245, 281
Mandela, Nelson 311
Manila, Philippines 154
Mannheim, Germany 196
Mansa Musa, king 135
Mantuan Succession, War of the (1629–31) 191
Manuel I of Byzantium (1143–80) 105
Manzikert, B. of (1071) 105, 132
Mao Zedong 276, 284, 292, 298–299
Maoris 24–25, 249, 250, 251
Maratha kingdoms 246
Marathas 171
Marathon, B. of (490 BC) xvi
Marconi, Guglielmo 343
Marcos, Ferdinand 304
Marcus Aurelius (161–80) 77
Margaret of Norway 142
Marib, Yemen 87
Mark Antony 63, 75, 76
markets, coastal (*wics*) 113
Marne valley 71
Marquesas islands 24, 258
Marquette, James 226
Marrakesh 133
Marseilles (Massilia), France 71, 184
Marshall Aid 324
Martinovics, Ignaz 209
Marx, Karl xviii, xxxiv, 219
Marxism 336
Mary Tudor, Queen of England (1552–8) 186
Masina 251–252
Massachusetts Bay 160
Massilia (Marseilles), France 71, 184
Masudi 125
Masurian Lakes 266
Maurya empire 67, 68

Maxentius 78, 80
Maximilian I, Emperor (1493) 195
"May 4th Movement" 275
Maya empire 146
Mayan people 20, 38, 84
Mayapán, Yucatán 146
Mayflower communities 160
Mazarin, Cardinal 188
Mazzini, Giuseppe 222, 224
Mecca, Arabia 87, 88
Medes people 55, 56
Median (formerly Yathrib), Arabia 87, 88
medicine: advances in xxi, xxiii–xxiv; Chinese
    xxii–xxiii; Greek xxiii
Mediolanum see Milan
Mediterranean trading posts 53
Mediterranean world (1494 to 1797) 189–191;
    Britain in 191; Italy and the Holy
    Roman Empire 190–191; Ottoman
    threat to 190
Megalithic Europe 14–15
Mehmed I (1413–21) 137
Mehmed II, Fatih, "The Conqueror"
    (1451–81) 106, 137
Meiji emperor 255
Mekong delta 29
Melaka, Sultanate of 131
Melanesia to the 1700s 23–25; island resources
    24–25; migrants, first 23–24
Memel, Lithuania 282
Mentuhotep of Thebes 33
mercenaries, Byzantine 105
MERCOSUR 318
Merneptah (1213–1203 BC) 35
Meroë 72
Merovingian Kingdom 94, 95
Merovingians 95
Merv 120, 169; B. of (651) 89
Mesoamerica, peoples of (300 BC to AD 1300)
    37–39; Maya, rise of the 38; rise of
    Teotihuacán 38; Toltecs, rise of the
    38–39
Mesoamerica on eve of European conquest (c.
    1300 to 1520) 144–146; outside the
    heartland 146; the Aztec 145–146; the
    Maya 145–146 see also Central America;
    South America

Mesopotamia 89, 92 see also Iraq
    Assyria controls 55
    Babylon rules 35
    as battle ground between rival empires 34,
        35
    construction of early canals 28
    early empires (c. 3500 to 1600 BC) 30–32;
        Agade empire 31
    early temples 13
    first cities 29, 30–31
    foundations of civilization 13
    Lakhmid Arab kingdom of Hira 58
    languages, early 31
    southern, marsh areas 11
    trade 29, 45
    writing, early, in 30
Messenians 60
metallurgy, early 15, 20–21
Methodius 91
Métis (mixed blood) communities 161
Metternich, Chancellor 223
Metz, French sovereignty over 197
Mexican labour in USA 235, 323
Mexican Revolution 319
Mexico
    since 1910 319–321; democratization
        320–321; revolution and intervention
        319–320
    after 1939 323
    early people establish capital 20
    early societies in 37
    on eve of European conquest 144, 145, 146
    independence (1825) 163
    industrial growth 239
    influence on North America 39–40
    insurgency in 238
    plants, domestication of 10
    Spanish settlement in 162
    US war with (1846–8) 231
Miao people 172
microchip, silicon, development of 343,
    344–345
Middle Ages 83–84, 92, 112
Middle East: Islam in (since 1945) 316;
    nationalism in (since 1945) 314, 315–316;
    secularism in (since 1945) 314–316
Midway, B. of (1942) 284

Miesko I (960–92) 100–101
migrants 218
    Asian 235, 236, 237, 249
    in Australia 249
    British 233–234, 236
    in Canada 235, 236–237
    Chinese 218
    Cuban 235
    in New Zealand 251
    in United States 233–235; controls and
        continuity 235; early 19th century
        233–234 ; "new" immigrants 234
Mikhailovich, Tsar Alexis (1645–76) 158–159
Milan (Mediolanum), Italy 77, 78, 190, 191
Mill, John Stuart: *On Liberty* (1859) xxxiii
Milosevic, Slobodan 333
Minamoto clan 116
Minas Gerais, Brazil 162
Mindanao, Philippines 260
Ming dynasty 44, 130, 150, 172, 174
    China at the time of (1368 to 1644)
        165–167; consolidation 165–166; overseas
        expansion 166–167
Minnesota 234
Minoan civilization (*c.* 3000 to 950 BC) 47–48
Minorca 191
Mishnah (AD 200) 93
missionaries 90, 102, 162
Mississippi, River 226, 232
Mississippi Valley, Middle 40
Missouri 227, 231
Missouri Compromise of 1820 231
Mitanni kingdom 34, 35
Mitannians 34
Mithradates I (171–138 BC) 57
Mithradates II (123–87 BC) 57
Moa (bird) 24–25
mobility, spatial xxxvi
Mobutu regime 311
Moche people 36
Modena, Italy 225
Mogollon culture 39, 40
Moháacs, B. of (1526) 167
Mohammad, Prophet 87, 88, 128
Mohammed Najibullah 338
Mohenjo-Daro, Indus valley 27, 29, 45
Moldavia 242

Moldova 330, 331
Moluccas 154
Mon rebellion 179
monarchies of Europe 187
monarchy in Britain and France (1154–1314)
    110–112
Möngke, Great Khan 123
Mongol empire (1206 to 1405) 121–124; and
    Christianity 122–123; conquests in
    Europe 122; emergence of 84; invasions
    107–108, 116, 117, 119; and Islam 122–123,
    133; last conquests 123–124; power,
    ebbing of 158
Mongolia 275
Mongolia, Inner 118, 275
Mongols 106; in China 165, 166; in India 128;
    invasion of Korea 44; retreat from
    Anatolia 136; sack of Samarkand xxvi
Monophysite Christians 90
Mont Lassois, France 71
Monte Albán, Mexico 20
Montenegro 222, 240, 332, 333
Montreal, fall of (1760) 200
Moravia 100, 282
Moravians 98
Morea 137
Mormons 226
Morocco 164, 274, 286, 294
Moscow 108, 214; Kremlin 158
Moselle valley 71
motor vehicles, development of 220, 343–344
Mozambique 155, 253, 295
Msiri, King 252
Mughal India, 16th-century resurgence of
    Muslim power 150
Mughal India, and growth of British power
    (1526 to 1803) 170–171; and East India
    Company 171; Mughal decline 171
Mughal painting 170–171
Muhammad, Prophet 87, 88, 128
Muhammad Ali 240, 252
Muhammad bin Tughluq (1325–51) 127
Muhammad Ghuri 127
Mukden, Manchuria 172
Multiculturalism Proclamation (1971) 237
Munich Pact (1938) 282
Murad II (1421–51) 137

Murat, Joachim 213
Mureybet, Euphrates 11
Murray River, Australia 8
Mursili I (*c.* 1620–*c.* 1590 BC) 34
Musa 89
Musandam peninsula 12–13
Muscovite armies in the Baltic 193
Muscovy, Grand Duchy of 148, 157–158, 193
    see also Russia
Muslim army 103; conquests 88–89;
    occupation of Sicily 97
Muslim Brotherhood 316
Muslim League 305
Muslim power, 16th-century resurgence of
    150, 151
Muslim suicide bombers 340
Muslim world
    800 to 1100 131–132
    1100 to 1350 132–134; the Crusades 133–134
Muslims 88, 89; in India 247, 305, 306; and
    Mongols 122–123; resist Russians in
    central Asia 259; Shi'ite xxx, 89, 123, 169,
    316, 339; Sunni xxx, 169, 316, 339; *see also*
    Islam; Islamic *entries*
Mussolini, Benito 278, 288
Muwatalli (1295–1271 BC) 35
Mwenemutapa empire 164
Myanmar *see* Burma
Mycenae, Greece 47–48, 58
Mycenaean civilization (*c.* 3000 to 950 BC)
    48–49
Myos Hormus, Red Sea 54
Mysore state 171

Na-Dene language speakers 17
Nabonidus (555–539 BC) 56
Nabopolassar (626–605 BC) 55
Nabta Playa, Egyptian Western Desert 16
Nadir Shah 169, 171
NAFTA (North American Free Trade
    Agreement) 323, 342
Nagasaki, Japan 155–156, 285
Nagorno-Karabakh 331–332
Nahua language 39
Nairobi, Kenya 312
Najran, Arabia 87
Nakhon Pathom, Thailand 129

Nalanda, India, Buddhist university 125
Namibia 73, 311
Nanak (1469–1539) 128
Nanking, China 166
Nantes, bishop of 98
Nantes, Edict of (1685) 198
Napata kingdom, Egypt 17, 72
Naples, Italy 183, 190, 191, 213, 225
Napoleon Bonaparte
    counter-revolution 209
    and Egypt 240
    and French revolution 210
    invades of Italy 191
    invades Russia (1812) 214
    plans to invade Britain 200
    and the reshaping of Europe (1799 to 1815)
        212–214; defeat and exile 214; military,
        primacy of 213–214
Napoleon III 225
Napoleonic Code xxix
Napoleonic Wars (1803–15) 213
Nara, Japan 115
Naram-Sin (2213–2176 BC) 31
Nariokotome, Kenya 3
Narva, B. of (1700) 194
Nasser, President 315
Natal 73, 258
National Action Party (PAN) (Mexico) 321
nationalism (1919 to 1941) 273, 274
nationalism, new 287–288
nationalism in Europe, rise of (1800 to 1914)
        221–223; independence, struggle for
        221–222; nationalism exported 222–223
Nationalist (Kuomintang) Party 275–276,
        277, 284, 297
nationalist movements 260–261, 274, 293,
        294, 295
NATO (North Atlantic Treaty Organization)
        292, 308, 324, 331, 333
Navarre, army of 103
Navigation Acts 204
Nazi Party 94, 279, 286
Ndebele people 255
Neanderthals 4, 5–6
Nebraska 231
Nebuchadnezzar (604–562 BC) 55–56
Nebuchadnezzar I (1126–1205 BC) 35

Negrais island 179
Nehru, Jawaharlal 274, 306
Nelson, New Zealand 250
Nemrik, Anatolia 11
Neo-Confucianism 174
neo-liberalism 318
Neolithic trade 12–13
Neolithic villages 12
Nero (54–68) 76, 80
Nestorian Christianity 90, 123
Netherlands: economic strength 183, 184;
    German occupation of (1940) 283;
    northern, republican tradition 148;
    opposition to Philip II 187, 188, 189, 191;
    see also Dutch; Holland
Neustadt as place-name 114
Neustria 95
Neuville as place-name 114
Neva, River 106; B. of (1240) 108
Nevali Çori, Anatolia 11
Nevers, Charles Gonzaga, Duke of 191
Nevsky, prince Alexander 108
New Amsterdam see New York
New Brunswick 236
"New Deal" recovery policies 280, 322
New Economic Partnership for African
    Development (NEPAD) 312
New Economic Policy (USSR) 272
New France 235
New Guinea 23–24, 258
New Mexico 39, 160, 231, 323
"New Order" 281, 286, 290
New Plymouth, New Zealand 250
New South Wales 248
New York (New Amsterdam) 160, 228, 234;
    al-Qaeda attacks 312, 326, 338, 340; stock
    market 279
New York state 234
New Zealand
    since 1800 249–251; economic and political
        development 250–251; migration and
        national consciousness 251; wars 250
    Britain claims sovereignty over 258
    charting of 154
    man reaches 4, 24–25
Newfoundland 236; fishing grounds 159–160
Newport as place-name 114

Newton, Isaac: Principia Mathematica (1687)
    xxxii
Nguom, Vietnam 20
Nicaea, church council (325) 81
Nicaea, Greek enclave at 106
Nicaragua 146, 320
Nicarao people 146
Nicholas I, Tsar (1825–55) 242
Nicholas II, Tsar (1894–1917) 243–244, 271
Nien rebellion 244
Nietzsche, Friedrich xxxix; Thus Spake
    Zarathustra (1888) xxx
Nieuwpoort as place-name 114
Niger delta 73
Nigeria 254, 258; since 1957 309, 310–311, 312
Nihavand, B. of (642 BC) 58
Nil Kham Haeng, Thailand 20
Nile, River 8, 134, 253; delta 16
Nile valley 15, 16, 27, 28, 32
Nimrud, Assyria 55
Nine Years' War (1688–97) 198
Ninevah, Mesopotamia 13, 55
Nishapur 120
Nixon, Richard 299, 325
Nizhniy Novgorod 107
Nok culture 73
nomads 83, 98, 106, 107 see also Mongols
Non-Cooperation Movement 247
Non Nok Tha, Thailand 20
Non U-Loke, Thailand 21
Norman Conquest of England (1066) 99
Normandy 98, 111
Normans 105, 106, 111
Norse people 98–99, 100
North America see also Americas
    300 BC to AD 1300, early peoples of 39–40;
        towns, first 40
    1500 to 1810: 151, 159–161; political hostility
        and military threat 161
    aboriginal peoples 160–161
    animal life 8
    ceremonial earthworks and burial places
        19
    conflict in 199–200
    colonists, Britain's restrictions on 199
    power, growth of xxxvii–xxxviii
    slave revolts 209

North America – *cont.*
waters of, Britain surrenders control of
200
North American Free Trade Agreement
(NAFTA) 323, 342
Northern Ch'i dynasty 67
Northern Chou dynasty 67
"Northern Expedition" (1926) 275
"Northern Rising" (1569–70) 187
Northern War, Second (1655–60) 201
Northern Wei dynasty 67
Norway 100, 221–222, 223, 283
Nova Scotia 161, 236; fishing grounds
159–160
Novgorod, Russia 99, 107, 108, 139, 158
Nubia 33, 72–73, 134
Nubians 16
nuclear weapons 292–293, 324, 325, 333, 341
see also atomic bombs, dropping of
Nupe 252
Nuremberg, Germany 139
Nyamwezi people 252
Nyasa, Lake 252
Nystad, Treaty of (1721) 159

Oc Eo 129
Octavian (later Augustus) 63, 75–76
October Manifesto (1905) 243
Oda Nobunaga (1534–82) 176
Odoacer, *magister militum* 78–79, 86
OECD (Organization for Economic
Co-operation and Development) 342
Ögödei, Great Khan 122, 123
Ohio 234
oil, reliance on 340
oil crisis (1973) 329
Okhrana secret police 243
Okinawa 284
Oklahoma 226; City bombing 336–337
Olmecs 20
Olympia, religious sanctuary 59
Olympic Games (2008) xv, xvi, 300
Omar, caliph 89
Omar, Mullah 338
Omo basin, Ethiopia 5
Ônin Wars (1467) 117
Ontario, Canada 236

"Operation Desert Storm" 316, 326, 338
opium trade 173, 244
Opium War, First 244
"oppida" fortified settlements 71
Orange Free State 253
Ordos region, China 41
Oregon Trail 226
Organization for Economic Co-operation
and Development (OECD) 342
Organization for European Economic
Cooperation 290
Ormuz 155
Orthodox Church 91, 108, 185, 186
Osaka, Japan 177
Osama bin Laden 336, 340
Oslo Accords (1993) 314
Osman 136
Ostrogoths 79, 85, 86
Otranto, Italy 137
Ottar 113
Otto I, German emperor 98
Otto I, king of Saxony (936–73) 100,
108–109
Ottoman empire
1281 to 1522, rise of 106, 136–138, 189; defeat
and reconstruction 137
1522 to 1800 167–168, empire under
pressure 168
1648 to 1795, revival and decline 201–202
1800 to 1923, disintegration of xxxvii,
240–241, 260, 261–262; Turkey,
modern, creation of 240, 241
conquers Egypt 164
defeated by Russia (1876–7) 262
expansion in the Middle East 138
Muslim power, 16th-century resurgence of
150–151
struggle for control in 148
threat to Mediterranean world 190
Ottoman navy 137, 167
Ottoman-Spanish truce (1577) 190
Ottoman Turks 84
Ottoman-Venetian war (1499–1502) 137
Ottonians 109
Oudh province 171
Overland Mail 227
Oxus valley 68

Oyo 163
ozone layer 347

Pachuca, Mesoamerica 38
Pacific, Second World War in (1941–5)
      283–285; Allied build-up 284; final defeat
      284–285
Pacific islands, colonization of 4
Pacific Islands, emigration from 251
Pacific islands to the 1700s 23–25; island
      resources 24–25; migrants, first 23–24
Paekche, Korea 43, 115
Paekmagang River, B. of (668) 115
Pagan, Myanmar 130
Pakistan 294, 305–306, 307, 341
Pala family 125, 126
"Pale of Settlement" 94
Palestine 54, 89, 92, 132; since 1918: 312–313;
      Arab uprising 273; British trusteeship of
      272; British withdrawal from 294, 313,
      336; Egyptian trading expeditions to 33;
      European Jews demand national state in
      223; see also Israel
Palestine Liberation Organization (PLO)
      313–314, 336
Palestinian National Authority 314
Pallava dynasty 125, 126
Pan Ch'ao, China 53
Pan-p'o, China 41
Panama 144, 146; canal 152
pandemics xxii see also individual entries
Panikkar, K. M. 149
Panipat, B. of (1526) 170
Papacy, the 91–92
      962 to 1250, apogee of papal power 110;
            and the German empire 109–110
      centralization 141
      concordats 147
Paramara dynasty 125–126
Paris:, Bastille, storming of (1789) 210;
      Germans occupy (1870) 225;
      improvements in 198; Louis XIV driven
      from 188; population 183, 196
Paris Peace Conference (1919) 257, 275
Park Chung Hee 297
Parrattarna 34
Parthia 68

Parthian empire 52, 53, 57, 58
partition, age of: Eastern Europe (1648 to
      1795) 201–203; Ottoman revival and
      decline 201–202; Poland, partitions of
      202–203
Pasargadae, B. of (550 BC) 56
Passarowitz, peace of (1718) 202
Passau 98
Pasteur, Louis xxiii
Pataliputra, India 47, 68, 69
Pearl Harbor (1941) 283, 284, 324
peasants and feudalism 182
Peasants' Revolt (1381) 140
Pechenegs 107
Pedro I of Brazil 238
Pegu, Myanmar 130
Peipus, Lake, B. of (1242) 108
Peking 245, 275 see also Beijing
Peking Man 41 see also Homo erectus
Peloponnesian War (431–404 BC) 60
Penang, Malaya 179
penicillin xxiv
Pennsylvania 229–230
Pentagon, attack on (2001) 340 see also
      Washington, terror attacks on
People's Liberation Army (PLA) (Chinese)
      298, 299
"People's Will" group 243
Pereyaslav, Treaty of (1654) 158
Pernambuco, Brazil 157
Perón, Juan D. 317
Persian empire 89 see also Iran
      Alexander the Great's conquest 61
      aspects of Greek culture adopted 62
      empires of (550 BC to AD 637) 56–58;
            Parthian empire 52, 53, 57, 58; Sasanid
            Persia 57–58, 77
      Safavid, 16th-century resurgence of
            Muslim power 150–151
      Sasanid, rulers of 104
      war in (540–62) 79
Persian Gulf, settlement in 12–13
Persian shipping 153
Persians 54, 56, 59, 60; Sassanid 57–58, 77, 87,
      104
Peru 162, 238, 317, 337
Peruzzi banking house 139

Peter I (the Great) of Russia 159, 194, 202;
    political acumen 202
Petrograd (St Petersburg) xx, 159, 271
Petrograd Soviet (elected assembly) 271
pharoahs 32
Philadelphia 234
Philip II, king of Macedon 60–61
Philip II, King of Spain 187, 190
Philip IV, King of France (1285–1314) 111,
    112
Philip IV, King of Spain 187, 188
Philip V, King of Spain 191, 198
Philip Augustus (1180–1223) 111
Philippine Sea, B. of (1944) 284
Philippines: since 1975 304; Christianity
    enforced 151; early man in 20; resistance
    to US 259, 260; spread of Islam into 129,
    131; trade with 154; US annexation of
    214, 215, 259; US forces reoccupy 284;
    US leaves 300
Phoenicians 58–59, 72, 73; colonies 70;
    trading posts 53
Phrygia 55
Phung Nguyen, Vietnam 20
Piast dynasty 101
Picts 100
Piedmont-Sardinia 224–225
Pike, Zebulon 226
Pilgrimage of Grace (1536) 187
Pipil people 146
Pippin II 95
Pippin III 95
piracy 117, 204
Pisa, Italy 114
plague, bubonic xxi–xxii, 138, 139, 140, 217
Plains of Abraham, B. of (1760) 161
plants, domestication of 9–10, 14, 16, 18
Plassey, B. of (1757) 200
Plawangan, Java 21
Pliny (AD 23–79) 53
PLO (Palestine Liberation Organization)
    313–314, 336
plough, farming by 15, 151
Po valley xx, 114
Podolia 201
Pohai, Manchuria 41, 43
Pol Pot 302, 303

Poland 101; in 14th century 142; democracy
    suspended in 278; Germans invade
    (1939) 282, 289; Germans living in 287;
    Jewish migration to 92, 93; Mongol
    attack on 122; and Napoleon 213;
    nationalist agitation in 221–222; political
    protests in (1953) 290; revolt in (1794)
    208, 209; Russian expansion into 159;
    Slav state in 100–101; state reconstituted
    278; struggle for control in 148; union
    with Lithuania 158
Poland-Lithuania 158, 201, 202–203; diet
    (Sejm) 202, 203
Polish migrant workers 218
Polo, Marco 122
Polovtsy 107
Poltava, B. of (1709) 159, 194
Polynesia to the 1700s 23–25; island resources
    24–25; migrants, first 23–24
Polynesian canoes 153
Polynesians in New Zealand 251
Poniatowski, Stanislaw, king of Poland 202,
    203
Pony Express mail service 227
population explosion xxi, xxvii, 217
population growth, 20th-century 339–340
population growth and movements (1815 to
    1914) 216–218; movement 218;
    population explosion 217
Portugal 133; clashes with Spain 199;
    democracy in (1974) 330; independence
    (1668) 188; megalithic tombs 15;
    Napoleonic invasion (1808) 238; new
    dynasty in 142; opposition to Philip IV
    187, 188
Portuguese: in Africa 135, 136, 164, 252, 253,
    254; in the Americas 162, 163; in
    southeast Asia 178–179, 180; Jews
    (Sephardim) 93; possessions outside
    Europe 155, 156, 237; royal family 238;
    traders 155–156, 157; voyages of discovery
    from (1487 to 1780) 153–154
Poson, B. of (863) 105
potatoes 10, 18, 181
Potsdam conference (1945) 290
pottery: early European 14; Moche 36;
    Painted Grey Ware 46; Saladoid 37

Prague 93, 142
Prakrit 68
Prambanan, Java 130
Pratihara empire 125
Pøemyslid dynasty 101
PRI party 321
Princip, Gavrilo 262
printing press, invention of 185
Protestantism xxx, xxxiv, 186
Prussia, Duchy of 192, 203, 213, 224, 225
Prussians 104
Pskov, annexation of (1510) 158
Ptolemaic Egypt 61, 62
Pu Yi 281
Puerto Rico 37, 214
Pulakesin II 125
Punic War, First (264–241 BC) 74
Punic War, Second (218–201 BC) 74
Punjab 127, 305
"Puranas" 126
Purusapura 68
Pushyabhuti, Harsha 125
Pushyabhuti dynasty 125
Putin, Vladimir 328
Pydna, B. of (168 BC) 63
Pyongyang, N Korea 43
pyramids, Giza 32
Pyramids of the Sun and Moon 38
Pyrenees, Peace of the (1659) 197

Qajar dynasty 168–169, 170
Qazvin, Iran 169
Qermez Dere 11
Qubilai Khan 122, 165
Quebec, Canada 160, 200, 236, 237
Quechua language 143
Quentovic, France 113
Quetzalcoatl, Temple of 38
Quiberon Bay, B. of (1759) 200
Quito 209
Quraysh tribe 87
Qutbuddin Aibak 127

racism (1919 to 1953) 288–289
radio, invention of 343
Raffles, Sir Stamford 180
railways: expansion of 220, 264; first 206,

207, 219; transcontinental 152, 264; US
226, 228, 229, 230
Rajput princes, Hindu 170
Rajputs 125
Ram Mohan Roy 247
Ramayana 126
Ramses II 33, 35
Ramses III (1184–1150 BC) 33, 35
Rashtrakuta empire 124, 125
Ravenna, Italy 79
Re, sun god 33
Reagan, Ronald 325
record-keeping, early 12
Red Army 286
Red Brigades 336
"Red Guards" 298–299
Red Sea 87
Reformation, the (1517–1670) 92, 185–186;
       Protestantism, challenges to 186
refrigeration, development of 264
Regensburg, Germany 98, 195
religion xxvii–xxxi, 43, 44, 45, 47, 52; in
       Europe xxxiv; martyrs xxx; psychological
       power xxix; rifts xxix–xxx; and rise of
       terror 340; and scientific advances
       xxxii–xxxiii; and violence xxv–xxvi,
       xxxiv; 'wisdom literature' xxx–xxxi;
       see also individual entries
religious buildings xxix
religious resistance movements 260
religious wars (1493 to 1806) 195–196
Renaissance in Europe (1450 to c. 1600)
       147–148
Republican party, US 231, 232, 233
resistance movements 259–261
resources, natural, depletion of xxi
Reval, Estonia 192
revolt, age of (1773 to 1814) 207–209; counter-
       revolution 209; revolution, spread of
       208–209
Rhine, river 78, 114
Rhineland 114, 183, 282
Rhodes, Cecil 254, 255
Rhodes 167
Rhodesia 258, 273
Rhodri Mawr 100
Rhône, river 114

Rhône valley trade-route 71
Ribe, Denmark 113
Richard I (the Lionheart), King of England 102
Richard II, King of England 141
Richmond, Virginia 232
Rift Valley 15
Rig Veda 46, 47
Riga, Latvia 159
Rights of Man, Declaration of the (1789) 209, 210–211
Rim-Sin of Larsa 31
Rio de Janeiro, Brazil 162, 238
Rio de Janeiro agreements (1992) 347
river valleys, fertile, exploitation of 27, 28
Rivera, Primo de 278
Robert the Bruce 112
Robespierre, Maximilien 211
Rocky Mountains 226
Rollo 98
Roman Empire xvii, xx, 52, 53
    in Africa 72
    Antonine plague xxii
    army xix
    barbarian incursions 78
    Egypt, annexation of 63
    Gaul, conquest of 71–72
    Greek influence 74–75
    invasion of Greece and Asia Minor 62–63
    and Parthian empire 57–58
    power, expansion of (to 31 BC) 73–75; expansion to the east 74–75; from republic to empire 75; Punic wars 74; Rome, nature of 77; stability and strife 76–77
Roman power, height of (31 BC to AD 235) 75–77
    technologies xxxi–xxxii
Roman missionaries 90, 102
Romania: conquest of 266; democracy suspended in 278; independence (1878) 222, 240, 262; Jewish community in 94
Romanian Orthodox Church 186
Rome 73–74; attacked by Celts (390 BC) 71; becomes capital of Italy (1870) 225; and expansion of Christianity 90–91, 106;

Jews in 94; nature of 77; sack of (1527) 190; Senate 74, 75, 76, 79
Rome, B. of (312) 78
Rome to Byzantium, from (AD 235 to 565) 77–79; reconquests of Justinian 79, 86; rise of Christianity 78, 80–81
Romulus Augustulus 78–79, 86
Roncesvalles, B. of (778) 96
Roosevelt, Franklin D. 280, 322
root crops, domestication of 10, 18
Roskilds, Peace of (1658) 193
Rouen, France 98
Rousseau, Jean-Jacques xxiv, xxxiii; Social Contract (1762) 208
Roussillon 197
Royal Niger Company 255
Ruhr mines 218
Rukh, Shah (1405–47) 121
Rupert's Land 235, 236
Rus (or Vikings) 102, 105, 106–107; kingdom of 99
Rus, Kievan 107, 157–158
Rus, western 108
Russia: and Balkan crisis 262; becomes dominant in Baltic 194; Christianity in 91, 107; civil war 288; defeat of Ottoman empire by (1876–7) 262; economy 342; emigration 258; First World War 266, 270–271; invasion of central Asia 259; migrant workers in 218; Mongol invasion of 122, 123; Napoleon invades (1812) 213, 214; railways in 220, 264; Turkey, assault on 260; voyages of discovery from (1487 to 1780) 154; war over Chechnya 332; see also Muscovy; Soviet Union; USSR
Russian empire
    expansion and modernization (1815 to 1917) 242–244; reforming tsars 243; revolution and war 243–244
    expansion in Europe and Asia (1462 to 1815) 157–159; growth of empire 158–159
    Jewish community in 94
Russian Federation 328
Russian Revolution (1917 to 1929) xx, 267, 269, 270–272, 291; civil war 271; second revolution 271

Russian state, first: Kievan Russia (882 to 1242) 106–108; expansion of 107; Mongol invasions 107–108
Russians, Tsarist 170
Russo-Japanese War (1904–5) 175, 243, 256–257
Ruthenians 186
Rwanda 164; genocide (1994) 311
Ryuku islands 256

Sabi Abyad 12
"Sacred War" (356–46 BC) 61
Sadat, Anwar 313
Saddam Hussein 315, 316, 337, 338, 339
Sadowa, B. of (1866) 225
Safavid dynasty 168, 169
Safavids 121, 138, 167, 168
Saffarid dynasty 120
saffron 139
Sahara 4, 15, 16, 134, 135
Sahul (greater Australian continent) 21
Saivism 126
Saiyid Ahmad Khan 247
Sakhalin, southern 257
Saladin 103, 133
Salem, Massachusetts xxx
Salendra kingdom 130
Salian emperors 109
Salinas, Carlos 321
Salt Lake City, Utah 227
Salvador (formerly Bahia), Brazil 162
Samanid dynasty 120
Samanids 131
Samarkand, Iran xxvi, 120, 121, 169
Samoan region 24
Samory 252, 254, 259–260
Samos 59
Samudragupta 69
samurai 116
San Francisco, California 227
San Martín, José de 238
Sanskrit 46, 68, 129
Santarem, Amazonia 144
Santiago military order 103
Sappho 59
Saracens 95, 97
Sarajevo 265, 332–333

Sardinia 97, 141, 190, 191
Sarekat Islam 260
Sargon (c. 2296–2240 BC) 31
Sargon II (721–705 BC) 55
Sasanid family 56, 57–58
Sasanid Persia, rulers of 104
Sassanid Persians 77, 87
Satavahana dynasty 125
Satavahanas 68, 69
satellite communications 345
Savoy, duchy of 85, 190
Saxons 86, 96, 102
Saxony 98, 183, 196, 219
Saxony, elector of 195–196
Sayyid dynasty (1414–51) 127
Scandinavia 100, 112–113, 142, 233–234 see also individual countries
Scandinavian Union of Kalmar 192, 193
Scandinavian world 113
Scandinavians 112, 113; conversion to Christianity 102
Scanian War (1676–9) 194
Schiller, Johann von 196
Schlieffen Plan 266
Schliemann, Heinrich 47
Schmalkaldic League, Protestant 195
Schmitt, Carl xxv
science, advancement of xxxii–xxxiii, xxxv–xxxvi
Scotland 100, 112, 218
Scots 100, 233
Scythian tribes 68
"sea peoples" 35
SEATO (South-East Asian Treaty Organization) 292, 300, 301
Seddin, King's Grave 70
Seine, river 114
Sejong, King (1418–50) 174
Seleucia 62
Seleucid Asia 61, 62
Seleucid kingdom 57
Seleucus Nicator 68
Selim I (1512–20) 138
Selim III, sultan 240
Selim the Grim 167
Seljuk family 120
Seljuk period (1055–c. 1200) 120

Seljuk Turks 105, 106, 119; Sunni 131, 132, 133
Sembiran, Bali 21
Senegal 258
Senegal River 15; French on 252, 254, 258
Sennacherib (704–681 BC) 55
Seoul, Korea 175
Septimius Severus (193–211) 76–77
Serb nationalists 262, 265
Serbia 86, 202; and Austria 262–263, 265–266; conflict (1991–5) 330–331, 332; conquest of 137, 266; independence 222, 240, 262, 333
Serbians 136–137
Seven Years' War (1563–70) 192–193, 202
Seven Years' War (1756–63) 161, 200
Severus, Septimius (193–211) 76
Severus Alexander (222–35) 76–77
Seville, Spain 133
Shabwa, Yemen 87
Shahjahan (1629–57) 171
Shaka tribe 57, 68
Shalmaneser III (858–824 BC) 55
Shamash, Babylonian sun god 32
Shamshi-Adad I 31
Shang dynasty (c. 1520–1030 BC) 29–30, 41–42
Shans 307
Shantung 275
Sharia law 312
Sharifian dynasties 164
Sharon, Ariel 314
Shattiwaza 35
sheep farming 139, 181
Sher Shah 170
Sherman, Gen Philip T. 232
Shih Huang-ti 64
Shi'ite Fatimids 131, 132, 133
Shi'ite Muslims xxx, 89, 123, 169, 316, 339
shiki (Japanese land-rights) 115–116
Shining Path movement 337
Shiraz, Iran 120, 169
Shiva (god) 126
Shona people 255
Shu kingdom 66
Shutruk-Nahunte (1185–1155 BC) 35
Siam see Thailand

Siberia 151, 152
Siberians 17
Sicilian Vespers, War of the 140–141
Sicily 109–110; Allies invade (1943) 286; Aragonese rule 142; Austria holds 191; Muslim occupation 97, 131; Normans in 111; Spanish viceroy rules 190
Sierra Leone 254, 311
Sigismund, king of Poland 193
Sihanouk, Prince 301
Sijilmassa, Africa 134
Sikhism 128
Sikhs 245, 306
Silesia 183, 196, 199, 202;
Silisian army 122
Silistra, B. of (971) 105
Silk Road 53, 64, 120
silk trade 53, 64, 69
Silla, Korea 43, 44
Sillan armies 115
Sinan, architect 167
Sind, India 89
Sindhis 245
Singapore 180, 258, 302, 304
Sinkiang, China 53
Sino-Japanese War (1894–5) 245, 256, 260
Sinop, Turkey 242
Sivaji 171
Slave Kings (1206–90) 127
slave revolts 209
slave trade 71, 75, 152, 156, 157, 162, 203, 204–205, 218, 233, 252; Europeans and 164–165
slavery in United States 230–232
Slavs 85, 91, 100, 102
Slovakia 282, 330
Slovenia 332
smallpox 217
Smith, Adam: The Wealth of Nations (1776) xxxvi
Smolensk 107, 158, 193
Sobieski of Poland-Lithuania, John III (1674–96) 201, 202
Social Contract (1762) 208
Social Revolutionaries 271
Social War (91–89 BC) 75
Society Islands 24

Sofala 156
Sogdiana 58, 118
Sögüt 136
Sokoto 252
Solferino, B. of (1859) 225
Solomonids 136
Soma, deity 47
Somalia 295, 311
Somaliland, Italian 258
Somme, B. of the (1916) 267
Somme-Bionne, France 71
Somoza clan 320
Song Empire 44
Songhay empire 84, 135, 163, 164
Sonora, Mexico 39
Sophocles 60
South Africa 309, 311
South African War (1899–1902) 255
South America see also Latin America;
    Mesoamerica
  c. 1300 to 1535, on eve of European
    conquest 142–144; Amazonia 144; the
    Incas 143–144
  since 1910, search for stability and
    development 316–319; war and
    depression 317; urbanization, populism
    and violence 317–318; violence,
    democracy, neo-liberalism and
    globalization 318–319
  peoples of (300 BC to AD 1300) 36–37
South-East Asian Treaty Organization
    (SEATO) 292, 300, 301
Southampton, England (formerly Hamwic)
    113
Southern Cult religion 40
Soviet communist bloc, collapse of (1989–91)
    xxxix, 293
Soviet Union see also Russia; USSR
  break-up of 324, 326, 328, 330
  and Cold War 324–325
  deportations 288
  development of (since 1929) 326–328; cost
    of modernization 327–328; protest and
    reform 328
  German non-aggression pact with (1939)
    282
  and Middle East 315

  in Second World War 283, 286, 287, 289,
    327
Soviets (elected assemblies) 271
space programme 344
Spain: Arab conquest of (711) 89; Basque
    independence movement 291, 331, 336;
    Christian invasion of 132, 133; clashes
    with Great Britain and Portugal 199;
    concordat with Papacy (1523) 147;
    democracy in (1975) 330; and Dutch
    rebellion 187, 188; early farming 14; in
    Great Depression 280–281; Islam in 131,
    133; Jews in (Sephardim) 93, 142; Latin
    American revolt against 238; megalithic
    tombs 15; migrant workers in 218;
    military rule imposed (1923) 278;
    Napoleonic invasion (1808) 238;
    northern, cave paintings 8; revolts 188,
    213–214; ruled by Aragon and Castile
    148; voyages of discovery from (1487 to
    1780) 153–154
Spain, Reconquista of 102, 103, 185
Spanish Civil War (1936–9) 282
Spanish colonies 237
Spanish Habsburgs 197
Spanish in North America 160
Spanish in the Americas 161–162, 163
Spanish Inquisition xxv–xxvi
Spanish Netherlands 197
"Spanish Road" 191
Spanish Succession, War of (1701–14) 191,
    198
Sparta 60
Spengler, Oswald: The Decline of the West
    xviii
Spice Islands 179
spice trade 155, 156, 178
Spinola family 190
Spiz (Zips) 203
Sri Ksetra, Myanmar 129
Sri Lanka (Ceylon) 294, 306–307
Sri Vijaya empire 84, 178
Srivijaya, Sumatra 130
Ssu-uma family 66
St Ambrose 78
St Helena 214
St Louis, Missouri 227

St Paul 80
St Petersburg (Petrograd) xx, 159, 271
stagecoaches 227, 228
Stalin, Josef 272, 326, 327
Stalingrad, B. of (1942) 286
Stanislaw Poniatowski, king of Poland 202, 203
Stanley, H. M. 254
Starya Ladoga, Russia 113
Staufen emperors 109
steam power 206
steamships, development of 229, 263–264
steel output 220
Stephen, king of Hungary (997–1038) 98, 101
Strategic Arms Limitation Treaty (SALT) (1972) 293, 325
Stuttgart, Germany 196
Su-chou, China 166
Sudan 135; British conquest of 258; British reconquest of 255; civil war in 316; Nile valley 15; war in 309, 311, 312
Sudan, Nilotic 252
"Sudanic belt" 134, 135
Sudetenland 282
Sueves 85
Suez, Egypt 167; canal 152, 246; invasion (1956) 295
Sufi saints 128
sugar, cane 152, 181
sugar trade 203, 204
Suhar, Yemen 87
Suharto, President 301, 304
Sui dynasty (581–618) 65, 67, 117
suicide bombers, Muslim xxviii–xxix, 340
suicide (kamikaze) pilots 285
Sukarno, Achmed 274, 300–301
Sukarnoputri, Megawati 304
Sukhothai, kingdom 130
Suleiman the Magnificent (1520–66) 138, 167, 168
Sultaniya, Azerbaijan 120
Sumatra 5, 180
Sumerian civilization xxxi
Sumerian language 31
Sumitomo family 177
Sun Yat-sen 245, 274, 275

Sunda shelf 23
Sung dynasty 66, 117, 118–119
Sung-chiang, China 166
Sunni Ali, king of Songhay 135, 163
Sunni Muslims xxx, 169, 316, 339
Sunni Seljuk Turks 131, 132, 133
Superior, Lake 229
Suppiluliuma (1344–1322 BC) 34
Surat, India 157
Susa, Mesopotamia 30, 31
Susilo Bambang Yudhoyono 304
Sven, king of Denmark 100
Svyatoslav, Grand Prince (c. 962–72) 107
Svyatoslavich, Vladimir (980–1015) 107
Swahili-Arabs 252
Sweden: 900 to 1050 100; Baltic empire 192–193; breaks away from Scandinavian Union 192; power, decline of 194; wars with Denmark (1643–5, 1657, 1658, 1676–9) 193, 194
Swedes 99, 108
Swedish migrants 233
Swiss Confederation 141
Swiss migrants 233
Syria 33, 55, 87–88, 132, 272
"Syrian jugglers" 53
Szechwan, tribal risings in (1746–9, 1771–6) 172

Tabon Cave, Palawan 20
Tabriz, Iran 120, 122
Tahiti 258
T'ai-p'ing rebellion 244
Taika revolution (645) 115
Taino people 37, 145, 146
Taira clan 116
Taiwan (Formosa) 256, 259, 277; early cultures in 41; since 1945 296, 297
Taj Mahal, India 171
Tajikistan 120
Takauji, Ashikaga 116, 117
Taliban 308, 338
Talmud (AD 500) 93
Tamerlane (Timur) 120–121, 124, 128, 137, 170; followers of 119
Tamil Tigers (LTTE) 307
Tamils 307

T'ang Chinese armies 115
T'ang dynasty 43, 117–118
Tanganyika 254, 260, 272
Tanganyika, Lake 252
Tangier 191
Tanguts 118
Tannenberg, B. of (1914) 266
Tanzania, "Ujamaa" policies 310
Tanzimat reforms 240–241
Taoism xxii
Tapajós chiefdom 144
Taranaki, New Zealand 250
Taranto, Italy 97
Tarim Basin 118
Tariq ibn Ziyad 89
Tashkent 170
Tasmania (Van Diemen's Land) 248
Tatar Chin 119
Tatar invasions xxxiv
Taxila 69
tea trade 205
technologies: development of xxxi–xxxii,
    xxxv–xxxvi; early 3; Western, export of
    xxxviii
Teheran conference (1943) 287
Tehran, Iran 169
telecommunications 344–345
telegraph service, US 227–228
telephone, invention of 343
Tell 'Uqair, Mesopotamia 30
Templars 103
temples: Central Andes 19; early 13
Tenasserim 180
Tenedos 201
Tennessee River 232
Tenochtitlán xxxv, 145, 146
Teotihuacán, Mesoamerica 38
Ternate 131, 156
terror, rise of, and religion 340
"terror, war on" 326, 335
terrorism, world, since 1945 335–337; and
    nation-building 336; and social
    revolution 336–337
Tertry, B. of (687) 95
Teutonic Knights 104, 108, 140
Teutonic Order 192
Texas 160

Texcoco, Lake 145
textile industry 206, 219, 229
Thailand: 1954 to 1975 301; since 1975;
    Buddhist shrines in 129; early man in 20,
    21; French in 179; military coup (2006)
    305
Tham Khuong, Vietnam 20
Thebes, Egypt 33, 55, 60
Theodoric 86
Theodosius 81
Thera, volcano 48
Theravada Buddhism 131; teachings 68–69
Thessaly 61, 106
Third Department 242
Thirteen Years' War (1654–67) 158
Thirty Years' War (1618–48) 93, 191, 193, 194,
    195
Thomson, Joseph 343
Thorn, burghers rebellion 192
Thorn, Peace of (1466) 192
Thrace 61, 85, 106
Three Feudatories, rebellion of (1674–81)
    172
Thucydides 60
Ti people 66
Tiahuanaco, Bolivia 36
Tiber, River 73
Tiberius (14–37) 76
Tibet 275
Tidore 131
Tiglath-pileser III (744–727 BC) 55
Tigris valley, lower 27, 28, 30
Tikulti-ninurta I (1233–1197 BC) 35
Tilsit, Treaty of (1807) 213
Timbuktu, Niger 135, 163
"Time of Troubles" (1605–13) 158
Timur see Tamerlane
Tipu Sultan 171, 209
Titicaca Basin, Bolivia 36
Tito, Marshal 290
Titus (79–81) 76
Tlatelolco 145
Toba volcano, Sumatra 5
tobacco 152; trade 203, 204
Tocharians 57
Togoland 254, 272
Tokugawa Ieyasu 176

Tokugawa Shogunate xxxvii, 176–178
Toltecs, rise of the 38–39
Tongan region 24
tools, early xxxi, 3, 22, 15; Asian 20
Tordesillas, Treaty of (1494) 154, 162
Toronto, Canada 236
Toul 197
Toulouse, France 85
Toungoo, Myanmar 130
Touraine 111
Tournai, France 95
Toxandria 85
Toynbee, Arnold: *A Study of History* xviii
Toyotomi Hideyoshi (1536–98) 176
trade, Baltic 192
trade, global (*c.* 1775) 203–205; Asia, trade
    with 205; mercantilism 203–204; slave
    economy 204–205; and "triangular"
    152, 203, 204
trade, Neolithic 12–13
"trade diasporas" 53
trading, early, in Eurasia 29, 30–31
trading empires, expansion of (1500 to 1700)
    155–157; Dutch expansion 156–157;
    European rivalries 157; Portugal's
    trading empire 156; trading routes,
    Eurasian 52–54, 64
Trafalgar, B. of (1805) 213
Trajan (98–117) 76, 77
Trang Khen, Vietnam 20
Trans-Siberian Railway 264
Transjordan, British trusteeship of 272
transport, motorized, development of
    343–344
transport revolution (1870 to 1914)
    263–264
Transvaal 253, 255
Trasimene, Lake, B. of (217 BC) 74
Trent, Council of 186
Triple Alliance (1907) 261
Tripoli 132, 190, 258
Troy 47, 49
Troyes, France 85
Truman, Harry S. 324
Truman Doctrine 292
Tsarist Russians 170
Tudhaliya I (*c.* 1420–1400 BC) 34

Tudor dynasty 148
Tughluq dynasty (1320–1414) 127
Tukharistan 118
Tulagi 284
"Tulip Age" 168
Tulunids 131
Tunis 168, 190
Tunisia 132, 274, 294
Tupac Amaru 144
Turco-Mongol tribes 121, 122
Turcoman states 136
Turcoman tribes 138
Turkestan 118
Turkey 131 *see also* Anatolia
    modern, creation of 240, 241
    Ottoman (1522 to 1800) 167–168; empire
        under pressure 168
    Russian assault on 260
turkeys 18
Turkish Black Sea Fleet 242
Turkish wars (1768–74, 1787–92) 159
Turkmenchay, treaty of (1828) 169
Turkmenistan 120
Turks 102, 104, 131; in India 124, 126, 127; and
    Persian empire 58 *see also* Ghuzz Turks;
    Seljuk Turks 105
turnips 181
Tuscany 141
Tushpa, Lake Van 55
Tushratta 34–35
Tutankhamun (*c.* 1390–3127 BC) 34
Tutsi people 311
"Twenty-one Demands" (1915) 257, 275

U-Boat war 286
U-Thong, Thailand 129
Uganda 254, 258
Ugarit 35
Uí Néill 99
Ukraine 159, 201, 209, 288
Ulster Scotch-Irish migrants 233
Ulugh Beg 121
Umayyad Caliphs 89
Union, US Federal 232, 233
United Fruit 320
United Nations (UN) xxxvii, 175, 290, 295,
    306, 311, 334–335; coalition force 316;

Economic Commission for Latin
America 317
United States *see also* Americas; North
America
1783 to 1890, making of: western
expansion 226–228; communications,
development of 227–228, 229;
industrialization 229–230; railroad,
arrival of 226, 228, 229, 230
1776 to 1924, nation of immigrants
233–235; controls and continuity 235;
early 19th century 233–234; "new"
immigrants 234
since 1939, age of abundance 321–323;
immigration, trade and NAFTA 323;
post-war boom 322; race and urban
deprivation 323
since 1945, as world power 324–326;
communism, collapse of 325–326; policy
of containment 324–325; Vietnam War
325
annexation of islands 214, 215
Census Bureau 228
and Cold War 291, 292, 293, 324–325
Congress 232, 234
in First World War 267, 269
in Great Depression 280
and 'greenhouse gases' xxi
independence (1783) 226
market revolution in (1800 to 1880)
228–230
Mexican immigrants 323
Mexico, war with (1846–8) 231
migrants to 218
and nuclear weapons 341
Pacific Fleet 284
Philippines, resistance in 259, 260
Philippines acquired 259
population 217, 228
railways 152, 226, 228, 229, 230, 264
reconstruction after Civil War 232–233
in Second World War 284, 285
slavery in 230–232
support in Middle East 315
Uppland, kings of 100
Ur, Mesopotamia 30
Ur, Third Dynasty (2047–1940 BC) 31

Ur-Nammu 31
Urartu state 55
Urban II, Pope (1088–99) 102, 103, 109
"Urnfield culture" 69, 70
Uruguay (Banda Oriental) 199, 239
Uruk, Mesopotamia 30–31
USSR 272, 290, 291, 292, 293 *see also* Russia;
Soviet Union
Usuman dan Fodio 252
Utah 39, 226, 231
Utrecht, Treaty of (1713) 161, 199
Uttaranchal state 306
Uzbek Khanates 169
Uzbek Shaybani Khans 169, 170
Uzbekistan 120

Vaisnavism 126
Vajji mahajanapada 67
Valencia, Spain 133, 139
Valens 85
Valois 189
Van Diemen's Land (Tasmania) 248
Vandals 78, 79, 85–86
Varanasi 68
Vargas, Getúlio 317
Varna, Black Sea coast 15
Vasco da Gama 149, 151
Vedas 45, 46, 47
Vedas cult 45, 47, 67, 68
vehicles, first wheeled, in Europe 15 *see also*
cars, first
Venetia 225; power 137
Venezuela, chiefdoms 143
Venice 94, 106, 114, 137, 140, 201
Verazzano 154
Verdun, B. of (1916) 266–267
Verdun, France 197
Versailles, France 198
Versailles, Treaty of (1919) 275, 277–278, 279,
282
Vespasian (69–79) 76
Victor-Emmanuel II, king of Italy 225
Victoria, Lake 73
Vienna 93, 168, 196, 201, 209
Vienna Congress and Settlement (1815) 209,
214, 223
Viet Khe, Vietnam 20

Viet Minh 274

Vietnam (Annam) 166, 179, 259; since 1975
302, 303; early man in 20, 21; French
withdraw from 294, 301; Han invasion
of 64; Hindu temples in 129, 130; rise of
130–131; US withdraws from 334

Vietnam, South, collapse of (1975) 235, 334

Vietnam War (1961–73) 292, 293, 301–302,
324, 325

Vietnamese "boat people" 303

Vietnamese migrants 235, 303

Vijaya, Vietnam 130

Vijayanagar empire 128, 129

Vikings (or Rus) 100, 102, 105, 106–107; in
9th and 10th century Europe 97, 98–99;
kingdom of 99; see also Rus, Kievan;
Rus, western

Villafranca, Treaty of 225

villages: development of 12; early European
agricultural 13–14

violence, human xxiv–xxvii; indiscriminate see
terrorism, world, since 1945

Virginia 232

Visconti, Giangaleazzo, duke of Milan 141

Vishnu (god) 126, 129

Visigoths 85–86

Vix, France 71

Vladimir I 107

Vladimir Svyatoslavich (980–1015) 107

Vladimir-Suzdal 108; princes of 107

Volga, river 107, 158

Volgar Bulgars 107–108

Volkhov, river 106

Voyage around the Red Sea, A 54

voyages of discovery, European (1487 to 1780)
xxxv, 153–155; French, British and
Dutch 154–155; Spanish and Portuguese
153–154

Wæadysæaw, son of Sigismund 158

wagon trains 226

Waikato, New Zealand 250

Waitangi, Treaty of (1840) 250

Waitangi Tribunal 251

Wakefieldian "scientifically planned" colonies
250

Walata, Mali 134

Wales 100, 112, 233

Wallace, William 112

Wallachia 242

Waltham, Massachusetts 229

Wang Kon 44

Wang Mang 65

warfare xxiv–xxv, xxvi–xxvii
Hellenistic advances in 62
since 1945 333–335; new ways of warfare
334; peacekeeping 334–335

Warring States period (475–221 BC) 63

"Wars between Eight Princes" 66

wars of religion (1493 to 1806) 195–196

"Wars of the Roses" (1455–85) 148

Warsaw, Grand Duchy of 213

Warsaw Pact 292

Wash, the 114

Washington, al-Qaeda attacks 326, 338,
340

Washington, George 208

Washington Consensus 318

Wastergarn, Gotland 113

Waterloo, B. of (1815) 214

Watt, James 206

wealth, use of xxxv, xxxvi, xxxvii

weapons: early man 5; advances in xxxiv,
xxxviii; modern 334; nuclear 292–293,
324, 325, 333, 341 see also atomic bombs,
dropping of

"Weapons of Mass Destruction" 339,
340–341

Wearmouth-Jarrow, N.E. England xxxi

Wei dynasty 63

Wei kingdom 65–66

Wei valley, China 42

Weimar, reform programmes in 196

Wellington, New Zealand 250

Wells, H. G.: Outline of History (1920)
xvii–xviii

Welsh migrants 233

Weltpolitik (global foreign policy) 261

Wenzel of Bohemia 141

Wessex, kings of 99

west, reaction against the (1881–1917)
259–261

West Bank 313, 314

"West Hallstatt system" 71

West Indies 257–258, 274
Western Chin dynasty 66–67
Westphalia 213; Peace of (1648) 195, 197
White Australia policy 249
White Lotus rebellion (1796–1805) 173
Whitman, Walt 235
Whitney, Eli 230
wics (coastal markets) 113
William the Conqueror (1066–87) 111
Wilson, Woodrow 277
Wisconsin 234
witchcraft xxx
Witte, Sergei 243
women, emancipation of xxxvii, 250
wool, Spanish 182
world economy, formation of (1870 to 1914)
    263–265; commerce and banking
    264–265; transport revolution 263–264
world in 21st century 339–341; religion and
    rise of terror 340; weapons of mass
    destruction 339, 340–341
World Trade Center 340 *see also* New York,
    terror attacks on
World Trade Organization 299–300
World War, First (1914–18) xxvi, 234,
    265–267, 333; cause 287; in the east
    266–267; New Zealanders in 251;
    Ottoman empire in 240, 241; outbreak
    of 261, 266; Russia in 242, 244; stalemate
    266; victory in the west 267; weakens
    world economy 280
World War, Second (1939–45) xxxviii, 274,
    333
    in Asia and the Pacific 283–285
    in Europe (1941 to 1945) 285–287;
        Germany, defeat of 286–287; turn of the
        tide 286
    New Zealanders in 251
    outbreak of (1931 to 1941) 281–283; German
        expansion 282; war in Europe 282–283
    Soviet Union in 327
Worms, France 85; cathedral 114; Concordat
    of (1122) 109
Wright, Orville and Wilbur 343
writing: development of 29–30; Indus culture
    45; Linear B 48
Wu kingdom 66

Wu-ch'ang revolt (1911) 245
Wu-hsi, China 166
Wu-ti (140–87 BC) 64, 65
Württemberg 225
Wyclif, John 92, 141

Xerxes (486–465 BC) 57, 59
Xicalango 145

Yalta conference (1945) 287, 290
Yamamoto, Admiral 284
Yamana family 117
Yang Chien 67
Yangtze, lower, provinces of 276
Yangtze delta 41
Yangtze valley 41–42, 118
Yao people 172
Yarim Tepe 12
Yarim-Lim of Yamkhad 31
Yarmuk river, B. of (636) 89
Yathrib (later Medina), Arabia 87, 88
Yazdigird 89
Yellow River 27, 28, 41, 42
"Yellow Turbans" religious movement 65
Yeltsin, Boris 328
Yemen 87
Yerevan, Armenia 168
Yoritomo, Minamoto 116
Yorktown, blockade of 200
Yorubaland 252, 254
Yoshino, Japan 116–117
Yoshinori, *shogun* 117
Young Italy movement 224
"Young Turks" 241, 260
Yuan dynasty 122
Yuan Mongols 123
Yüan Shih-k'ai 274, 275
Yüeh kingdoms 64
Yüeh-chih horde 68
Yugoslavia
    collapse of 332–333
    conflict in (1991–5) 330–331; and religion
        340
    democracy suspended in 278
    after Second World War 290
    state created 278
Yung-cheng, emperor (1722–35) 172

Yung-lo emperor 166
Yunnan rebellion (1726–9) 172

Zagwe dynasty 136
Zaitun, China 122
Zama, B. of (202 BC) xix, 74
Zanzibar 218
Zapotecs 20
Zaragoza, Spain 133
Zaria city state 135

Zartonk 240–241
zemstvo (local government) 243
Zimbabwe, Great 136, 164
Zimri-Lim of Mari (c. 1714–1700 BC) 31
Zionism 312–314 see also Jews/Jewish entries;
    Judaism
Zionist Congress, First (1897) 223, 312
Zips (Spiz) 203
Zoroastrianism 52
Zwingli, Huldrych (1484–1531) 185